THE GLANCE OF THE EYE

SUNY series in Contemporary Continental Philosophy
Dennis J. Schmidt, editor

THE GLANCE OF THE EYE

Heidegger, Aristotle, and the Ends of Theory

WILLIAM MCNEILL

State University of New York Press

Published by
State University of New York Press, Albany

For information, address State University of New York Press,
State University Plaza, Albany, N. Y., 12246

Production by Marilyn P. Semerad
Marketing by Fran Keneston

Library of Congress Cataloging-in-Publication Data
McNeill, William, 1961–
    The glance of the eye : Heidegger, Aristotle, and the ends of
theory / William McNeill.
        p.   cm. — (SUNY series in contemporary continental
philosophy)
    Includes bibliographical references and indexes.
    ISBN 0-7914-4227-6 (hc : alk. paper). — ISBN 0-7914-4228-4 (pbk.
: alk. paper)
    1. Heidegger, Martin, 1889-1976—Contributions in philosophy of
theory. 2. Theory (Philosophy)—History—20th century.
3. Aristotle—Influence.   I. Title.   II. Series.
B3279.H49M376   1999
121'.35'092—dc21   98-48871
                                                                          CIP

10 9 8 7 6 5 4 3 2 1

Liberation from the tradition is an ever new appropriation of its newly recognized strengths. (GA 29/30, 511)

Contents

I Theoria and Philosophy: Heidegger and Aristotle

II The Transformation of Theoria

III The Threshold of Representation: The Augenblick in Heidegger's Reading of Nietzsche

IV Originary Theoria

Preface

The present study is an attempt to understand the phenomenon of the *Augenblick* in Heidegger's thought, and in particular its relation to the primacy of seeing and of *theōria* in Aristotle and in our philosophical and scientific tradition. In the title of the book, "the glance of the eye" is thus intended in both a broad and a narrow sense. In a broad sense, it refers to seeing and to the look, encompassing also the original sense of *theōria* as a "seeing" or pure beholding. In a narrower sense, it translates the German word *Augenblick,* and carries both a visual and a temporal sense, conveying the "momentary" character of seeing.

The origins of this study may be traced to a question and a suspicion. On the one hand, there was the question of what exactly was at stake in the experience of the *Augenblick* that seemed to me to occupy the very center of Heidegger's thought from early to late. While it seemed apparent that the *Augenblick* marked an experience of limit—of the limits of human understanding and of the intrinsic finitude of historical being—as an experience it nevertheless seemed to verge on the incomprehensible. Furthermore, although the phenomenon of the *Augenblick* lies at the heart of Heidegger's thinking of being as time (so much so that one prominent commentator has described *Being and Time* as the attempt to elaborate a "philosophy of the *Augenblick*"),[1] it also tends to be largely neglected even by those studies claiming to focus on Heidegger's thinking of temporality.[2] On the other hand—and perhaps not unrelated to this relative neglect—the very word *Augenblick* arouses a certain suspicion in the modern, and especially "postmodern" philosophical ear, namely, the suspicion that this word carries or testifies to a continued complicity with the recognized primacy of the

---

[1] Otto Pöggeler, "Destruktion und Augenblick," in *Destruktion und Übersetzung,* ed. T. Buchheim (Weinheim: VCH, Acta Humaniora, 1989), 18.

[2] A neglect recently noted in a fine study by Hans Ruin. See *Enigmatic Origins* (Stockholm: Almqvist & Wiksell International, 1994), 176-77.

visual metaphor for knowledge that has allegedly dominated our philosophical tradition.[3] Thus there arose also a further question: Was the experience
of the *Augenblick* in Heidegger perhaps a last testimony to the problematic
hegemony of vision and of *theōria* in our Western philosophical tradition?
To what extent was Heidegger's thinking of the *Augenblick* complicit with
the history of *theōria?*

It thus became evident that it would be impossible to consider adequately the phenomenon of the *Augenblick* in Heidegger without also considering its broader philosophical context: that of the history of *theōria* and
of its instability at the beginning and end of philosophy. The *Augenblick* in
Heidegger's thought, as the present study will show, manifests both continuities and disjunctions with the history of philosophy considered as a
history of *theōria*. But the nature of the primacy of *theōria* for philosophy also meant that the status of *theōria* could not be considered on its
own, but had to be understood in relation to those moments against which
theōria delimits itself in establishing its definitive primacy, namely, *praxis*
and *poiēsis*. This delimitation, definitive for the subsequent tradition, occurs most decisively in Aristotle.

An early encounter and preoccupation with Aristotle's thought has long
been recognized as important for Heidegger's work. But it is only with the
recent publication in the *Gesamtausgabe* of a number of Heidegger's lecture courses dealing with Aristotle that the extent of his indebtedness to
Aristotle has begun to be more fully acknowledged. Such acknowledgement,
which is still in its initial stages, can itself arise only out of an equal appreciation of the extent to which Heidegger's phenomenological readings
illuminate Aristotle's own texts in an original manner, letting them shine
in unforeseen and unforeseeable ways. It should be noted, however, that
the present study does not attempt to undertake a systematic interpretation of Heidegger's readings of Aristotle, but remains guided by its leading focus on the *Augenblick* and its relation to *theōria*. As the study will
show, Heidegger's understanding of the *Augenblick* is influenced not only
or primarily by his phenomenological encounter with Husserl (who remains
guided by the primacy of a theoretical and scientific approach), or by the
significance of this term in a number of thinkers who seek to resist the
philosophical hegemony of theory (Kierkegaard, Nietzsche, Jaspers), but

---

[3] This primacy of vision as a manner of access to beings has been investigated in
relation to different kinds of seeing by David Michael Levin in *The Opening of Vision*
(New York: Routledge, 1988). See also his edited collection of essays *Modernity and
the Hegemony of Vision* (Berkeley: University of California Press, 1993). The postmodern suspicions concerning vision have recently been surveyed with particular relation
to French thought by Martin Jay in *Downcast Eyes* (Berkeley: University of California
Press, 1993).

most decisively by Aristotle, and in particular by Aristotle's understanding of *praxis*. Yet while the *Augenblick* in Heidegger's thought can indeed be understood as the "glance of the eye" pertaining to originary *praxis*, such *praxis* should not—as I also try to indicate—simply be opposed to either *theōria* or *poiēsis*. Rather, it puts such oppositions into question, unsettling them even as it acknowledges their critical importance. The *Augenblick* itself carries for Heidegger a primarily *critical* import. It is itself the site of *krinein*, of finitude and of the possibility of critique.

The present study, written over a number of years, necessarily conveys shifts in style and emphasis that I hope are not overly obtrusive. It thus represents a documentation of work in progress, rather than a polished thesis. Likewise, due also to the complexity of the topic, it has no single thesis, but circles around a number of these central issues which find a certain focus in the *Augenblick*. Furthermore, the study was not conceived in accordance with an initial plan or framework, but was led by a series of questions that arose along the way. It is not, therefore, an attempt to treat systematically all of Heidegger's claims concerning the *Augenblick* or *theōria* throughout his work, but rather to approach and phenomenologically open up the experience of the *Augenblick* in Heidegger's work and some of the central issues that serve to situate it both phenomenologically, textually, and historically. It should become apparent in the course of the investigation that the *Augenblick* does not name a single, immutable experience in Heidegger's thought, but designates a site or locus that is also historically and hermeneutically determined and transformed. Thus, while in the early phenomenological work it designates a moment intrinsic to the finite *praxis* of the individual, from the mid-1930s on the *Augenblick* is thought increasingly as a site of the event (*Ereignis*) of worldly presencing and of possible transformations in the history of being. As such a site, it is characterized throughout by two fundamental traits: the trait of finitude, whereby it is open for the sudden, nonmediated, unforeseeable irruption of beings into presencing, and the trait of being held in such openness in such a manner as to be delivered over, always already, to historical time, to being with others, and to the claims of a tradition.

The study is divided into four parts. Part 1 considers the problem of the genesis of theory and of the relation of *theōria* to *praxis* in Heidegger's early work from 1922 to 1933. Here Heidegger's 1924 interpretation of Aristotle (chapter 2) sets the scene for a double reading of *Being and Time*, first from the perspective of a theoretical aspiration (chapter 3), and then from the perspective of a primacy of *praxis* (chapter 4). A certain tension in the early work between theory and *praxis* also provides the occasion for some reflections on the philosophical and political status of the 1933 Rectoral Address from this Aristotelian perspective (chapter 5). In part 2,

I look at some of Heidegger's interpretations of *theōria* in its modern, scientific and technological forms. From the mid-1930s, Heidegger's thought becomes increasingly attentive to the intrinsically historical character of *theōria*, whose transformation into modern scientific and technological theory essentially governs the dominant political reality of the modern "world picture." Heidegger's analyses, I suggest, highlight the limits and ends of scientific and technological seeing in such a way as to manifest the originary finitude of the *Augenblick* as what is not only refused in such "technovision," but approaches us as thus refused. Part 3 of the study attempts to illuminate retrospectively an early, and for Heidegger quite pivotal, encounter with such limits in the work of Nietzsche by turning back to Heidegger's 1937 interpretation of Nietzsche's thought of the eternal recurrence of the same. This thought, in thinking the *Augenblick,* opens itself in a decisive manner to the limits of the *theōria* of modern representation and (in its proximity to the "will to power") intimates its technological mutation into the attempted self-production of the will to power as the "will to will," albeit in a manner that for Heidegger's questioning remains problematic. Finally, in part 4 I try to open a perspective on some traces of a pre- or proto-philosophical *theōria* and "seeing" in Heidegger's work, traces that are not unrelated to the *Augenblick.* As a preparation for this, I turn first to consider the originary sense of ancient *theōria,* prior to its philosophical appropriation, drawing on the work of other scholars. From this perspective, I then try to read several texts of Heidegger in which something of this ancient sense of *theōria* and of seeing is in play: "The Origin of the Work of Art" (1936), the discussion of the look of the Other in the *Parmenides* lecture course (1942/43), and "The Anaximander Fragment" (1946).

I implied earlier that the present study had its origins in a suspicion and a question of mine. That is untrue. Its origins certainly lie elsewhere: in an invitation by David Wood to present a series of seminars at the University of Warwick some years ago, which led to a first draft of chapter 1, and sent me further than I could have at that time foreseen; and beyond that, in my philosophical apprenticeship with David Farrell Krell, who first seduced me to enter the *Augenblick;* and with Robert Bernasconi, without whose continual support and inspiration this project would have been impossible. This study is further indebted to my parents and family for their continual support over many years, and to Ruth Oliver, who encouraged me to finish it. I owe special thanks also to David Krell and to Daniel Price, both of whom read an early draft of the book and made numerous helpful suggestions, and to Daniel Selcer and Keith Peterson for their painstaking work on the proofs. Finally, I am grateful to DePaul University for a research grant and for a period of leave from my teaching responsibilities that enabled me to bring this project to fruition.

Abbreviations of Works Cited

Works by Aristotle

DA   *On the Soul.* With a translation by W. S. Hett. The Loeb
      Classical Library. Cambridge: Harvard University Press, 1957.

EE   *The Eudemian Ethics.* With a translation by H. Rackham. The
      Loeb Classical Library. Cambridge: Harvard University Press,
      1952.

M   *The Metaphysics.* 2 vols. With a translation by H. Tredennick.
      The Loeb Classical Library. Cambridge: Harvard University
      Press, 1933/35.

NE   *The Nicomachean Ethics.* With a translation by H. Rackham.
      The Loeb Classical Library. Cambridge: Harvard University
      Press, 1934.

P   *Politics.* With a translation by H. Rackham. The Loeb Classi-
      cal Library. Cambridge: Harvard University Press, 1944.

Works by Gadamer

GW   *Gesammelte Werke.* 10 vols. Tübingen: J.C.B. Mohr, 1985ff.

Works by Heidegger

BSD   *Zur Frage nach der Bestimmung der Sache des Denkens.* St.
      Gallen: Erker-Verlag, 1984.

BW   *Basic Writings.* Edited by David Farrell Krell. New York:
      HarperCollins, 1993.

EM   *Einführung in die Metaphysik.* Tübingen: Niemeyer, 1953. Translated by Ralph Manheim under the title *An Introduction to Metaphysics.* New Haven: Yale University Press, 1959.

FD   *Die Frage nach dem Ding.* 3rd ed. Niemeyer: Tübingen, 1987. Translated by W. B. Barton, Jr. and Vera Deutsch under the title *What is a Thing?* Chicago: Henry Regnery, 1968.

G   *Gelassenheit.* Pfullingen: Neske, 1959. Translated by John M. Anderson and Hans E. Freund under the title *Discourse on Thinking.* New York: Harper & Row, 1966.

GA 9   *Wegmarken.* Gesamtausgabe vol. 9. Frankfurt: Klostermann, 1976. Translated under the title *Pathmarks,* edited by William McNeill. New York: Cambridge University Press, 1998.

GA 17   *Einführung in die Phänomenologische Forschung.* Gesamtausgabe vol. 17. Frankfurt: Klostermann, 1994.

GA 19   *Platon: Sophistes.* Gesamtausgabe vol. 19. Frankfurt: Klostermann, 1992. Translated by Richard Rojcewicz and André Schuwer under the title *Plato's Sophist.* Bloomington: Indiana University Press, 1997.

GA 20   *Prolegomena zur Geschichte des Zeitbegriffs.* Gesamtausgabe vol. 20. Frankfurt: Klostermann, 1979. Translated by Theodore Kisiel under the title *History of the Concept of Time.* Bloomington: Indiana University Press, 1985.

GA 21   *Logik: Die Frage nach der Wahrheit.* Gesamtausgabe vol. 21. Frankfurt: Klostermann, 1976.

GA 24   *Die Grundprobleme der Phänomenologie.* Gesamtausgabe vol. 24. Frankfurt: Klostermann, 1975. Translated by Albert Hofstadter under the title *The Basic Problems of Phenomenology.* Bloomington: Indiana University Press, 1982.

GA 26   *Metaphysische Anfangsgründe der Logik im Ausgang von Leibniz.* Gesamtausgabe vol. 26. Frankfurt: Klostermann, 1978. Translated by Michael Heim under the title *The Metaphysical Foundations of Logic.* Bloomington: Indiana University Press, 1984.

GA 29/30   *Die Grundbegriffe der Metaphysik: Welt – Endlichkeit – Einsamkeit.* Gesamtausgabe vol. 29/30. Frankfurt: Klostermann,

	1983. Translated by William McNeill and Nicholas Walker under the title *The Fundamental Concepts of Metaphysics: World, Finitude, Solitude.* Bloomington: Indiana University Press, 1995.
GA 33	*Aristoteles, Metaphysik Θ 1-3: Von Wesen und Wirklichkeit der Kraft.* Gesamtausgabe vol. 33. 2nd ed. Frankfurt: Klostermann, 1990. Translated by Walter Brogan and Peter Warnek under the title *Aristotle's* Metaphysics Θ *1-3: On the Essence and Actuality of Force.* Bloomington: Indiana University Press, 1995.
GA 34	*Vom Wesen der Wahrheit: Zu Platons Höhlengleichnis und Theätet.* Gesamtausgabe vol. 34. Frankfurt: Klostermann, 1988.
GA 45	*Grundfragen der Philosophie: Ausgewählte "Probleme" der "Logik."* Gesamtausgabe vol. 45. Frankfurt: Klostermann, 1984. Translated by Richard Rojcewicz and André Schuwer under the title *Basic Questions of Philosophy: Selected "Problems" of "Logic".* Bloomington: Indiana University Press, 1994.
GA 53	*Hölderlins Hymne "Der Ister."* Gesamtausgabe vol. 53. Frankfurt: Klostermann, 1984. Translated by William McNeill and Julia Davis under the title *Hölderlins Hymn "The Ister"* Bloomington: Indiana University Press, 1996.
GA 54	*Parmenides.* Gesamtausgabe vol. 54. Frankfurt: Klostermann, 1982. Translated by André Schuwer and Richard Rojcewicz under the title *Parmenides.* Bloomington: Indiana University Press, 1992.
GA 55	*Heraklit.* Gesamtausgabe vol. 55. Frankfurt: Klostermann, 1987.
GA 56/57	*Zur Bestimmung der Philosophie.* Gesamtausgabe vol. 56/57. Frankfurt: Klostermann, 1987.
GA 60	*Phänomenologie des Religiösen Lebens.* Gesamtausgabe vol. 60. Frankfurt: Klosterman, 1995.
GA 61	*Phänomenologische Interpretationen zu Aristoteles. Einführung in die phänomenologische Forschung.* Gesamtausgabe vol. 61. Frankfurt: Klostermann, 1985.

GA 63   *Ontologie (Hermeneutik der Faktizität).* Gesamtausgabe vol. 63. Frankfurt: Klostermann, 1988.

GA 65   *Beiträge zur Philosophie (Vom Ereignis).* Gesamtausgabe vol. 65. Frankfurt: Klostermann, 1989.

GA 79   *Bremer und Freiburger Vorträge.* Gesamtausgabe vol. 79. Frankfurt: Klostermann, 1994.

H   *Holzwege.* Frankfurt: Klostermann, 1950.

ID   *Identität und Differenz.* 8th ed. Pfullingen: Neske, 1986. Translated by Joan Stambaugh under the title *Identity and Difference.* Bilingual edition. New York: Harper & Row, 1969.

KPM   *Kant und das Problem der Metaphysik.* 4th ed. Frankfurt: Klostermann, 1973. Translated by Richard Taft under the title *Kant and the Problem of Metaphysics.* Bloomington: Indiana University Press, 1990.

NI, NII *Nietzsche.* 2 vols. Pfullingen: Neske, 1961. Translated by David Farrell Krell under the title *Nietzsche.* 4 vols. in 2. New York: HarperCollins, 1991.

PIA   "Phänomenologische Interpretationen zu Aristoteles (Anzeige der hermeneutischen Situation)." *Dilthey Jahrbuch für Philosophie und Geschichte der Geisteswissenschaften* 6 (1989): 235-74. Translated by Michael Baur under the title "Phenomenological Interpretations with Respect to Aristotle: Indication of the Hermeneutical Situation," in *Man and World* 25 (1992): 355-93. References are to the original manuscript pagination, as indicated in both the German and the English text.

QT   *The Question Concerning Technology and Other Essays.* Translated by William Lovitt. New York: Harper & Row, 1977.

SA   *Schellings Abhandlung Über das Wesen der menschlichen Freiheit (1809).* Tübingen: Niemeyer, 1971. Translated by Joan Stambaugh under the title *Schelling's Treatise on the Essence of Human Freedom.* Athens, Ohio: Ohio University Press, 1985.

SD   *Zur Sache des Denkens.* Tübingen: Niemeyer, 1976. Translated by Joan Stambaugh under the title *On Time and Being.* New York: Harper & Row, 1972.

SDU   *Die Selbstbehauptung der deutschen Universität.* Frankfurt:
        Klostermann, 1983. Translated by Karsten Harries under the
        title "The Self-Assertion of the German University. The Rec-
        torate 1933/34: Facts and Thoughts." *Review of Metaphysics*
        38 (1985): 467-502.

SG   *Der Satz vom Grund.* 6th ed. Pfullingen: Neske, 1986. Trans-
        lated by Reginald Lilly under the title *The Principle of Reason.*
        Bloomington: Indiana University Press, 1991.

SZ   *Sein und Zeit.* Halle a. d. S.: Niemeyer, 1927. Translated by
        John Macquarrie and Edward Robinson under the title *Being
        and Time.* Oxford: Blackwell, 1987. Where reference is made
        to marginalia, I have used *Sein und Zeit,* 15th ed. Tübingen:
        Niemeyer, 1979.

TK   *Die Technik und die Kehre.* 6th ed. Pfullingen: Neske, 1985.

UK   *Der Ursprung des Kunstwerkes.* With an Introduction by
        Hans-Georg Gadamer. Stuttgart: Reclam, 1978.

US   *Unterwegs zur Sprache.* 6th ed. Pfullingen: Neske, 1979.

VA   *Vorträge und Aufsätze.* 5th ed. Pfullingen: Neske, 1985.

VS   *Vier Seminare.* Frankfurt: Klostermann, 1977.

W   *Wegmarken.* Frankfurt: Klostermann, 1967.

WD   *Was heißt Denken?* 4th ed. Tübingen: Niemeyer, 1984. Trans-
        lated by J. Glenn Gray under the title *What is called Thinking?*
        New York: Harper & Row, 1968.

WDP   *Was ist das—die Philosophie?* 7th ed. Pfullingen: Neske, 1981.
        Translated by Jean T. Wilde and William Kluback under the
        title *What is Philosophy?* Bilingual edition. Albany: N.C.U.P.
        Inc.

ZS   *Zollikoner Seminare.* Frankfurt: Klostermann, 1987.

A Note on Terminology

Being In the following essay the German *Sein* has been translated as "being" (in the lowercase) and should be understood in a verbal sense. The noun *das Seiende* has generally been rendered as "beings," or occasionally as "an entity" or "entities." Where "a being" is used, the meaning will generally be that of "an entity in its being," unless the context indicates otherwise.

Praxis Where the word *praxis* is italicized, it refers to the Greek πρᾶξις, which, as the essay will explain, may itself carry a number of different senses (see chapter 2, note 14). Where the term appears as praxis or "praxis," it is meant in the loose, modern sense of the word, which refers to any direct involvement with the world and is generally opposed to "theory" (see chapter 3 for further discussion). The Greek *praxis*, by contrast, can also include theoretical activity.

Beginning Throughout the present study, the German word *Anfang* will be translated as "beginning." It should be noted that this term does not imply a determinate point of onset in either a spatial or temporal sense for Heidegger, but has the sense of a more remote, more indeterminate gathering that leads to the emergence of an action or of a historical epoch. In this sense it may be compared to Heidegger's thinking of a destiny or "destining" of being. In his 1934/35 lecture course on Hölderlin, Heidegger equates *Anfang* or "beginning" with *Ursprung,* "origin," and distinguishes it from the ordinary sense of the "start" of something (in German, *Beginn*) as the onset of an event:

> The 'start' is something other than the 'beginning' [*Anfang*]. A new weather situation, for example, starts with a storm. Its beginning, however, is the complete change of air that brings it about in advance. A start is the onset of something; a beginning is that from which something arises or springs forth. The world war began centuries ago in the political and spiritual history of the Western world. The world war started with battles in the outposts. The start is immediately left behind, it vanishes as an event proceeds. The beginning, the origin, by contrast, first appears and comes to the fore in the course of an event and is fully there only at its end. (GA 39, 3)

Compare Heidegger's discussions of *Anfang* in the Rectoral Address and in "The Origin of the Work of Art" (see chapters 5 and 8 of the present study).

Chapter 1

Introduction: Of an Ancient Desire

Pantes anthrōpoi tou eidenai oregontai phusei, "All human beings by nature desire to know," begins Aristotle's *Metaphysics*. The translation offered by Heidegger in *Being and Time*, "The care for seeing is essential to man's being,"[1] is—like many of his translations of Greek texts—unorthodox, but in this context relatively unproblematic. As the footnote in the English translation by John Macquarrie and Edward Robinson indicates, Heidegger here is understanding *eidenai*—connected with *eidos,* the visible form of something—in terms of its root meaning, "to see."[2] And Aristotle indeed proceeds to identify our tendency to prefer vision (*horan*) over all the other senses, whether in respect of action (*prattein*), or even when no action is anticipated. For, Aristotle continues, "of all the senses, sight best brings about [*poiei*] knowledge of things and reveals many distinctions."

Yet what kind of seeing is at stake in the "knowing" referred to in this first sentence of the *Metaphysics*? It is clearly not a matter of mere sense-perception. The esteem in which we hold such perception or *aisthēsis* in general is merely a sign or indication (*semion*) of our desire to see or to know in some "higher" sense of the word. Aristotle does not immediately specify what this higher sense of seeing is. The seeing referred to has not yet been differentiated in accordance with the five forms of knowledge or intellectual virtue through which the soul can attain truth: *technē,* the kind of know-how pertaining to artisanship; *epistēmē,* theoretical or "scientific" knowledge; *phronēsis,* practical wisdom; *sophia,* wisdom in the highest

---

[1] "Im Sein des Menschen liegt wesenhaft die Sorge des Sehens" (SZ, 171).
[2] *Being and Time,* trans. John Macquarrie & Edward Robinson (Oxford: Blackwell, 1987), 215 n. 2.

1

sense; and *nous,* pure apprehending—each of these having their own kind of seeing.[3] We do not yet know, in these opening paragraphs, which kind of seeing will be the subject of the *Metaphysics;* we merely have a "sign" that it will not be mere sensory apprehending.

Two comments should be made here on Heidegger's appropriation of this statement from Aristotle.

First, it should be noted that Heidegger translates the Greek *oregontai* (from *orexis,* usually rendered as "desire") by *Sorge,* care. Care is of course the term used in *Being and Time* to designate the being of *Dasein,* the being of that entity which we ourselves are. Existing as care, Dasein is not only already in the world, in a certain disclosedness and alongside (*bei*)[4] whatever worldly things it is involved with. Over and above this, before all this, it is always already stretched out ahead of itself: it is essentially futural. In terms of its practical activities, it has already anticipated and thus in in its very being already knows, or has already "seen," what it is about to do, that which has not yet been accomplished and is yet to come. Its seeing is a foreseeing. This, as Macquarrie and Robinson indicate, is in keeping with the literal meaning of the Greek word *orexis:* to "reach out for." Reading with Heidegger, then, all humans in their being not merely desire to see, but, prior to all practical activity and all comportment toward each and every being, have already seen.

What is most striking here is that what is thus presented in *Being and Time* as an interpretation of a traditional Platonic-Aristotelian model of knowledge (namely a prior sighting or vision) also seems to accord exactly with what Heidegger, some years later, will appear to pronounce unambiguously as his own definition of knowledge. It runs: *Wissen heißt: gesehen haben.* "To know means: to have seen." We shall comment on this "definition" in a moment. For now, it suffices to raise the general question of whether Heidegger's definition is in fact the traditional definition of knowledge underlying Western metaphysics.

That the answer is no, or—more cautiously—yes and no, should be apparent from a second comment that ought to be made. Heidegger, as the context indicates, is well aware of the primacy accorded to vision in the philosophical tradition from the Greeks onward. His citation of this first line of the *Metaphysics* occurs in §36 of *Being and Time,* and serves to introduce a discussion of this very tradition. Heidegger remarks that the philosophical primacy accorded to vision was recognized particularly by Augustine in Book X of his *Confessions,* which discusses the *concupiscentia oculorum,* the desire of the eye. "Originary and genuine truth," as Heidegger

---

[3] See NE, 1139 b14ff.

[4] The German preposition *bei* does not primarily have a spatial sense, but implies being "with" in the sense of being "in the presence of" something or someone.

puts it, "lies in pure beholding [or intuiting: *Anschauung*]. This thesis has remained the foundation of Western philosophy ever since" (SZ, 171). Yet is it not quite remarkable that Heidegger should here locate a discussion of this tradition and its emphasis upon seeing within a section that bears the simple title "Curiosity" (*Die Neugier*)? A section which, in a few sentences, spans Parmenides, Aristotle, Augustine, and Hegel: Western philosophy from its first beginnings to its culmination! Is Heidegger implying that the whole of Western philosophy can somehow be reduced to curiosity? It is difficult to avoid this impression, notwithstanding the assertion that curiosity does not seek to understand what is seen, but seeks "*only* to see," or "*only* to see and to have seen," as Heidegger later puts it (SZ 172, 346). Notwithstanding also the assurance that "Curiosity has nothing to do with contemplating beings and marvelling at them—with *thaumazein*." For it could be that an originary *thaumazein* was precisely what died out when philosophy entered the scene. This might indeed be read into the beginning of Aristotle's *Metaphysics*. Book I, chapter two of the *Metaphysics* remarks:

> It is through wonder [*thaumazein*] that men now begin and orig- inally began to philosophize, wondering in the first place about the aporias at hand.... Now he who wonders and is perplexed feels ignorance [*agnoein*] ...therefore it was to escape ignorance that men studied philosophy.... (M, 982 b12)

Yet would not an escape from ignorance necessarily entail the disappearance of *thaumazein?* Is not the association of *thaumazein* with ignorance already symptomatic of the appropriation of *thaumazein* by philosophy?[5] Is there perhaps a more originary "contemplation" of beings belonging to the pre- philosophical experience of *thaumazein*—more originary, that is, than the *theōria* or contemplation of the philosophers?

***

Let us leave some of these questions suspended for now. But what of this apparent alignment between the philosophical desire to see and that of curiosity? Is such an alignment too hasty? Alternatively, perhaps, one might complicate matters by insisting on the necessity to distinguish between curiosity as an everyday desire to see, and the philosophical desire to see,

---

[5] This weakening of the experience of *thaumazein* in Aristotle has been suggested by Hannah Arendt in *The Life of the Mind*, vol. 1 (New York: Harcourt Brace Jovanovich, 1978), 114. On philosophy and wonder, see also John Sallis, *Double Truth* (Albany: State University of New York Press, 1995), chapter 11; and especially his essay "...A wonder that one could never aspire to surpass," in *The Path of Archaic Thinking*, ed. K. Maly (Albany: State University of New York Press, 1995), 243–74. See also Walter Bröcker, *Aristoteles*, 5th ed. (Frankfurt: Klostermann, 1987), 18–23.

of which our everyday tendency would be a reflection or "indication," yet by no means identical to it. And neither of these, perhaps, would be the same as Heidegger's later conception of knowing as having seen. If this division were to prove tenable, we would thus have three conceptions of the desire to see:

(1) The first and most obvious of these would be the *everyday* desire to see, as manifest in our everyday curiosity. The desire behind this "seeing," as a mode of Dasein's understanding, is not restricted to seeing with one's eyes (SZ, 170). It also encompasses, for example, a desire to hear and to have heard. Yet nor is it restricted to a pure sensory apprehending, if by sensory apprehending we mean the straightforward apprehending of a given object that affects our senses. This is not to say, however, that this everyday form of the desire to see is directed toward a suprasensible "beyond." For it indeed remains a general orientation toward the sensible realm, yet in this orientation is directed beyond those objects given as present, directed toward something not yet visible, something not yet present. The desire behind the vision of curiosity is, quite simply—as the German *Neugier* implies—a desire for the new. Its vision is a seeing in the sense of a kind of understanding, as §31 of *Being and Time*, "Da-sein as Understanding," has already made clear. Yet it is not an understanding that seeks to understand in the sense of to know (*Wissen*) or to be "knowingly in the truth." It is a seeing that seeks *only* to have seen, a knowing that seeks "merely to have known" (SZ, 172). The word *have* is important here. For it indicates that in curiosity, we somehow evade our own having-been. And this is why Heidegger, when later analysing the temporality of curiosity, will describe it in terms of Dasein's fleeing before its own thrownness, before the mortality of its own being-toward-death: ultimately, as a fleeing in the face of the *Augenblick*, of a vision immanent in the "glance of the eye" and belonging to the originary and primordial time of our existence.[6]

(2) The interpretation of this everyday curiosity as a desire only to have seen already points to a second possible conception, which would be that of the *philosophical* desire to see, as represented by the history of ontology or metaphysics. This desire would indeed seek to see, but this time in a nonsensory manner of apprehending, and would do so in order to understand or gain knowledge of the truth. To that extent it would not be mere curiosity; it would not seek *merely* to have seen, but precisely to hold fast to its object, to secure its vision, to remain in pure contemplation of the truth. This second form of desire differs from the first, therefore, not only in its directedness, but in its desire to remain in the presence of its object. Yet in another respect this philosophical desire may be nothing other than

---

[6] See SZ, §68c, 346ff.

a reflection, or the repetition on another level, of the everyday tendency.[7] For it remains, first, a desire to see; and, second—as we shall indicate in a moment—a desire *to have seen*. Moreover, with the emergence of this kind of understanding, a priority of vision or of the visual metaphor comes to impose itself in the domain of human knowledge: the seat of knowledge is ultimately located in the "eye of the soul" (*omma tēs psuchēs*) referred to by Plato and Aristotle.

It seems that Heidegger, in this section on curiosity, provides us with a sketch of the initial genesis not only of curiosity, but also of philosophical knowledge. It is when our everyday concern with worldly things is interrupted, writes Heidegger, when we rest or take a break from things, that the vision (*Sicht*) pertaining to our everyday circumspection (*Umsicht*) becomes freed. Ontologically, this means that care then becomes a tarrying alongside these worldly things; it seeks to see them merely in their "outward appearance" (*Aussehen*) (SZ, 172).

Now this "freeing" of vision that Heidegger describes here is not yet that of a developed philosophical desire (it does not yet seek the nonsensible *idea* or *eidos*); but nor is it as yet the desire that characterizes curiosity, for a description of the latter, without any further account of its genesis, is introduced only in the subsequent paragraph bearing the reservation "however" (*aber*). Curiosity is the opposite of a tarrying alongside: it is a nontarrying that brings about "the continual possibility of dispersion [*Zerstreuung*]" (SZ, 172). In other words, this initial account of the desire to see the world merely in its look is not yet a description of curiosity, if the latter is to be understood as a desire *merely* to see, for it has not yet

---

[7] The unsettling similarity between the two is noted in Plato's *Republic* (475c–e):

> "But the one who feels no distaste in sampling every study, and who attacks his task of learning gladly and cannot get enough of it, him we shall justly pronounce the lover of wisdom, the philosopher, shall we not?"
>
> To which Glaucon replied:
>
> "You will then be giving the name to a numerous and strange band, for all the lovers of spectacles [*philotheamones*] are what they are, I fancy, by virtue of their delight in learning something. And those who love to hear some new thing are a very strange lot to be reckoned among philosophers. You couldn't induce them to attend any kind of serious debate or discussion, but as if they had farmed out their ears to listen to every chorus in the land, they run about to all the Dionysiac festivals, never missing one, either in the towns or in the country villages. Are we to designate all these, then, and similar folk and all the practitioners of the minor arts as philosophers?"
>
> "Not at all," I said, "but they do bear a certain likeness to philosophers."
>
> "Whom do you mean, then, by the true philosophers?"
>
> "Those for whom the truth is the spectacle of which they are enamoured [*Tous tēs alētheias ... philotheamonas*]," said I.

been interpreted in contrast to possible knowledge of the world, in terms of possible truth. Only then can this phenomenon be regarded as the desire *only* or *merely* to see, as opposed to "grasping" and "being knowingly in the truth."

Yet the outward appearance or "look" of something, which somehow comes to excite and arouse in advance the desire of curiosity, enigmatically giving rise to its emergence, is also at the starting point of the philosophical desire. *Aussehen,* the outer appearance, look, or aspect of something, is Heidegger's translation of the Greek *eidos,* which, via Plato and Aristotle, comes to be interpreted as the nonsensible idea or primary form. That Heidegger is indeed also alluding to the genesis of philosophical knowledge here is supported by a more detailed, though still concise account of cognitive knowledge (*Erkennen*) provided early in §13, whose title identifies this kind of knowledge as a founded mode of being-in-the-world. It is an account which, moreover, has its precedent in Aristotle. How does such cognitive knowing arise? Seeing as theoretical, "scientific" knowing, *eidenai* qua *epistēmē,* Aristotle tells us, began with leisure, when practically all the necessities of life had been provided.[8] Heidegger, paraphrasing, writes that cognitive knowledge arises on the basis of a "deficiency" in our involvement with things, a holding oneself back, an interruption of our being captivated by worldly activities:

> In holding back from any kind of producing, manipulating, and the like, concern puts itself into what is now the sole remaining mode of being-in-the-world, a merely tarrying alongside.... *On the basis* of this way of being toward the world—one which now lets us encounter entities within the world merely in their pure *outward appearance* (*eidos*)—and *as* a mode of this way of being, an explicit looking at [*Hinsehen auf*] what we thus encounter is possible. This looking *at* is in each case a specific way of taking up a direction toward something, a setting our sights on what is present-at-hand. It takes over an "aspect" [*Gesichtspunkt*] in advance from the entity which it encounters. Such looking-at itself enters the mode of dwelling autonomously alongside entities within the world. (SZ, 61)

An early formulation of the same account, in the 1922 treatise "Phenomenological Interpretations with Respect to Aristotle," actually identifies such "merely looking at"—which "is accomplished as a determinative looking at, and can organize itself as science"—with curiosity. The German *Neugier,* Heidegger there adds parenthetically, means *cura, curiositas.* It is

---

[8] M, 981 b14f.; 982 b23f.

thus a mode of caring, of *Sorgen* as *curare*.[9] Significantly, this early account from 1922 makes no attempt to distinguish between a merely looking-at in the everyday sense that would seek only to have seen, and a scientific or philosophical contemplation that would desire to see a more concealed truth of things.

Being and Time, in any case, here provides a concise account of the genesis of philosophical and theoretical comportment, of the life of *theōrein:* a possibility which, Heidegger goes on to say, can develop into science and as such may come to govern our being-in-the-world.

And this is indeed what has happened. What was once philosophical knowledge became science, today subservient to technology which orders the contemporary world. Our present existence is overwhelmingly dominated by technology. As is well known, one of Heidegger's later concerns is that our contemporary, technological understanding of being—of being as a particular configuration and ordering of presence—is unduly and perhaps dangerously restrictive, and that this understanding has arisen because philosophical knowledge was itself unduly restrictive from the beginning. It arose, Heidegger alleges, in the light of a reductive understanding of *technē*, namely *technē* considered in terms of productive activity as craftsmanship. Yet why and how this reductive understanding of *technē* itself came to dominate is less easy to ascertain. Its ascendancy occurred—as Plato's *Republic* documents clearly enough—under the pressure of a certain political necessity, a "necessity" that is becoming more and more worthy of question for us today.

Philosophical knowing as founded by Plato and Aristotle was not, of course, a sighting of the *eidos* as the sensible outward appearance of something. Such seeing is merely the sensory apprehending of a particular thing, but not yet an explicit knowledge of the essence (*ousia*), or of what the thing truly is as such. This essence must be given (as Heidegger indirectly indicates in the passage just quoted) by the sighting of a particular "aspect" or *eidos* "in advance." This is the nonsensible *eidos* that can be "seen" by the eye of the soul. The exemplary vision of such an *eidos* is the form sighted in advance by the artisan before producing his actual product. This form or *eidos* is not reducible to an image, and, moreover, is independent of all the particular examples that the craftsman may produce of his product. As such, it is at once common to all (*koinon*), universal (*katholou*), and yet not bound to any particular image or sense-perception. Furthermore, unlike the actual thing produced, the *eidos* is what is most constant, even "eternal": it is not (or not yet) subject to material decay in the realm of the sensible. Finally, and most importantly in view of subsequent historical

---

[9] PIA, 7–8. Cf. GA 63, 103.

developments, it is that which is earlier or prior to the particular product: the *eidos* as essence is what Aristotle characterizes as the *to ti ēn einai:* that which the thing already was before its actualization. As such, it constitutes the *genos* or origin of the product and determines its *morphē*, its eventual figure or form in each instance. The *eidos* is cause, *aition*. The genesis of beings comes to be sought in their nonsensible and primary form.

Philosophical knowledge, then, according to this model which finds its exemplary moment already latent within the activity of artistic production, is understood as a seeing, a pure *theōrein* of the nonsensible *eidos* in the soul. Such knowledge lies in the sighting of the *eidos* that comprises the universal origin and determinative essence (*essentia*) of each sensible object as that which already was: the apriori. Because the artisan's sighting of the nonsensible *eidos* (which is already a *theōrein*, although not yet "pure" or disinterested, since it is part and parcel of the productive activity) governs in advance the being of the eventual product, the vision that truly sees this *eidos* will know in advance what governs the order of being.

Much of this is familiar enough. Yet why in the first place did seeing and vision come to be the privileged manner of access to things in the explicit unfolding of knowledge, whether of cognitive knowledge or of the more essential knowing ascribed to wisdom? Why not hearing or smelling, touch or taste? Elsewhere, Heidegger argues that the priority of vision comes about not only (as Aristotle claims) because things appear to be most clearly delimited through vision, in terms of their outline, figure, or form, but also because they thereby appear most constantly present (GA 34, 102). For only sight grants the simultaneity of what is present and what has been (the *hama* of which Aristotle speaks in *Metaphysics* Book IX), holds them together in one vision, as opposed to the mere sequential apprehending that occurs through the other senses.[10] Of all the senses, only vision grants the possible apprehending of a relative constancy of presence, even while allowing for change. The act of seeing, as Aristotle explains in Book X of the *Nicomachean Ethics*, is intrinsically complete and perfected at the moment of seeing: "...the act of sight [*horasis*] appears to be perfect [*teleia*] at any moment of its duration; it does not require anything to supervene later in order to perfect its form" (NE, 1174 a14f.). Seeing was regarded as the most powerful of the senses, according to Heidegger, because it was, for the Greeks, the most powerful way in which things could be given *us present:*

Seeing, having or keeping something in view, is indeed the predominant, most obvious, most direct and indeed the most

---

[10] M, 1048 b23. For an extensive discussion of this simultaneity which inheres in vision, see Hans Jonas, "The Nobility of Sight," *Philosophy and Phenomenological Research* 14, no. 4 (June 1954): 507–19.

impressive and extensive way of having something present. On account of its exceptional way of *making-present,* sensible vision attains the role of the exemplary model for knowing, knowing taken as an apprehending of entities. The essence of vision is: it makes and holds things present, holds something *within* presence, so that it is *manifest, there* in its unconcealment. (GA 34, 159–60)

Only because the Greeks implicitly understood the being or givenness of beings as *presence* could the *eidos,* as that which can be most constantly present amidst the flux of things, come to dominate over the event of unconcealment as such, determining the unconcealment of whatever appears.

Yet for vision truly to see, and thus to be a genuine knowing, it must precisely remain with its object, in the presence of what it sees; what it sees must be that which abides in presence. It cannot immediately pass on to something else, like the productive activity of the artisan, who must put his hands to work, or the restlessness of the merely curious, who desire only to have seen. Like mere curiosity, the philosophical desire is certainly a desire to see. And to see is always already to have seen—the Greek word *eidenai* conveying precisely this perfect tense. Thus, translated more literally, the first line of the *Metaphysics* reads, "All humans by nature desire to see and to have seen."[11] Yet there is a decisive difference between seeing and having seen only to have seen, and seeing and having seen while remaining in the presence of what is thus disclosed. Only the latter can constitute a knowing that allows the seer to take a stand amidst the flow of appearances, to stand before what he sees, and thus to truly know and dispose over it. Only such tarrying in which one at the same time has seen and continues to see fulfils the sense of genuine knowing once conveyed in the Greek word *epistēmē* (literally, to stand before, over and against something).

The philosophical desire is, therefore, in its very beginnings, also a desire to have seen, but to tarry in the presence of its (nonsensible) vision: such is the Greek determination of the life and activity of *theōrein* as understood in its most decisive and influential form in Aristotle.

Let us interrupt for now these preliminary remarks concerning this second form of the desire to see, the philosophical desire. The many complexities of this problematic will occupy us in the course of the present study. But it should be emphasized from the outset that Heidegger, in drawing attention to the interruptions of our involvement in worldly concerns, is not necessarily claiming that the *technē* pertaining to productive comportment is the ultimate ground of philosophical knowledge. This is not a claim that

---

[11] This point is made by Hannah Arendt in *The Life of the Mind,* vol. 1, 58, 87.

"theory" is grounded in "praxis." Rather, we shall see Heidegger argue that
"praxis"—in the quite broad sense of concern with worldly things and its
corresponding circumspection—is itself a *founded* kind of presence, founded
in care, which may harbor a more originary kind of vision.

(3) Is there a more primordial kind of vision? This brings us back to the
question of a third kind of desire to see, the question of what appears to be
Heidegger's own "definition" of knowledge. *Wissen heißt: gesehen haben.*
"To know means: to have seen," he announces. It is again an identification of knowing with seeing (one that implicitly recalls *videre* as the Latin
root of *Wissen*), and once more a matter of *having* seen. The statement
appears in "The Origin of the Work of Art" (1936), but it is a "definition"
Heidegger will repeat throughout his later work, his insistence upon the
importance of "listening" to language notwithstanding. In knowing as having seen, the "seeing" in question is not simply opposed to hearing, for it
is not reducible to sense-perception by the eyes as opposed to the ears or
other sense organs. In the essay "Logos" (1951), for example, when speaking of the *sophia* of the Presocratics, Heidegger asks what is meant by such
knowing. "If such knowing remains a having seen whose seeing is not that
of the eyes as senses—just as having heard is not at all a hearing with the
instruments of hearing—then having heard and having seen presumably
coincide" (VA, 209). As this later context of a pre-philosophical *sophia* indicates, such having-seen, although it is not reducible to sense-perception,
is also not that of the philosophical sighting of the nonsensible.[12]

Now this definition of knowing as it appears in "The Origin of the Work
of Art" explicitly identifies such knowing with *technē*. And the kind of seeing
intended, Heidegger tells us, is to be taken "in the broad sense of seeing,
which means: apprehending something present as such." Yet *technē* in this
sense is not simply the making or producing accomplished by the artisan.
Technē, says Heidegger,

> as a kind of knowing experienced by the Greeks, is a bring-
> ing forth [*Hervorbringen*] of beings in that it brings forth [*her*]
> what is present as such out of concealment expressly before
> [*vor*] us and into the unconcealment of its outward appearance
> [*Aussehen*]; *technē* never means the activity of making. (H, 48)

Technē is not simply an activity of making, undertaken by a human
"subject." It is a *poiēsis*, a "bringing forth," but a bringing forth from out
of *concealment*. Concealment itself is thus intrinsic to *technē* as a knowing
having-seen. Such *technē* is of course not the same as philosophical knowledge. Yet we have noted that Heidegger's readings of the Greeks suggest

---

[12] On this point, see especially the discussion in *Der Satz vom Grund*, SG, 85ff.

that it was indeed a particular, restrictive interpretation of *technē* that provided the model according to which such knowledge developed. Here, in "The Origin of the Work of Art," Heidegger appears to be seeking a broader, less restrictive understanding of *technē* via the context of a meditation on art, which, as he recalls, was also called *technē* by the Greeks. Thus, he continues:

> The artist is not a *technitēs* because he is also a craftsman, but rather because both the setting-forth [*Her-stellen*] of works and the setting-forth of items of use occur in that bringing-forth-before us which in advance lets beings come before us [*vor kommen*] into their presencing in terms of their outward appearance. (H, 48)

Technē is not mere human activity, but a bringing forth that responds to a *"letting* come before us," which is to say: to a coming, a future, an arrival that has somehow already occurred "in advance." The outward appearance of the work, the presencing of its "look" which arouses our desire, would thus also have to be understood in terms of this letting.

We shall not analyse this definition of knowledge any further at this point; we would have to approach the topic of that desire which the Greeks called *erōs* in the context of Heidegger's discussion of art and the beautiful—something to which we shall have to return. Let us for now conclude these remarks on this third kind of desire to see by recalling that Heidegger goes on to relate it to the ecstatic existence of Dasein as resolute openness (*Ent-schlossenheit*), a theme already broached in *Being and Time*. Knowing as having-seen is described as a preservation of the work, a letting-be, an ability to "let the work be a work"; it means both an openness toward being as unconcealment, and assuming a stance within what Heidegger calls *das Ungeheure* of this unconcealment as it occurs in the work (H, 54–55).

What is *das Ungeheure,* the "extraordinary"? We shall meet it again. By way of anticipation, we may already suspect that it announces an opening onto otherness, onto an otherness perhaps unthought—or unforeseen—in the philosophical tradition hitherto. In marked contrast to the withdrawal from worldly concerns that came to characterize the *theōria* of the philosophers, "The Origin of the Work of Art," which is concerned primarily with the "great" work of art, that is, with the role of the artwork beyond its philosophical-political demotion (such as we find in Plato's *Republic*), emphasizes the work's relation to *world,* the way in which the work "opens up" a world and a vision of the world, giving things their "face" and human beings their "outlook" upon themselves (H, 32).

***

By way of conclusion, let us return to the question of *thaumazein* and its relation to curiosity. The threefold conception of "having seen" which may already be in play in *Being and Time,* and the analysis of *thaumazein* that we have suggested, are further illuminated by some remarks made by Heidegger in a lecture course delivered in 1937/38 under the title *Fundamental Questions of Philosophy.* Speaking of the origin of philosophy, Heidegger there states the following:

> The customary accounts of the provenance [*Herkunft*] of philosophy from *thaumazein* usually give the impression that philosophy arises from curiosity [*Neugier*]—a feeble and pitiful determination of its origin, and one that is possible only where one has never given thought to what it is that is here to be determined in its "origin" [*Ursprung*]. . . . (GA 45, 156)

Thaumazein, then—as *Being and Time* already indicated—is not to be identified with curiosity. If there is a certain desire pertaining to such wonder or "astonishment" (*Er-staunen*)—for the latter is experienced only insofar as human *technē* turns toward and runs up against *phusis,* against the self-emergent prevailing of beings as a whole—this desire and attunement intrinsic to *thaumazein* nevertheless conceals an inherent danger, the danger of its own self-destruction. It can happen, Heidegger remarks,

> that the craving [*Gier*] to acquire knowledge and to be able to calculate takes the place of the fundamental attunement of astonishment. Philosophy itself now becomes *one* undertaking among others; it is made subordinate to an end that is all the more dangerous the higher it is set—as, for example, in Plato's *paideia,* a word that is poorly translated as "education" [*Erziehung*]. Even the fact that in Plato's *Republic* the "philosophers" are called upon to be the highest rulers, the *basileis,* is already an essential demotion of philosophy. As the grasping of beings, our acknowledging them in their unconcealment, unfolds into *technē,* those aspects [*Anblicke*] of entities that are brought into view in such grasping—the "ideas"—inevitably and increasingly become that which alone provides the measure of things. Grasping becomes a knowing familiarity with ideas, and this requires constant conformity to these ideas. . . . (GA 45, 180–81)

This vocation of philosophy whereby the supremacy of *theōria* becomes subservient to the end of governing the *polis* (a tendency consolidated, as we shall see, by Aristotle), and eventually to the *technē* of calculative production, is not merely something that *can* happen; it has already happened as the history of metaphysics, the history of Western science and technology. What is the upshot of this dislodging of the unconcealment of beings into the realm of the idea? Philosophy itself becomes an oddity, "a curiosity," *eine Kuriosität*. What does it mean, Heidegger asks, that philosophy has become a curiosity? It means

> that philosophy stands at the end of its first beginning [*Anfang*], in that situation which corresponds to its beginning—albeit only as its *final predicament* [Endzustand]. Once philosophy was that which was most strange and seldom and singular—now it is the same, but now only in the form of a curiosity. (GA 45, 182–83)

The very success of philosophy's offspring, science and technology, in the end brings about the end and legitimate completion of philosophy itself, which becomes increasingly marginalized and powerless, paradoxically subsumed by that which it once sought to resist. And this process, Heidegger argues, goes hand in hand with the loss or occlusion of the originary essence of *alētheia*, of "unconcealment."

In what follows, we shall try to follow the complex trace of this desire to see and its mutations in Heidegger's work. We shall begin by considering the philosophical response, that of *theōria*, in the light of Heidegger's reading of Aristotle and in the perspective of *Being and Time*. In part 2, we shall examine the modern transformation of this same desire as manifest in the essence of modern science and technology, a transformation that brings the history of philosophy, as the history of *theōria*, to a definitive and very specific end. After considering Heidegger's reading of a decisive intimation of this end in Nietzsche's thought of the eternal return of the same (part 3), we shall turn, finally, back toward the Greek beginning in an attempt to better understand what the establishment of the philosophical *theōria* itself entailed (part 4).[13]

---

[13] An early version of chapter 1 has appeared under the title *Heidegger: Visions* (University of Warwick, England: Center for Research in Philosophy and Literature, 1993).

Part I

Theoria and Philosophy: Heidegger and Aristotle

Reaching back to Aristotle becomes an authentic recollection only if we philosophize in the *Augenblick*. (GA 26, 18)

Compared to the duration of the *kosmos* in general, human existence and its history is indeed most fleeting, only an *'Augenblick'*—and yet this transiency is nevertheless the highest manner of being when it becomes an existing from out of freedom and for freedom. (GA 26, 23)

Only individual action itself—the *Augenblick*—can dislodge us from the most extreme brink of possibility into actuality. Philosophizing, on the other hand, can only ever lead us to the brink and always remains something penultimate in this respect. Yet it can only ever lead us this far if it actually runs ahead into this penultimate domain and thus grasps its own entirely precursory character and finitude. (GA 29/30, 257)

Chapter 2

Vision in Theory and Praxis: Heidegger's Reading of Aristotle (1924)

The interpretation of curiosity outlined in *Being and Time* situates itself firmly within the existential-ontological perspective of the analytic of Dasein, "and not," Heidegger emphasizes, "within the restricted orientation toward cognition":

> Even at an early date, and within Greek philosophy, it was no accident that cognitive knowledge [*Erkennen*] was conceived in terms of the "desire to see." The treatise which stands first in the collection of Aristotle's treatises on ontology begins with the sentence, *pantes anthrōpoi tou eidenai oregontai phusei:* the care for seeing is essential to man's being. (SZ, 170–71)

This 1927 analysis was, however, preceded by an earlier analysis, dating from 1924, in which Heidegger engaged with precisely this more restricted question, albeit in a manner already informed by a developed existential-ontological problematic. The 1924/25 lecture course on Plato's *Sophist* was in fact introduced by an extensive interpretation of Aristotle, one that in retrospect appears crucial for understanding the extent to which an immanent "destruction" of the history of ontology—and especially of Aristotle—is already being undertaken in the published divisions of *Being and Time*.[1]

---

[1] Throughout the present study, the German word *Destruktion* will be rendered as "destruction." *Destruktion* does not have a merely negative sense for Heidegger, but entails the recovery of the originary sources of the philosophical tradition by dismantling those interpretations that tend to conceal the fundamental issues. See SZ, 22–23.

Some of the far-reaching consequences of that "destruction" will be
discussed in the following chapters. One immediate consequence, however,
is that *Being and Time* should not simply be read (as even today tends
to be the case) as another "theory" of human existence, or for that matter of the meaning of being. A failure to appreciate the extent to which
the foundations of ancient philosophy are being taken up again, critically
reinterrogated, and thereby interpretatively transformed means that even
a careful and astute reading of *Being and Time* may discover only the
repetition of traditional, deep-rooted philosophical "prejudices," without
paying attention to the way in which such "prejudices"—which certainly
are present, only not as something negative, but rather as the positive basis of the treatise itself—are also critically problematized and unsettled by
the interrogative thrust of the inquiry. To mention only one such issue that
will concern us in the present study, it is sometimes argued that *Being
and Time* offers a theory of existence or *Dasein* that, for all its apparent
radicality, merely repeats the most traditional philosophical prejudice of
Platonic-Aristotelian thought: the view that contemplative, philosophical
knowledge, existing in the splendid isolation prescribed by the authentic
existence of Dasein, ought to govern the inauthentic, fallen life of the many
who exist in the fleeting realm of mere opinion and dispersed activity. The
life of everyday *praxis* in the *polis* can be grounded and given meaning
only via the pure *theōrein* of the philosopher, whose contemplation of the
good in itself is not just one *praxis* among others, but the highest and most
authoritative of all. Despite his profound attentiveness to the importance
of plurality and to the inevitable contingency and situatedness of the good
in the realm of ethico-political human reality, even Aristotle (it is claimed)
ultimately betrays a certain "Platonic" preference for the authority of the
theoretical life. *Being and Time* if anything reinforces this "Platonic bias." [2]

This reading of *Being and Time* remains problematically one-sided,
however, to the extent that it highlights the repetition of traditional ontology without fully appreciating or acknowledging the radicality with which
Being and Time simultaneously undermines these dichotomies centered
around the "theoretical" life as opposed to the "practical." Indeed, the publication of the *Sophist* lectures might even seem to reinforce this reading
insofar as it already employs much of the terminology of *Being and Time*
in order to translate many key terms of Aristotle's ontology. [3] The term

---

[2] See Jacques Taminiaux, *Lectures de l'ontologie fondamentale* (Grenoble: Millon,
1989), 149–89. See also Dana R. Villa, *Arendt and Heidegger: The Fate of the Political*
(New Jersey: Princeton University Press, 1996).

[3] Taminiaux, for example, appeals in this manner to a transcript of the *Sophist*
lectures—since published as GA 19—in support of his interpretation. See *Lectures de
l'ontologie fondamentale*, 182–89.

"authenticity" (*Eigentlichkeit*), for example, is used by Heidegger in the *Sophist* lectures to designate the theoretical, contemplative life of *sophia* as distinguished from the ethical and practical disclosure of being in *phronēsis*. Nevertheless, as we shall see in chapters 3 and 4, extreme caution should be exercised in any attempt to translate these correspondences into the analytic of Dasein in *Being and Time,* and this despite, or even because of the terminological similarities. In order to help us appreciate the critical distance that *Being and Time* takes with respect to the decisive foundations of Greek ontology—and particularly with respect to what Heidegger calls "their highest and purest scientific stage in Aristotle," a Temporal interpretation of which "cannot be presented" in *Being and Time* (SZ, 26)[4]—the present chapter focuses on one thread of Heidegger's reading of Aristotle as presented in the *Sophist* course. Because the foundations of Aristotle's ontology are ultimately inseparable from a certain privilege accorded to the activity of *theōrein,* we shall try to trace Heidegger's reading of this privileging of *theōria* in relation to *praxis* and *technē.* In particular, what exactly is the relation between *theōria* and *praxis* in Aristotle, as Heidegger presents it? And how are we to assess the status of Heidegger's own analysis?

As Heidegger points out in §36 of *Being and Time,* Aristotle's *Metaphysics* is concerned with uncovering the origin of our *scientific* investigation of beings and their being "in terms of this specific manner of being of Dasein," that is, in terms of the "desire to see." It provides a Greek interpretation of "the existential genesis of scientific knowledge." "Scientific knowledge" here translates *Wissenschaft.* Although the character of the knowledge in question (i.e., Greek *epistēmē* and *theōria*) is clearly not reducible to that of modern science, translating *Wissenschaft* in any other way would obscure the essential connection Heidegger sees between the two. Yet it is not only, indeed not primarily the origin of modern science that is in question here. The development of modern science parallels the fate of philosophy itself. On the one hand, *Wissenschaft* in the context of Aristotle translates *epistēmē.* At stake, therefore, is a kind of investigative knowing or *Wissen* in the broad sense, which also includes philosophical knowledge. Yet this epistemic knowledge, Heidegger suggests, may be traced back to the "restricted" perspective of cognition or cognitive knowledge (*Erkennen*), which for its part appears to be the "natural" outcome of a primacy of perception when it comes to orienting oneself toward the world. On the other hand, the term *Wissenschaft* also points to what Heidegger already

---

[4] Following convention, we shall translate *Temporalität* as Temporality and *temporal* as Temporal, reserving the lower case to translate *zeitlich* and its cognates. The German *Zeitlichkeit,* temporality, is used by Heidegger to refer to the *ecstases* of time, while *Temporalität* refers more specifically to the *horizonal* dimension of ecstatic temporality. On this point see GA 24, 436.

regarded as the culmination and completion of philosophy in German Idealism (in particular in Hegel's *Science of Logic,* the *Wissenschaft der Logik*). Yet within German Idealism itself, the primacy of a contemplative model of knowing remains. Having recalled philosophy's beginnings in Parmenides' statement, *to gar auto noein estin te kai einai* ("for being and apprehending are the same"), Heidegger notes:

> Being is that which shows itself in pure, contemplative apprehending [*im reinen anschauenden Vernehmen*], and by such seeing alone is being uncovered. Original and genuine truth lies in pure beholding [or pure "intuition": *in der reinen Anschauung*]. This thesis has remained the foundation of Western philosophy ever since. The Hegelian dialectic found in it its motivating conception, and is possible only on this basis. (SZ, 171)

The history of Western philosophy, from Parmenides to Hegel, would thus tell the story of a singular desire.[5]

In the *Sophist* lecture course of winter semester 1924/25, Heidegger attempts to trace the genesis of the supreme form of "scientific" knowledge or *epistēmē,* namely, the *sophia* beloved of the philosophers, a genesis depicted in the first two chapters of *Metaphysics* Book I.[6] There, Aristotle presents his inquiry as starting from the generally held opinions and judgments about knowledge and its different levels. As Heidegger remarks, this account presents the self-interpretation of an understanding implicit in the "natural" or "everyday" *Dasein* of the Greeks.[7] *Sophia,* Heidegger stresses, bears witness to a specific orientation of Dasein: to Dasein's being oriented solely toward things being uncovered and made visible, toward their visibility (GA 19, 69). This intrinsic orientation of Dasein toward visibility culminates in an understanding of the highest possibility of human knowledge

---

[5] In *The Basic Problems of Phenomenology* (1927) Heidegger indeed credits Hegel with having brought philosophy to its completion. It is again a matter of *having seen:* "With Hegel philosophy, that is, ancient philosophy, has in a certain sense been thought to its end.... Hegel has seen everything that is possible. Yet the question is whether he has seen it from the radical center of philosophy, whether he has exhausted all possibilities of the beginning so as to be able to say he is at the end" (GA 24, 400).

[6] Note that Heidegger had presented an (as yet unpublished) interpretation of the first two chapters of *Metaphysics* Book I more than two years earlier, in a course on Aristotle delivered in summer semester 1922. For details see Theodore Kisiel, *The Genesis of Heidegger's* Being and Time (Berkeley and Los Angeles: University of California Press, 1993), 238ff.

[7] Heidegger does not define *Dasein* terminologically in the *Sophist* course. While it might be translated as "existence" (and on occasion will have to be thus translated), we have generally preferred to retain the German word, partly in order to preserve a certain continuity with *Being and Time.* It will become apparent in the course of our reading that *Dasein* is, already in 1924, *also* being understood from the perspective of the question of being as it will be developed in the later treatise.

as pure contemplation, or *theōrein.* Given that philosophy is nothing other than a love (*philein*) of *sophia,* this implies that the "restricted orientation toward cognitive knowledge," once it is referred back to an underlying "desire to see," is the manifestation not merely of a particular tendency within philosophy, but of the philosophical desire itself in its entirety, from its *archē* to its *telos.*

Nevertheless, the brief discussion of the first line of the *Metaphysics* provided in the *Sophist* course is not quite the same as the subsequent discussion in *Being and Time.* Not only is Heidegger's translation somewhat different, but more importantly, the immediate context of his interpretation is different:

> Because *sophia* is determined as pure *theōrein,* Aristotle in the first line of the *Metaphysics* takes this way of existing [*Dasein*] as his point of departure: *pantes anthrōpoi tou eidenai oregontai phusei....* "All human beings intrinsically strive to see." To existence [*Dasein*] there belongs "seeing," apprehending in the broadest sense; what is more: to existence there belongs *orexis,* a pursuit of seeing, of being familiar with.... (GA 19, 69–70)

Here, *oregontai* and *orexis* are not yet translated by "care," as they will be in *Being and Time,* but by "striving" and "pursuit."[8] A second difference of translation is that Heidegger here refers to "human beings" rather than to "man's being." Nonetheless, it is clear that for both Heidegger and Aristotle it is the *phusis,* that is, the intrinsic nature of human beings that is at issue, and Heidegger indeed goes on to refer to this as "the being of humans."

Yet the horizon of Heidegger's interpretation, though certainly ontologically informed, is not yet that of an explicitly *existential* interpretation of *Dasein,* although Heidegger does note that the method of the interpretation is grounded in a "phenomenology of Dasein" that cannot be explicitly presented in the present context (GA 19, 62). Rather, the context of this part of the 1924/25 course is an attempt to trace the genesis of *sophia* as the ultimate possibility of pure contemplation, or *theōrein.* Here, Heidegger will read the desire to see in terms of the ultimate possibility of contemplative knowledge. In the discussion of the first line of the *Metaphysics* in *Being and Time,* by contrast, we find no explicit mention of either *theōrein* or *sophia.* At most, we find a reference to *Wissenschaft* and to the Greek interpretation of its "existential" genesis. And this may suggest that the desire to see

---

[8] The German for pursuit, *Aussein auf ...,* which suggests a being directed toward something, is used in the 1922 treatise "Phenomenological Interpretations with Respect to Aristotle" to convey the meaning of "care" (*Sorgen, curare*). Care, as the fundamental meaning of the factical movement of life, is directed toward its respective *world* in each case (PIA, 6).

is being submitted to a different horizon of interpretation in the existential analytic—a horizon that is neither simply that of *theōrein* nor that of its corollary *philosophia*. For both these, as we have noted, would seem to fall within the logic of that "restricted orientation" toward cognitive knowledge from which Heidegger distances the existential analytic in *Being and Time*. In other words, perhaps the ultimate horizon of the "desire to see" will, in *Being and Time*, prove to be something other than pure *theōrein*, the supreme fulfilment of *sophia*. Perhaps it will point accordingly to another horizon of knowledge, of *Wissen*, and to a different genesis of *Wissenschaft*.[9] Perhaps it already points toward a horizon of seeing and knowing that is neither that of curiosity, nor that of the philosophical tradition described in the *Sophist* course.

A third discussion of the first line of the *Metaphysics* appears in the course directly following the *Sophist* lectures: the *Prolegomena to the History of the Concept of Time*, delivered in the summer semester of 1925 and destined to be reworked into the first division of *Being and Time*. As in the magnum opus, the discussion again occurs in the context of an analysis of curiosity, but the analysis of curiosity is here embedded within an interpretation of "falling" as a way in which Dasein is "moved" in its being (GA 20, 378). Although a translation identical to that in *Being and Time* is offered, the interpretation displays significant deviations from the 1927 treatise. Most importantly, Heidegger in the 1925 course appears to criticize Aristotle for understanding metaphysical knowledge—still referred to as *theōrein*—in terms of the desire to see. This desire is here explicitly identified with curiosity. But Aristotle's interpretation, Heidegger now objects, is one-sided, even "out of place" or "wrong":

> The treatise that stands first in the collection of Aristotle's writings on ontology begins with the sentence: *pantes anthrōpoi tou eidenai oregontai phusei:* the care for seeing is essential to man's being. Aristotle places this sentence at the beginning of his metaphysics, where this way of putting it is really out of place [*verkehrt*]; at any rate, this sentence begins his introductory remarks which have the task of clarifying theoretical comportment in respect of its origin as the Greeks then saw it. For him curiosity [*Neugier*] becomes an altogether originary comportment from which theoretical comportment, *theōrein*—taken solely in the Greek sense—receives its motivation. That is an

---

[9] A possibility that would also challenge the thesis of Jacques Taminiaux, namely, that Heidegger leaves unquestioned "the idea that perception ... is nascent science." See *Lectures de l'ontologie fondamentale*, 129. In chapter 3, we shall attempt to trace this other genesis of science in showing how Heidegger's conception of an *existential* genesis of science disrupts the very order of derivation that it attempts to thematize.

altogether one-sided interpretation, yet one that is motivated
by the Greek way of seeing things. What is important for us is
simply that *eidenai* (which is not to be translated as knowing
[*Wissen*]) is indeed constitutive for the *phusis* of human beings.
(GA 20, 380–81)

The term *verkehrt* seems in this context to mean simply "wrong" or
"mistaken" in the sense of "out of place." However, it more literally implies something being upside down or the wrong way round (as in Hegel's
"inverted world," *die verkehrte Welt*). The implication here seems to be
that the desire to see—at least if we take it in the sense of curiosity—does
not amount to an "originary" manner of comportment in terms of which
the origin and genesis of *theōrein* could be explained. It does not, perhaps,
constitute the *phusis* of human beings. And if *eidenai* is not to be rendered
as "knowing," then this is presumably in order to retain and emphasize the
original visual connotation of the word. One reading of this passage would
be to understand it as repeating a classical gesture often made whenever
an order of founding is at stake: the "higher" may not be explained by the
"lower." *Eidenai* would not yet be metaphysical knowledge or *Wissen;* the
latter would be achieved only in a consummate *theōrein*. Accordingly, the
order of founding implied by Aristotle would have to be reversed. Curiosity,
the desire to see, would have to be understood on the grounds of the apriori
constitution of *theōrein* as its intrinsic "condition of possibility," and not
vice versa. Curiosity would be a lesser stage of a consummate *theōrein,* it
would not yet have attained the ultimate object of its desire, an object that
would always already determine it from the beginning. The appearance of
this sentence at the outset of Aristotle's *Metaphysics*—which presumably
ought to identify the origin of metaphysical knowledge in the *phusis* of
human beings—would therefore be out of place.[10]
     Such a reading, however, might have to be tempered by another. Es-
pecially if, already at this early stage of Heidegger's work, knowledge or
genuine *Wissen* no more amounts to theoretical comportment than it does
to curiosity. And especially if the "desire to see" should ultimately—that
is, from the beginning, in its very origins—prove to be something other
than curiosity. For could it not be that Heidegger is here pursuing the suspicion that to understand the origin of *theōrein* in terms of curiosity—or
indeed vice versa, in Hegelian fashion, where pure *theōrein* or intellectual
intuition finally sees itself as the historical, albeit retrospective completion
of its lesser stages—is to misunderstand what is ultimately at stake in the
desire to see, thus to misunderstand that desire itself?

---

[10] Such a reading is suggested by Hans Blumenberg in *Das Lachen der Thrakerin: Eine
Urgeschichte der Theorie* (Frankfurt: Suhrkamp, 1987), 152–53.

The End of Desire

Again, everything depends upon the horizon of interpretation. For already in Heidegger's *Sophist* lectures the interpretive horizon of this desire is in fact not reducible to that of *theōrein*, as will become apparent. Yet since the horizon of the *Metaphysics* is indeed that of *theōrein*, let us first accompany Heidegger in surveying, within the perspective of that horizon, what is said at the beginning of Aristotle's treatise.

Aristotle begins Book I of the *Metaphysics* by discussing five different levels or degrees of "seeing" or knowing: *aisthēsis, empeiria, technē, epistēmē,* and *sophia.* The first of these, *aisthēsis* or sensory apprehending, is said to belong by nature to living beings in general. A second level of knowledge is that of *empeiria*, "experience." Whereas sensory apprehending is dependent at each moment on the givenness of an immediate object presented to it, experience implies having assumed a certain stance—an orientation or *Gestelltsein*, as Heidegger puts it (GA 19, 73)—and a relative constancy amid the alternation of sense data; it implies having already gathered a given manifold of sensations with respect to an underlying unity, that is, being able to hold together in a certain continuity what would otherwise be dispersed temporal moments of sensory apprehension. In short, it entails the ability to retain phenomena, to hold things present (*Gegenwärtighalten*) over and across a span of time.

Aristotle grants a measure of experience—which by implication arises from a combination of sense-impressions and memory (the latter entailing also *phantasia*, "imagination")—to other animals as well as to humans. Yet having assumed a stance and orientation in the midst of other beings does not yet entail being able to relate to that very stance as such, that is, to attain selfhood in the sense of having freed oneself for one's own being. Such is possible only through the distance granted by *logos*, only through a "seeing" that sees beyond what appears in the experiential unity of sense-perception. Thus, Aristotle continues, "humankind lives also by art and reasoning." The terms "art" and "reasoning" (*technē kai logismois*) are used in a fairly broad sense here, which is difficult to render in English. *Technē* means knowledge; it is clearly different from both sensory apprehending and from experience, while not yet being defined in the narrow sense of productive (as opposed to practical) knowledge. *Logismois* for its part refers to the faculty of *logos*, and recalls the Greek definition of the human being as *zōion logon echon*. The two indeed go together: the implication is that the move to the level of *technē* entails having *logos*. Unlike human beings, animals and other living beings by implication have neither *logos* nor *technē*.

At this point Aristotle mentions a fourth level of knowledge, though without indicating more precisely what it means. It is through experience, he says, that humans acquire both art (*technē*) and "science" (*epistēmē*). *Technē*, Aristotle explains, first comes about when, out of many impressions (*ennoēmatōn*) arising from experience, "a single universal judgment is formed with regard to like objects." Both experience and *technē* are kinds of knowing (*gnōsis*): experience is knowledge of particulars; *technē* of universals. And yet, Aristotle states, "we consider that knowledge [*eidenai*] and proficiency belong more to *technē* than to experience, and we assume that artisans are wiser than people of mere experience ..." (M, 981 a24). The specific knowing to be found in *technē* is an *eidenai*, the "seeing" that in the opening sentence is identified as the specific goal of human striving. Experience, as Aristotle notes, certainly belongs to *technē* in the sense that such knowledge arises through experience: without experience, there could be no *technē*. Nevertheless Aristotle indicates that there is a qualitative leap from the seeing of particulars to the seeing of universals. Although experience is also a having-seen (and indeed a kind of having-seen that is crucial for the development of *phronēsis*),[11] namely, a having run through and assimilated a number of "perceptions," this having seen remains as such a knowledge of particulars (of particular events, "facts," perceptions), of sensory experience, and is not yet a seeing of universals. Such "seeing" of universals, of the "forms" or *eidē*, is implicit within *technē*, and it is on the basis of such universals that scientific knowledge or *epistēmē* can first develop.

In his analysis of *Metaphysics* Book I, Heidegger emphasizes that in *empeiria* the particular phenomenon that appears is indeed present in its *eidos*, but this *eidos* is embedded in a referential context of involvement. This implies that it is experienced from out of whatever is presenting itself in a particular context, but is not explicitly anticipated or foreseen as such. In the development of *technē*, by contrast, that which can present itself is precisely *anticipated* in its *eidos* as *archē*, as that which is already there, that starting from which something arises (*aition*) and comes to presence. "That which the making-present [*Gegenwärtigung*] of the context ultimately anticipates is: putting the being in its presence [*Anwesenheit*] (*ousia*) at our disposal in uncovering it by going back to what is already there, the *archē*" (GA 19, 77). In this process of seeing more (*mallon eidenai*) by foreseeing, by anticipation, the *eidos* becomes increasingly separated out—increasingly set into relief over and against its particular instantiation and appearance, even though it has not yet become the object of an independent and thematic contemplating, which first occurs at the level of *epistēmē* as rigorously defined by Aristotle. The *eidos* in this proto-independence is initially

---

[11] Thus, Aristotle indicates, even animals may be said to have a kind of *phronēsis* (M, 980 b22).

"simply there," implicit within *technē* itself. Its increasing separation—precisely via the Platonic-Aristotelian determination of being—is nevertheless indicative, as Heidegger points out, of an increasing independence of the Greek *logos* itself. Within the process of dealing with things, of doing and making, *"legein* becomes *more and more independent"* (GA 19, 91). The *eidos* is, as it were, "read off" (*abgelesen*) from—which also means it is read into—the things themselves in their contextual presence (GA 19, 77); it is selected and gathered (*legein*) as such: it is anticipated *as logos*. What is at stake in this process is thus nothing less than the advent of the Greek-Western *logos* of scientific-technical rationality that claims to be the *logos* of beings themselves. Yet—as we shall see much later in our study—one of the things that Heidegger's thinking of being (the *logos* of *Sein*) will try to show is that this specific anticipation (this specific foreseeing as a prediction, a fore-telling of something in "how it comes to its being": GA 19, 91) does a certain violence to things themselves, to beings in the uniqueness of their self-showing. The *eidos*, as being (*Sein*), is not originarily *logos*.

The fifth and final stage of knowledge discussed by Aristotle in the first chapter of Book I is *sophia*, wisdom. The general assumption that the artisans are wiser than people of mere experience further implies, says Aristotle, that *sophia* "in all cases depends rather upon knowledge [*eidenai*]" (M, 981 a26). Aristotle also gives his reason for assuming that artisans are wiser: it is because they "know," that is, have seen (*isasin*, related to *eidenai*) the "cause" (*aitia*). Knowledge as *eidenai* is thus a particular tendency lying within *technē*, a tendency that points already in the direction of *sophia*. In *technē*, as Heidegger puts it, *sophia* is already prefigured (GA 19, 77).

This brief and very schematic outline already indicates something essential with respect to the distinction between experience, in its directedness toward *aisthēsis*, and *technē*, and in particular with respect to the different kinds of apprehending involved. It points to something that will be crucial for Aristotle's distinguishing between *theōria* and *phronēsis*, between contemplation and practical wisdom. Whereas in *technē* that which has yet to come into presence (the *ergon*, the "work" to be produced) has already been seen in advance in its determinative *eidos*—whereas the seeing in *technē*, as an *eidenai*, is a seeing *and having seen*—the particular object of sense-perception that contributes to experience has not been seen in advance; in its singularity and uniqueness, it has always yet to be seen. Whereas the antecedent sighting (*theōrein*) of the *eidos* in *technē* in principle already *has* the being (*ousia*) of its object at its disposal (barring the inevitable contingencies to which the actual process of making is exposed), this is not at all the case at the level of the *aisthēsis* of experience, where that which presents itself has precisely not been seen in advance. This "already having present at one's disposal" is elsewhere identified by Heidegger as the primary meaning of being that comes to the fore in Greek philosophy: *ousia, parousia,* presence.[12] It is a sense of being already inscribed within the Greek *eidenai.*

The development of this sense of "seeing" as a freely disposing over is further illuminated by Aristotle when he contrasts the person of experience, the craftsman, and the master craftsman or *architektōn.* The person of experience sees the "fact," the "that it is" (*to hoti*), but not the "wherefore" (*dioti*). He sees that this is the case here and now, as the situation presents itself in a particular context, but does not see or know whence it arises, how it has come to be. The craftsman or artisan, by contrast, sees the wherefore, the "cause" (*aitia*). The master craftsman, however, sees more and is wiser than the mere craftsman. And this superiority is associated with the fact that the master craftsman has developed the ability to teach. To this extent, his knowledge already foreshadows the possibility of *epistēmē,* for (unlike that of the artisan) it has been freed from direct involvement in the productive process. Like the epistemic knowledge foreshadowed by it, the ability to teach is a possibility already latent within *technē,* a possibility which the master craftsman explicitly develops. Yet the master craftsman is still to some extent a craftsman. The vision of the master craftsman remains oriented toward the end of making and of production. And if wisdom is to be associated with being free and independent (*eleutheros*)—with freedom from involvement, with freedom for *theōrein,* for overseeing and surveying existence as a whole—then there may be a knowledge that is still wiser and more free. The hierarchy of knowledge outlined by Aristotle at the close of the first chapter of Book I is thus summarized as follows: "the person of experience is held to be wiser than the mere possessors of any power of sense-perception, the artisan than the person of experience, the master craftsman than the artisan, and speculative knowledge [*de theōrētikai*] more learned than productive [*poiētikōn*]" (M, 981 b31).

The reason for this discussion of knowledge, Aristotle reminds us, is that we are investigating what is meant by *sophia.* General opinion has it that the kinds of knowledge discussed represent ascending stages of wisdom, because it is generally assumed that *sophia* is concerned with "the primary causes and principles" (*ta prōta aitia kai tas archas:* M, 981 b29). *Sophia* is implicitly understood to mean knowledge of the first causes and principles, and this is identified with the developed tendency toward pure *theōrein.*

What is the ultimate object or end of the desire to see? According to Aristotle's analysis of the natural tendency, it is to be found in *sophia,* in that kind of knowledge in which we find a distinctive *theōrein* and which constitutes an end in itself. Aristotle considers this ultimate mutation of

---

[12] See SZ, 25–26; also KPM, 233; GA 24, 214–15; and GA 26, 182–84.

eidenai in the second chapter of Book I of the *Metaphysics*, again by way
of recollecting the various opinions and judgments as to what characterizes
this supreme seeing and those who possess it.

Sophia, Aristotle tells us, is an exceptional kind of *epistēmē*. For it
entails knowing (*epistasthai*) all things, "so far as it is possible, without
having knowledge of every one of them individually" (M, 982 a8). Such
knowledge is therefore not an "empirical" knowledge, not *empeiria*. It is
not a matter of experiencing all things and thereby having knowledge of
them, but rather of seeing the universal (*katholou*). This of course does not
preclude its starting from experience in the sense of being acquired through
(*dia*) experience, as are *epistēmē* and *technē* (M, 981 a3). However, wisdom
is concerned with knowledge of "difficult things" (*ta chalepa*)—things that
are difficult for most people to see, because they lie furthest removed from
the senses (M, 982 a25). It is concerned with knowledge of the causes;
indeed, as Aristotle has already indicated, with the primary causes and
principles. And among the "sciences" or kinds of *epistēmē*, Aristotle states,
that *epistēmē* which is desirable in itself, for the sake of itself (*de tēn autēs*
heneken) and for the sake of *eidenai* (*tou eidenai charin*) is more nearly
wisdom than that which is desirable for its results (M, 982 a15).

Several points follow from this. First, as Aristotle has indicated, wisdom
will belong to the theoretical or speculative sciences rather than to the
productive sciences, for the latter aim at some result. Second, if we desire
wisdom for the sake of *eidenai*, this is because such seeing is at root the very
essence of *sophia*. Third, since we desire it for the sake of itself, *sophia* must
be self-sufficient, self-grounding (although certain factical preconditions are
of course required in order for it to emerge): it must be its own object or
end.[13] And fourth, the same point is reflected again in the very structure of
the *hou heneka:* the "for the sake of which," Aristotle will shortly indicate,
is one of the causes (M, 983 a33). *Sophia* is to see the causes, and thereby
also to see itself as self-caused, existing for the sake of itself and having
no cause beyond itself. *Sophia* is thus the only free or independent science
(M, 982 b27). For it is that seeing in which all "causality" begins and ends,
in which the *phusis* of the human being first comes to itself and flourishes
as such, in which it first attains its proper independence and freedom, its
proper end. Such "seeing" first brings the human being explicitly into his
own proper being, into his own proper end in relation to beings as a whole.
Thus, wisdom as supreme knowing is said by Aristotle to know "the end of
each action [*prakteon*], which is the good in each particular case," as well
as "the highest good as a whole in all of nature" (M, 982 b5). The good

---

[13] See NE, 1177 a27f., where Aristotle ascribes self-sufficiency (*autarkeia*) to the
activity of *theōrein* that belongs to *sophia*.

means the end as that for the sake of which something exists; as such, notes Aristotle, it is one of the causes.

What are the implications of all this for the knowledge under investigation? The inevitable conclusion has in fact already been drawn. It is already clear, Aristotle concludes in chapter one, that the knowledge of first principles and causes will be an *epistēmē,* and as such a specific form of *theōrein* (M, 982 a3). It is clear (*dēlon*), because the knowledge at issue is something being investigated, that is, it is being explicitly sought after, pursued; and this seeking is itself nothing other than our pursuit of the "natural" human tendency and desire to see, the desire for *eidenai.* Given this "natural" desire, the question naturally follows: What is the highest or supreme seeing (*malista eidenai*) attainable by human beings? Aristotle finds the answer in the supreme *theōrein* of *sophia,* in a pure *nous* which, as he clarifies in Book XII, moves our being as the primary object of desire (*hōs erōmenon*) (M, 1072 b4). What is seen in this ultimate contemplation is nothing other than the permanent presence of the world as a whole, of the highest and divine good as it moves our being. *Theōrein,* as a *noein,* an activity of *nous,* can see the being of particular beings (in the *dianoein,* the discursive *noein* found in *epistēmē*) only because it has always already somehow seen this whole. And this presence of world is simply the divine work of (an "active" or poietic) *nous* in us, to which our finite ("passive" or responsive) human *nous* can ascend in an ultimate activity of *theōrein.*

In one sense, then, the object of this sought-after knowledge is in fact already given and ultimately cannot be in question, insofar as Aristotle takes the "natural" attitude—ordinary understanding or opinion (*doxa*)— as his starting point, as the *archē* of his own investigation. What is sought is already there, already given—but only as the concealed end of natural desire. Yet paradoxically, therefore, it has not yet been given, precisely insofar as that desire has not yet reached its end, has not yet been fully unfolded and fulfilled. Aristotle's investigation into *sophia* merely makes explicit what is already presupposed in this natural desire, inscribing itself within that *archē* and *telos,* his *logos* thereby itself fulfilling and accomplishing that very desire. As Heidegger notes in his commentary, "this idea of *sophia,* which proceeds toward the *aitia* as such, and indeed in the direction of *ta ex archēs,* that is, of the *archai,* makes explicit what Dasein implicitly strives for in a manner as yet unclear to itself" (GA 19, 96).

The Complication of Praxis

Book I of the *Metaphysics* thus narrates the story of an uninterrupted unfolding of vision from its most primitive and basic stages of sense-perception into its supreme and highest form found in the *theōrein* belonging to *sophia*. It tells the story of what we may call the *natural genesis* of theoretical comportment, a genesis that unfolds by way of a seemingly unproblematic teleology of desire, of a desire that supposedly belongs to the "nature" of human beings. The philosophical desire itself, as the striving for *sophia*, would do nothing other than explicitly enact the stages prescribed by this natural genesis. Yet this genesis is itself threatened in its very principle when we consider that human comportment does not unfold merely in accordance with the necessity of innate or natural desire, but in accordance with desire that can be modified through *logos*, in other words, in accordance with human *praxis*. Theoretical contemplation, after all, is itself a *praxis*, a comportment freely chosen by human beings who are not simply subject to laws of natural necessity.

The complication of *praxis* thus threatens to interrupt the story of a purely natural genesis of theoretical life. If there is a natural hierarchy of human vision and knowing, then such a hierarchy must first be grounded with respect to the *logos* itself. More precisely, it must demonstrate its legitimacy with respect to the relation between *logos* and desire, that is, with respect to the nature of the intrinsic possibilities and limits of human *praxis*. In the 1924/25 *Sophist* course, Heidegger investigates precisely this complication via a reading of Aristotle's *Nicomachean Ethics* that focuses on Books VI and X. The entire interpretation hinges on the question of the relative priority of practical or theoretical wisdom, of *phronēsis* or *sophia* as discussed by Aristotle at the end of Book VI. Indeed, Heidegger's reading of *Metaphysics* Book I occurs within an interpretation of the *Nicomachean Ethics* oriented toward understanding the respective claims of *phronēsis* and *sophia* to be the highest mode of ontological disclosure. In the current section, we shall follow Heidegger's initial analysis that seeks to locate *phronēsis* in a preliminary manner with respect to the other forms of knowledge examined in Book VI of the *Ethics*. We shall then be in a position to examine Heidegger's interpretation of the relation between theoretical and practical knowledge with regard to their modes of "seeing," considered as modes of disclosure.

Book I of the *Metaphysics* indeed appears to allude to the *Nicomachean Ethics* as explicating the distinction between *technē, epistēmē,* and other forms of knowledge (M, 981 b26). Practical knowledge and its most excellent form, *phronēsis* or practical wisdom, seems to differ in principle from theoretical or speculative knowledge, simply because practical knowledge is always already involved in a particular *praxis*. It does not have time to turn away or take a contemplative distance from the concrete situation of its immediate involvement. The horizon of *praxis* thus seems to lie outside that of *theōrein*. And we might therefore expect practical knowledge to be different in principle from that "desire to see" which marks the starting point or *archē* of Aristotle's investigation into speculative knowledge. But is this in fact the case?

For Aristotle, *praxis* is the highest and most distinctive possibility of human existence.[14] Unfolding in the midst of the temporal and the contingent, such existence can in no sense transcend the intrinsic finitude of its situation so as to attain directly an outside perspective on itself. Such a perspective would be possible only if one were to commit the *hubris* of identifying the human condition with that of the divine. Aristotle's account of the *praxis* of human life emphasizes the worldly character of human involvements and the inevitable unpredictabilities to which such an existence is exposed. Nevertheless, it remains striking that Aristotle will ascribe the fullest disclosure of human existence as such not to the kind of vision that remains attentive to and most fully apprehends such contingencies—the vision of *phronēsis* or practical wisdom—but to the "theoretical" vision belonging to the *sophia* of the philosopher. The philosophical vision sees most transparently what human existence is as such. And yet, the relation between theoretical knowledge and *praxis* is not a simple opposition for Aristotle. As a kind of knowing, *theōria* may indeed be contrasted with *phronēsis,* but, as we shall appreciate more fully later, this contrast is not an opposition. Aristotle not only identifies the activity of *theōrein* as itself a *praxis;* he regards it as the highest *praxis.* Yet it is not as though *theōria* were merely one possibility or form of human *praxis* among others; rather, as we shall try to show, *theōria* is that kind of vision which first sees and thereby knows what *praxis* itself most truly is. *Theōria* as a *praxis* is so far from being severed from *praxis* and *phronēsis* that it proves, on Aristotle's account, to be the most originary self-disclosure of *praxis* as such.

---

[14] There are of course a number of different usages of the term *praxis* in Aristotle. At least three can be initially discerned: (1) *Praxis* is sometimes used to characterize the nature of "biological" life and its associated activities, as found in both humans and animals. (See, for example, *De partibus animalium,* 645 b15ff.; also *Historia animalium,* 589 a3.) Here, the *praxis* of life has the sense of an activity that maintains itself as such despite its dependence on environment and on other beings generally. Life in this organic sense is an end in itself. Thus, Aristotle also extends the term *praxis* to cover those subordinate activities which serve the overall activity of life, including generation, feeding, growth, copulation, waking, sleep, and locomotion. (2) *Praxis* is also used to refer to specifically human actions or activities, although still in a quite broad sense that includes making (*poiēsis*) and contemplating (*theōria*) as well as ethical and political activity. (3) *Praxis* is used in a more restricted meaning to refer primarily to ethical and political life, to "deeds and words" as the truly human activities. Factual freedom from the necessities of life, including freedom from enslavement, is a precondition of human *praxis* in this sense.

Of these three different registers, we shall be concerned only with the second and third in the present chapter. As will become clear, these two senses cannot always be clearly distinguished from one another, and this for fundamental reasons.

We shall follow some of the details of this argument in the remainder of this chapter. But let us begin by situating, in a preliminary way, Aristotle's understanding of *praxis* and of practical wisdom in relation to theoretical or speculative knowledge. We shall do so within the context of Heidegger's reading.

Heidegger's discussion of *phronēsis* concentrates initially on Book VI of the *Nicomachean Ethics*, where Aristotle describes five ways in which the soul attains truth (*alētheia*) in affirmation or denial, that is, by way of the *logos*. These are identified as *technē, epistēmē, phronēsis, sophia,* and *nous*. Judgment (*hupolēpsis*) and opinion (*doxa*) are said to be capable of error or falsity. All these belong to the virtues of the "intellectual" or "noetic" part of the soul (*noētikōn*) (NE, 1139 b12).

Truth is here considered insofar as it can be apprehended by the soul itself. The soul, according to Aristotle, has two parts, one having *logos*, the other without it (NE, 1139 a5). Furthermore, there are two ways of having *logos:* a) *epistēmonikon*, the epistemic or "scientific" faculty, and b) *logistikon*, the deliberative faculty. The first is concerned with *epistēmē;* the second with deliberation (*bouleuesthai*). The distinction is made on the basis of the kind of knowledge that each provides. The epistemic faculty is concerned with the contemplation (*theōrein*) of those things whose *archai* are invariable, the deliberative faculty with things that are variable: not simply things that can "change" or move, as Heidegger explains, but things that in their very being can be otherwise than they are.

Heidegger frames his reading of Book VI in the following manner. With respect to these two faculties, the task is to ascertain which disposition (*hexis*) of each faculty is best. The criterion for this will be the question of which disposition best discloses the ultimate *archē* or being of things. In the case of the epistemic faculty it will be shown to be *sophia;* in the case of the deliberative faculty, *phronēsis*. The question will then arise of which of these two dispositions has priority. A comparative examination of the different kinds of knowing as dispositions of having *logos* is thus entailed.

Aristotle begins his comparative investigation by considering *epistēmē*. Epistemic knowledge has as its object something that exists of necessity and is eternal (*aidion*). Its object cannot be subject to growth or decay (it is *agenēta*) (NE, 1139 b24). And this means that its being must remain constant even when the object is not being observed or contemplated: epistemic knowing must dispose over its object even *exō tou theōrein*, "outside of an actual beholding at any given moment," as Heidegger puts it. The knowing characteristic of *epistēmē*, as a manner of disclosure, can thus be seen as the preservation of the discoveredness of its object. It uncovers and preserves in such disclosedness the being of its object, yet in a very specific way. Heidegger states:

It is a *being disposed* [Gestelltsein] toward the beings of the
world that disposes over the *look* [Aussehen] of those beings.
Epistēmē is a *hexis of alētheuein* (b31). In this *hexis* the look
of beings is preserved. (GA 19, 32)

This mode of preservation, however, by its very nature entails that the
beings accessible to it and known in this way "can never be concealed."
They cannot become other in their essential being, even when they are
not purely present to our contemplation. "Scientific" knowing thus fundamentally denies the possible self-concealment of beings in its claim to
knowledge, even though it must presuppose that very concealment as its
own raison d'être. The broader implications of this will become apparent
as our study progresses.

In addition to being a *hexis* of disclosure or discovery, *epistēmē* is a *hexis*
of demonstration. It proceeds by deduction or "syllogism" rather than by
induction (*epagōgē*), since the knowledge pertaining to *epistēmē* can be
taught, and "all teaching proceeds from that which is already known."
In other words, *epistēmē* presupposes our already being in explicit possession of certain *archai* (NE, 1139 b18).[15] As learnable and teachable,
epistēmē constitutes an independent kind of knowledge—its *logos* remains
true whether or not its objects are present for it, and yet precisely because
of this it does not in itself provide access to the ultimate disclosedness or
true being of its objects (GA 19, 31f.). Such truth can be apprehended
only by *nous,* for it concerns a truth of *being* and not merely a "logical" or
apophantic truth.

The second form of knowledge Aristotle considers is *technē,* here understood in the restricted sense of know-how that pertains to making or
producing. *Technē* has as its object something that undergoes change. Its
object (the product) undergoes change in the specific sense that prior to the
productive process it does not yet exist in its eventual form. In this sense,
the object of *technē* is something that can be other than it is. *Technē,* like
epistēmē, entails a kind of *theōrein,* but one specifically concerned with
how to bring a thing into existence (NE, 1140 a13). Yet unlike *epistēmē,*
this kind of seeing apparently contains the ultimate *archē* of its object
within itself. Heidegger here refers to Aristotle's account from Book VII
of the *Metaphysics.* Before producing something, a kind of deliberation is
required which entails that the artisan must first contemplate how the product will look in its *eidos.* In the *Metaphysics,* Aristotle states that "that
which properly produces [*to poioun*], that from which movement [*kinēsis*]
begins, is the *eidos* in the soul" (M, 1032 b22). More precisely, it is the
"seeing" of this *eidos,* its presence in the soul, which is there referred to

---

[15] Cf. NE, 1140 b31f. For a more detailed account, see *Posterior Analytics,* 99 b15ff.

as *noēsis* (M, 1032 b15f.). This means, however, that the *archē* does not lie in the work or artifact itself, as does the *archē* of those things which exist "by nature" (*kata phusin*) (NE, 1140 a16). Furthermore, the end of the activity of making is other than the activity itself (NE, 1140 b4); the finished work lies outside (*para*) the productive process (NE, 1094 a6). As finished and completed, the artifact thus no longer falls within the purview of *technē*, but has been set forth and freed for other ends. In other words, the knowledge or *theōrein* specific to *technē*, as concerned with *poiēsis*, with the process of making, cannot wholly preserve within it the full *archē* of its object. The object of *technē*, as something made, is other than *technē* and as such already falls prey to contingency and chance (*tuchē*) in the very process of making. The product may turn out to be a failure, even though the artisan had a clear vision of what he or she wanted to make (cf. NE, 1140 a19). The disclosure in *technē* of the being of its object is intrinsically deficient.

Both the *theōrein* found in *epistēmē* and that found in *technē* thus fall short in their ability to disclose the being of their respective objects. In the case of *epistēmē*, the deficiency is due to the fact that it necessarily refers to objects that lie beyond immediate observation (*exō tou theōrein*), proceeding via deduction on the basis of universal principles (*logoi*) already appropriated. The truths it discloses are thus in principle open to being regarded as merely "logical" truths, without any immediate or direct sighting (*epagōgē*) of their object being required. A prime example, as Aristotle notes, is the ability of the young to learn mathematics, for the purely formal, deductive truths of mathematics do not require any direct experience on the part of the individual (NE, 1142 a15f.). And this amounts to saying that the *theōrein* of *epistēmē* is distanced from an immediate access to and presence of the things themselves. "The first principles from which scientific truths are derived," as Aristotle concludes, "cannot themselves be reached by science" (NE, 1140 b32). In the case of *technē*, the deficiency is due to the contingency that attends the translation of the *eidos* into material existence. As a result, the end product may not accord in its being (*eidos*) with the *eidos* seen in advance. In each case, therefore, there is a spatio-temporal *removal* from immediate presence that limits (but also enables) the disclosive ability of the *theōrein* involved.

Precisely such removal seems not to obtain, however, in the case of the third kind of knowledge considered by Aristotle. *Phronēsis* refers to knowledge belonging to human *praxis* insofar as such activity constitutes an end in itself. It is described as "a disclosive disposition that occurs by way of *logos* [*hexis alēthē meta logou*], concerned with action in relation to what is good and bad for human beings" (NE, 1140 b7). Like *technē*, *phronēsis* belongs to the deliberative faculty of the soul, since the latter apprehends objects whose *archai* are variable. However *phronēsis* is not the same as *technē*, because "*poiēsis* aims at an end that is other than itself, whereas in doing [*praxis*] the end is not other; doing well [*eupraxia*] is in itself the end" (NE, 1140 b4). In *technē*, knowledge is directed toward the finished product as the end or *telos* of that knowledge. In *phronēsis*, on the other hand, knowledge is directed toward action itself as constitutive of the being of the *phronimos,* the person of practical wisdom. *Phronēsis* is a knowledge attuned to human beings in their singularity and communal being with one another, concerned with the human being as "an origin of actions [*archē tōn praxeōn*]" (NE, 1112 b32).[16] Accordingly, the ontological disclosure of the object of *phronēsis*, the disclosure of the being of the self as an acting, is preserved in this direct and immediate relatedness. *Phronēsis* discloses the being of the *phronimos* in its ontological "truth"; it discloses the truth of my own being as acting here and now. Unlike the ontological disclosure of true being in *epistēmē*, this disclosure is bound to the finite temporality of the moment; it is not a general truth already accessible in principle to an independent or supposedly neutral observer.

Aristotle notes that *phronēsis* too is commonly associated with a kind of *theōrein* concerned with what is good for oneself and for human beings in general (NE, 1140 b10). Yet since the object of *phronēsis* is none other than oneself, Aristotle points out that this kind of knowing does not constitute an independent body of knowledge in which we might come to excel. *Phronēsis* is not like *technē* in this regard; it is not an independent knowledge that could be applied to different cases. We cannot therefore speak of excellence *in phronēsis,* as we can in the case of *technē;* rather, *phronēsis* itself *is* an excellence or virtue (*aretē*) (NE, 1140 b22f.). One cannot be in error in the sense that one's "seeing" would not in some way disclose one's ownmost being—even if only in an implicit manner not transparent to oneself. This also implies that *phronēsis,* unlike *technē,* cannot simply be learned from others; it requires experience of oneself.[17] Furthermore, whereas *technē* is learned and perfected by a process of trial and error, this is not the case in *phronēsis:* In ethical action, one cannot, fundamentally, experiment with oneself in the manner in which a *technē* experiments with its object, namely, in such a way as to be capable of an indifference toward that object (cf. GA 19, 54). For *phronēsis* is a seeing ("knowing") of oneself *as an acting self,* as the self that is acting in any particular situation, and not a seeing

---

[16] Cf. NE, 1139 b6. That the actions and, accordingly, the kind of knowing in question are not those of an isolated "subject," but already embedded in a communal being with others, is indicated by Aristotle when he notes that actions done through our agency, or by us as individuals, may also include those done by our friends, "since the origin of their action is in us" (NE, 1112 b27).

[17] On this point, see Hans-Georg Gadamer, GW 1, 322ff.

of oneself as an object whose very being is *other* than that of oneself. Nevertheless, the acting self in question is not at all a "subject" in any modern sense—not least because it cannot be represented.[18] *Phronēsis* is an intrinsic relation to one's own being. To formulate it in terms that parallel Heidegger's characterization of Dasein in *Being and Time*—a parallel we shall investigate further in chapter 4—*phronēsis* entails a seeing in which the being of the human being that I myself am is *in question* (and thus in some sense open, at stake, yet to be decided). It entails a kind of seeing whose own mode of being is not indifferent to it; its activity is structured as an ontico-ontological care for self.[19] Insofar as the *archē* and *telos* of *phronēsis* coincide, *phronēsis* thus seems to be a complete and self-contained form of knowing, which Aristotle will thus describe as a "seeing of oneself [*to hautou eidenai*]" (NE, 1141 b35). In our doing and acting, we "see" ourselves and are thus in a sense present to ourselves immediately, without any contemplative distance or objectification.

Nevertheless, our originary, worldly relation to ourselves as acting beings not only presupposes concealment; this relation and its attendant concealment can themselves become concealed and covered over in and through our guiding interpretations of ourselves and of the world. *Phronēsis* is disclosive—it is an *alētheuein*—precisely because concealment is intrinsic to the being of the self as acting. As Heidegger puts it, "Insofar as the human being himself is the object of the *alētheuein* of *phronēsis,* the human being must be in a situation of being covered over from himself, of not seeing himself, so that an explicit *a-lētheuein* is required in order to become transparent [*durchsichtig*] to oneself" (GA 19, 51). Self-disclosure, attaining transparency, is relative to the practical situation; it is radically finite and, as such, an infinite task, one that must be accomplished ever anew.[20] Furthermore, concealment of oneself is not only a possible result of a particular self-interpretation. As Aristotle indicates by reference to pleasure and pain, a mood or attunement can conceal the human being from himself, so that the *archē* "does not show itself" (*ou phainetai*) as such.[21] And for this reason, *phronēsis* must repeatedly be retrieved (*sōizei*) by a certain composure (*sōphrosunē*) (NE, 1140 b10f.).

Heidegger thus initially sums up *phronēsis* as follows:

> *Phronēsis* is thus nothing self-evident, but is a *task that must be seized in a prohairesis.* . . . *Phronēsis* is a *hexis* of *alētheuein,*

---

[18] See part 3 of the present study, "The Threshold of Representation."

[19] Cf. our remarks in "Care for the Self: Originary Ethics in Heidegger and Foucault," *Philosophy Today* 42, no. 1/4 (Spring 1998): 53–64.

[20] GA 19, 56; see also chapter 4 below.

[21] GA 19, 51–52; NE, 1140 b17.

"a kind of disposition of human Dasein in which I dispose over
the transparency of myself." [22] (GA 19, 52)

But the fact that *phronēsis* remains a task, and not a perfected accomplishment, points to something else that is important, namely, the fact that this
kind of knowing is not an independent *hexis* or mode of disclosure:

> *Phronēsis* is thus itself *indeed an alētheuein, but not an inde-
> pendent one, rather it is an alētheuein in the service of praxis;*
> it is an *alētheuein* that makes an action transparent in itself.
> Insofar as the transparency of a *praxis* is constitutive thereof,
> *phronēsis* is co-constitutive of the proper accomplishment of
> action itself. *Phronēsis* is an *alētheuein,* but, as noted, not in-
> dependent; rather it guides an action. (GA 19, 53)

In other words, the disclosure that occurs deliberatively in *phronēsis,* by way
of *logos,* is itself dependent upon and directed toward, that is, subservient
to, a more originary disclosure. *Phronēsis,* as we shall see, indeed guides an
action, but in its deliberative capacity neither first discloses the practical
situation of action, nor indeed does it disclose the primary end toward which
an action is directed in advance.

This is merely a preliminary situating of *phronēsis* with respect to the
other intellectual virtues, and a more careful analysis of *praxis,* and in particular of its specific seeing, will be required. Before proceeding to analyse
phronēsis in greater detail, Aristotle briefly considers the two remaining
ways in which the soul attains truth by way of the *logos,* namely, *sophia*
and *nous.*

Sophia belongs to the epistemic faculty. In Book VI of the *Nicomachean
Ethics,* Aristotle begins his consideration of *sophia* by reminding us that its
counterpart, *epistēmē,* is itself unable to apprehend the first principles from
which it demonstrates scientific truths. Nor do *technē* or *phronēsis* enable
us to apprehend these *archai,* for they deal with variable objects, whereas
the epistemic faculty is concerned with objects that are invariable and exist
of necessity. Yet somewhat surprisingly Aristotle then adds: "Nor is *sophia*
the knowledge of first principles either, for whoever has wisdom has to arrive
at some things by demonstration" (NE, 1141 a1). Recalling the dispositions
whereby we attain truth and are never led into falsehood (*technē* is now
omitted, and this, Heidegger suggests, is because it now appears that *technē*
may indeed lead us into falsehood), Aristotle insists that the first principles
or *archai* must be apprehended by *nous.* The implication is that *sophia*

---

[22] The citation is Heidegger's paraphrase of NE, 1140 b20f., where Aristotle describes
phronēsis as a *hexis meta logou alēthē.*

is not merely a direct apprehending of first principles, for it also entails demonstration (*apodeixis*). And this because human apprehending is not a *pure nous*, but a *nous* that, in order to disclose itself (whether to itself or to others), must pass through the *logos*, that is, a *nous* that is a *dianoein*. It is an apprehending that apprehends things in their unity (in the *archē* of their respective being) only by way of separating out their being in relation to one another, by seeing things *as* being this or that and not something else. "On the basis of *logos*, of addressing something *as* something, *noein* becomes a *dianoein*" (GA 19, 59). Human *nous* is in need of *logos:* only by becoming dianoetic can it "demonstrate," that is, let things be seen in their being, as being this or that. Demonstration, we noted, is the method of *epistēmē*, which proceeds by deduction on the basis of certain *archai* already given. The principles themselves, however, are given through induction (*epagōgē*), that is, via an immediate apprehending enabled by *nous* (NE, 1139 b28f.). *Sophia* directs itself toward the being of particular beings, toward particular beings insofar as they *are*, that is, toward their *archai* (their being) *as such* (and not *only* toward their being this or that, as do the particular sciences); but it can do so only because it is also a *dianoein*, only because it is able to separate and gather those beings as such via *logos*. The *archai* as such, however, are not purely "logical," for they can be apprehended only in a singular and finite act of *noein*. Thus, Aristotle continues, the wise man must see (*eidenai*) both what follows from first principles (*ta ek tōn archōn*), that is, dianoetically and deductively, and (via *nous*) truly disclose (*alētheuein*) the first principles themselves. *Sophia* must be a combination of *nous* and *epistēmē*, it must be "a consummated knowledge [*epistēmē*] of that which is most exalted [*timiōtatōn*]" (NE, 1141 a17). It must be a knowledge of being itself as such and as a whole, of that which "most is" in all beings.

"That which is most exalted" is here, as in Book I of the *Metaphysics*, identified with the divine (*to theion*) (M, 983 a5). In that treatise, however, Aristotle expresses doubt as to whether knowledge of the divine could be considered something within human power, "since in many repects human nature is slave-like" (M, 982 b30). The desire for *sophia*, however, strives precisely for a freedom and independence from human necessity; it is a striving that unfolds solely for the sake of itself, and thus most approximates and approaches divine freedom. Knowledge of the divine is *sophia;* yet *sophia* can be divine in only two ways, notes Aristotle: either it is the possession of god, belonging to the divine, or it has the divine as its object. Is this supreme, divine vision of something ever-enduring (*aei*) possible for human beings? Is not human existence bound to the finitude of the concrete situation, thus thoroughly dependent and constantly changing? Is not all human seeing bound to and limited by the contingencies of *praxis?* Is it not in *praxis* and its specific virtue, *phronēsis,* that the human "desire to see" finds its inevitable end? Yet what exactly is this "seeing" intrinsic to human *praxis?*

The Glance of the Eye

Central to *phronēsis* is what Aristotle in the *Nicomachean Ethics* identifies as a practical *aisthēsis,* a practical vision or "perception" that discloses the ultimate *archē* and *telos* of *praxis,* namely the concrete situation of action in all the particularity of its givenness. *Phronēsis,* as Aristotle puts it, "concerns what is ultimate [*eschatou*], and this is the object of *praxis* [*to prakton*]" (NE, 1142 a24). Yet the kind of *aisthēsis* in question is not that of the mere sense-perception of sense-objects, but is something like the sort of *aisthēsis* whereby "we perceive that the ultimate figure [*eschaton*] in mathematics is a triangle." Two things are distinctive of the kind of *aisthēsis* belonging to mathematics: First, we perceive the object—the figure of the triangle—as a whole; and second, our perceiving reaches a kind of end or stop (*stēsetai*) in this perception.

Aristotle emphasizes, however, that "the term *aisthēsis* applies in a fuller sense to mathematical intuition than to *phronēsis;* the practical intuition of the latter belongs to a different species" (NE, 1142 a30). The *aisthēsis* intrinsic to *praxis* clearly cannot be the same as the *aisthēsis* at work in mathematics, given that the objects of mathematics and geometry are unchanging and universal. By contrast, the kind of perception found in *phronēsis* must pertain to *praxis* itself in all its particularity and contingency. As Heidegger remarks, it is not a theoretical or contemplative seeing, not a "mere looking," but a "circumspective looking" (*umsichtiges Hinsehen:* GA 19, 163) that is guided in advance by the end of *eupraxia,* acting well. This end is not a particular or determinate good, but the highest good for human existence as a whole (*to eu zēn holōs:* NE, 1140 a28). Good circumspection sees a situation not just in one determinate respect, but above all with respect to this more general good, as a good not just for me, but for human beings in their plurality and worldly belonging together (NE, 1140 b7–21). Yet for Aristotle the good is not a universal, but relative to the finite situation and circumstances of the actor (cf. NE, 1096 a11ff.). The seeing of the situation must thus be *circum*spective, at once encompassing and open. Yet such circumspection has something in common with the mathematical *aisthēsis* in that it both perceives its object as a whole and reaches an end or stop in this perception. As Heidegger puts it, what *phronēsis* must perceive is the whole factical situation within which we have to act, and this situation, as the ultimate limit of such perception, also constitutes the end or "ultimate facts" within which deliberation (as an accomplishment of *logos*) can occur. It is thus the entire factical situation of action, the situation as a whole in its unique particularity, and not any particular sense-object, that constitutes the *eschaton* of practical *aisthēsis*.

But what exactly is the role of the practical *aisthēsis* in *phronēsis?* *Phronēsis* is described as a *hexis meta logou;* it occurs by way of deliberation, of talking something through in the *logos*.[23] This deliberation follows the form of a practical "syllogism" or deduction. However, as Heidegger constantly emphasizes in his interpretation of Book VI, it is crucial to keep in mind that this syllogism, as the way in which *phronēsis* unfolds, is not something undertaken independently of our actions.[24] The practical syllogism is what happens in and as *praxis*, it *is praxis* in its very accomplishment, in the movement of its unfolding and actualization. A practical syllogism consists of the following steps: (1) The particular action or immediate end desired, that is, held in advance in a *prohairesis* (for the sake of some further end or good, a *hou heneka* or *agathon* that we wish for and have set via *boulēsis*) (cf. NE, 1111 b10ff.; 1113 a15ff.) is such and such (major premise); (2) The concrete situation is this (minor premise); (3) Therefore, I shall act in the following way (conclusion) (GA 19, 159). Yet it is not only the minor premise—that is, whatever is disclosed in the moment of practical *aisthēsis*—that first has to be given in order for deliberation to occur. The major premise—the end projected or intended— also has to be given; indeed it is prior to, and even appears to organize the

---

[23] Nevertheless—and this will be crucial for understanding the eschatological nature of disclosure in *phronēsis*—Aristotle insists that *phronēsis* is not a *hexis meta logou monon,* not simply a disposition of *logos* (NE, 1140 b28). And this is because a purely "logical" disposition can become concealed or forgotten, "whereas *phronēsis* cannot." It is on account of this impossibility of "falling" (*Verfallen*) into forgottenness or concealment (*lēthē*) that Heidegger in this 1924 course identifies *phronēsis* with the phenomenon of conscience (*Gewissen*)—a phenomenon that will be analyzed at length in *Being and Time* (GA 19, 56; cf. 139). For some of the background to this identification of *phronēsis* with *Gewissen*—an identification we shall examine in greater detail in chapter 4—see Robert Bernasconi, "Heidegger's Destruction of Phronesis," *The Southern Journal of Philosophy* 28, Supplement (1989): 127–47.

[24] Robert Bernasconi suggests more provocatively that "Aristotle does not appeal to the practical syllogism to explain the workings of *phronēsis*," the so-called practical syllogism being a schema introduced, rather, "from another realm" to help explain "cases where *phronēsis* is not operative." See "Technology and the Ethics of Praxis," *Acta Institutionis Philosophiae et Aestheticae* 5 (1987): 93–108. Heidegger's analysis in the *Sophist* course, by contrast, appears to accept that *phronēsis* does unfold as a kind of syllogism. The two interpretations are not entirely at odds, however, since what Bernasconi is resisting is the notion of a syllogism that would operate extrinsically, at a distance from the unfolding accomplishment of *praxis* itself. Likewise, Heidegger emphasizes the embeddedness of deliberation in *praxis* by stressing that the so-called minor premise is not at all a piece of propositional knowledge or information, but the moment of practical perception.

practical *aisthēsis* itself: I "see" the present situation in the light of a projected end. We thus find the following moments intrinsic to *praxis:* (1) the particular end or action projected or "chosen in advance" (*prohairesis*) as the specific goal of desire; (2) the disclosure of the factical situation, via a practical *aisthēsis,* with respect to this end; (3) the projected end as modified via deliberation, this third moment marking the beginning of a particular action, the moment of correct deliberation and decision (*orthotēs boulēs*) when desire is correctly directed toward the appropriate action in accordance with the *logos* of the one deliberating (NE 1142 b1ff.). The *logos* thus belongs to the action; the action itself, if appropriate, should unfold as a true disclosure (*alētheia*) that is *homologōs tēi orexei,* homologous with desire (NE, 1139 a30). This moment at which deliberation has been correctly accomplished and is conclusively directed toward the end desired is the moment of judgment that enables a decision. Heidegger thus translates *boulē* as "open resolve" or "resolute openness" (*Entschluß, Entschlossensein*) comprising the "transparency" (*Durchsichtigkeit*) of an action.[25] "Insofar as this resolute openness has indeed been appropriated and achieved, that is, insofar as I am openly resolved, the action is there in its most extreme possibility." Openness here means a disclosedness, being resolved in a certain disclosedness. Yet this conclusion of the syllogism, Heidegger indicates, is also a closure (*Schluß*) or coming to an end: "it is not some proposition or piece of knowledge, but the *breaking-forth of whoever is acting as such* [das Losbrechen des Handelnden als solchen]" (GA 19, 150–51).[26]

---

[25] The Greek *boulē* suggests resolve following deliberation or taking counsel with oneself. But "following" here does not mean that one first deliberates and then acts, as though the two were separate; rather deliberating—and particularly deliberating well—is intrinsically an acting and deciding, and decision is intrinsically deliberative. Both share the same element, namely, the being of the *phronimos.* This is conveyed in the Greek, *hē ara toiautē orthotēs boulēs euboulia, hē agathou teuktikē:* "Therefore it is this kind of correctness of resolve that is deliberative excellence, namely, attaining something good." As H. Rackham, translator of the Loeb edition, rightly notes, "No distinction seems to be made between arriving at the conclusion of a practical syllogism, that is, inferring correctly what is to be done as a means to some End, and actually achieving that End by action." *The Nicomachean Ethics* (Cambridge, MA: Harvard University Press, 1982), 354–55 n. d. And this is because the practical syllogism is not a purely "logical" inference. On the connection between deliberation (*boulesthai, bouleuesthai*) and resolve (*boulēs*), see Gadamer, GW 10, 42–43 (in connection with Heidegger); and Helene Weiss, *Kausalität und Zufall in der Philosophie des Aristoteles* (Basel: Verlag Haus zum Falken, 1942), 129 n. 106. See also the *Greek–English Lexicon* of Liddell and Scott (Oxford: Oxford University Press, 1989).

[26] The German *Entschluß,* a resolve that implies decision, thus has the sense of acting from out of and on the basis of a certain closure, that is, it implies a *finite* action. The prefix *Ent-* suggests at once opening (an opening for the onset of a particular action) and closure (the closure of a temporal moment of insight). *Entschlossensein* here does not, however, imply deciding in a manner that closes off other possibilities; rather one remains open even as one acts. (Cf., in another context, the helpful comments by John

This schema is undoubtedly correct. And yet the relation between prior choice (*prohairesis*), deliberation (*bouleuesthai*), and the practical *aisthēsis* warrants closer attention. For the major premise of the practical syllogism, the particular end chosen, is itself in fact subservient to some further end or good. This entails that any particular end of *praxis* is itself only a means to some further end (as Aristotle notes, both choice and deliberation in the sphere of action are concerned not with ends, but only with means (*tōn pros ta telē:* NE, 1111 b4ff.)—an order of implication that would appear to regress ad infinitum were there not some supreme or ultimate end (NE, 1094 a19f.). As Aristotle remarks in Book I, "a thing chosen always [*aei*] as an end and never as a means we call absolutely final or complete [*haplōs dē teleion*]" (NE, 1097 a34).[27]

Aristotle points out that whereas a *prohairesis* is a choice that bears on the immediate unfolding of a situation in such a way as to be held open in its futural character (it has at one and the same time—the time of action— already been chosen and is yet held open to modification via deliberation: NE, 1139 b6f.), there are more primary choices or commitments that are relatively fixed (such as one's profession: NE, 1112 b12f.), and may be considered ends in themselves (for example, promoting health insofar as one is a doctor). But even these are in principle open to change and deliberation (if, for example, the doctor loses his job). Furthermore, their contingency is indicated by the fact that, as *particular* ends, they too may be viewed as means to some further end (e.g., making money), and are thus not the ultimate or truly primary end of a particular existence. What, then, is the ultimate end or supreme good (*telos haplōs, ariston*) for us human beings (*pros hēmas*)? According to Aristotle, the human good is the *ergon*, the action and activity (*energeia*) of the soul in its most proper excellence or virtue (*aretē*), which will be shown to be that of *nous* (NE, 1097 b21ff.). The ultimate end of a particular existence is that existence itself as such, in what is most proper to it as an origin of *praxis*, that is, in its own finitude. For every chain of deliberation comes back to oneself in the end, that is, to one's own being as an *archē* of *praxis*. We carry our reasoning back to the *eschaton*, to its ultimate end (1112 b19), which is the beginning of the action (*prōton en tēi genesei:* 1112 b24); we stop (*pauetai*) enquiring how to act when we have brought the origin of action back to ourselves and to the dominant part of ourselves (1113 a5).

Sallis on the translation of this term, BW, 131, note.) This double sense is similar to that present in the term *Entwurf*, "projection," which carries much of the same sense as *prohairesis*, and could indeed, with certain reservations, be regarded as a translation of the latter. Cf. Heidegger's comments on *Entwurf* in GA 29/30, 527.

[27] On Heidegger's reading, the ontological priority of that which "always" (*aei*) is as it is will prove decisive in deciding the priority of *theōrein* and *sophia* over *phronēsis*.

Yet how, if at all, is *praxis* as an end in itself, as an unconditional end, present in *phronēsis?* Is it something toward which we orient ourselves in advance in the *logos* of a more primary projection or *prohairesis*—the result, perhaps, of a prior philosophical, theoretical, or calculative-technical reflection on the nature of the good? If such were the case, *praxis* could not be an end in itself, distinct from *poiēsis,* as Aristotle argues, but would become subservient to an extrinsic end, thereby inscribing itself within the means-end schema of calculative deliberation characteristic of *technē.*[28] Is such an end then accessible in, or via, the practical *aisthēsis* which discloses the momentary existence of the *phronimos* in the particular situation?

What the practical *aisthēsis* discloses is, more precisely, the various "givens" (the various factors to be taken into account in deliberation) within the temporal particularity—what Heidegger calls the *Jeweiligkeit*—of this or that situation. The particular situation, moreover, is something ultimate, something so singular and unique that it cannot be apprehended by *logos,* but only by the practical *aisthēsis.* It constitutes the proper end or *eschaton* of the practical vision, and thereby of *praxis* itself. What Heidegger finds especially significant is that Aristotle describes this practical *aisthēsis* as a form of *nous*—a term otherwise reserved for the pure apprehending, in *sophia,* of universals that remain constant:

> For *nous* apprehends what is ultimate [*eschaton*] in both re-
> spects, since ultimates and primary delimitations [*prōtōn horōn*]
> are grasped by *nous* and not by *logos.* In demonstrations, *nous*
> apprehends the immutable and primary delimitations, in prac-
> tical inferences it apprehends the ultimate fact [*eschatou*] that
> can be otherwise, the minor premise, since these are the first
> principles [*archai*] from which the end [*hou heneka*] is inferred.
> And the universal is drawn from the particular; hence we must
> have perception [*aisthēsis*] of particulars, and this perception is
> *nous.* (NE, 1143 a35f.)

Nous is present in both *sophia* and *phronēsis.* And what is grasped by *nous* is in each case something ultimate: either the universal delimitations or *archai* that remain the same and comprise the starting point of demon-stration in scientific knowledge, or the ultimate fact or state of affairs that can be otherwise and at which all deliberation in the *logos* ends. Practical

---

[28] This threat to *praxis* has been discussed extensively by Robert Bernasconi, "The Fate of the Distinction between *Praxis* and *Poiesis,*" in *Heidegger in Question* (New Jersey: Humanities, 1993), 2–24. See also his essay "Technology and the Ethics of Praxis." More recently, this issue has been placed in a broader context by Dana R. Villa in *Arendt and Heidegger: The Fate of the Political.*

vision is intrinsically *eschatological* in that it discloses, and thus itself comprises, in its very operation, an *eschaton* that marks the limit of *logos,* an end that *logos* itself cannot reach. The *nous* of *phronēsis* is an apprehending of beings that intrinsically "exceeds the *logos*" (GA 19, 158). Although *phronēsis* guides and directs the entire action of the *phronimos,* it remains dependent on something other than itself, namely, "the action itself," and is thus (unlike the *theōrein* of *epistēmē* or *sophia*) not an independent form of disclosure. As Heidegger puts it, *"Phronēsis* lies more in *praxis* than in the *logos"* (GA 19, 139). Whether we are concerned with deliberation, calculation, or demonstration, discursive thought can only set to work on what has already been disclosed via a finite and unique act of *nous.*

What this means, on Heidegger's reading, is that the intrinsic structure of *phronēsis* is "the same" as that of *sophia:* both are an *alētheuein aneu logou,* a true disclosing without *logos:*

> *Phronēsis is structurally the same as sophia;* it is an *alētheuein aneu logou;* this is what *phronēsis* and *sophia* have in common. Yet in the case of *phronēsis,* pure apprehending is to be found on the *opposite side.* We have here *two possibilities of nous: nous in its most extreme concretion and nous in the most extreme katholou, in its most universal universality.* (GA 19, 163)

The practical vision that informs *phronēsis* occurs in a momentary glance; it is a moment of "most extreme concretion," a moment that, as Heidegger puts it, orients or directs itself toward "what is most extreme" (*das Äußerste*), catches sight of the absolute *eschaton:*

> The *nous* of *phronēsis* aims at what is most extreme in the sense of the absolute *eschaton. Phronēsis* is a *catching sight of the here-and-now* [Erblicken des Diesmaligen], of the concrete here-and-now character [or uniqueness: *Diesmaligkeit*] of the momentary situation. *As aisthēsis, it is the glance of the eye, the momentary glance* [der Blick des Auges, der Augen-blick] *at what is concrete in each specific case and as such can always be otherwise.* The *noein* in *sophia,* by contrast, is a contemplating of that which is *aei, that which is always present in its sameness.* (GA 19, 163–64)

In his 1922 treatise "Phenomenological Interpretations with Respect to Aristotle," Heidegger had already identified the moment of practical insight or *Augenblick* as translating Aristotle's conception of the *kairos* of the practical situation (PIA, 35–36). Later, in the 1927 course *The Basic Problems of Phenomenology,* he would remark that "Aristotle already saw the phenomenon of the *Augenblick,* the *kairos,* and delimited it in Book VI of his *Nicomachean Ethics,* although without succeeding in connecting the temporal character specific to the *kairos* with what he otherwise knows as time (the *nun*)" (GA 24, 409).[29] The *kairos* refers to the opportune moment, the temporal moment of decision at which action engages, the moment in and around which everything turns. What is "seen" (for the most part only implicitly) in the kairotic moment of insight is the *eschaton,*

---

[29] Theodore Kisiel situates the 1922 treatise in the context of Heidegger's early lecture courses on Aristotle in part 2 of his study *The Genesis of Heidegger's* Being and Time, 221–308. Heidegger's analyses of the *kairos* in Aristotle are also crucially informed by his readings of the *kairos* in early Christianity; in particular, the 1920/21 course "Introduction to the Phenomenology of Religion" (GA 60) is important here. (See Kisiel, 149–219.) This course centers on the meaning of early Christian eschatology as documented in St. Paul's Epistles to the Thessalonians. In Pauline eschatology, Heidegger emphasizes, the *eschaton* is not a future event, and *parousia* does not have the sense of "arrival" or "presence" found in Greek, Platonic-Aristotelian thought (GA 60, 98ff.). The *kairos* of the *parousia*—the *Augenblick,* as Heidegger translates it (GA 60, 102)—is experienced only in an *eidenai* that implies an already having seen one's own having come to be (*genesthai*) (GA 60, 93–95). It is a knowing experience of the radical finitude and uncertainty of one's being before the unseen God, a "wakefulness" of factical existence. (For an excellent and insightful account of this course, see Thomas Sheehan, "Heidegger's 'Introduction to the Phenomenology of Religion,' 1920–21," *The Personalist* 60, no. 3 [July 1979]: 312–24. John van Buren, in *The Young Heidegger* [Bloomington: Indiana University Press, 1994], provides a rich account of Heidegger's interpretations of the unsettling eschatology of the *kairos* in "primal Christianity," as opposed to the eschatological prophecy found in later Christian and Scholastic thinkers under the influence of Greek philosophy and its prioritizing of the theoretical, contemplative life. See part 2 of his study, chapter 8 [157–202]. See also Van Buren's discussion of the *kairos* in Heidegger's readings of Aristotle [228–34]. In connection with the theoretico-scientific approach to history, see Charles Bambach, *Heidegger, Dilthey, and the Crisis of Historicism* [Ithaca: Cornell University Press, 1995], 211–38. Otto Pöggeler's *Der Denkweg Martin Heideggers* [Pfullingen: Neske, 1963] is still an important resource for understanding Heidegger's theological background. See also Hugo Ott, *Martin Heidegger* [Frankfurt/New York: Campus Verlag, 1988].) Heidegger's readings of primal Christianity thus suggest a very different experience of the *kairos* from the sense of "fullness of time" or "fulfiled time" in later and modern Christianity. (Cf. Kierkegaard's *The Concept of Anxiety,* trans. Thomte [New Jersey: Princeton University Press, 1980]; also the essays by Paul Tillich, "Kairos," and "Kairos und Logos," in *Kairos,* ed. P. Tillich [Darmstadt: Otto Reichl Verlag, 1926]. For an overview of the diverse philosophical and theological meanings of *kairos,* see M. Kerkhoff and E. Amelung, in *Historisches Wörterbuch der Philosophie,* ed. J. Ritter & K. Gründer [Darmstadt: Wissenschaftliche Buchgesellschaft, 1976], 667–69. Kerkhoff's essay "Zum antiken Begriff des Kairos," *Zeitschrift für Philosophische Forschung* 27, no. 2 [1973]: 256–74, gives a rich and detailed overview of the history of this word.) Nevertheless, Heidegger does not simply read the early Christian sense of the *kairos* that he finds in St. Paul into Aristotle's *Nicomachean Ethics.* Rather, it is surely Aristotle (mediated by Luther, and, of course, in conjunction with Husserl) who first provides Heidegger with the phenomenological eye and conceptuality with which to analyse the temporality of the *kairos* in a manner attentive to "the things themselves."

"the most extreme point [*das Äußerste*], in which the concrete situation
that is seen in a determinate manner peaks [or culminates: *sich zuspitzt*] in
each case" (PIA, 35).[30]
    Certainly, the moment of vision or glance of the eye intrinsic to *phronēsis*
has, by virtue of a guiding *prohairesis,* always already let the situation be
seen in a determinate respect. *Praxis* itself, human existence (the *prakton*)
as the hesitant yet ongoing transformation of *praxis* in each case, is thereby
always already seen with respect to a guiding "not yet," a futural possibility
and directionality for its transformation. Yet amid this "kairotic" vision in
which, in the unfolding of *praxis,* what has been has always already turned
into and toward the future, practical insight peaks in opening onto something that cannot be calculated or appropriated by deliberation. As deliberative, *phronēsis* is, as Heidegger (echoing Aristotle) puts it, "epitactic":
it issues commands, it orders and directs what is seen in the *Augenblick,*
giving it a determinacy, letting it be seen in a particular light. But this
"epitactic illumination" only brings our *praxis* into a "readiness for" something, a "breaking-forth toward" something (*der Bereitschaft zu ...,* des
Losbrechens auf ...) (PIA, 36). For the *eschaton* of the practical vision,
the point at which the latter stops and comes to an end or halt, is also the
end of *logos,* a standstill (*Stillstand*) and a stilling. It is "that moment of
being [*Seinsmoment*] which is concerned with concrete beings and at which
the intervention of the doctor engages [*einsetzt*], and, conversely, that moment at which deliberation and talking things through come to a standstill"
(GA 19, 157–58).[31] This *eschaton* is "the most extreme limit" (*die äußerste
Grenze*) of deliberation, at which "an action engages."
    In *phronēsis,* the practical *aisthēsis* informs every moment in the on-
going transformation of *praxis* that human existence is. It discloses *praxis*
itself in its momentary character, its exposure to a particular situation. Yet
does the practical *aisthēsis* thereby disclose *praxis* itself *as such, praxis* as

---

[30]Note that the interpretation of the *Augenblick* as a *Zuspitzung,* that is, as culminating in a peak or extremity (*Spitze*), returns in the 1929/30 course *The Fundamental
Concepts of Metaphysics* as marking the proper or authentic essence of time (GA 29/30,
§31ff.). The *Augenblick* is there identified with the "look of resolute openness" (*Blick
der Entschlossenheit:* 224); it constitutes the "simultaneous whole" or unity of Dasein's
vision (*Sicht*) that is otherwise dispersed into the three perspectives (*Sichten*) of present,
having-been, and future (GA 29/30, 218). This "simultaneity" obviously invites comparison with the *hama* of seeing and having seen in Aristotle's *Metaphysics* Book IX. We
shall examine this "peaking" of the *Augenblick* in more detail in chapter 4.
[31]This formulation recalls *Metaphysics* Book VII, which depicts the moment of *praxis*
in poiēsis (M, 1032 b6ff.). The notion of the *kairos* is pertinent in particular to medical
practice; Aristotle also mentions war and navigation as actions in which the opportune
moment is critical. The notion of the *kairos* was also widely discussed by rhetoricians.
For an overview, see Pierre Aubenque, *La prudence chez Aristote* (Paris: Presses Universitaires de France, 1963), 98 nn. 3, 4.

praxis? The glance of the eye that informs *phronēsis* sees what it sees in terms of a "good" that has already been decided upon beforehand; but this may be just a particular end or good (e.g., promoting health in the case of a doctor), or it may be the good in itself (*haplōs*), that is, the absolute good with respect to human existence as a whole (*pros to eu zēn holōs:* 1139 b28), the practical good as an end in itself. Only if it deliberates with a view to the latter will deliberation be the kind of deliberation appropriate to *phronēsis,* namely, deliberating well (*euboulia*) (NE, 1142 b28f.). As deliberating well, *phronēsis* must already have the *agathon* "in view" (*im Blick*) at every moment; it must act knowingly with a view to the good. Yet this means that *phronēsis* itself (as deliberating on what is disclosed in the practical *nous*) is powerless to decide the ultimate end or good toward which it is directed; *phronēsis* is possible only for someone who is *already* good (NE, 1144 a34; GA 19, 166f.). And this in turn implies that the practical *aisthēsis,* oriented in advance toward a particular end, yet given over to the particularity of a here-and-now situation, is in itself unable to disclose the practical good (*praxis* itself) as such. The disclosure of the latter, rather, is contributed by *sophia.*

In other words, the glance of the eye belonging to genuine *phronēsis* (as deliberating well) has already seen *more* than what is given in any practical situation. It sees the "givens" in the context of a whole (the temporal particularity of the situation), but this "whole" has itself been seen in advance in a very specific respect: not just with a view to any particular good, but with respect to the practical good as such, to *praxis* as an end in itself: presence or actuality itself as fleeting, unstable, open to the possibility of change (*metabolē*) at any moment. But this implies that intrinsic to *phronēsis* there is a vision that already "sees" not only the possibility of change, but actuality itself as that which remains constant, that which always returns as the same, that is, *as presence,* in and throughout all change. Yet as we shall see, this understanding of actuality in Aristotle, explicitly accomplished in pure *nous* as a *theōrein* of presence, always risks becoming a purely formal-ontological conception of presence if the *bios theōrētikos* and *bios politikos* become separated out from one another.[32]

Athanatizein

In Book I of the *Nicomachean Ethics,* Aristotle had noted that the highest good with respect to human *praxis* must be conceived as that at which all *praxis* aims, and which constitutes an ultimate end (1097 a15f.).

---

[32]See below: "Retrospect on the 1922 Treatise on Aristotle" (chapter 4); and "The Theoria of the Ancients" (chapter 8).

Eudaimonia (well-being), he remarked, appears best to fit this requirement of being something chosen always (*aei*) as an end in itself and never as a means to something else. As such, it constitutes the final and self-sufficient end of *praxis*. Moreover, Aristotle notes, *eudaimonia* seems to be divinely given, "one of the most divine things [*theiotatōn*] that exist ...something divine and blissful" (NE, 1099 b9ff.).

Yet does *phronēsis* itself aim at this end? Does it disclose this end as such? On the contrary, the problem, as we have indicated, is that *phronēsis* must always presuppose such an end. The *prohairesis* that guides *phronēsis* as a *hexis meta logou* (i.e., as discursively regulated) is directed toward a *particular* end within a given situation in each case, and not toward the ultimate end of *praxis* as such. The supreme good (*to ariston*), Aristotle notes, can show itself (*phainetai*) as such only within an existence that is already good (NE, 1144 a34). And this, as Heidegger remarks, entails that *phronēsis* is not completely independent. *Phronēsis* can be an authentic disclosure of human existence only if its practical vision is already informed by the supreme good (GA 19, 166–67); deliberating well must have the good "in view" at every moment. Merely having at our disposal the end we have chosen to pursue, and having practical insight in the sense of seeing the right means to that end does not make us morally good. The end itself must be good; it must be determined by moral virtue, that is, by a *hexis* that is continually guided by an anticipatory view of the supreme good, a view or "seeing" that is somehow at work in the finite *praxis* of the *phronimos*.

According to Aristotle, this seeing of the supreme good is most purely attainable and most fully actualizable in the *theōrein* belonging to *sophia*. Yet such vision not merely *discloses* the ultimate end of human existence as such and as a whole; it *accomplishes* it (*poiein*) in and by its very activity. It is this accomplishment or *poiēsis*, Heidegger notes, that decides the ontological priority of *sophia* over *phronēsis*. For whereas the *nous* of *phronēsis* is dependent upon something other than *phronēsis*, namely, the action itself (i.e., the ontological disclosure of the *phronimos*, of his being in the factical situation of the moment), "The philosopher's pure contemplation indeed accomplishes something, *poiei*, and does so *tōi echesthai kai tōi energein* (cf. 1144 a6), 'by our having it and actively engaging it', thus not through results, but *merely by my living in this theōrein*" (GA 19, 169). What the *theōrein* of *sophia* accomplishes or "produces" is *eudaimonia*, not as something other than its own activity, but as this very activity itself.

But why is the *energeia* of pure *theōrein* the "accomplishment" or *poiēsis* of *eudaimonia*? Aristotle considers this issue in Book X of the *Nicomachean Ethics*. *Eudaimonia*, as the ultimate end and completeness of human existence, constitutes, as Heidegger describes it, "the authenticity [*Eigentlichkeit*] of the being of human Dasein." It cannot therefore be a mere possibility, in the sense of a *hexis* or disposition that may or may not be actualized on particular occasions, but must be "a [way of] being of human beings that at every moment [*Augenblick*] constantly is what it is" (GA 19, 172). *Eudaimonia*, if it is to fulfil the criterion of being the ultimate and most complete possibility of human existence, that is, the authentic being of the human being, must be a potentiality for being that is being actualized and thus is present as the ultimate possibility of itself: "not a mere potentiality for being, but this potentiality for being in its being present [*Gegenwart*], *energeia*" (GA 19, 172). *Eudaimonia*, as *energeia*, means nothing other than presence alongside that which always is as it is, that whose being is most self-complete; it is the "independent presence [*Vorhandensein*] of the living [human] being in the world . . . the *teleiōsis* [completeness] of the being of such a being as being-in [*In-sein*]" (GA 19, 172–73).

According to Aristotle, *theōrein* is the activity (*energeia*) that best fulfils this conception of *eudaimonia*. Heidegger concludes his discussion of this Greek conception of the authentic being of human Dasein by enumerating and discussing the arguments provided in Book X of the *Nicomachean Ethics* (1177 a12ff.). Here we can offer only a brief, point by point synopsis of this discussion.

(1) *Eudaimonia* must be activity in accordance with the highest virtue in us, that which governs (*archein*) us "by nature," and this is *nous*, whose proper virtue or excellence is *theōrein*.

(2) *Theōrein*, as the activity of *nous* in us, apprehends the highest of those things that are knowable, the things that "always" are.

(3) As such, *theōrein* is the most continuous (*sunechestatē*) form of activity, "for we can contemplate more continuously than we can carry on any form of action" (NE, 1177 a21f.). Whereas the practical *nous* of *phronēsis* is always directed toward something different and changing, something ever new, pure contemplation is comparatively uninterrupted, for, as Heidegger expresses it, it "dwells alongside" a being that cannot be otherwise than it is. "Whereas beings that are the concern of *praxis* can be otherwise in each case and demand a resolute decision [*Entschluß*] in the moment [*Augenblick*], pure contemplation of that which always is remains, as it were, within an enduring Now" (GA 19, 174).

(4) Such activity, furthermore, as activity in accordance with *sophia*, is generally acknowledged as the most pleasurable activity. As contemplating and dwelling alongside that which is constant, human existence also finds a constancy in its disposition and attunement. It enters the "pure tarrying" of *diagōgē*, as opposed to the unease of seeking and searching (such as we find in *phronēsis*). Whereas such searching seeks to first uncover what is concealed, "the pure tarrying of knowing, of seeing, of having in view, is a dwelling alongside beings in their unconcealment" (GA 19, 175).

(5) *Theōrein* is that activity which is most self-sufficient (*autarkeia*). Once the necessities of life have been supplied, those who practise wisdom can contemplate independently of others, whereas the exercise of other virtues (such as justice or bravery) requires the presence of others. By contrast, activity in accordance with the highest virtue can be independent. The pure contemplation of the philosopher is indeed a finite activity, a matter that only the individual can accomplish. Yet this does not preclude it being a way of being with one another, a matter of community. The philosopher, Heidegger notes, can be a philosopher only if he sees things for himself: "No one can see things for others. . . . Pure seeing is a matter for the individual, although precisely whoever sees for himself, if he sees the same thing as others, is with those others in the manner of *sumphilosophein,* of philosophizing with one another" (GA 19, 177).

(6) *Theōrein* is the only activity that can be loved for its own sake, for it produces no result beyond (*para*) the actual activity of contemplation. *Theōrein* as an activity is truly an end in itself (and thus *praxis* in the most proper sense), whereas other forms of *praxis* (Aristotle mentions politics and war as being the most virtuous and noble) indeed aim at something over and beyond themselves. As such, *theōrein* has the intrinsic leisure of being able to tarry alongside its object, while other forms of *praxis* entail pursuit of some further end (NE, 1177 b17).

(7) The activity of *theōrein* is genuine only whenever it extends over a complete lifespan. It must strive to sustain itself as an activity that is maintained throughout human life, and is not merely undertaken on occasion. This indicates, notes Heidegger, "the peculiar tendency to measure human Dasein, with regard to its temporal existence, according to the permanence [*Immersein*] of the world" (GA 19, 177). In striving to maintain themselves in the constant activity of contemplation, human beings have the possibility of a certain *athanatizein* (NE, 1177 b33), of striving for immortality.[33] The contemplative possibility of one's activity being an end in itself opens up the possibility of, as Heidegger formulates it paradoxically, "not reaching an end" (GA 19, 178).

A few remarks by way of conclusion. This paradoxical formulation just cited is indicative of a particular tension at issue in this "peculiar tendency" noted by Heidegger, namely the emerging tension between a *theōrein* in

---

[33] Heidegger leaves the Greek word *athanatizein* untranslated; it carries the sense of a kind of active striving to become immortal. Hannah Arendt renders it as "immortalizing": see *The Life of the Mind,* vol. I, 129ff.; also *Between Past and Future* (New York: Penguin, 1993), 71 n. 26. Nicholas Lobkowicz explains it as "a sort of active immortality," and points out its contrast to *anthrōpeuesthai,* existing and acting as a human being, which is associated with politics. See *Theory and Practice* (Indiana: University of Notre Dame Press, 1967), 27.

service to *praxis* and *phronēsis,* intended to ground ethical and political
praxis even in exceeding them, and a *theōrein* that (seeking to dwell in
proximity to a nonhuman divinity) becomes increasingly opposed to and
separated from ethical and political existence, establishing itself instead as
an independent *praxis* and way of life, that of the *bios theōrētikos* withdrawn from the world of the political.[34] This separation, however, does
not yet occur in Aristotle, who maintains *theōria* and noble ethico-political
praxis in a relation of close and mutual complementarity.[35] With the emergent tension highlighted by Heidegger, however, the *temporality* of *theōria*
tends to become that of "an enduring Now," as Heidegger puts it (GA 19,
174), one whose endurance is measured according to "the entire duration
of human existence" (GA 19, 177), and is opposed to the time of ethical and political *praxis,* the time of the *Augenblick* intrinsic to *phronēsis.*
And yet, once severed from the philosophical *theōria,* from philosophical
insight, *phronēsis* can no longer be *phronēsis:* it can no longer be what it
is supposed to be, namely deliberating well, with a view to a good that
exceeds the exigencies of the immediate situation. *Phronēsis* can be good
deliberation only if it attends not only or exclusively to immediate ends
and circumstances, but sees beyond these in such as way as to fully see
itself as such, in the perspective of the world as a whole, as intrinsic to the
accomplishment of *praxis* regarded as an end in itself. The glance of the
eye inherent in *phronēsis* must see not only the presencing of the current
situation that can be otherwise at any moment, but the intrinsic stability
of presence in which it itself is already held and "is," in such a way as to be
open to otherness, to the presencing of alterity. The *Augenblick* of *phronēsis*
must itself be held in an anticipatory openness directed toward the divine
being of the world that exceeds it, and from this openness first be open
to and see itself as such, attuned in the felicitous manner of *eudaimonia.*
But this being held in an anticipatory *theōrein* not yet removed from the
sensible or turned toward another realm is neither the accomplishment of
logos (of an *epistēmē* or learned *technē*), nor a mere *hexis,* but an activity

---

[34] On the emergence of this tension, see Lobkowicz, *Theory and Practice,* chapter 2.

[35] Thus, while one should certainly acknowledge a tension and a tendency toward
separation, such separation is still for Aristotle more of an analytical than a real one.
And it is certainly an exaggeration to claim, as does Werner Jaeger's developmental
thesis, that by the end of the *Nicomachean Ethics* we are left with two "separate worlds."
See W. Jaeger, *Aristoteles: Grundlegung einer Geschichte seiner Entwicklung* (Berlin:
Weidmannsche Buchhandlung, 1923), 424. Similarly, the close relation between *phronēsis*
and *theōrein* in the *Protreptikos* is not necessarily indicative of a developmental split
in Aristotle's understanding of *phronēsis,* contrary to Jaeger's claims. For a discussion,
see the criticisms by Hans-Georg Gadamer, "Der aristotelische 'Protreptikos' und die
entwicklungsgeschichtliche Betrachtung der aristotelischen Ethik" (GW 5, 164ff.), and
Pierre Aubenque, *La prudence chez Aristote,* 15ff.

that must be enacted *in* the living moment. The pure *theōrein* of *sophia* is not just (among other things) an apprehending of *praxis* as such, as though action were always already an end in itself and needed only to be apprehended correctly. Rather, such *theōrein* is intrinsically poietic: It first brings about *(poiein) praxis* as an end in itself, participates in its very accomplishment and coming to presence.[36] This pure *theōrein*, as *nous*, is not pure self-production (which remains a phantom of modernity), but rather a kind of protoethical response, itself an action, to a world that is already there. In it, the *nous* of *praxis* "sees itself" in the manner of a *theōrein* that is not at all self-centered, but open to the world as a world of divine otherness.

Certainly this sense of a *theōrein* that remains attentive to sensible immediacy even while exceeding it is already receding by the time of Aristotle. *Theōria* as such an openness to otherness is transformed in its essence when being and the divine comes to be interpreted as the One, in a "monotheistic" manner. The being of the world increasingly comes to be regarded as a constant presence-at-hand of that which is essentially the same; the "eternal" character of this constant sameness of presence (available for contemplation in the *bios theōrētikos*) comes to be opposed to the never-ending unease and disruption of the life of ethico-political *praxis*. But even then, in Aristotle himself, the philosophical life is concerned not merely with the contemplation of truth, but "with *phronēsis* and the contemplation [*theōrian*] of truth" (EE, 1215 b3). Even then *theōria* is not opposed to *praxis* or *phronēsis*, but stressed as the originary and properly "ontological" element of *praxis*, not only in *Metaphysics* Book IX, but also in the *Politics*, where Aristotle himself takes issue with those who regard only the "exoteric" actions carried out in the presence of others as *praxeis:*

> For the life of action [*ton praktikon*] is not necessarily active in relation to other human beings, as some people think, nor are only those processes of thought practical that are pursued for the sake of things that result from action, but far more those kinds of *theōria* and thought that have their end in themselves and are pursued for their own sake; for the end is to do well [*eupraxia*], and therefore is a certain form of *praxis*. (P, 1325 b17f.)

On the one hand, *theōria* is here emphasized as a supreme form of *praxis*, conducive to acting well,[37] even while, on the other hand, it is already seen as withdrawn from the immediate realm of the political.

---

[36] Cf. the poietic role of *nous* in *De Anima* (DA, 430 a10ff.).

[37] Cf. the close conjunction of *theōrein* and *praxis* in Book I of the *Nicomachean Ethics*, where Aristotle writes that he who attains or strives for *eudaimonia* will "always [*aei*] or most often be employed in doing and contemplating [*praxei kai theōrēsei*] the things that are in conformity with virtue" (1100 b19).

The extent to which *sophia* and *phronēsis* ought to mutually imply one another for Aristotle is perhaps also seen in Book I of the *Metaphysics,* where he actually refers to *sophia* as a kind of *phronēsis* (M, 982 b24). *Phronēsis* does not simply have a rigorous technical sense for Aristotle. This very tension is intrinsic to Aristotle's thought, which thus calls for multiple readings. What Heidegger's reading in the *Sophist* course emphasizes is the tendency toward a separation of *theōria* from the *Augenblick* of *praxis* that can be read especially in Book X of the *Nicomachean Ethics.* Commensurate with this emphasis on the tendency for *theōria* to become an independent *praxis* is Heidegger's choosing largely to circumvent (particularly in these closing sections) the divine aspect of *theōrein.*[38] By contrast, the emphasis is on the emergence of *theōria* as an increasingly human activity. Such humanization itself becomes increasingly established when, via Stoicism and Neoplatonism, "science" becomes "practical" theory—theory oriented toward practical life, leaving the divine *theōria* to the Christianized-monastic *vita contemplativa.*[39]

Yet emphasizing in this way the tendency of *theōrein* to develop into an independent human manner of comportment must also be considered in the light of Heidegger's impending project of a "destruction" of the history of ontology, even if that project was not yet explicitly outlined as such. The emergence of *theōrein* as an independent *praxis* is, after all, precisely what happens in (indeed as) the subsequent history of philosophy and science. And it is this tendency toward separation that Heidegger is implicitly criticizing when he stresses that what comes to the fore in the prioritizing of *theōrein,* according to the arguments which he lists from Book X, is the Greek tendency toward understanding being as "absolute presence" (GA 19, 178). On the other hand, if the "authenticity" of human existence, on this reading of Aristotle, is to be aligned with an implicit understanding of being as "absolute presence," with a striving for immortality in a direction divergent from the mortality of human *praxis* amid its worldly activities, then is it not part of the subsequent project of *Being and Time* to relocate the authentic being of human Dasein in the midst of mortality, and to understand Dasein's most proper being otherwise than in terms of pure presence? To understand it, rather, in terms of the *Augenblick* which here in the *Sophist* course is understood as intrinsic to *phronēsis?*

Heidegger's 1924 reading of Aristotle—of which we have presented only a very partial view here—on the one hand might appear to be a sustained

---

[38] This neglect of the divine aspect of *theōria* is, however, intentional, and was prefigured by some earlier remarks which we shall consider later. (See "Theoria and Divinity: The Philosophical Turn" in part 4 of the present study.)

[39] We cannot pursue these developments within the scope of the present study; a rich and suggestive account is provided in Lobkowicz, *Theory and Practice,* chapters 3–5.

and incisive effort to follow Aristotle in making the case for a prioritizing of *theōrein*. On the other hand, as we can see more clearly in the retrospect of *Being and Time*, it prepares the terrain for a critique of this very prioritizing as indicative of a desire for pure presence. One could, however, as we have suggested, regard this imminent critique not so much as a critique of Aristotle per se, but of a particular reading of Aristotle, a reading that becomes that of the metaphysical tradition and that increasingly emphasizes the separation of "theory" from other forms of "praxis" (including making), to which *theōria* eventually becomes altogether subservient. Nor should one hasten to conclude that because the discourse of "authenticity" in the *Sophist* course designates the theoretical life as opposed to the practical, Heidegger is also following this desire for the "theoretical" ideal in *Being and Time*. In the later treatise, as we know, the *Augenblick* will characterize the most authentic, ecstatic, and "held" presence of *Dasein* as being-in-the-world, its most extreme possibility (SZ, 338). Yet precisely the presencing of, or in, that authentic presence will be increasingly problematized; it will be shown to entail the phenomena of concealment and withdrawal, of absence and finitude of time that any *logos* premised on theoretical seeing—at least in its post-Aristotelian form—can only occlude. In *Being and Time*, a phenomenology of concealment emerges via a focus on mortality, on the most extreme (*äußerste*) possibility of existence as Dasein's being-toward-death. In the *Sophist* course, on the other hand, Heidegger, arguing that the Greeks implicitly came to understand being as presence (*Gegenwart, Anwesendsein*), traces the "desire to see" that issues in the prioritizing of pure *theōrein* back to the *Augenblick* as the critical moment in which mortality and presence confront one another, in which we "see" a presence that can "always" (*aei*) be otherwise. Yet this very reading is possible only from the perspective of a thinking for which the understanding of being as presence has already become problematic. Where Aristotle finds in *theōrein* "a certain possibility of *athanatizein*," of approaching immortality—this being the "most extreme position to which human *Dasein* was brought by the Greeks" (GA 19, 178)—Heidegger's subsequent vision of mortality will problematize and rethink this very extremity of the Greek vision of being. Such "critique," when seen in terms of the "destruction" of the history of ontology, need not—as we have suggested—preclude the possibility of a certain rehabilitation of *theōria*, and thus also of *phronēsis*; nor indeed does it preclude another reading of Aristotle, one that might resist Heidegger's emphasis here on "absolute presence."

Chapter 3

The Genesis of Theory: *Being and Time* (1927)

Aristotle's account of the ascendancy of *theōria* in its philosophical and scientific form explains this ascendancy by recourse to what we have termed a "natural genesis." According to this account, theoretical comportment arises when the necessities and immediate pleasures of life have been satisfied (the beginning of the *Metaphysics* thus suggests that the mathematical sciences began in the neighborhood of Egypt, where the priestly class was granted leisure). It arises via a withdrawal from immediate involvement in the world concerned with worldly needs and desires, a withdrawal that opens a new time, a time for tarrying in pure contemplation, a time for "scholarship." This natural genesis thus follows a path that moves increasingly away from basic sense-perception, immediate experience, and artisanship, toward the pure "seeing" of the nonsensible forms, eventually reaching its natural end in the contemplation of the presence of the world or *kosmos* as a whole, insofar as the latter can be present for human existence. The world is present in the moment of contemplation (of the *theōria* of *sophia*), as the pure presence or actuality, the sheer actualization and enactment that this pure seeing itself is. This activity and actuality of *theōrein* is not to be understood as opposed to *praxis;* rather, as sufficient unto itself it *is* the highest *praxis* that human life, as an end in itself, can be at its limit. This intrinsic limit also marks the most proper delimitation of the human being as such: it assigns man his proper place in the world in relation to other beings and to the world itself as divine, circumscribing the horizon of his very being; it constitutes the actuality of his ownmost possibility, his proper *ergon*, and assigns him in advance his *ēthos*, the place where he stays and where he must dwell, the site of his habitation in the world. And since human beings are not themselves divine, since they are continually beset by other possibilities, needs, and desires, to dwell in this place requires a continual striving to actualize or help bring about (*poiein*) the actuality of this constant possibility. To be fully human, to flourish and fulfil one's ultimate nature, is to desire to see one's ultimate ends, to strive for wisdom.

For Aristotle, *theōrein* as pure *praxis* thus marks the limit-possibility of the being of human beings in the world, the attainment of their proper independence and freedom. But does such theoretical activity or comportment itself have limits that were not discerned as such by Aristotle? And what sort of limits come to impose themselves in the course of the increasing independence of *theōrein* in its *scientific* mode, where the diversification of the special sciences gradually institutes a separation of *theōria* from *praxis* and *technē*, a separation that distances the sciences from their foundation in the philosophical experience of a divine yet worldly *theōrein?* The contemplation belonging to the special sciences is oriented toward particular *archai* or delimitations of knowledge, in such a way that, once distanced from its ethico-philosophical foundations, it increasingly overlooks its own activity as such, the immediacy of its own *praxis* in the face of the world. No longer directed toward a finite ethical dwelling in relation to the actuality of the world as a whole, this contemplation of the constant and "eternal" *archai* of things (of their being) increasingly opposes itself to the realm of becoming and of "practical" involvement (even as it remains directed toward that very realm in its desire to know it). "Theory" and "praxis" become separated off from one another; their relation eventually comes to be seen as one of "application," whereby theory is "applied" to praxis, and "praxis" is taken to mean any direct involvement with the world.

The present chapter examines the problematic origins of this separation between the theoretical comportment of science—but also of philosophy itself, insofar as the latter (from Descartes, through the speculative metaphysics of German Idealism, to Husserlian phenomenology)[1] itself becomes "scientific," severed from the immediacies of human *praxis*—and so-called "practical," circumspective involvement as traced in Heidegger's *Being and Time* (1927). To this end, we shall attempt to follow two different accounts of the genesis of theoretical comportment. The first appears to be merely a reworking of the story of "natural genesis" that we find in Aristotle. The second concerns what Heidegger himself terms the "existential genesis" of theoretical comportment, a genesis which, as we shall examine, has its ultimate roots in the ecstatic temporality of Dasein, or, more precisely,

---

[1] Kierkegaard and Nietzsche represent the most notable rebellions against this scientific-speculative aspiration of philosophy, although in ways that, from a Heideggerian perspective, do not adequately fathom the historical determination of metaphysics. On Heidegger's reading of Nietzsche, see part 3.

in the Temporality of being itself. In addition to raising hermeneutic concerns about the "scientific" and thematizing aspirations of *Being and Time* itself (aspirations that Heidegger would subsequently acknowledge as inappropriate), the present chapter also leads us to examine Heidegger's early understanding of science as a thematizing objectification of beings (an issue that will be further investigated in part 2). Finally, this context provides the opportunity for an initial orientation regarding the place of *praxis* in *Being and Time* (an issue we shall address more closely in the next chapter).

The Natural Genesis of Theory

We have already drawn attention to one account provided by Heidegger, in *Being and Time,* of the genesis of the foundation of philosophical and scientific knowledge in the sense of theoretical contemplation. This account is presented in §13, where Heidegger argues that knowledge in the sense of cognition represents a founded mode of being-in-the-world. Heidegger also refers to the cognitive knowledge (*Erkennen*) of world as an "existential 'modality' of being-in" (SZ, 59). Cognitive knowledge of world is here to be understood broadly as the cognitive apprehending of intraworldly beings in their being, although the clear distinction between world as constitutive of Dasein's being and "world" in the sense of intraworldly beings will be made only in the following section. Such knowledge, Heidegger goes on to point out, can develop autonomously once it has emerged; it can become the specific undertaking of science, and assume authority over Dasein's being-in-the-world (SZ, 62).

Cognitive knowledge, in other words, although it is a form of theoretical comportment, is not yet science; for one thing, it has yet to establish its own procedure in terms of method, which would first grant it the requisite autonomy, distance, and independence from involvement with other beings in the world, that is, from "praxis" in a broad sense. Heidegger's phenomenological account, however, seeks to question the nature of the severing that would take place at that very moment when theoretical comportment in the form of science would establish its autonomy from such involvements. His reflections on cognitive knowledge and its genesis are introduced, he explains, because cognitive knowledge of the world is mostly or even exclusively taken to represent the phenomenon of being-in. This is the case not merely in the epistemological approach of *Erkenntnistheorie;* rather, quite generally for the most part "practical comportment is understood as '*non*theoretical' or 'atheoretical' comportment" (SZ, 59). Dasein's understanding of itself as being-in-the-world, Heidegger argues, is misled by its according such priority to cognitive knowledge.

Heidegger's interpretation of the genesis of cognitive knowledge is opposed to those models that seek to understand cognition as arising out of
the "transcendence" of an independently existing subject with respect to
an object. It aims, in effect, at attaining a more originary, phenomenologically more adequate understanding of transcendence itself. It does so by
arguing that Dasein's modes of being, as ways of being-in-the-world, are
ontologically prior to any "transcendent" relation toward either a "subject" or an "object." For one thing, the way in which a being manifests
itself to us in its phenomenal appearing is determined in part by the manner of our comportment toward it, that is, by a particular mode of our
being in each specific case. A being or "object" appears quite differently
to us depending on whether we are involved with it in a process of producing something, or merely contemplating it free from any involvement.
Different again are the ways in which we encounter and relate to another
human being. This indicates that there is no such thing as an object *per se*
or an object *in general,* independent of its appearing. And the same goes
for the notion of a "subject." We as "subjects" appear very differently to
ourselves—we have a very different relation toward ourselves—depending
on whether we are actively involved in or given over to some task of making,
engaged in a relationship with other human beings, or merely reflecting on
ourselves by way of philosophical or scientific contemplation. Dasein in its
metaphysical "neutrality"[2] is ontologically prior to any subject or object,
indeed to any being or entity whatsoever, because it first constitutes the
site of our possible relationality toward any entity: the way in which Dasein exists co-determines the way in which an entity is given to and for
us; it co-determines the kind of being that an entity has in each particular
case. The being of Dasein, that is, being-in-the-world, determines at least
in part both what an entity is for us (its whatness or *essentia*) and the
way in which it is appears in any given instance (its *existentia*). Cognitive knowing, as one possible ontic relating toward beings, is ontologically
founded in being-in-the-world, in which beings are first uncovered. And if
there is indeed something like a *transcendence* implied in every relationality
toward something, then such transcendence, Heidegger argues, demands to
be understood not in terms of a "subject," but in terms of our ontologically prior being-in-the-world, that is, in terms of Dasein as a "clearing"
(*Lichtung*) or site of disclosure. Furthermore, these reflections suggest that
the *world* is not simply "nature" in the Kantian sense of the totality of beings existing before us, as though they were independent objects given for

---

[2] On the metaphysical neutrality of Dasein, see GA 26, §10, 171f. For a discussion of this neutrality, see Jacques Derrida, "Geschlecht: différence sexuelle, différence
ontologique," in *Psyché: Inventions de l'autre* (Paris: Galilée, 1987). See also our remarks
in "Care for the Self: Originary Ethics in Heidegger and Foucault."

our cognition (SZ, 60). Rather world must belong to transcendence itself; indeed, Heidegger will later interpret it as the "horizon" of transcendence.

The analysis of cognitive knowing as a founded mode of being-in-the-world is thus intended to point toward the unitary phenomenon of *world* and of Dasein's *transcendence* as ontologically prior to any distinction between "theory" and "praxis"—understanding the latter now in the broad sense of doing and making, as opposed to theoretical contemplation. How does Heidegger's initial, extremely condensed account of the genesis of cognitive knowledge unfold?

Knowledge in its cognitive mode is said to have its prior grounding in our already being alongside or in the presence of (*bei*) the world, which does not simply mean a "fixed staring" at something purely present-at-hand. Being-in-the-world is initially a kind of concern, where concern (*Besorgen*) does not refer to the economic or "practical" activities of Dasein, but is employed as an ontological term to designate a particular way of being-in-the-world (SZ, 57). Broadly speaking, *Besorgen* refers to any mode of comportment concerned primarily with "things." In its concernful existence, Dasein, according to Heidegger, is *"captivated* by the world of its concern" (SZ, 61). And this kind of captivation belongs intrinsically to our involvement. In order for cognitive knowledge to be possible as a "contemplative determining of what is present-at-hand," there must first be what Heidegger refers to as a "deficiency" of our concernful involvement. In our holding back from our involvement in producing and manipulating things, concern transposes itself into the sole remaining mode of being-in, a mere tarrying alongside (*Verweilen bei* ...). It is *on the basis* of this kind of ontological relation to world, Heidegger explains, that we can then encounter intraworldly beings simply in their pure look (*Aussehen*) or *eidos,* and explicitly view or look at them as such. Such mere looking at beings (*Hinsehen*) is a mode of being-in-the-world; indeed, it remains a mode of concern, albeit a "deficient" one. Moreover, as a looking *at,* it always entails a particular way of taking up an orientation toward something, a "setting our sights upon" whatever is present-at-hand. This directionality or orientation of vision occurs prior to our encountering beings as this or that; it takes over a "viewpoint" (*Gesichtspunkt*) *in advance* from the beings it encounters (SZ, 61). We see beings always already in this or that respect.

Dasein's vision must thus be oriented in advance in terms of the particular "viewpoint" it looks at and the perspective it adopts toward things. In the case of merely looking at things, our seeing must have a prior directive to contemplate those beings solely in terms of their outward appearance or *eidos,* and not, for example, in terms of the end that these beings are to serve in a process of making. In "merely looking" at a hammer with respect to its form or shape, its purpose remains irrelevant. The way in which we

see particular beings is in general dependent upon the end at which our seeing aims in advance. In the specific case of making or producing something,
the end or perspective in terms of which we see things is the final product
or work itself, the *ergon* as *telos* of the productive process. Yet as *telos,*
our vision of the work to be produced is also *archē,* in the sense that such
vision orients and regulates the entire activity of production in advance. In
technē, that is, in the specific knowledge that guides the involved process of
making or producing something, this end or purpose must also be taken up
into, or taken account of in, our prior "seeing." For Plato and Aristotle,
this antecedent seeing, this prior "vision," is of course the nonsensible
eidos or *idea* sighted in the soul of the craftsman, the idea contemplated
by the "eye of the soul." The thrust of Heidegger's argument in §13 seems
to be that because that activity which appears to be a nonproductive,
disinvolved contemplation of things nevertheless still contemplates objects
in terms of their *eidos,* such contemplation remains derivative, dependent
upon the kind of knowing pertaining to productive comportment. It appears
to take as its model a key moment of productive knowledge or *technē:* the
antecedent sighting (*theōrein*) of the *eidos.* Furthermore, the question arises
as to whether this allegedly "disinvolved" contemplation is really as disinvolved as it tends to claim. Is it not also guided in advance by a specific
end, a certain purpose and ideal? Its end is precisely that prescribed and
made possible by the kind of seeing intrinsic to *technē:* the releasing or
freeing (*Freigabe*) of an entity into an independent self-subsistence, a lying
present-at-hand before us. The pure contemplation of things would thus be
merely a mode of concern, the extraction of the theoretical moment within
technē, and in its essence no different from the latter. What we think of as
"theoretical" contemplation, cognitive knowledge, would *in essence* be no
different from productive comportment.

Heidegger proceeds to outline, very concisely, how such pure contemplation of something can in turn establish itself as an independent or au-
tonomous way of being-in-the-world. Looking at things can become an independent way of dwelling alongside beings in the world. In such *dwelling,*
which is a holding back from manipulation or utilization, there occurs an
apprehending of what is present-at-hand. Such apprehending occurs by way
of addressing and discussing something *as* something. It is a way of *interpreting* things that allows us to determine them as this or that, and the
resulting interpretations can be retained and preserved in sets of asser-
tions. In short, science becomes possible as one particular development of
theoretical apprehending.

It seems clear, as we noted in chapter 1, that Heidegger is here presenting us with a concise account of the genesis of theoretical comportment.
It is not so easy, however, to assess what status this account is intended

to have; in particular, what its implications are for the Aristotelian distinctions between *theōria, praxis,* and *poiēsis.* One temptation would be to read the passage as an attempt to reverse the prioritizing of "theory" over "praxis." Theory would merely be a founded mode of praxis. Such a reading might indeed seem to be suggested by the closing paragraph of §12, where Heidegger indicates that the traditional "priority" of the cognitive mode of knowledge has led to practical comportment being understood as *non*theoretical, that is, still in terms of theory as primary. Heidegger's account might thus be seen as undermining such primacy by instituting a reversal. However, this reading would not only leave intact the same oppositional structure; it would also overlook Heidegger's insistence that concern (*Besorgen*) is not equivalent to "practical" activity, even if we take the term "practical" in a broad sense that encompasses both doing and making. Theoretical contemplation is also a mode of concern. Furthermore, the exemplary mode of concern discussed here is certainly not *praxis* in the narrow (ethico-political) sense understood by Aristotle, namely, that of doing as opposed to making, but *Herstellen,* "producing," *Hantieren,* "manipulating" or "handling" things, "and so on" (SZ, 61). In Aristotle's terms, the know-how pertaining to such modes of comportment is *technē,* not the *phronēsis* of *praxis.* What seems clear from these considerations is that Heidegger, while emphasizing the way in which theoretical contemplation emerges within the context of a worldly involvement with things, and specifically with producing or making, is not indicating any ontological order of founding with respect to these two modes. The initial goal is to make both forms of comportment visible as modes of worldly concern.

Given these preliminary considerations, what does Heidegger's account of cognitive knowledge as a founded mode ultimately tell us? It tells us nothing. Nothing, that is, concerning the *ontological* genesis of cognition or theoretical comportment. What it provides is merely an account of the *ontic* genesis of cognitive knowledge. If cognitive knowledge is grounded in concern in the broad sense of a worldly comportment with things, then such concern must, as prior to any differentiation into particular modes, first be understood by the analytic in terms of being-in-the-world as the apriori, existential-ontological constitution of Dasein. It demands to be understood in terms of Dasein's being as a transcendence that first makes possible all such comportment. Thus Heidegger, pointing to what is implicit in even the most provisional thematizing of the phenomenon of cognition, reminds us that "Cognitive knowledge is a mode of being of Dasein as being-in-the-world, it has its *ontic founding* in this ontological constitution" (SZ, 61, emphasis added).

If, therefore, cognitive knowledge of world is announced in the title of §13 as a "founded mode," then the founding at issue is *ontic,* and, as the

title indicates, merely intended to "exemplify" or provide an illustration of
Dasein's being-in. Indeed, so little does this account clarify the ontological
genesis of cognitive or theoretical knowledge that it seems (as we noted
earlier, in chapter 1) to accord entirely with Aristotle's account of the genesis of knowledge as presented in Book I of the *Metaphysics*—to accord, in
other words, with that account of the genesis of theoretical comportment
which Heidegger in the 1924/25 *Sophist* course described as arising from
the "natural" or everyday understanding and interpretive tendency inherent in Greek existence (GA 19, 65ff.): theoretical contemplation began when
human beings had leisure (*scholazein, diagōgē*), when the necessities of life
had been fulfilled (M, 981 b21f., 982 b24f.). Just as Heidegger in the *Sophist*
course translates *diagōgē* as (among other things) *Verweilen*, "tarrying"
(GA 19, 68), so too in §13 of *Being and Time* the word *Verweilen* characterizes freedom from involvement in producing and manipulating things.

Ontologically, Heidegger's account here clarifies nothing. At most, it
serves to point toward the ontological dimension of being-in-the-world or
originary transcendence in terms of which the ontological problematic of
the genesis of *theòria* can first be raised in a phenomenologically appropriate manner. In particular, we should note that the account has given
no indication as to why precisely contemplation of the *eidos* came to serve
as the exemplary model for a thinking associated with leisure or tarrying
alongside things. Heidegger points more explicitly to this question in a later
note added to his text, precisely where the account might seem to offer an
explanation of how a contemplative looking at something in terms of its
eidos can arise. This marginal note reads:

> Looking away from ...does not in itself give rise to looking
> at. [...] Looking at ...has its own origin and has such look-
> ing away as its consequence; contemplation [*Betrachten*] has its
> own origination. The look at the *eidos* demands something else.
> (SZ, 61 n. a)[3]

What this "something else" is whereby contemplation originates is an
existential-ontological question that cannot yet be raised in this preliminary context of the analytic of Dasein. Yet our remarks on the genesis of
theoretical knowledge in the *Sophist* course already suggest that the answer has to do not only with the fact that the primacy of vision in Greek
thought is indicative of a desire for enduring presence, but—and perhaps

---

[3] The German *Betrachten* may be translated as either "contemplation" or "observation." For our purposes here, the two may be taken as equivalent, and as referring to
"theoretical" seeing (in general we have up to now used "contemplation" as the equivalent of *theòria*). In part 2, we shall see that such "theory" is still understood in too
general a sense that has yet to be more historically specified.

more importantly—that it has just as much to do with the possibility of independence (*Eigenständigkeit*) and self-subsistence, in particular, with the possibility of establishing a freedom and independence from immediate involvement and from all the absorption and captivation that such involvement entails.

Dispersions of Vision: Theory, Praxis, Techne

Our account thus far suggests that both theoretical contemplation and making or producing are to be understood as modes of a particular comportment of Dasein which Heidegger names *Besorgen*. *Besorgen*, or "concern," does not therefore refer to "praxis" in the loose sense (doing and/or making), as opposed to "theory." Nor does it refer exclusively to making or *poiēsis*.[4] It does, however, as we noted, refer to a broad sense of comportment that is primarily concerned with "things." But what exactly does the term "things" include? The possible objects of *Besorgen* are not just any entities regarded in whatever way.

Heidegger addresses this issue in a provisional manner in §15 of *Being and Time* when discussing which beings we should consider in attempting to make visible Dasein's everyday being-in-the-world. The beings we encounter within the world are generally "things." Yet Heidegger warns that if we understand things to be defined by their substantiality, materiality, or the extrinsic value they have, we may be led astray ontologically. Such ontological determinations only conceal our preontological understanding of these seemingly most proximate beings of our everyday concern. At this point Heidegger notes that the Greeks indeed had an appropriate term for "things":

> The Greeks had an appropriate term for "things": *pragmata*, that is to say, that which one has to do with in one's concernful dealings (*praxis*). But ontologically, the specifically "pragmatic" character of the *pragmata* is precisely what the Greeks left in obscurity; they thought of them "proximally" as "mere things." We shall call those beings which we encounter in concern *equipment* [Zeug]. . . . (SZ, 68)

---

[4] Taminiaux is overly restrictive in aligning Dasein's everyday comportment and understanding with *poiēsis* as opposed to *praxis*, and in suggesting that Dasein's circumspective seeing "has no eye for *Dasein* itself" (*n'a pas d'yeux pour le* Dasein *lui-même*). See *Lectures de l'ontologie fondamentale*, 157. A complete blindness to one's own being would be just as phenomenologically incomprehensible as a complete severing of *poiēsis* from *praxis*.

Praxis is here translated as *besorgender Umgang,* "concernful dealings." But does this mean that we should equate *Besorgen* with *praxis* in the narrow Aristotelian sense? Clearly not, for Aristotle's more narrow conception of *praxis* belongs to the realm of ethico-political affairs, concerned primarily with human beings and not with "things."[5] Yet perhaps it does indeed fall under the more general, less "technical" sense of *praxis* that was prevalent in Greek thought, and which is also found in Aristotle. *Praxis* in this more general sense could include doing (in the ethico-political sense), making, or even contemplating: in this sense, any human activity is a *praxis.* "Things" or *pragmata,* Heidegger would later note in another context, can indeed refer to this more encompassing sense of *"praxis* taken in a truly wide sense, neither in the narrow meaning of practical use (cf. *chrēsthai*), nor in the sense of *praxis* as moral action: *praxis* is all doing, undertaking, and sustaining, which also includes *poiēsis"* (FD, 54).[6]

Yet why does Heidegger say that *pragmata,* referring to the "objects" of *praxis,* is an "appropriate term" for "things"? The reason is presumably that such beings demand to be understood ontologically *from out of praxis* itself (and this means in terms of their properly *worldly* character), and not as independently subsisting entities, initially devoid of any worldly character. However this, it seems, is precisely what the Greeks did not accomplish.[7] They left the "pragmatic" or *praxis*-like character of these things *ontologically* obscure. And this, by implication, because they failed to achieve a sufficiently originary, ontological understanding of *praxis* in all its moments. As is now well-known in the light of the publication of the Marburg lecture courses from the period of *Being and Time,* this inadequate interpretation of the ontological character of "things," and by implication of *praxis* itself, occurred, on Heidegger's reading, due to the ascendancy of a "technical" way of thinking about things, one that, deriving from the experience of craftsmanship, came to understand "things" in terms of the *theōria* deriving from *technē,* while (most rigorously in Aristotle) reserving *praxis* and its specific kind of knowledge (*phronēsis*) for the realm of human ethico-political affairs.[8] This derivation is corroborated by a marginal note that Heidegger subsequently added to the expression "mere things":

---

[5] There are, as we have noted, a number of different senses of the word *praxis* in Aristotle. See chapter 2, 31n. 14.

[6] A point noted by Robert Bernasconi, "The Fate of the Distinction between *Praxis* and *Poiesis,*" 7. The same point is made by Heidegger in EM, 44. Cf. also GA 17, 45–46.

[7] Heidegger does not clarify precisely who these "Greeks" are, but it should be evident—as we shall explain in a moment—that Plato and Aristotle are intended primarily.

[8] On the derivation of this "technical" understanding of things, see in particular *Die Grundprobleme der Phänomenologie* (GA 24), 149ff. See also Taminiaux's commentary in *Lectures de l'ontologie fondamentale,* 108ff.

Why? *eidos—morphē—hulē!* coming from *technē,* thus an "artisan" [*künstlerische*] interpretation! if *morphe* not [interpreted] as *eidos,* [then as] *idea!*

If the objects of *praxis* or concernful activity were understood as "mere things," this occurred, on Heidegger's account, because they were viewed essentially as though they were material (*hulē*) to be worked upon by a craftsman. Material, as a natural resource of *technē,* came to be regarded as *mere* material, yet to be given shape and form (*morphē*) by the craftsman who in advance sights the *eidos* or visible look of the thing to be produced. Things thus come to be seen as "mere" things: the thing is only fully a thing when it has achieved its *telos* (the stamp of its *eidos*) as the completion of its form. Taken in itself, the thing is deficient with regard to its proper form, yet to be bestowed by human intervention.

But of course, this *telos* or end is not, properly speaking, the ultimate end of the material product or "thing." Once produced, the product is there to be acted upon again; it once more becomes subservient to human *praxis.* As Aristotle notes, the end of *poiēsis* is *praxis* (NE, 1139 b1). Subservient to the end of human *praxis,* the product is ontologically incomplete or underdetermined when considered independently of such *praxis.* For every human product is made *for* something; it finds its end in the realm of human affairs. In its very being, a product of human making is something that exists for some further human activity. Its way of being is constituted by an "in order to. . . ." Taken *in itself,* however, it can be viewed as a mere thing to be acted upon. This view of the object of *praxis,* the *pragma,* as a "mere" thing results from a technical interpretation or way of thinking that views things in respect of their self-subsistence as something present-at-hand.[9] Yet this also implies that the *praxis/poiēsis* distinction itself, when applied in too absolute a manner, lies at the root of a reductive understanding of "things." It is only because the *praxis*-like dimension of the making or producing, and indeed also of the *theōria* inherent in *technē,* is overlooked or eclipsed that the "thing" can be seen as having in itself no worldly or *praxis*-like character, and that this very seeing or *theōrein* can likewise disregard its own embeddedness in human *praxis,* become "unworldly."

A more originary interpretation of *praxis*—but also, presumably, of *theōria* and *technē*—is thus called for, one that remains attentive to the properly worldly character of all involvements. And this entails an interpretation of what, in general, being-in-the-world (or "Dasein") means. The phenomenon of concern, or *Besorgen,* will thus have to be understood in

---

[9] The nature of this reduction of the thing would later be considered in greater detail by Heidegger, and specifically in the context of *technē,* in "The Origin of the Work of Art" (1936). See part 1 of the essay, "The Thing and the Work."

terms of its ontological rootedness in being-in-the-world, in transcendence, in Dasein's originary being as care and as temporality. In *Being and Time,* Heidegger initially seeks to resist a merely technical-theoretical interpretation of things by focusing on things as equipment, in their readiness-to-hand, intrinsically constituted by an "in order to" or purpose and thus, in their being, referred to the ontological realm of Dasein, of the being that we ourselves in each case are. Such readiness-to-hand (*Zuhandenheit*), as the analysis clarifies, and not presence-at-hand (*Vorhandenheit*), constitutes the manner of being that such "things" properly have in themselves (SZ, 71, 75). This of course might be taken as a merely "subjective" interpretation of the being of independent entities, whose proper independence science would respect more carefully via the supposed neutrality of its theoretical vision that observes and contemplates things as self-subsistent in their "objective" presence-at-hand. Yet such an objection presupposes human *praxis* to be a realm of merely subjective activity, belonging to and under the control of individual human beings as subjects, and subsequently extended ontologically to include other things within it. In this perspective readiness-to-hand appears as a mere "aspect" ascribed by human "cognition" to things that already exist independently of any relation to us (SZ, 71). *Being and Time,* by contrast, opens itself to the possibility that "human activity" or *praxis,* properly understood, is not merely human at all in the modern subjectivist sense, but a kind of activity that demands to be understood more originarily in terms of the worldly disclosure of being that occurs in each case as a mode of being-in-the-world, or Dasein. The primacy of this disclosive relation to world is indicated in §16 when Heidegger shows that the being of things in their readiness-to-hand presupposes a certain "nonthematic" presence of world, a presence which, from the perspective of the supposedly pure presence-at-hand disclosed by the theoretical gaze, is rather an absence or withdrawal of world. The proper being of equipment, its readiness-to-hand, is graspable "only on the basis of the phenomenon of world" (SZ, 75–76).

This nonthematic presence of world in its absence belongs intrinsically to our "circumspective" concern with and absorption in our worldly involvements with things. It occurs in and amid the circumspection (*Umsicht*) that guides our understanding of our involvement with things. For all understanding, Heidegger will emphasize, is intrinsically constituted by "seeing" (*Sicht*) as a primary manner of access to beings in their being. Likewise, all Dasein's seeing or sighting of things in their being is intrinsically an understanding. But not all seeing is theoretical or thematic. We have already noted Heidegger's argument that concern in the sense of equipmental involvement cannot be thought adequately in terms of theoretical or cognitive knowledge. In §15 he underlines the point in the following way:

Just *looking at* the particular qualities of the "outward appearance" of things, however sharply we look, is incapable of discovering anything ready-to-hand. The gaze of the merely "theoretical" look at things is deprived of any understanding of readiness-to-hand. Yet our dealing with things by manipulating them and using them is not blind; it has its own kind of vision, by which our manipulation is guided and imparted its specific thingly character.[10] Our dealing with equipment subordinates itself to the manifold assignments of the "in order to." The vision [*Sicht*] with which it thus accommodates itself is *circumspection* [Umsicht]. (SZ, 69)

Circumspection, the seeing specific to equipmental involvements, should not, therefore, be analysed on the basis of *theōrein,* or starting from a theoretical perspective on things, but must be seen phenomenologically, in its own right. Theoretical and circumspective seeing, although both are ways of seeing as well as modes of concern in the sense indicated, should not be confused with one another. Yet nor, Heidegger continues, may they be understood by imposing the traditional, yet ill-defined opposition of "theory" and "praxis":

"Practical" comportment is not "atheoretical" in the sense of being sightless, and its difference from theoretical comportment is not simply due to the fact that in theoretical comportment one contemplates, while in practical comportment one *acts,* and that action must apply theoretical cognition [*Erkennen*] if it is not to remain blind; for just as contemplation is originarily a kind of concern, so too action has *its* vision. Theoretical comportment is a noncircumspective merely looking at things. But the fact that this looking is noncircumspective does not mean that it follows no rules: it constructs a canon for itself in the form of *method.* (SZ, 69)

As we have noted, the fact that Dasein's theoretical comportment is noncircumspective does not preclude the possibility that it is a (ontically) founded or derivative mode of circumspective concern. Contemplation, as noncircumspective, remains a kind of concern. Heidegger therefore seeks to emphasize that one should not view "theoretical" and "practical" comportment as mutually exclusive ways of being that reciprocally supplement one another. Theoretical comportment is itself a form of acting, of comportment, just as practical comportment (or "action" in a broad sense) is also

---

[10] Here we follow the first edition. Later editions have *Sicherheit,* "security," in place of *Dinghaftigkeit,* "thingly character."

a seeing, indeed one that does not first need "theory" to inform it. Is not the kind of interpretation that posits "theory" and "practice" as existing independently of one another and then subsequently entering into a relation of hierarchy or supplementarity itself already the result of a theoretical perspective?

Heidegger's point, then, is not that there is no difference between theoretical and circumspective comportment, between "theory" and "practice." Quite to the contrary. His point is simply that this difference must be understood in terms of its unitary ground, as a distinction between different modes of (concernful) being-in-the-world, different ways of uncovering beings within the world. Another way of putting this, in more temporal terms, is to say that the difference between these different modes of comportment is not a difference that simply obtains *within* the horizon of an already existing presence. Rather, such difference occurs as a disclosive, intrinsically differential and finite happening in which the disclosure of world itself is at play. But what exactly is "world"? What is the strange presence-in-absence of world that marks the very difference or differentiation between circumspective and theoretical seeing?

Before approaching the answers to such questions, we must attempt to clarify further what is being asked. Heidegger indicates that the difference between these different modes of concern, namely, theoretical and circumspective comportment, is to be understood phenomenologically in terms of dispersion (*Zerstreuung*):

> With Dasein's facticity, its being-in-the-world has in each case already dispersed or even split itself into particular ways of being-in.... (SZ, 56–57)

> Our dealings have already dispersed themselves into a multiplicity of ways of concern. The kind of dealing that is closest to us is, as we have shown, not a merely cognitive apprehending, but rather that kind of concern which manipulates things and puts them to use; and this has its own kind of "cognition" [*Erkenntnis*]. (SZ, 67)

Circumspection and theoretical contemplation are dispersed, already differentiated ways of concern. This dispersion is not only factical, but also historical, that is, it occurs as the concrete enactment of certain interpretations of the being of beings. From the point of view of the analytic, however, the difficulty remains of how to access Dasein's being prior to such dispersion. In terms of what can we recognize such dispersion *as dispersion?* The analytic of Dasein aims to uncover the originary being of Dasein which, far from being reducible to any of these dispersed modes, would constitute the ground on which they could first be understood as such. These dispersed modes of Dasein's being, as ways of concern, of *Besorgen* (but also of "solicitude," *Fürsorge,* which we shall consider in the next chapter) that unfold factically as specific ways of relating to beings, will be understood more originarily on the ground of Dasein's being as care *(Sorge).* But in what sense does "care" constitute a "ground" of being-in-the-world? And in what sense is such a ground to be conceived as "unitary"?

It is important to understand that this is not an instance of positing the One as the ground of the Many in a manner which we find throughout the history of philosophy. Ground and its unity here, in the analytic of Dasein, are not opposed to or set over against dispersion; and such dispersion is not posited as something that could or should be overcome. Traditionally, ground is understood philosophically as that which already is, that which is most constantly present, that which already underlies a possible multiplicity of (temporally or contingently dependent) determinations: in Aristotle, it is *to ti ēn einai,* "that which already is (has been) in being"; it is primary *ousia* or "substance"; and the same understanding of being is employed in Aristotle's understanding of the "soul" *(psuchē)*[11]—notwithstanding the fact that the *human* soul is also an *archē* of *praxis,* an *archē* determined as *hou heneka,* an "origin" that can freely relate to and anticipate itself, its own being, as its end. As our previous chapter indicated, this end of the human soul, of human being as such, itself tends—with the ascendency of theoretical contemplation—to be understood as an already existing, already present ground *(nous),* a ground that "always" already endures and needs only the act of theoretical contemplation to come into its own (authentic) being, into its ownmost *ergon,* its ownmost self-enactment and end *(en-ergeia, entelecheia),* its ownmost self-presence. The *being* of the "self" thus tends to be understood already in Aristotle, and henceforth in the history of philosophy, as an already present ground. The understanding of the soul in Aristotle is of course not at all identical to the determination of the self in modern subjectivity: The Aristotelian "soul" comes into its ownmost being not by a reflective intuiting of itself as the ground of thinking, as in Descartes—a thinking that then relates all worldly beings back to itself as their unitary ground whose temporal self-oblivion and fallibility is made good by the Christian Creator-God—but rather by its contemplation of the divine presence of the world itself. And yet there is a certain sameness and continuity here from Aristotle to modernity in the determination of true being by way of *theōria.*

By contrast to this traditional understanding of ground, the analytic of Dasein does not conceive of the unitary ground of Dasein's being—

---

[11] See DA, 412aff.

its being-a-self as being-in-the-world—as an already existing or already present, apriori ground that transcends temporal determination or is attained contemplatively in transcending the temporal and finite. Rather, the unitary ground of Dasein's being, *as transcendence,* is itself shown to be intrinsically temporal, factical, and historical. In other words, transcendence, as the originary ground of Dasein's being, is not a transcendence *of* (in the sense of exceeding or going beyond) dispersion, but a transcendence *already in* dispersion. Transcendence and dispersion, ground and multiplicity, are not mutually exclusive, precisely when Dasein's being is seen as *praxis* and not conceived in a theoretical or speculative manner. But *praxis* in this sense is to be conceived in a broad sense, more originarily than in the narrow Aristotelian sense of ethico-political *praxis* that tends to oppose such *praxis* to *theōria* (as well as to *poiēsis*). Theoretical contemplation, as a mode of dispersion, is already a *praxis:* a kind of concern, grounded in Dasein's own being as care. And here we can already discern the overall thrust of the analytic of Dasein compared to Aristotle's understanding of human existence, namely, to problematize the privileging of *theōria* and of presence in the Greek understanding of existence by giving priority to the finitude of Dasein's existence as *praxis,* yet in a manner that does not simply oppose this level of *praxis* to *theōria,* but interprets its intrinsic temporality in a more radical sense than that allowed by merely contrasting it with the theoretical disclosure of time and presence in terms of the "now" (*nun*) and the "eternal" (*aei*). The authentic disclosure of the presence pertaining to Dasein's existence will be granted by the *Augenblick,* the glance of the eye of a finite temporality, and not of a theoretical transcendence.

We shall explore this more originary self-disclosure of Dasein's being in the next chapter. For now, it suffices merely to raise again the question of how to access Dasein's being as an originary and unitary ground of all its dispersed modes of comportment, including theoretical and circumspective. It should now be clear that what is entailed in this task is *not* to access Dasein's being *prior to* its dispersion, as we expressed it above. The task, rather, is to access it—to let it be seen beyond, or even in, its self-concealment—in and amid such dispersion, in the finite temporality of this very dispersion. Dasein's transcendence in dispersion is *unitary* in the manner of its temporalizing, and not as a prior, already existing ground. In already being dispersed into (being "alongside" [*bei*] and involved in) one possibility of concern, Dasein is also presented (as already being in-the-world) with other possibilities, which it holds "present," and it maintains itself in an openness (ahead of itself) for other possibilities of its being that have yet to emerge. This already being presented with and holding itself open for other possibilities (other possible modes of comportment and dispersion) is *not closed off* by Dasein's existing in dispersion, but as a primordial or originary way of being, is already maintained as such in and throughout all factical existing.

Yet what manner of access is appropriate to this originary and unitary phenomenon of Dasein's being as care? What kind of phenomenological "seeing" will disclose Dasein's being as such even in its dispersion? What is required, according to Heidegger, is a "*unitary* phenomenological look" at Dasein's being as a whole, a "complete look through" the whole of Dasein's being in all its structural (ultimately temporal) moments. And this can be neither the kind of theoretical or circumspective looking that remain directed toward beings (as present-at-hand or in their readiness-to-hand) but not toward being; nor can it be an "immanent perceiving of experiences," which likewise remains oriented toward that which is merely present. It must, rather, be a seeing intrinsic to "one of the *most far-reaching* and *most originary* possibilities of disclosure," a mode of disclosure lying in Dasein itself (albeit for the most part dormant), namely, the fundamental attunement of *Angst* which discloses being-in-the-world as such (SZ, 180–82). The seeing intrinsic to this manner of disclosure will subsequently be interpreted as the phenomenon of the *Augenblick*, which we shall examine in the next chapter. Yet is not the disclosure granted by the *Augenblick*, which grounds and informs the entire analytic of Dasein, itself in a certain tension with the proposed phenomenological nature of the investigation? For phenomenology, Heidegger has indicated, is "primarily a *concept of method*" (SZ, 27). And as such it is science (*Wissenschaft*): "science of the being of beings—ontology" (SZ, 37). Its task is to make being as such, and initially the being of Dasein, explicit or thematic. Yet are the scientific and thematizing aspirations of such phenomenology ultimately appropriate to disclosing the being of Dasein? Are they not remnants of the theoretical desire, itself already in dispersion, and requiring the construction of method in order to guide it?

***

For the moment, we shall merely leave these as questions. The present section has served to indicate the centrality of the unitary problem of transcendence and world for understanding the status of theoretical comportment in *Being and Time*. This will become more apparent in what follows. The issue of the temporal finitude of Dasein's being, as a being-in-dispersion, will prove crucial to the problem of accounting thematically for the ontological genesis of theoretical comportment.

The Existential Genesis of Theory

The question of the *existential-ontological* possibility of science or theoretical knowledge is not properly broached by Heidegger until the analytic has
elucidated the ontological meaning of Dasein's being as temporality. If Dasein's being, articulated as care, is ultimately to be understood as temporality, and if such being is essentially a being-in-the-world, then world and its
transcendence must also be thought in terms of their temporal possibility.
We noted earlier that cognitive knowledge as a theoretical comportment
toward beings is ontologically founded in being-in-the-world. Heidegger's
preliminary analysis in §13 argued that if a transcendence is implied in all
comportment toward beings, then such transcendence must itself be understood in terms of the prior, ontological structure of being-in-the-world, and
not in terms of an independently existing "subject" that then "transcends"
itself in the direction of an "object." "Theory" and "praxis" as traditionally comprehended ways of relating to beings presuppose that those beings,
and we ourselves, are already given, that is, understood *in advance* of any
possible ontic comportment or relationality. Dasein has already projected
and understood being, the being both of itself and of those beings it wishes
to deal with in concernful comportment. This prior projection of Dasein's
own being together with the being of intraworldly beings is entailed in what
Heidegger understands by *transcendence*. Since Dasein's being is being-in-
the-world, and beings are given as beings "within" the world, world itself
must belong to Dasein's transcendence. It is from out of such transcendence, that is, from out of a prior understanding of world, that Dasein can
relate to beings in the manner of theoretical or practical comportment.

If Dasein's being is temporality, how does that temporality allow for an
understanding of transcendence, that is, of world? Heidegger investigates
this issue in §69, "The temporality of being-in-the-world and the problem of the transcendence of world." It is one of the most difficult sections
in *Being and Time*. Heidegger begins the section with some introductory
remarks concerning the disclosedness or "openness" of Dasein for its possibilities. This disclosedness is a kind of clearing (*Lichtung*). Whatever has
"cleared" (*gelichtet*) Dasein must not be interpreted as some kind of ontic
power or source that is simply present, but rather is itself temporalized in
Dasein's ecstatic temporality. This "clearedness," Heidegger tells us, "first
makes possible all illumination and illumining, every apprehending, 'seeing,'
and having of something.... *The 'There'* [the *Da* of *Da-sein*] *is originarily
cleared by ecstatic temporality*" (SZ, 350–51).[12] Here, not just "seeing" but

---

[12] "Diese Gelichtetheit ermöglicht erst alle Erleuchtung und Erhellung, jedes Ver-
nehmen, 'Sehen' und Haben von etwas.... *Die ekstatische Zeitlichkeit lichtet das Da
ursprünglich*."

also "having" is referred back to Dasein's ecstatic temporality. Seeing itself is, as we noted, one way of having, of having something present.

Heidegger's introductory remarks draw to a close with a series of questions and a warning, which together serve to suggest in advance that certain questions—most importantly that concerning the *being* of world—will not be adequately resolved in this section. Instead, the analysis must be content to accomplish "the necessary prior clarification of those structures with regard to which the problem of transcendence must be posed" (SZ, 351). Commensurate with the context of our present inquiry into the ontological possibility of theoretical comportment, the following account will focus on §69b, "The temporal meaning of the modification of circumspective concern to the theoretical discovery of what is present-at-hand within the world."

Heidegger begins §69b by emphasizing straightaway that the inquiry is not now interested in the ontic history or development of science, but in "the *ontological genesis* of theoretical comportment." The inquiry seeks to attain "an *existential concept of science*" (SZ, 357). It is important to note that Heidegger does not confine such theoretical comportment to the investigation of beings or entities. Rather, he is here pursuing a broad conception of science that allows for two fundamentally different orientations: Science is to be understood as a "way of existence and thereby as a mode of being-in-the-world that can discover or disclose beings or being." The second of these possibilities is crucial for Heidegger's own undertaking if the phenomenological investigation of *being* is to be a science. Heidegger indeed hints as much, while intimating that his present account of the ontological genesis of science will be subject to a certain incompleteness and thus can be only preparatory:

> A fully adequate existential interpretation of science, however, can be carried out only after the *meaning of being and the "connection" between being and truth have been clarified* in terms of the temporality of existence. The following deliberations are preparatory to the understanding of *this central problematic,* within which, moreover, the idea of phenomenology, as distinguished from the preliminary conception of it, which we indicated by way of introduction, will be developed for the first time. (SZ, 357)

What kind of truth pertains to being itself, and accordingly, what kind of knowledge is appropriate to it, remains an open question. Heidegger at this stage indeed understands the scientific, phenomenological investigation of being as a kind of theoretical undertaking. One which, therefore, as only one particular mode of comportment, must inevitably fall prey to a certain facticity and dispersion. Even if this conclusion seems to follow with

a certain inevitability, however, it would be premature to make any judgment as to what the consequences of such facticity and dispersion might
be. If Dasein's being is temporality, the facticity and dispersion in question can be understood only via the temporal analysis of the dispersion of
Dasein's being into distinctive kinds of comportment such as theory and
circumspection.

Heidegger describes the modification from circumspective to theoretical
concern in terms of a "change-over," in German, *Umschlag:* a term used
elsewhere to translate the temporal sense of *metabolē* or change.[13] The
questions posed by §69b are: What sort of account can we provide of the
ontological possibility of such a change-over? In terms of what are we to
interpret it?

> In characterizing the change-over from the manipulating and us-
> ing and so forth which are circumspective in a "practical" way,
> to "theoretical" exploration, it would be easy to suggest that
> merely looking at beings is something that emerges when con-
> cern *holds back* from any kind of manipulation. What is decisive
> in the "emergence" of theoretical comportment would then lie in
> the *disappearance* of praxis. So if one posits "practical" concern
> as the primary and predominant kind of being which factical
> Dasein possesses, the ontological possibility of "theory" will be
> due to the *absence* of praxis, that is, to a *privation.* (SZ, 357)

The account that Heidegger sketches here, however, seems suspiciously
close to one we have already encountered, namely, that proposed in §13.
The emergence of cognitive knowing was there apparently traced precisely
to a "holding back" from all concernful involvement, a "deficiency" of our
concernful having-to-do with the world. Yet Heidegger is now critical of
such an account:

> But the discontinuance of a specific manipulation in our con-
> cernful dealings does not simply leave the guiding circumspec-
> tion behind as a remainder. Rather, our concern then diverts
> itself specifically into just looking around [*Nur-sich-umsehen*].
> Yet this is by no means the way in which the "theoretical"
> attitude of science is reached. On the contrary, the tarrying
> that arises when manipulation is discontinued can take on the
> character of a more precise kind of circumspection, such as "in-
> specting" [*Nachsehen*], checking up on what has been attained,
> or looking over the "operations" that are now "at a standstill."

---

[13] See, for example, GA 24, §19; GA 26, 199; GA 33, passim; W, 355.

Holding back from the use of equipment is so far from being
"theory" that the kind of circumspection that tarries and "contemplates" remains wholly bound to the ready-to-hand equipment with which one is concerned. "Practical" dealings have
their *own* ways of tarrying. And just as praxis has its specific
vision ("theory"), theoretical research is not without a praxis of
its own. (SZ, 357–58)

Tarrying alongside things, which (as §13 already indicated) arises when
one holds back from manipulating and using, is not yet theoretical comportment. Looking back at the earlier account of cognitive or theoretical
knowing, we can see that such tarrying corresponds to an *"apprehending
of what is present-at-hand,"* and that the theoretical, cognitive mode of
comportment presumably emerges only when "apprehending becomes a
determining." As we remarked when commenting on §13, this account
merely indicates a nexus of ontic founding which could be valid *if* what
is initially and most proximally given—Dasein's concernful absorption in,
or captivation by, the world—were to be taken as the phenomenological
ground for interpreting its other modes of comportment. However, the ontological interpretation of Dasein's being must put into question precisely
whatever is initially and most proximally given or "shows itself."
     We can now better appreciate what the earlier account of cognitive
knowledge as a founded mode was intended to accomplish. Although it clarified nothing of the ontological grounds of theoretical knowing, it effectively
disarmed the traditional priority of theoretical contemplation. Heidegger's
reason for including §13 was that the "priority of cognitive knowledge" was
misleading for understanding Dasein's being-in-the-world (SZ, 59). Hence
§13 argued, in effect, that the priority of theoretical comportment over
"praxis" could just as well be reversed. In part, this was in preparation
for the analysis of Dasein's concernful dealings: the point was to see such
concernful comportment phenomenologically, without the phenomenological vision being clouded by traditional approaches. As Heidegger put it
in §15, "Achieving phenomenological access to the beings we encounter
consists rather in warding off those interpretative tendencies which thrust
themselves upon us and accompany us, and which cover over not only the
phenomenon of such 'concern', but even more those beings themselves *as*
encountered of their own accord *in* and for our concern" (SZ, 67). Yet the
reversal from the theoretical approach to "praxis," that is, to what *seems*
to be phenomenologically first, by no means guarantees that this initial
"given," namely, "practical" concern, constitutes the *ontological* ground in
terms of which theoretical comportment could be understood in its genesis. The reversed order of founding appealed to by Heidegger's preliminary

account is thus no less tenuous than the traditional order. All these considerations, however, serve little more than to remind us, as §69 now expresses
it, "that it is by no means evident where the ontological boundary between
'theoretical' and 'atheoretical' comportment really lies" (SZ, 358). What is
called for is a closer analysis of the ontological relation between circumspective seeing and the kind of seeing that announces itself in the traditional
priority of theoretical contemplation:

> One will point out that all manipulation occurring in science
> is merely in the service of pure observation [*Betrachtung*]—
> the investigative discovery and disclosure of the "things them-
> selves." "Seeing," taken in the broadest sense, regulates all "pro-
> cedures" and retains priority. "In whatever way and by whatever
> means knowledge [*Erkenntnis*] relates to objects, *intuition* [An-
> schauung] is that by which it relates to them immediately, *and
> toward which all thinking as a means is directed*."[14] Whether
> it is factically attainable or not, the idea of the *intuitus* has
> guided all interpretation of knowledge from the beginnings of
> Greek ontology until today. If we are to exhibit the existential
> genesis of science in accordance with the priority of "seeing,"
> then we must begin by characterizing the *circumspection* that
> guides our "practical" concern. (SZ, 358)

Heidegger analyses the kind of seeing belonging to circumspection as
itself guided by an overview (*Übersicht*) of the equipmental totality and
its worldly context. This overview—which receives its "light" from Dasein's own being and is thus grounded in care—is not a surveying of things
present-at-hand, but a "primary understanding of the totality of involvements" within which concern operates. Such an overview, as a kind of understanding, is able to bring things nearer by interpreting what has been
sighted. Heidegger terms this operation "deliberating" (*Überlegung*), and
accords it the "peculiar schema of the 'if—then'." Circumspective deliberation lets us see that *if* something is to be achieved, *then* we require this or
that means. Such circumspection is therefore never simply a taking note of
what is given and present-at-hand. It can bring something nearer that is
not at all present within our immediate field of vision (SZ, 359).

In order to remind ourselves of the broader perspective at issue here, it
may be helpful at this point to draw a brief parallel and contrast between
this analysis and the account of practical vision in the 1924 interpretation
of Aristotle. It should be clear that the "overview" described by Heidegger

---

[14] The quotation is from Kant's *Critique of Pure Reason*, A 19; the italics are
Heidegger's.

here is not to be straightforwardly equated with the vision of practical *aisthēsis* that informs *praxis* in the Aristotelian sense. The vision described in the present instance is part of a context of equipmental involvement in a task of making or producing something; in short, it is concerned with the being of "things" and not of Dasein itself. A "circumspective overview" is thus the kind of retentive-attentive vision appropriate to *technē*, namely, a "seeing" or making-present of an already given context of involvements with respect to a particular (futural) possibility for transforming something within that context (i.e., a possibility of *poiēsis*). The antecedent sighting of, or attentiveness to (*Gewärtigen*) such a possibility is what has traditionally been understood as the sighting of the *eidos*. Heidegger's description here emphasizes the *embeddedness* of such sighting within a more general, and yet quite determinate context.

The interpretive movement and appropriation of what is sighted circumspectively in such a contextualized overview is in §69 conceived as a process of deliberation by way of the "if—then" schema. Significantly, Heidegger's 1924 reading of Aristotle had attributed this schema of deliberation to the development of *technē* within the "natural" genesis of theoretical knowing. Whereas *empeiria* is a "quite primitive making-present" in terms of the schema '*as soon as* this *then* this,' *technē* depends on this schema being modified to '*if* this *then* this'—that is, it marks the opening up of a futural dimension, and thereby an increased freedom from presence (although Heidegger does not indicate this here). Experience depends on a context of events being retained and kept present, while *technē* has an insight into this *context* of presence as such. This entails that things come to be seen in the possible constancy of their presence, that is, in their *eidos*. According to Heidegger, it is on account of the *repetition* of a sequence of events that a view of the *eidos*, the "constantly recurring look," emerges. What is distinctive about the kind of understanding belonging to *technē* is the *"presentation of the look,"* of the outward appearance or *Aussehen* of that with which we are concerned. The "new phenomenon" distinctive of *technē*, Heidegger emphasizes in the 1924 interpretation, "lies in the direction of its *seeing*, not in what it does" (GA 19, 74–78).

What emerges from the 1924 analysis as significant for our purposes is that the schema of deliberation described here in *Being and Time* as intrinsic to our involvement in an equipmental context, that is, to *technē*, is also precisely the schema of deliberation that we seem to find in *phronēsis*. The "if—then" schema is, as Heidegger indicates, nothing other than the means—end schema: *if* (we are to achieve such an end) *then* we require such and such means. The difference between *technē* and *phronēsis* lies not in the possible engagement of a deliberative, means—end schema as such, but in the kind of futural projection or *seeing* of being that the ensuing deliberative process is dependent upon and subjects itself to in advance. In the circumspective overview pertaining to *technē*, what is foreseen is a particular possibility (or range of possibilities) pertaining to the independent being or presence of intraworldly entities or "things." In the practical vision of *phronēsis*, what is anticipated (in a *prohairesis*) is a possible *praxis*, that is, the possible being of the *phronimos*, a possible way of being-a-self. The primary projection is different in each case: in the one instance, the projection of the being of an independent entity, the work to be produced; in the other, a projection of a way of being that itself is its own activity, existing as a futurally oriented, and yet momentary *praxis*. Moreover, whereas the "glance of the eye" is limited to the disclosure of the particularity of a specific situation of action, the circumspective overview of *technē* is a disclosure precisely of the possibility of repetition: it discloses a possibility in the possible constancy of its being; the projected possibility must be re-produced in the actual work, and it stands in the possibility of being repeatedly actualized in subsequent works. *Technē* sees a possible universal. The practical vision of *phronēsis*, by contrast, discloses a singular, unique, and unrepeatable possibility of *praxis*. "The glance of the eye" of *praxis* concerns precisely the singularity of the unrepeatable, and therein lies its intrinsically finite, "eschatological" character.

The existential meaning of circumspective deliberation, Heidegger argues in *Being and Time,* is making-present (*Gegenwärtigung*). Bringing something closer that is not physically present is also a possible mode of making-present: envisaging something as present (*Vergegenwärtigung*). In envisaging it as present, our deliberation is able to "bring into view" something needed that is un-ready-to-hand (e.g., I need something with which to drive in these nails) (SZ, 359). However, circumspective making-present in general is said to be a phenomenon that is *founded* in at least two respects. In the first place, it "belongs in each case to a complete ecstatic unity of temporality." It must both retain (*behalten*) the equipmental context (I am building a table ...) and be attentive to (*gewärtigen*) a particular possibility of concernful involvement (I need something to secure the table legs). Thus, circumspective making-present is founded in the sense that it can only bring nearer what has *already* been laid open (i.e., what has already come to presence) by the temporalizing of a retentive attentiveness. In other words, circumspective making-present does not give rise to itself, but is enabled by and springs from a unity of retention and attention. This also implies that as an activity, it is not purely present to itself, nor is it self-originating.

The second sense in which circumspective deliberation is founded is that it is dependent upon interpretation. Whatever is addressed via the 'if—then' schema must in advance have been understood *as such and such,* that is, it must already have undergone interpretation. The schema 'something as something' is more originary than the 'if—then' schema, yet is itself founded ontologically in the temporality of understanding. Deliberative circumspection lets us see the ready-to-hand *as* having an involvement in a certain task (we see the hammer as being something for hammering nails; if I use the hammer then I can drive in the nails), but it does not first discover the ready-to-hand itself. Whatever can be interpreted as something must already have manifested itself; it must already have been sighted by the vision belonging to Dasein's understanding, prior to any interpretation.

Both senses in which circumspective making-present is founded thus amount to the same phenomenon: the "rootedness" of the present in future and having-been, a rootedness Heidegger identifies as the "existential-temporal condition of the possibility" of circumspective seeing.

Thus far, the temporal analysis of circumspection has served merely to clarify the situation or *ontological context* in which the change-over to theoretical comportment must occur. Heidegger next attempts to analyse what is implied in the change-over itself by way of an *assertion* whose meaning may be modified according to whether the context is circumspective or theoretical. He takes as an example the assertion "The hammer is heavy." The meaning of an assertion is dependent upon our interpretation of it, and each interpretation implies a latent or prior understanding. In the case of our present example, the assertion may be interpreted as meaning that the hammer is unsuitable for the task in which we are involved. In this instance, then, it is understood within a context of circumspective concern, involved in making or repairing something. The assertion is made and understood in advance with respect to an equipmental context that is retained and with a view to an end or purpose, an 'in order to . . .' to which we are attentive. However, the assertion could also be understood as meaning that the hammer has the property of heaviness. Here the hammer is understood as a body having mass, subject to the law of gravity. Such understanding no longer operates in the "horizon" of a circumspective, attentive retaining. It has a different view of things:

> Why is it that in this modified kind of discourse what we are talking about—the heavy hammer—shows itself differently? It is not because we are keeping a distance from manipulation, nor because we are looking *away* [ab*sehen*] from the equipmental character of this entity, but because we are looking *at* [an*sehen*] the ready-to-hand thing which we encounter, looking at it in a "new" way as something present-at-hand. *The understanding of being* by which our concernful dealings with beings within the world are guided *has changed over* [umgeschlagen]. (SZ, 361)

This change-over in our understanding of being entails a *new* way of looking at things, a new kind of seeing. *How is this new way of seeing possible?* We now contemplate and observe the piece of equipment as something present-at-hand. But surely, Heidegger points out, even this does not yet in itself constitute theoretical or scientific comportment. Furthermore, we can contemplate the ready-to-hand as an "object," in a scientific manner, without that object losing its equipmental character.

> The modification in our understanding of being does not seem to be necessarily constitutive for the genesis of theoretical comportment "toward things." Certainly not—if this modification is taken to mean a change in the kind of being understood as belonging to those beings lying before us. (SZ, 361)

The point here seems to be that if we take the being of an entity to be something possessed by or intrinsically belonging to that entity itself—as though it were an independent entity lying before us with its own, independent kind of being—then our understanding of what that entity in itself is need not change when we move from circumspective to theoretical comportment. The entity in question would be independently given, and we could simply look at it in different ways. But the *way* in which an entity is given is precisely what is at stake here. Heidegger's point is that the modification at issue in our understanding of being is not concerned with what kind of independent being we ascribe to beings themselves—for is not the very conception of independent being a *result* of the theoretical attitude in the first place?—but precisely with these *different ways of seeing and looking at things.* In other words, the modification in our understanding of being also entails a modification in Dasein's understanding of its own being and of its world: Dasein understands ("sees") itself *as* dealing with things in the manner of making, *as* observing them scientifically; it sees the world as the immediate environment (*Umwelt*) within which it has to make something for someone, or as a totality of beings independently "there" for exploitation, and so on. The modification in question thus entails a change in our understanding of *being in general,* for such understanding is what guides and makes possible this or that factical comportment of Dasein toward things. What is at stake, ultimately, is a modification of *horizon:* of the horizonal unity of Temporality in which Dasein understands its own being *together with* the being of beings within the world. The happening of this modification is thereby implicitly associated with the "destiny" of Dasein's being, with its *facticity* and *historicality.* The concept of facticity entails "the being-in-the-world of an 'intraworldly' being [i.e., Dasein] such that this being can understand itself as bound up in its 'destiny' with the being of those beings it encounters within its own world" (SZ, 56).

The Thematizing Projection of Things

Heidegger does not pursue the temporality of horizonal modification in this context. The remainder of §69b is content to shed indirect light on the issue by elucidating what is further implied in the genesis of theoretical comportment. Compared to the situation of circumspective concern, a scientific understanding of the assertion that the hammer is heavy entails our overlooking (*übersehen*) not only the equipmental character of the ready-to-hand, but also the specific, environmental context of involvement. "The beings of our environment become altogether *decontextualized*. The totality of what is present-at-hand becomes thematic" (SZ, 362). This decontextualizing for its part also allows us to delimit various "regions" of what is present-at-hand, in order to investigate them theoretically.

What kind of understanding of being makes possible this decontextualizing and thematizing? Heidegger attempts to clarify this question by examining the "classical example" both for the historical development of science and for its ontological genesis: mathematical physics. The decisive factor in the genesis of mathematical physics is the "mathematical projection of nature itself." This projection entails the opening of a new horizon:

> This projection [of nature] discovers in advance something constantly present-at-hand (material) and opens the horizon for the guiding respect in which its quantitatively determinable constitutive moments (movement, force, place, and time) are to be viewed. Only "in the light" of a nature thus projected can such a thing as a "fact" be found and posited for an experiment regulated and delimited in terms of this projection. The "grounding" of "factual science" became possible only because researchers understood that in principle there are no "mere facts." (SZ, 362)

This projection of nature *as* that which is constantly present-at-hand (thus, a particular interpretation and uncovering of nature) opens the horizon for the "guiding respect" in which it is to be viewed in advance: that of quantitative determinability. The understanding that essentially there are no "mere facts" amounts to the understanding that being, understood as the way of being or manner of givenness of things, does not belong to independent objects in themselves, but is co-dependent upon our projective understanding of it. For the purposes of the ontological analysis of the intrinsic possibility of science, the particular *respect* (here, the mathematical) in terms of which we interrogate and investigate beings is not in itself decisive. Rather, as Heidegger puts it, what is decisive is that the mathematical projection of nature "discloses an apriori." Natural science discovers "the thematic beings *in the only way* that beings can be discovered: in the prior projection of the constitution of their being." It is in terms of this primary projection that the ensuing procedural and conceptual moments of scientific inquiry may be worked out, moments that, taken as a whole, constitute "the full existential concept of science" (SZ, 362–63).

The guiding understanding of being constitutive of the scientific project is essentially a thematizing projection. *Thematization* is the term Heidegger chooses to designate the scientific projection in its entirety. Thematization means "objectifying." It is a way of releasing beings within the world so that these beings can be made to respond to a process of pure discovery. Thematization does not first posit beings, but merely releases them or frees them in such a way that they can be subsequently interrogated and determined in a particular respect; here, for being determined objectively via the mathematical projection of nature. But what is the temporal sense of such objectification? In what kind of presence are beings to present themselves? Heidegger explains it thus:

> This objectifying being alongside beings that are present-at-hand within the world has the character of a *distinctive making-present*. It is distinguished from the present of circumspection mainly by the fact that the discovering belonging to the science in question is attentive [*gewärtig ist*] solely to the discoveredness of what is present-at-hand. (SZ, 363)

This is an important statement which must be read carefully. A first reading might suggest that this explanation fails to find anything essentially distinctive about theoretical comportment. After all, Heidegger has just pointed out that scientific comportment is by no means attained merely by looking at something as present-at-hand (as opposed to ready-to-hand). And of course something present-at-hand can announce itself *within* circumspective concern, for example, when a tool breaks or is too heavy for the task in hand. The making-present characteristic of scientific understanding is attentive *solely* to the *discoveredness* of present-at-hand beings. It is attentive to the manner of their discoveredness (their presence), to the way in which they can be made to lie before us as objects of contemplation and observation. By contrast, even when in circumspective concern we become attentive to something broken and thus suddenly present-at-hand, that attentiveness is still bound up with, and is part of, our attending to the task in which we are involved. We seek to repair the broken tool, to restore the interruption, and to continue with the task to be accomplished. This kind of presence-at-hand is thus still tied to the possibility of that readiness-to-hand in the equipmental context which lets us get on with the task of doing or making something. As Heidegger had earlier clarified,

"This presence-at-hand of something that cannot be used is not yet entirely devoid of all readiness-to-hand whatsoever; equipment that is present-at-hand *in this way* is not yet just some thing that happens to appear somewhere before us" (SZ, 73).

In other words, not all presence-at-hand is the same. There are different kinds of presence-at-hand, and the specific kind characteristic of unreadiness-to-hand must be understood as a "deficient" mode of circumspective concern. The kind of making-present distinctive of our scientific comportment, by contrast, seeks to *maintain* a way of discoveredness or presencing to which beings have to respond. That is, beings are made or challenged to respond to a particular prior projection of their being as constant presence-at-hand. In the projective vision of theoretical discovery, beings are challenged to show their particular "aspects" as present-at-hand determinations of a "thing" projected as an independently subsisting substratum. Beings become thematic, present-at-hand before us, "objects" or "mere things" to be interrogated and determined.

A crucial remark appears here in a footnote to the claim that theoretical, thematizing comportment takes the form of a distinctive or exceptional making-present. Heidegger, referring back to earlier comments on the priority of seeing in traditional accounts of knowledge (with specific allusion to Kant: SZ, 358), now interprets the *temporal meaning of this priority of seeing:* "The thesis that all cognitive knowledge has 'intuition' [*Anschauung*] as its end has the temporal meaning that all cognitive knowing [*Erkennen*] is a making-present." The scientific desire to see, in other words, reflects the desire for a certain kind of presence. However, Heidegger adds a qualifier: "Whether every science, and indeed philosophical knowledge [*Erkenntnis*], aims at a making-present here remains as yet undecided" (SZ, 363 n. 1). This qualifier on Heidegger's part seems to entertain the possibility that a phenomenological "science of being" (as opposed to the ontic sciences concerned with beings) may somehow escape this priority of making-present in the manner of the presentation of the present-at-hand—a priority which, Heidegger argues, reflects a limited understanding of being, an understanding that, in particular, is inappropriate to the being of Dasein and of the phenomenon of world. Yet if thematization is essentially a making-present, then how can a thematizing science of being manage to avoid falling prey to the same concealment of Dasein's fundamentally finite and historical world-involvement? Is not science itself a particular, historically co-determined praxis on the part of finite beings? Is not the thematizing projection as such (whatever its object or theme), as decontextualizing, a concealing of the worldly context of finite action, including its own activity? Does it not conceal the essential dispersion and facticity of all actions?

Toward the end of the 1927 course *The Basic Problems of Phenomenology,* Heidegger explicates the conception of phenomenological ontology as a
scientific objectification of being. Yet he also there concedes that the very
act that grounds the objectification of being (the projection of being upon
the horizon of its understandability), "and precisely this grounding act,"
is exposed to uncertainty (GA 24, 459). The uncertainty is not due merely
to the danger that Heidegger mentions, namely that the objectification of
being always risks being confused with the objectification of beings (in the
positive sciences) and with everyday comportment toward beings. Rather,
his own Temporal analysis of being in that course has by then implicitly undermined the very possibility of bringing to presence the intrinsic grounds
of any thematizing projection—grounds which lie in the finitude of Dasein
itself, and thus in the finitude of time. Somewhat earlier in the 1927 course,
one could perhaps already detect a certain sense of uncertainty as Heidegger
identified the aspirations of a scientific phenomenological ontology with the
very possibility of philosophy:

> There is no explicit ontology in our experiencing beings; pre-
> sumably, however, an understanding of being in general in the
> preconceptual sense is the condition of our being able to objec-
> tify, that is, thematize at all. It is in the objectification of being
> as such that the fundamental act is accomplished in which ontol-
> ogy constitutes itself as science [*Wissenschaft*]. What is essential
> in every science, including philosophy, is that it constitutes it-
> self in the objectification of something that is somehow already
> revealed, that is, pregiven.... If being is to be objectified—if
> an understanding of being is to be possible as science in the
> sense of ontology— *if there is to be philosophy at all,* then that
> upon which our understanding of being, as understanding, has
> already projected being preconceptually must be revealed in an
> explicit projection. (GA 24, 398–99, emphasis added)

The underlying uncertainty presumably concerns, at root, a suspicion
that the "grounds" of any thematizing projection are *existentiell:* preontological, preconceptual, not purely present, and conceptually irrecoverable.
This problematic foreshadows what in 1928 Heidegger will characterize as
the *Umschlag* or turning of fundamental ontology into "metontology." As
Heidegger explains, the Temporal analysis of being is in itself "the *turning*
in which ontology itself explicitly turns back into the metaphysical ontics
in which it implicitly always stands" (GA 26, 201). At the very moment in
which ontology, the science of being qua being, would attempt to ground
itself thematically, it recoils back into its ontic foundations in "the finitude

of Dasein," whereby philosophizing comes to acknowledge itself as a "matter of finitude" (GA 26, 198). Thus, when Heidegger in the 1927 course writes that "The founding act [*Grundakt*] of objectification ...has ...the function of *explicitly* projecting what is pregiven upon that [horizon] upon which it is *already* projected in prescientific experience and understanding" (GA 24, 399), "what is pregiven" in the case of fundamental ontology is the being of Dasein as being-in-the-world; and the horizon upon which it is already prescientifically projected is the finite and futural having-been of being-in-the-world, that is, the primary projection of being or world out of which Dasein understands itself. The founding "act" of objectification, precisely as an act, of necessity resists all objectification.[15]

Modification

Heidegger's account in *Being and Time* may well have arrived at a "full existential concept of science," and even determined ontologically what is distinctive about theoretical comportment by tracing that comportment back to its rootedness in a particular temporalizing of ecstatic temporality. Yet are we any clearer as to the *ontological genesis of science?* Are we any closer to understanding what makes possible the "change-over" or "modification" of circumspection to theoretical comportment? Clearly, the existential-ontological question of the genesis of science has to account for *how* the temporalizing of making-present becomes modified or changes over from temporalizing the presence of readiness-to-hand, and of non- or prescientific presence-at-hand, to temporalizing the *specific* presence-at-hand that is distinctive of the theoretical-scientific understanding of being. From the perspective of circumspective concern, this change-over appears to be a *rupture* or radical break from the context of circumspection. On the other hand, we have seen that this rupture might seem to be prepared or prefigured already within the circumspective context, in which a kind of presence-at-hand announces itself. Yet may we understand the presence specific to science in terms of that presence-at-hand which can appear within circumspection? What provokes the change-over to a different kind of attentiveness guiding our understanding of being? The change-over is a modification of temporal *horizons:* as Heidegger noted, the scientific projection of being "opens the horizon" for a *new* way of looking at things (SZ, 362). The ontological genesis of science must be traced in its possibility to horizonal

---

[15] On the subject of metontology, see David Farrell Krell, *Intimations of Mortality* (University Park: The Pennsylvania State University Press, 1986), chapter 2; also Robert Bernasconi, *Heidegger in Question,* chapter 2; and our remarks in "Metaphysics, Fundamental Ontology, Metontology," *Heidegger Studies* 8 (1992): 63–79.

Temporality (to what Heidegger calls *Temporalität*), and to the way in which temporal horizons can be modified.

Heidegger chooses not to pursue the existential origin of science any further in *Being and Time,* although he does indicate that the particular kind of attentiveness in question (i.e., the particular projection of the future) is "existentielly grounded" in a resolute openness (*Entschlossenheit*)—that is, in one particular kind of *Entschlossenheit*—and thus in the "authentic existence" of Dasein (SZ, 363). This should not, presumably, be taken to imply that science factically presupposes an *explicitly appropriated* authentic self-understanding of Dasein (doing science need not entail any explicit understanding of the ultimate foundations of such activity), but that it can be seen to be grounded in Dasein's *Existenz* proper, once we (phenomenologists) understand the latter appropriately. Yet what if that existentiell ground should prove groundless, or rather, grounded in a finitude beyond presence and yet intrinsic to Dasein authentically understood as originary *praxis?* Would this not preclude making such a "ground" present to and for the thematizing, scientific projection of being? For the moment, Heidegger is content to show that thematization, as theoretical comportment toward beings, *presupposes* Dasein's ontological constitution of being-in-the-world. That is, it presupposes *transcendence.* In order to thematize any entity, Dasein must already have transcended that entity. Indeed, all ontic comportment toward any entity presupposes transcendence. Accordingly, even our "practical" dealings with the ready-to-hand presuppose Dasein's transcendence. Transcendence, as we have already noted, makes possible all concernful being alongside beings, whether that concern is theoretical or practical (SZ, 364).

Heidegger makes a further important point at the end of §69b. Given that thematizing "modifies" our understanding of being, this implies that being itself must *already* have been understood. Yet what understanding of being is it that is modified? As argued, it appears that we cannot understand the thematizing-scientific projection of being in terms of our circumspective understanding of being as readiness-to-hand (together with the presence-at-hand bound up with it). This means that it is not just our understanding of being as readiness-to-hand and presence-at-hand that is modified. Heidegger indicates this when he asserts that "our understanding of being can remain neutral. Readiness-to-hand and presence-at-hand have then not yet been distinguished, still less ontologically conceptualized" (SZ, 364). In other words, a more originary, and as yet undifferentiated understanding of being in general is at work, in terms of which both presence-at-hand and readiness-to-hand could be modified. And such must be an understanding of *world,* that is, of transcendence itself: an understanding of the being (presence) of intraworldly beings as *bound up with* the being of Dasein itself (existence), a *unitary* understanding of being-in-the-world that guides all ontic comportment toward things and toward oneself and others. In §69c Heidegger traces the temporal possibility of the transcendence "of" world (i.e., of world as the horizon disclosed in and through Dasein's transcendence—world is itself "transcendent": SZ, 365–66) to "temporality as an ecstatic unity having something like a horizon." The unity of horizonal "schemata" makes possible "the original connection of the 'in-order-to' relations with the 'for-the-sake-of-which'," that is, of equipmental being (readiness-to-hand) with the futural being of Dasein (SZ, 364–66). As an undifferentiated "horizon," "world is neither present-at-hand nor ready-to-hand. It 'is there' together with the ecstases that are 'outside themselves'" (SZ, 365). World is always already "predisclosed" in all circumspective concern (SZ, 76).

The temporal possibility of horizonal *modification*, however, is not thematically investigated by Heidegger until the 1927 course *The Basic Problems of Phenomenology.* Toward the end of that course, Heidegger gives a very condensed and restricted, and yet telling account of what the horizonal modification of our understanding of being entails. Given the already achieved insight that being is primarily understood as presence (*Anwesenheit* or *Praesenz*), what is at stake is the modification from one kind of presence to another. The particular modification Heidegger considers in the 1927 course is not that from circumspective concern to theoretical comportment, but a preliminary stage thereof, one that remains bound to the context of circumspective concern, namely, the modification through which we come to notice something absent or missing. From the perspective of our involvement with the ready-to-hand, such an entity is "un-ready-to-hand."

How can we come to notice that something is missing? Within our involvement with the ready-to-hand, there must be a certain interruption or suspension of such involvement. There is a momentary shift of horizon, from the presence of something we are manipulating to a different kind of presence: the presence of something missing, absent, not there within our immediate environment—something that does not simply present itself. Heidegger terms this modified presence "absence" (*Absenz*). Absence according to this meaning does not mean not being present at all, it is merely a different kind of presence: the missing tool is precisely present to us *as* missing or *as* absent. It is present in and through its very absence. The role of the "as" here is indicative of the fact that the discovery of what is present in its absence is intrinsically discursive, involving interpretation.

How is such a modification of presence itself possible in terms of ecstatic-horizonal temporality? Heidegger considers that the ecstasis of the future has priority in our understanding of being. When Dasein is involved in the circumspective presence of making or manipulating something, that

presence and Dasein's understanding of it are determined primarily by Dasein's *attending* to the end or 'in order to' of the task in hand. This end or
goal of the process in which we are involved is not itself something purely
"before the mind's eye," as we say; it is not something we hold purely
present before us as an intentional object of our "consciousness." Rather
we know of it, we have it in view as something we have seen already, something retained in such a way as to orient in advance the context and every
step of our procedure within that context. It governs our entire presence
within that context—and yet is "absent," not directly or immediately before me. It is not an intentional object lying before a subject, but rather
co-constitutes the "subject" that I am in that situation in the sense that my
actions are determined only through my *subjecting* myself to it in advance,
in a prior subjection. Dasein comes toward or into this presence from out of
a prior, that is, futural projection of what it is aiming at in accomplishing
this task. This also entails Dasein's retaining the equipmental context as
that to which it comes back; presence is also dependent upon the context
retained. The way we view and retain that context, however, is primarily
dependent on the futural ecstasis of attending. In order for any given presence to be modified, there has to be a modified temporalizing of the futural
ecstasis. Dasein must come toward what is already there (the equipmental
context and prior orientation of our involvement) from a different perspective. Specifically, in order for circumspective presence to become modified
to the presence of something absent, in order for circumspection to reorient
itself, Dasein must first have become *attentive to* what is missing. Heidegger
is able to explain, relatively straightforwardly, how this is possible, simply
on the basis of the ecstatic *unity* of temporality. The futural projection
of what is missing itself arises from out of the presence of the equipmental context in which we are already involved. Dasein becomes attentive to
something as missing because it is already missing *from,* that is, *within,*
the given contextual presence.[16] This is consistent with the way in which
the temporality of our involvement with things in the world temporalizes
primarily from out of the present. The origin of our attentiveness to what is
missing, and, accordingly, the origin of a new or altered horizon of presence,
is in this respect unproblematic.

    In another respect, however, there is indeed a problem for Heidegger's
analysis here. It concerns the very possibility of horizonal modification.
The more pressing question, which Heidegger himself only gestures toward,
is what happens at the very moment when the ecstasis of the future is
modified—when, that is, the horizon shifts from one possible presence to
another. Insofar as that moment is a moment of closure, the closing off

---

[16] This also presupposes, of course, a prior familiarity with the missing item.

of one presence and the opening of another, it seems that negation and closure—withdrawal of the presence in which we already find ourselves, of the presence that seems to be present to us—must belong to the way in which the future temporalizes, that is, the way in which it opens presence and holds it open. In other words, in the very moment of modification—as its very possibility—something like a missing future announces itself. At the moment when presence becomes modified to absence, we, Dasein, are neither one presence nor the other; indeed, at such a moment, there is no pure presence at all, or more precisely no self-presence, if by self-presence we mean the way an already existing Dasein comes (futurally) toward itself, conceived as a horizonal presence that has already been there. But this "missing future" is precisely the phenomenon of the originary future, of futuricity and origination as such. Yet all of this implies that the coming into presence of Dasein, the temporalizing of the originary future, does not *belong* to Dasein's being, or more precisely, to Dasein at the purely *ontological* level, as pure Da-sein: it does not belong to this Dasein conceived purely ontologically and in its (existential/categorial) *difference* from the being of other beings. In other words, it now appears that the temporalizing of the originary future does not belong to Dasein in its ontological difference, but to the happening of world as the undifferentiated, unitary horizon of being/time. The existential/categorial distinction, as a *purely ontological* distinction, is unsustainable—but this is because the ontological difference itself, as *difference*, is unsustainable. Conceived at the ontological-Temporal level, Dasein turns out to be Nothing; at the level of the existentiell, it thus shows itself to be a being held out into Nothing.[17]

Such considerations suggest, therefore, that there is no fully constituted (or closed) presence in the first place, not even in readiness-to-hand or presence-at-hand, given that any such presence must allow for the possibility of modification and, simply to be open for another possibility, must already have closed off the futural horizon belonging to that presence. Making-present may not only be "enclosed" (*eingeschlossen*) in future and having-been in the sense of a horizonal containment (SZ, 328), but closed off, en*closed* in these other ecstases, closed off by an originary future that does not arrive (i.e., whose temporalizing "is," or rather happens as the event of its nonarrival), thereby precisely opening the horizon of what has been, allowing having-been to be, letting it be. This letting-be, in that case,

---

[17]Cf. "What is Metaphysics?" (1929) (W, 1ff.), where being attuned to the Nothing is said to happen "seldom enough—only for *Augenblicke* in the fundamental attunement of anxiety" (111). On undifferentiatedness (*Indifferenz*) and the necessary collapse of the "ontological difference" see the 1929/30 course *The Fundamental Concepts of Metaphysics* (GA 29/30, 512ff.). Dasein's being the ground of a "nullity" (*Nichtigkeit*) is of course already intimated in the analysis of conscience (*Gewissen*) in *Being and Time*.

would also no longer be a letting be *purely present*. The originary future is originary in the sense of poietic: it lets world emerge.

Such a closure of the futural ecstasis of attending is already implicit in some of the remarks in §69a of *Being and Time*. Not so much in the temporality of missing something, which—as in the *Basic Problems of Phenomenology* (GA 24, 441)—is attributed to a deficient mode of the present that Heidegger terms *ungegenwärtigen:* letting something be present in its nonpresence (absence); but more tellingly in the temporality of our being surprised by something:

> the possibility of *being surprised* by something is grounded in the fact that our *attentive* making-present of something ready-to-hand is *unattentive* to something else that stands in a possible context of involvement with the former. The nonattending [*Ungewärtigen*] of our lost making-present first discloses the "horizonal" leeway [*Spielraum*] within which something surprising can befall Dasein. (SZ, 355)

The implication again is that a futural closure of the presence belonging to Dasein's being as being-in-the-world is at work in every presence. Earlier in *Being and Time*, the same phenomenon of closure was intimated in the analyses of fear which, in its threatening character, is described as "closing" Dasein's being precisely *in* letting it be seen in a particular respect (SZ, 141). Such closure is a precondition of experiencing something terrifying (of *Erschrecken*), in which something threatening that is "not yet [present], but [possible] at any moment [*Augenblick*]" irrupts suddenly into the concernful presence of our being-in-the-world (SZ, 142). The *Augenblick* is precisely a being held open for the possible presencing of another worldly being, which we may or may not expect, and which can irrupt suddenly.[18] It is precisely the finitude of this openness for one's ownmost being, this finitude of the *Augenblick,* that is "anticipated" in an authentic being-toward-death, toward the indeterminate possibility of impossibility that is itself "possible at any moment," at any *Augenblick* (SZ, 258). For in this anticipation of its own finitude Dasein "holds itself" within an openness for "a constant *threat* springing from its 'there'," for a threat that "arises from its ownmost individuated being" (SZ, 265).[19]

---

[18] Note that the character of "suddenness" (*Plötzlichkeit*)—in Greek, *exaiphnēs*—the sudden irruption (*Hereinschlagen*) of something into presence, or the sudden onset of an action, can therefore be associated with the *Augenblick,* yet need not be. We shall take up these themes in more detail in chapter 4. On the significance of *Erschrecken* as an attunement of thinking at the end of philosophy, see GA 45.

[19] Contrary to what is sometimes claimed, the *Augenblick* referred to on SZ, 142 is therefore one and the same phenomenon as the *Augenblick* of originary, ecstatic

In the present context, Heidegger does not shy from indicating, albeit tentatively, the consequences of this insight into the closure of the futural ecstasis for the horizonal analysis. He points out, firstly, that missing something is not merely the discovering of something un-ready-to-hand, but also an "explicit making-present of precisely that which is already, and at least as yet ready-to-hand." The modification from presence to absence in this instance "lets precisely that which is ready-to-hand be conspicuous" (GA 24, 442). If we recall that the analysis in §16 of *Being and Time* associated the conspicuousness of the ready-to-hand with presence-at-hand announcing itself, we can understand these remarks as implying that the condition of the possibility of any presence-at-hand whatsoever is this temporal modification of horizons. And insofar as there is always a certain presence-at-hand bound up with readiness-to-hand, the closure or moment of "negation" at work in such modification would belong to readiness-to-hand itself:

> A fundamental yet difficult problem is announced here, namely, to what extent precisely a negative moment comes to be constituted within the structure of such being, that is, initially within readiness-to-hand, if formally we may call what pertains to ab-sence [*das Ab-sentiale*] a negation of whatever pertains to presence [*des Praesentialen*]. Posing the question in a fundamental way: To what extent does there lie in Temporality in general, and also in temporality, something negative, a 'not' [*ein Negatives, ein Nicht*]? Or even: to what extent is time itself the condition of the possibility of nullity [*Nichtigkeit*] in general? Because the modification of presence to absence ...belonging to temporality (both to the ecstasis of the present and to the other ecstases) has a character of negativity, of a 'not,' not-present, the question arises of where the root of this 'not' lies in general. A closer consideration shows that even the 'not' and the essence of the 'not,' nullity, can likewise be interpreted only from out of the essence of time, and that from here the possibility of modification, for example, from presence to absence, can first be clarified. (GA 24, 442–43; cf. SZ, 285–86)

It appears that nullity and closure pervade not only the ecstasis of making-present, but all the ecstases, together with the very horizon of presence they open up. It is not just the modification from presence to

temporality, and thus has the same structure as the authentic anticipation of the *Augenblick;* the same is also true of the "appropriate *Augenblick*" (i.e., for the onset of an action) referred to in §36 (SZ, 172). See Günter Seubold, "Bemerkungen zu 'Destruktion und Augenblick'" (a response to Otto Pöggeler), in *Destruktion und Übersetzung,* ed. T. Buchheim (Weinheim: VCH, Acta Humaniora, 1989), 31–38.

absence that entails closure; rather, the implication is that there is no fully
constituted presence (such as that of readiness-to-hand) there in the first
place—an insight that threatens to disrupt the entire Temporal analysis of
being, which appears to be premised on the possibility of understanding
temporality in terms of the modification of *already* temporalized ecstases
and their horizons. Heidegger effectively concludes—or rather interrupts—
the analysis of horizonal modification with the words, "We are not adequately prepared to penetrate into this obscurity" (GA 24, 443).[20]

What is at issue here is ultimately the possibility of the new. What is
required in order that a new understanding and a new kind of comportment
may appear, such as theoretical comportment? How is it possible for an
understanding and form of comportment to occur that has never before
occurred historically as such? From where can the guiding projection of
scientific-theoretical activity be drawn? It cannot be drawn from the already
disclosed possibilities of an already existing world. It cannot happen from
out of the world as already transcendent or ecstatically disclosed. For it is a
possibility that precisely has never been there before. Heidegger's analyses
are able to show that if concernful involvement, comporting oneself toward
beings, were primary with respect to disclosure, it would be impossible
for anything like theoretical understanding to arise. Both circumspective
involvement and theoretical understanding are possible only as "modes" of
being-in-the-world, that is, of transcendence. Theoretical comportment is
possible only if being has already been projected and understood in a new
way. And for different kinds of understanding to be possible, world must
not only be something already disclosed, it must also be *disclosive,* poietic,
allowing for the possibility of the new.

---

[20] For an initial exploration of the issue and consequences of modification, see our
doctoral thesis, "Heidegger and the Modification of *Being and Time*" (University of
Essex, 1986).

Chapter 4

Originary Praxis: The Trace of Phronesis in *Being and Time*

We have now examined something of what is at stake in Heidegger's "destruction" of an ontic or "natural" genesis of *theōrein*, a genesis that provides the guiding thread of Aristotle's inquiry into the supreme form of human knowledge in the *Metaphysics,* but is complicated by the account of *praxis* in the *Nicomachean Ethics.* Heidegger's investigation tracing the *ontological* genesis of *theōrein* as part of the analytic of Dasein seeks to understand, in terms of temporality and its horizonal structure, the genesis of *theōrein* in its Aristotelian, epistemic form that despite manifold historical transformations was destined to remain paradigmatic for scientific and philosophical knowledge from Aristotle to the present. In so doing, the ontological inquiry effectively undermines, through its attention to temporal finitude and the interplay of absence and presence, the very possibility of theoretical contemplation contemplating itself either in the full and immediate presence of an absolute intuition, or as a thematic object present before a subject. It thus undermines the traditional, foundational primacy of pure *nous* or intuition (*Anschauung*), from the *noēsis noēseōs* of *sophia* as conceived by Aristotle (albeit with the reservations indicated in chapter 2) to the intellectual intuition of German idealism, the Husserlian intuiting of essences (*Wesensschau*), and by extension, the ground of self-presence that the derivative forms of *epistēmē* presuppose.

The scientific projection of the world can thus be seen as theoretically groundless—unable to ground itself anywhere other than in the finitude of human *praxis,* whose ultimate grounds are inaccessible to theoretical contemplation. A closure of vision, irreducible to the enclosure of ecstatic making-present within future and having-been that Heidegger had hoped to thematize conceptually and objectify in terms of its horizon, announces itself already in Dasein's circumspection, in its involvement and captivation with the world of its concern. Heidegger's attempt to trace a more radical, ontological genesis of theoretical comportment is itself curtailed, and appears to founder on the very desire to found, to explain, and thematically to account for the temporal and historical emergence of contemplation and its outgrowth, modern science. As Heidegger himself would later concede in the "Letter on 'Humanism'" when addressing the originary meaning of *ēthos, Being and Time* "does not yet succeed in retaining what is indeed the essential help of phenomenological seeing, but dropping the inappropriate intention to do 'science' and 'research'." The thinking of being as the being of Dasein has trouble "bringing to language" its proper "dimension," its "primordial element," which is that of "originary ethics" (W, 187). An implicit tension within *Being and Time* is thus evident between phenomenological seeing conceived as an objectifying, thematizing science of being, and a more originary, more finite moment of vision intrinsic to circumspective involvement in the broadest sense.[1] It is not as though phenomenological seeing is simply to be renounced; rather, its essential help must be retained while freeing phenomenology from its scientific and objectifying aspirations. Presumably, bringing to language this more originary, finite "moment of vision" would itself be a freeing of phenomenology in this sense. But how does one bring a phenomenon to language or make it explicit as such—let it be seen as what it is—without thematizing or objectifying it? Another kind of saying is called for (i.e., can already be heard): language must attend more originarily to the manner of its own saying, to its own element, its own being. This transformation of language must attend more appropriately to its own, historically "destined" coming to presence in the finite element of human *praxis,* in the speaking of "mortals."

We shall not pursue this later path of Heidegger here. For the moment, our task is to follow a second thread of the analytic: that of the selfhood of Dasein and of the existentiell, which is the proper dimension of *praxis* conceived in a more originary manner. Insofar as the attempt to account thematically for the horizonal modification of presence seems necessarily to have recourse to *already* temporalized ecstases and horizons, it is difficult to see how the supposedly more radical, ontological account of the genesis of theoretical comportment could ultimately avoid collapsing back into the kind of "natural" or ontic account which Heidegger seeks to problematize. The undoubted radicality of the existential undertaking consists,

---

[1] With regard to what follows regarding *phronēsis,* we might recall Gadamer's remark that it was in and through his discovery of *phronēsis* in Book VI of the *Nicomachean Ethics* that Heidegger "took his first, decisive distance from 'philosophy as a strict science'"—the latter phrase alluding, of course, to Husserl (GW 3, 286–87).

rather, in its tracing all foundational accounts back to their rootedness in temporality. Yet ecstatic temporality itself, as the transcendence of Dasein's being-in-the-world, cannot be maintained in any ontological purity of being as presence. It is founded in the *existentiell*, in the finite, factical, and historical existence of Dasein in each case. The entire existential analytic, Heidegger emphasizes, is rooted in the existentiell; it arises from that dimension and recoils upon it (SZ, 13, 38, 436).

We have already attempted a provisional analysis of how the Aristotelian conception of *praxis* seems to be displaced in the existential analytic of *Being and Time*. We noted in chapter 3 that *poiēsis* and the knowledge pertaining to it (*technē*), as well as *praxis* in the narrow Aristotelian sense, both appear to be understood by Heidegger in terms of a broader and perhaps more originary sense of *praxis*, translated as "concernful dealing" (*besorgender Umgang*). However, we remarked further that although theoretical cognition is also to be understood as a kind of concernful dealing, thus as a *praxis* in the broad sense, Heidegger's account still allowed for a distinction between theory and the remaining forms of *praxis* in terms of different kinds of *seeing:* concernful dealing that entails an involvement or absorption in doing or making is a circumspective kind of *praxis*, whereas the *praxis* of theoretical comportment is (or claims to be) a more independent kind of vision: the gaze of "pure contemplation" or "observation." These different kinds of *praxis*, we argued, can therefore be understood as *dispersions of vision.* Yet thematizing such vision in terms of an apriori or transcendental ground, as a seeing prior to dispersion, would necessitate vision contemplating itself, thus apparently reinscribing the blindness of the already dispersed theoretical moment. Such blindness consists in theoretical contemplation overlooking its own finitude as rooted in *praxis*. This is not yet to say that such blindness is the "fault" or "effect" of the theoretical desire. In fact, it should become apparent that it is nothing other than an irretrievable closure that is essential to and constitutive of theoretical activity as such. The "blindness" of the theoretical desire—its reductionism, but also its power—consists in the way in which it seeks to maintain, to reinscribe or retrieve that moment of dispersion, of the closure and finitude intrinsic to all *praxis*. In part 2, we shall examine one form of this attempted recuperation of closure with respect to modern scientific and technological comportment.

The comparative considerations of the previous chapter thus invite us to read the traces of *theōria, praxis,* and *technē* in *Being and Time* along the following lines. The circumspective overview characteristic of *technē*, oriented as it is toward the primary projection of the independent being of entities other than Dasein (other Dasein-like entities, or other human beings, could of course also be understood in terms of this projection, but this—which would be an inauthentic understanding of others—is not Heidegger's immediate concern in the analytic), is also a closure of vision, a kind of non-seeing or disregarding (*Nichtsehen, Absehen:* SZ, 55) of the being of Dasein itself, or more accurately, of the way in which the being of Dasein is also implicated (in its "destiny") in the being of intraworldly entities. The originary dimension of *praxis* becomes concealed and closed off. And this is a concealment of Dasein's own being, which is also why Dasein, subjected to this primary projection of being, tends to understand itself (albeit implicitly) in terms of the presence of things, or inauthentically. When it comes to interpret itself explicitly, it tends to regard itself as yet another object of the theoretical contemplation that is indeed now extracted from its former embeddedness in *technē*, yet (as a modification of circumspection) still sees objects in terms of their independent presence-at-hand. Dasein's authentic understanding of itself as originary *praxis*, by contrast, would consist in its retrieval of its ownmost being, in its seeing, in the "glance of the eye" or *Augenblick*, the singular and momentary character of its own presence as Dasein.

Yet is there an original presence proper to Dasein, simply there to be retrieved? What can be meant by a retrieval of one's ownmost being, if such being does not consist in a permanent or constant presence that would be Dasein's own by virtue of its return, as identical, throughout or across different "moments" of time—since this would entail precisely a leveling of the *Augenblick*, of the temporality of *praxis*, into a series of present-at-hand "moments" seen from the theoretical perspective once more? What kind of presence is *proper* to Dasein as such, as Dasein, whether a particular Dasein sees its own presence in a phenomenologically appropriate manner or otherwise? What grants Dasein the measure of its own presence in the moment? What horizon delimits it, thus opening Dasein to itself in view of its ownmost end? In terms of what does Dasein ultimately "see" and thereby understand itself as it acts? What, ultimately, is the "selfhood" of Dasein? Have we not seen in chapter 3 that, at the purely ontological level, there is no presence proper to Dasein itself—that Dasein in its "practical" involvements understands "itself," rather, from out of a horizon of world, a horizon that at once discloses and closes our worldly involvements in an aletheic occurrence of presence and absence?

These questions must be asked with vigilance, for there is a temptation to read the ontological inquiry into Dasein's authentic being-a-self in *Being and Time* as reinscribing a theoretical ideal, either in the form of a quasi-constant transcendental or metaphysical selfhood (perhaps a kind of temporalized version of Kant's transcendental unity of apperception), or in terms of a continual yet unfulfilable desire for self-presence. Such readings might appear to find support, moreover, in the fact that Heidegger himself describes Dasein in terms of an existential "solipsism" and individuation (SZ, 188), and later (in 1928) more explicitly in terms of metaphysical "neutrality" and "isolation" (GA 26, §10). Although the context makes it clear that this "solipsism" and individuation are to be thought in terms of the disclosure of *world* as such (and not as that of an isolated or empty subject withdrawn from the world), when coupled with worries about the role and place of the political and of plurality in *Being and Time* such references might seem to lend weight to the arguments of those who see a heroic solipsism and "Platonic bias" in the emphasis on selfhood and individuation in *Being and Time,*[2] or else regard the *Augenblick* as an "empty" "nothing," devoid of any worldly content.[3] On the other hand, the fact that the *Augenblick* refers to Dasein's authentic or proper *presence* promotes the suspicion that the theoretical ideal of the desire for pure self-presence is indeed still active in the analytic of Dasein. And when one recalls that the "modification" of Dasein's understanding into the mode of disclosure of its authentic and proper being is supposedly a "retrieval" and "repetition" of Dasein's being that wrests it back from *dispersion,* and that such retrieval is to occur precisely through the ("scientific") methodology of phenomenological seeing, then the evidence seems overwhelming.[4]

---

[2] See Jacques Taminiaux, "La réappropriation de l'*Ethique à Nicomaque:* ποίησις et πρᾶξις dans l'articulation de l'ontologie fondamentale," in *Lectures de l'ontologie fondamentale;* and Dana R. Villa, *Arendt and Heidegger: The Fate of the Political.* Taminiaux reads Heidegger's reappropriation of the *Nicomachean Ethics* as evidencing a "Platonic bias" in favor of an existential solipsism of the theoretical life to the exclusion of a pluralistic Aristotelian *praxis,* with all the attendant political implications that such a bias would entail. Moreover, this "Platonic bias," on Taminiaux's reading, is maintained throughout Heidegger's later thought. Both Taminiaux and Villa appeal to Heidegger's displacement and repetition of the *praxis/poiēsis* distinction in support of their arguments concerning the suppression of political plurality.

[3] See Otto Pöggeler, *Der Denkweg Martin Heideggers,* 209–11. As Friedrich-Wilhelm von Herrmann argues, this reading of the *Augenblick* results from an unwarranted conflation of being-alongside . . . and falling, that is, from an overlooking of the worldly character of the *Augenblick.* See F.-W. von Herrmann, *Subjekt und Dasein,* 2nd ed. (Frankfurt: Vittorio Klostermann, 1985), 198–224. The same tendency to simply oppose worldly absorption and involvement, including being with others, to authentic being-in-the-world is also found in Taminiaux's reading.

[4] David Krell expresses the suspicion succinctly in noting that Heidegger's analysis must summon "the 'unbroken discipline' of a 'gaze' that will 'understand existentially' the whole of Dasein's appropriate being without dispersion or distraction (SZ, 323). . . . That unblinking *Blick* will of course have everything to do with the moment, *der Augenblick,* in which there-being twists free from oblivion and remembers who it is. Yet how will such a gaze differ from the insistent gape of theory? How will such a moment or blink of an eye differ from the traditional phenomenological presentification that in Heidegger's own view is egregiously inappropriate?" See *Of Memory, Reminiscence and Writing* (Bloomington: Indiana University Press, 1990), 243.

Yet is the "retrieval" from dispersion a recollective modification or "recovery" that would *overcome* the oblivion or concealment of being that permeates everydayness?[5] Does Heidegger's phenomenological seeing in *Being and Time* reinscribe, or does it not rather *undermine,* by the radicality of its very enactment, the traditional aspirations of phenomenological method? Everything here depends on how we interpret what Heidegger calls Dasein's anticipatory and resolute openness (*vorlaufende Entschlossenheit*) and the repetition or retrieval (*Wiederholung*) that it enacts. If the anxious, anticipatory resolve that temporalizes the *Augenblick* brings us—as David Krell's careful analyses pointedly remind us—face to face only with the *possibility* of retrieval or repetition, what precisely is the character of such possibility? Is it to be contrasted or opposed to actuality, as Krell implies when he writes that "In anxiety, the glance of an eye or moment of vision in which Dasein confronts its mortality is possible, yet not actual"?[6] Or does such possibility have to be understood as intrinsic to the actualization of actuality (and thus to the *en-ergeia* of a *poiēsis* that is "at work" in all *praxis,* even the purest, that of seeing)[7] in a sense that does not merely oppose it to the "category" of actuality? What kind of seeing is called for in the *Augenblick* or "glance of the eye"?

In the preceding chapter we have seen Heidegger's interpretation of the genesis of the theoretical stance confront a moment of dispersion in the closure of temporal horizons. In the present chapter, we shift our focus back to the question of *phronēsis* in *Being and Time.*[8] We shall begin by reconsidering the practical moment in the light of Heidegger's 1924 reading of Aristotle, in order then to suggest that *Being and Time,* in translating and transforming Aristotle's conception of *sophia,* makes explicit something that the 1924 interpretation left unsaid.

---

[5] Cf. Krell (ibid.), 252–53.

[6] Ibid., 252.

[7] Cf. our remarks on *theōrein* in chapter 2 above.

[8] For discussions of this theme in existing scholarship see Taminiaux, "Poiesis and Praxis in Fundamental Ontology," *Research in Phenomenology* vol. 17 (1987): 137–69; and "La réappropriation de l'*Ethique à Nicomaque:* ποίησις et πρᾶξις dans l'articulation de l'ontologie fondamentale" in *Lectures de l'ontologie fondamentale.* See also Walter Brogan, "Heidegger and Aristotle: Dasein and the Question of Practical Life," in *Crises in Continental Philosophy,* ed. Arleen B. Dallery & Charles E. Scott (Albany: State University of New York Press, 1990), 137–46; Franco Volpi, "*Dasein* comme *praxis:* L'assimilation et la radicalisation heideggerienne de la philosophie pratique d'Aristote," in *Heidegger et l'idée de la phénoménologie,* F. Volpi et al. (Dordrecht: Kluwer Academic Publishers, 1988), 1–41; Robert Bernasconi, "The Fate of the Distinction between *Praxis* and *Poiesis,*" in *Heidegger in Question;* also his essay "Heidegger's Destruction of Phronesis," and the response by Walter Brogan, *The Southern Journal of Philosophy* 28, Supplement (1989): 149–53.

Originary Praxis and Authenticity

We have seen in chapter 2 that for Aristotle the highest activity possible for human life is that of an exceptional *theōrein:* that *theōrein* whereby mortal life contemplates its final end as the divine actuality of *nous*. This vision of divine *nous* is even interpreted by Aristotle as "the self that each [truly] is," insofar as it surpasses and dominates what can be achieved concretely by human *praxis*. As Aristotle himself expresses it, "it would be a strange thing if a man should choose to live not his own life, but the life of some other than himself" (NE, 1178 a2).

The idea of living the life of another bears more than a passing resemblance to Heidegger's interpretation in *Being and Time* of how everyday Dasein, at first and for the most part, is not its proper or authentic self, but has been relieved of its being by others. Everyday Dasein stands in subjection to others: "It itself *is* not; its being has been taken away by others" (SZ, 126). Everyday Dasein has already abdicated its own being to that of others. The similarity to Aristotle's formulation is even more striking in Heidegger's 1925 course *Prolegomena to the History of the Concept of Time:*

> Dasein as being-with *is lived* by the *Mitdasein* of others and by the world with which it is concerned in whatever way. Precisely in its ownmost everyday activity Dasein as being with others is not itself; rather *it is others who live one's own Dasein.* (GA 20, 337, emphasis added)[9]

Aristotle's comment on the difference between living one's true self and living the life of another follows his discussion in Book X of the *Nicomachean Ethics* of why the contemplative life (the life of *theōrein*) comes closest to fulfilling the actuality of *eudaimonia* as the ultimate end of human life. This discussion supplements the analysis in Book VI that argued for the need for *sophia* to inform *phronēsis,* that is, for the primary insight of theoretical contemplation to infuse the remaining forms of *praxis*. The implication of Aristotle's comment is that to immerse oneself in everyday ethical and political *praxis* to the exclusion of the life of contemplation would be to live one's finitude and mortality without seeing it as such, without having glimpsed the possibility of "divine" worldly presence that constitutes one's ultimate and ownmost possibility of being. To see and to have seen (from the perspective of the highest actuality, of *energeia*) the constant, that is, recurrent presencing of the frailty of *praxis*, of human finitude and mortality, would be to know in the highest sense, to know in the manner

---

[9] Cf. SZ, 299.

of a living *sophia* not yet severed from (or posited above and beyond) the contingencies of *praxis*. It would be to "see oneself" in the *Augenblick* of *phronēsis*, of a practical knowing always already attuned to philosophical insight. *Phronēsis* can be *phronēsis*, a virtue and an excellence, only if it is also already *sophia,* only if the latter always already infuses and informs it. Not to know in the manner of this supreme knowing would be to lose oneself in the particular absorption "of the moment," to lose the measure of one's own existence. To put it in terms of Heidegger's analytic of Dasein, to thus immerse oneself in the forgetful dispersions of *praxis,* to the oblivion of oneself, would be to exist inauthentically, to overlook one's ownmost being.

Although Heidegger does not cite this comment of Aristotle's in the 1924/25 *Sophist* course, an initial reading of that interpretation in the light of the subsequent work of *Being and Time* and the Marburg lectures of 1924–28 might readily conclude that Heidegger's analyses of the authenticity and inauthenticity of Dasein are merely a reworking, or retranslation, of the interpretation of human existence that emerged from this earlier reading of Aristotle. From this perspective, as we have just noted, *Being and Time* might well be read as an attempt to retrieve the Aristotelian privileging of the contemplative life, albeit while radicalizing the theoretical moment in the direction of a rigorous, phenomenological vision directed not toward the "eternal" being of the *kosmos,* but toward *praxis.*[10] Indeed, we have already traced how the phenomenological eye that accompanies the analytic of Dasein appears to reinscribe a very traditional, theoretical ideal via the desire for thematization. Furthermore, it seems that such a reading can only be reinforced when Heidegger in the 1924/25 course identifies *.eudaimonia* as "the authenticity of the being of human existence" (GA 19, 172),

---

[10] An argument advanced by Jacques Taminiaux, who claims in *Lectures de l'ontologie fondamentale* that "Heidegger subscribes unreservedly to the ontological privilege of the *bios theōrētikos,* as a philosophical existence devoted to a vision of being...." In undermining the Aristotelian privileging of presence, however, in favor of the finite time of *praxis,* the only task that remains for the "thinking of being" is "to think the finite time of *praxis*" (189). Yet Taminiaux's argument precisely maintains and reinscribes the opposition of thinking and acting, of *theōria* and *praxis* even in their phenomenological transformation, and thus regards the "thinking of being" as a *mere thinking* opposed to practical involvement, withdrawn from the world, and removed from the realm of political plurality. Thus, Taminiaux reads even the later Heidegger's claim that thinking is the accomplishment (*Vollbringen*) of action as another symptom of a "Platonic" leaning, "oriented toward a mode of the *bios theōrētikos,*" and still opposed to human plurality (180). The same claim is maintained in *La fille de Thrace et le penseur professionnel* (Paris: Éditions Payot, 1992), where it is argued that *theōria* in *Being and Time* is simply "redoubled," directing its view back upon *praxis,* but maintaining all of its problematic privilege (18ff., 62ff.). In the present chapter, by contrast, we shall try to show how and why these very oppositions are already undermined in Heidegger's early thought, and why the thinking of being cannot be adequately or fully understood in terms of the Platonic-Aristotelian privileging of *theōria.*

and *theōrein* as that which "brings existence [*Dasein*] into the authenticity of its being" (GA 19, 174). Moreover, it is not only such references to authenticity (*Eigentlichkeit*) that are present in that course, but much of the terminology that would become notorious with the publication of *Being and Time* is already present in the *Sophist* course, and it is used precisely to translate the analyses from Aristotle's *Nicomachean Ethics*.[11]

Nevertheless, we should not be too quick to draw such a straightforward parallel between Heidegger's interpretation of Aristotle and the analytic of Dasein presented in *Being and Time*. Evidently, there is a parallel, yet one that must be complicated in the light of the 1927 treatise. Just as Aristotle's privileging of the theoretical life need not be seen as advocating a withdrawal from the political and ethical realm, nor as compromising his insistence that human life is properly *praxis,* exposed to instability and to the political plurality of words and deeds, so too there is no intrinsic reason to read Heidegger's analysis of the authenticity or proper being of Dasein along such lines. It would be short-sighted to argue that just because Heidegger in *Being and Time* does not provide any detailed, concrete account of the political or of its inherent plurality, authentic Dasein must be essentially apolitical and solipsistic.[12] It is simply not within the immediate (and highly restricted) scope of *Being and Time* to provide any detailed analysis of everyday being with others in political life. If Dasein's proper or authentic being-a-self is only a "modification" of the "one" (*das "Man"*), this should not be read as meaning that it is withdrawn from or simply opposed to this realm of plurality, of everyday interpretation and opinion. It does, however, mean that the dominant, everyday self-interpretations of Dasein are to be put in question. It is as a practice of *critique* that the project of *Being and Time* maintains a profound continuity with the historical role of philosophy, repeating philosophy's original vocation. Yet this "repetition" not only critically questions prevailing opinion (*doxa*); it also critically interrogates the traditional philosophical conception of what such *doxa* itself is; it critically interrogates, for example, the prevalent philosophical interpretation that simply opposes the self, conceived as an "I" or "subject," to the realm of "others." "*Authentic being-a-self,*" Heidegger emphasizes, "does not rest on an exceptional state of the subject, cut off from the 'one', but *is an existentiell modification of the 'one' as an essential existential*" (SZ, 130).

---

[11] One can certainly trace the genesis of Heidegger's terminology in earlier works as well, albeit in a more condensed form, most importantly for our purposes in the 1922 treatise "Phenomenological Interpretations with Respect to Aristotle." We shall draw on this early treatise later in the present chapter.

[12] This is argued, again, by Taminiaux in *Lectures de l'ontologie fondamentale*. See also Dana Villa, *Arendt and Heidegger*, 130, 140.

It may be helpful, at least initially, to understand authenticity and inauthenticity as reworking the Aristotelian concepts of, respectively, an understanding attuned to *praxis* as opposed to one attuned to the realm of
poiēsis and of those involved therein—a schema of comparison that has
been proposed by Jacques Taminiaux.[13] According to this schema, authenticity would correspond to what, in the *Metaphysical Foundations of Logic,*
Heidegger calls an *augenblickliches Sichselbstverstehen,* an understanding
of oneself in the moment or *Augenblick* (GA 26, 9). This understanding,
which would seem to correspond to Aristotle's conception of *phronēsis,* is,
moreover, explicitly aligned with the practice of philosophizing as "historical recollection" (*geschichtliche Erinnerung*). But to what extent does this
schema of comparison hold?

Both authenticity and inauthenticity are possibilities of Dasein's understanding. Specifically, they refer to ways in which Dasein understands and
"sees" *itself,* its own being, as it comports itself factically in the world.
Dasein's understanding of itself in such comportment, that is, in its relations toward other beings (whether equipment, other Daseins, or nature),
is termed an *existentiell* understanding. By this Heidegger means that such
understanding relates primarily to Dasein's *own being* (termed "existence"),
rather than to the being of other beings in the world. Heidegger also refers to
it as an "ontic" understanding. In *The Basic Problems of Phenomenology,*
he remarks that Dasein's self-understanding "relates to Dasein itself, that
is, to a being, and is therefore an ontic understanding. Insofar as it is
related to existence, we call it existentiell understanding" (GA 24, 395).
Such understanding not only relates to Dasein, to this specific entity in
its being; it is also factically grounded in each case, accomplished by a
particular existing Dasein. Furthermore, such self-understanding is implicit
and latent in Dasein's concrete existence; it does not, Heidegger emphasizes, entail any explicit self-reflection, "inner perception" in the Kantian
or Husserlian sense, or theoretical contemplation.[14] Dasein understands itself, in its own being, in and through its concrete activities, without taking
any distance from its involvements and absorption in the sense of standing
back and "thinking about" itself. It is in this sense of a self-understanding
implicit in all concrete existing that we must understand Heidegger's comments in §4 of *Being and Time,* where the distinction between existentiell
and existential is first introduced: "The question of existence never gets
straightened out except through existing itself. The kind of understanding of oneself that guides us *in this way* we call *existentiell.* The question
of existence is an ontic 'affair' of Dasein. For this, we do not require any

---

[13] *Lectures de l'ontologie fondamentale,* 155ff.
[14] See GA 24, 225–27.

theoretical transparency as regards the ontological structure of existence" (SZ, 12). One does not have to be a philosopher or theoretician to "see" and understand one's own being in some way.

Yet in what way does one see one's own being for the most part? For this understanding of one's own being is always already interpreted, it articulates itself in and through interpretations—themselves for the most part concealed, yet no less dominant on that account—that may be indicative of what, seen philosophically, is an "inauthentic" yet nevertheless genuine understanding, that is, interpretations (which may be everyday and/or philosophical) that tend to *conceal*, from oneself and from others, what one's own being ultimately is (in its potential for being). Such concealment arises through having interpreted one's own being in terms of the presence of other beings within the world. Or, our interpretations may indeed be indicative of a genuine self-understanding that is *disclosive* of one's ownmost potential for being as a being-in-the-world, yet without having appropriated explicitly in philosophical or ontological terms what is properly or "authentically" understood in such understanding.[15] The hermeneutic task of making explicit this more concealed and yet genuine self-understanding is that of the *existential* analytic of Dasein. Such interpretation, as an explicit appropriation (*Aneignung*)[16] of what is already latently understood in some manner in all existing, reveals the formal-ontological structure of a possible authentic self-understanding, of a possible authenticity. It thus also first makes

---

[15] In this context, it is important to note that "inauthentic" does not mean "nongenuine." On Heidegger's account, the determinations "authentic/inauthentic" and "genuine/nongenuine" intersect (SZ, 146, 148). But, as he indicates in *The Basic Problems of Phenomenology*, an "in-authentic self-understanding of Dasein does not at all mean a nongenuine self-understanding . . . as though not the self, but something else would be understood therein." Inauthentic self-understanding, he notes, still *experiences* authentic Dasein as such, and may do so in a genuine manner. By contrast, "all extravagant rooting about in the soul can be in the highest degree nongenuine or even pathologically eccentric" (GA 24, 228). What these remarks imply is that possible authenticity or inauthenticity, that is, the reference to authenticity in general, is to be understood at the philosophical-hermeneutic level of whether an implicit self-interpretation appropriately articulates and discloses the being proper to Dasein or not, whereas the genuine/nongenuine distinction concerns the existentiell manner in which one's own being is either engaged and invested in whatever is discursively disclosed, or (hypocritically or pathologically) avoids this self-engagement. The genuine/nongenuine distinction thus concerns the existentiell *Einsatz* or commitment of one's finite existence. Equally, one's existence could well be authentically understood in a formal-ontological manner, yet, as a lived existence, be nongenuine. Like the distinction between authentic and inauthentic (GA 24, 243), "genuine" and "nongenuine" are thus not mutually exclusive. Every nongenuine understanding is non-*genuine*, that is, it conceals a level of self-engagement, of self-commitment and involvement that is already "there" and implied. Such concealment may itself be deliberate or explicit, for example, in hypocrisy.

[16] Interpretation (*Auslegung*) has the task of appropriation (*Aneignung*), whether implicit or explicit: SZ, 148ff.

explicitly visible as such the possibility of in-authenticity.[17] An authentic
self-understanding of what oneself always already is in one's own being, and
indeed ultimately is, in one's ownmost possibility of being, is thus only a
"modification" of the understanding of "oneself" (*Man-selbst*) that is already understood in everydayness without any philosophical reflection.[18]
And yet the existential hermeneutic only reveals, in an explicit projection,
a *possible* authenticity or inauthenticity which, in order to be genuinely
and factically enacted, must be seized upon or taken up in the existentiell
engagement and commitment (*Einsatz*) of a particular, factically existing
Dasein that is "in each case mine," that is, in each case singular, unsubsti-
tutable. The possibility of authenticity or inauthenticity is itself grounded
in the fact that Dasein is in each case mine (*je meines*) (SZ, 42–43).[19]

In this sense, then, a parallel between Dasein's authentic or appropriate
existentiell self-understanding and *phronēsis* seems evident, for *phronēsis* is
concerned precisely with the non self-reflective understanding of the being
of the self as *praxis*. Dasein's understanding is a "seeing," and in *phronēsis*,
as Aristotle describes it, there lies a "seeing of oneself" (NE, 1141 b35). In
acting, we always already "see" and have seen ourselves in a certain way.
Yet in the light of our earlier comments on *Being and Time,* an immediate qualification is necessary. For, as we argued in chapter 3, the more
restricted Aristotelian conception of *praxis* that delimits it from *technē* and
from *theōria* is put into question via Heidegger's analyses of Dasein's concernful dealings in the world. Such dealings, on Heidegger's account, extend
beyond mere doing (*praxis*) to include theoretical contemplation (*theōria*),
as well as all making and producing (*technē, poiēsis*). Dasein's existentiell
understanding of its own existence (whether authentic or inauthentic) is
therefore essentially broader in scope than Aristotle's account of *phronēsis*

---

[17]Cf. SZ, 42–43, 268; GA 24, 242–43. The revealing of these fundamental possibilities,
however, does not and need not occur in the first instance through explicit, philosophical
interpretation. It occurs, Heidegger shows, more originarily through the fundamental
attunement of anxiety (*Angst*) whereby Dasein is brought before its being-in-the-world
as such. See SZ, §40.

[18]The translation of *das Man* and its cognates by "the they" is profoundly misleading
for just this reason: it perpetuates the misreading, so common among commentators in
the English-speaking world, that *oneself,* as a self, is somehow exempt from or set over
and against the "they," "them," "the others." This misunderstanding is clearly pointed
out by Heidegger. See SZ, 118, 126.

[19]These reflections also suggest that the "extreme construction" (GA 26, 176) or "factical ideal" (SZ, 310) of authentic existence is inextricably tied to the possibility of
philosophy, of philosophizing and of the philosophical life as a particular concretion of
existence. On the pivotal notion of existentiell *Einsatz*, see our remarks in "Care for the
Self: Originary Ethics in Heidegger and Foucault," and "The First Principle of Hermeneutics," in *Reading Heidegger from the Start,* ed. T. Kisiel and J. van Buren (Albany: State
University of New York Press, 1994), 393–408. See also Robert Bernasconi, *Heidegger in
Question,* chapter 2.

in the *Nicomachean Ethics* would appear to allow. Authentic and inauthentic understanding encompass *all* Dasein's activities and comportment toward beings.

If this is correct, then the extended scope that is implicitly accorded Dasein's self-understanding on Heidegger's account must reflect a doubt on Heidegger's part as to whether the rigid delimitations between *technē*, *phronēsis*, and the *theōria* of *sophia* can be maintained when one considers the properly ontological dimension of *praxis* (and likewise of productive and theoretical comportment). Of course, it is only after Aristotle that the distinctions and contrasts between *technē*, *phronēsis*, and *theōria* either become rigid delimitations lending themselves to oppositional and hierarchical difference, or, in the case of the *praxis/poiēsis* distinction, tend to disappear altogether. Nevertheless, compared to Aristotle's interpretation of *phronēsis*, we see in Heidegger's existential analytic the incursion of a transformed understanding of *world* into Dasein's self-understanding. Dasein in its activities understands *not only* its own being, but also the being of all other beings it encounters and relates toward (whether actually present or "merely" possible). As Heidegger expresses it in *The Basic Problems of Phenomenology:*

> In every existentiell understanding there lies an understanding of the being of existence in general. Yet insofar as Dasein is being-in-the-world, that is, insofar as, equiprimordial with its facticity, a *world is disclosed and other Daseins are co-disclosed, and intraworldly beings are encountered, the existence of other Daseins* and *the being of intraworldly beings is understood equiprimordially with our understanding of existence*. . . . In existentiell understanding, wherein factical being-in-the-world attains insight and transparency [*einsichtig und durchsichtig wird*], there already lies an understanding of being that has to do not only with Dasein itself, but with all beings that are in principle revealed together with our being-in-the-world. (GA 24, 395–96)

Being itself in general is latently understood in all existentiell understanding, which is why the analytic of Dasein's own being is able to prepare for an interpretation (or "laying bare," *Freilegung*) of the meaning of being in general. The horizon upon which Dasein understands being in general is *world*. Yet for Aristotle, world remains as it were the dark side of *phronēsis:* the horizon and truth of its situatedness, to be sure, but one that can be illuminated only by the light of another kind of knowledge, that of the theoretical contemplation of *nous* pertaining to *sophia*. *Sophia* is for Aristotle that realm of knowledge in which world can properly be understood. But is not the phenomenon of world thereby exposed to the danger of becoming leveled off into an already present, independent totality of beings, with a divine being posited as its existing, already present ground? The more *sophia* comes to be separated from *phronēsis,* the more the presencing of world *in phronēsis* comes to be obscured, and the more *praxis* opposes itself to the theoretical foundations that are required to inform it.

Heidegger's analytic, by contrast, will attempt to make explicit this transcendence of world—that is, of Dasein's being proper—via an ontological inquiry into Dasein's most originary understanding of its own being: its authentic understanding of itself as originary, mortal, death-bound *praxis,* glimpsed in the "eschatological" glance of the eye. As existentiell—oriented toward the existence of the self—this understanding will not be that of a theoretical contemplation. The authenticity of Dasein's being will belong not to a *sophia* already conceived on the *aisthēsis* versus *theōrein* distinction, as it did for Aristotle according to Heidegger's 1924 reading, but to the existentiell level akin to an originary *phronēsis* in which *nous* is interpreted eschatologically, beyond the view that merely opposes becoming to the permanence and constancy of being. In speaking of "originary" *praxis* or *phronēsis,* we mean to indicate not only that any pure separation of *praxis* and *phronēsis* from *theōria* and *poiēsis* is derivative and secondary (i.e., presupposes a perspective that is already theoretical in the narrow sense) but also that, just as originary *praxis* will later be seen to entail a more originary *theōrein,*[20] so too it entails a *poiēsis:* an originating, the advent of something new, unrepeatable, "eschatological."

Phronēsis, then, is to be transformed, interpreted less restrictively than in Aristotle. And yet—the very *possibility* of precisely this Aristotelian distinction of *phronēsis* must be reinvestigated and retrieved: the possibility of an understanding of one's own being or existence *as distinct from* the being of other, intraworldly things. For this is the possibility inscribed in the very idea or project of an analytic of the being *of Dasein,* in the idea of an existential analytic that will attempt to focus its investigation upon *Dasein's* being, and upon it alone, while bracketing, as it were (at least initially) the problem of conclusively determining the being of other, intraworldly beings.[21] That task does not entail the *exclusion* of the dimension of world. On the contrary—and this multi-dimensionality is, in part, what makes Heidegger's undertaking so difficult to grasp—Dasein is to be investigated precisely as being-in-the-world, in terms of its openness for world; its most originary being will be shown to be its transcendence, its continual exposure to the at once open and closed horizon termed "world."

---

[20] See part 4 of the present study.

[21] In this sense, Heidegger emphasizes that the analyses of readiness-to-hand and equipmentality, for example, are intended primarily to bring Dasein's transcendence into view. See his comments in a footnote to "On the Essence of Ground," W, 51 n. 55.

But equally, this incursion of world does not prevent the analytic from focusing on Dasein's understanding of *its own* being in distinction from that of other beings. Such a focus, again, does not entail any factical isolation of Dasein: on the contrary, it merely demands, as Heidegger puts it elsewhere, the "metaphysical isolation" of Dasein, the investigation of which must be all the more concrete on account of this, and indeed as a counter to the kind of ontological excess or "exaggeration" that Heidegger elsewhere attributes to Hegel (GA 26, 176).

Seeing Oneself

Aristotle, as noted, describes *phronēsis* as a "seeing oneself" (*to hautou eidenai*), catching sight of oneself in, or better, as *praxis*. But what kind of seeing is this exactly? What does one see as "oneself" in the vision intrinsic to *praxis?* To what extent is such seeing transparent with respect to itself? And how is this kind of seeing and transparency thought in *Being and Time?* To answer these questions, we must examine more closely the vision intrinsic to the *Augenblick.*

In the *Sophist* course Heidegger had drawn attention to the eschatological character of the practical *aisthēsis* or *nous* intrinsic to *phronēsis,* but had not really analyzed this eschatological character as such, and certainly not in its temporal implications, other than to point out its "momentary" character, its dependence on the uniqueness of the given context at a particular instant. By contrast, in following Aristotle's argument for privileging the theoretical life of *sophia,* Heidegger had emphasized that theoretical activity receives its privilege by its orientation toward pure presence:

> *Noein* as *energeia theōretikē* most fully satisfies the *energeia* of a living being, its pure being present [*Anwesendsein*] as such. To that extent, *noein* satisfies most authentically *eudaimonia.* It is in the latter that human life consists in the authenticity of its being [*in der Eigentlichkeit seines Seins*]. This authenticity is conceived in a radically ontological sense, in such a way that, as such, it is the ontological condition for the factical, concrete existence of the human being. (GA 19, 179)

For the Greeks, Heidegger had noted, the analysis of human existence is oriented purely toward the meaning of being itself, toward the possibility of human Dasein "always being," that is, achieving permanence. But the "authentic being" of Dasein according to this conception of human existence corresponds, he remarks, to *ēthos,* "stance" (*Haltung*) (GA 19, 178). Heidegger's reading, as we argued earlier, suggests that *phronēsis* can be an excellence only if it is already oriented toward the good, that is, only if it is already informed by insight into a possible constancy of human existence as a whole.

Heidegger's analysis, as we noted, here follows the tendency toward a *separation* of the theoretical vision from the ethico-political. On this interpretation, the disclosure of the moment in practical *nous,* as a disclosure of this particular presence that can at any moment be otherwise than it is, implies a prior, theoretical seeing and knowledge of presence itself as such, as that which remains or returns as the same throughout all change. But it is important to note the radically ontologizing schema on which the sustainability of this argument is based: it entails the separation of the *being* (presence) of an entity from the entity itself (i.e., what Heidegger would later call the "ontological difference"); in this instance, the separation between the concrete moment of this *praxis* here and now, and a more general, universal horizon from which the concrete, particular *praxis* may be viewed. In other words, in the very tendency to make the being of an entity dependent upon knowledge, upon a prior (theoretical) knowing and having seen, there also lies the tendency toward a homogenization and leveling out of radically finite temporal moments into a formal, universalized world-time.

Making *praxis* subservient to *theōria* in this way, which opens up a separation between them, naturally tends to obscure and conceal the intrinsically finite character of *praxis* in its originary sense, which is prior to this separation. And it is this originary sense of *praxis* that *Being and Time* seeks to retrieve in analysing Dasein in its possible authenticity as originary transcendence and as finite, ecstatic temporality. The *Augenblick* or authentic presence of Dasein is not to be understood as merely the practical correlate of a theoretical ideal, nor in terms of a "theory" of human existence; indeed, as Heidegger points out in *The Metaphysical Foundations of Logic,* the problem is that "transcendence was from early on regarded primarily in terms of *theōrein,* and that means: transcendence was not sought in its originary rootedness in the authentic being of Dasein. And yet the latter, as authentic action [*eigentliches Handeln*], as *praxis,* was of course not unknown to antiquity." The analysis of Dasein as transcendence must not conceive of transcendence as *praxis* in opposition to *theōria;* rather, "the problem is the common root of both intuition, *theōrein,* and action, *praxis*" (GA 26, 236). Transcendence, Heidegger indicates, *is* to be conceived as *praxis;* only the latter is not to be taken too narrowly.

These remarks are important for helping us to situate the analysis of the authenticity of Dasein in *Being and Time.* It is clear that the authentic being of Dasein is not to be understood primarily by theoretical contemplation, in the manner that authentic existence appears to be in the *Nicomachean Ethics,* at least on Heidegger's 1924 reading. But it is equally

clear from these remarks that the analysis of Dasein's authenticity in terms
of the *Augenblick* in *Being and Time* should not be taken as a mere reversal of Aristotle's argument, as though *Being and Time* merely wanted to
uphold the practical *nous* of *phronēsis* as opposed to the *theōria* of *sophia*.
Rather, the focus on the eschatological character of practical insight in the
1924 analysis presumably pointed the way for Heidegger to move toward a
more originary interpretation of *praxis*.

If the *Augenblick* as thematized in *Being and Time* indeed pertains to
Dasein as originary *praxis,* then the kind of "seeing" involved must—as we
indicated in chapter 3—exceed those dispersions of vision pertaining to circumspection (*Umsicht*), to its correlates considerateness (*Rücksicht*) and
forbearance (*Nachsicht*) and their opposites (these referring to the ways
in which we "see" or regard the Dasein of others within the world), and
to theoretical contemplation (*Hinsehen, Betrachten*), which are all kinds
of concern and solicitude (*Besorgen, Fürsorge*). This more originary seeing must be one not yet irrecoverably dispersed into the world (and the
"not yet" signifies here that it is futural), a seeing that "recovers" itself
in the very unfolding of dispersion. Moreover, as belonging to Dasein's authenticity, such seeing is existentiell and discloses Dasein's existence as a
whole, which has the ontological structure of care (*Sorge*). In the passage
cited earlier from *The Basic Problems of Phenomenology*, we have seen that
Heidegger identifies a certain insight and transparency of vision that belongs to factical, existentiell understanding. It is in existentiell understanding that Dasein, as being-in-the-world, "attains insight and transparency"
(GA 24, 396).[22] In *Being and Time,* Heidegger attempts to thematize such
transparency at the existential level, specifically in Division One, chapter 5,
when presenting the preparatory analysis of Dasein as disclosedness, as a
clearing or *Lichtung.* To say that Dasein has an understanding of its being
means that its being is disclosed to it via a futural projection. And such
understanding is Dasein's sight or vision:

> In its projective character, understanding goes to make up exis-
> tentially what we call Dasein's *sight* [Sicht]. With the disclosed-
> ness of the "there," this sight is existentially; and Dasein *is*
> this sight equiprimordially in each of those fundamental ways
> of its being which we have already noted: as the circumspection
> [*Umsicht*] of concern, as the considerate respect [*Rücksicht*] of

---

[22] Note that the term *Einsicht* was used, together with *Umsicht*, in Heidegger's 1924/25
interpretation of Aristotle precisely in order to translate a key moment of *phronēsis*
(GA 19, 21). See also the analysis of *Nicomachean Ethics* Book VI in the 1922 "Phenomenological Interpretations with Respect to Aristotle." The beginning of the 1922
treatise invokes transparency (*Durchsichtigkeit*) as the goal of the hermeneutics of the
factical situation of interpretation (PIA, 237).

> solicitude, and as that sight which is directed upon being as such, for the sake of which Dasein in each case is as it is. That sight which relates primarily and as a whole to existence, we name *transparency* [Durchsichtigkeit].... A being that exists sights "itself" [*sichtet "sich"*] only insofar as it has become transparent to itself with equal primordiality in its being alongside the world and being with others as the constitutive elements of its existence. (SZ, 146)

To understand the importance of this passage, we must distinguish between two kinds of transparency. On the one hand, we noted how, earlier in *Being and Time,* Heidegger appears to identify a certain transparency with the *theoretical* project of an existential analytic of Dasein: Dasein's existentiell understanding does not require any "theoretical transparency of the ontological structure of existence" (SZ, 12; cf. 86). In our preceding analyses we have attempted to trace that ideal of a theoretical transparency along the lines of the aspirations of a phenomenological science of being, with its attendant thematizing and objectifying desires. In the current passage, however, we are dealing with the thematization, on the formal-existential level, of an *existentiell* transparency concerned with Dasein's existence as a whole, and not that of an already dispersed, theoretical seeing.[23] We are considering what Heidegger calls a kind of "self-knowing" (*Selbsterkenntnis*) "in the well-understood sense," namely, in a sense that does not refer to the "inspection of a point called the self" (*Beschauen eines Selbstpunktes:* SZ, 146). This existentiell transparency pertains to Dasein's understanding of existence (i.e., its own being) as a whole, of being-in-the-world in and throughout all its constitutive elements.

This existentiell transparency, contrasted by Heidegger with a nontransparency or lack of transparency that may arise from lack of acquaintance with the world, can vary in degree and is presumably latent in all existence, even in Dasein's everydayness. As such it corresponds to the peculiar undifferentiatedness (*Indifferenz*) of everyday existence that was earlier thematized in §9. Yet this latent transparency, at once a transparency of Dasein's existence and an access to and openness for being in general, that is, world, tends to be partially covered up and even concealed as such when Dasein interprets its own being inauthentically, understanding itself inappropriately in terms of its absorption in particular dispersed activities (such as doing,

---

[23] Once again, Taminiaux reads this passage as evidence of "the privileged status of seeing" associated with the scientific aspirations of phenomenology; a privileging of phenomenological reduction over "deconstruction"; and, finally, of the Husserlian sense of the indivisible *Augenblick* of originary intuition (*Anschauung*) or "seeing" as self-presence. See *Heidegger and the Project of Fundamental Ontology,* trans. M. Gendre (Albany: State University of New York Press, 1991), 65–69.

making, or contemplating). *As such,* this transparency—as Dasein's transcendence or openness to world—is neither authentic nor inauthentic; but it may be understood and interpreted in an authentic or inauthentic manner. Authenticity, *Eigentlichkeit,* here refers to the attainment of an existentiell understanding, attuned to the *Augenblick,* that lets the existence of *Dasein* be seen in the very transparency that it is.

That such transparency is not simply to be *opposed* to nontransparency or concealment of one's own being is clear from the fact that Dasein, so long as it exists, is its disclosedness. Its own being is never entirely closed off or concealed from it. Yet the transparency of its own being, whatever its extent, is not simply given, but must continually be *brought about* in relation to its concrete being-in-the-world. It is in continual tension with concealment.[24] The phenomenological-hermeneutic analysis is concerned with making explicit precisely what is at issue in this play of un-concealment, of transparency and nontransparency, not with respect to any specific end or activity, but in the being of Dasein as a whole.

The existentiell transparency that discloses Dasein's being as a whole, as being-in-the-world, and transcends factical dispersion into the kinds of seeing that belong to doing, making, or contemplating and are concerned with beings, pertains to the originary being of factical Dasein as care. As in the *Sophist* course, Heidegger terms this originary transparency *Entschlossenheit,* resolute openness. This resolute openness which comprises Dasein's authentic being-a-self "first gives Dasein its authentic transparency" and brings the being of the *Da* into the determinacy of its factical situation (SZ, 298–300). The seeing characteristic of resolute openness is not a cognitive apprehending that places a situation before itself, but has already placed itself into the situation. Such seeing is already an acting. "As openly resolved, Dasein is already *acting*" (SZ, 300). Yet the term "action" is to be deliberately avoided, Heidegger remarks—not because it is not action that is at stake, but because such action must not be interpreted one-sidedly within the theory/praxis distinction, nor must it be taken as "activity" as opposed to "passivity." The action in question is *originary* action:

---

[24] Taminiaux, by contrast, reads it as equivalent to a theoretical self-transparency devoid of relations to others and leaving all concealment behind it: see *La fille de Thrace et le penseur professionnel: Arendt et Heidegger,* 92, 228. But this is to misunderstand the role of such transparency, as a task that must continually be accomplished anew with respect to Dasein's factical existence: only because Dasein is always in some respects concealed from itself is attaining a new transparency of its being an issue for it. Furthermore, as Heidegger here indicates, Dasein's being as a task is to "become transparent to itself" not in the metaphysical or ontological isolation of its being, but "with equal primordiality in its being alongside the world and being with others as the constitutive elements of its existence." Cf. our earlier analysis of *phronēsis* as having the task of making an action transparent (chapter 2).

> We are deliberately avoiding the term "action" [Handeln]. For
> on the one hand this term would once again have to be grasped
> in such a broad sense that activity would also encompass the
> passivity of resistance. On the other hand, it suggests a misun-
> derstanding with regard to the ontology of Dasein, as though
> resolute openness were a particular kind of comportment be-
> longing to our practical as opposed to our theoretical capacity.
> Care, however, as concernful solicitude, encompasses the being
> of Dasein as a whole in such an originary way that it must al-
> ways be presupposed as a whole prior to any separation between
> theoretical and practical comportment.... (SZ, 300)

Before we attend more closely to the trace of a seeing and a transparency pertaining to the more originary interpretation of *praxis* in *Being
and Time,* a few remarks may be in order regarding care as the originary
unity of "concernful solicitude." The remarks concern our earlier comment
that Dasein's understanding of *others*—of other Dasein-like beings within
the world—is not the immediate or direct concern of the preparatory analytic of Dasein in *Being and Time.*[25] The reason that this issue, which
readers find so absent from the analyses, is not Heidegger's *immediate* concern has to do with the extent to which our everyday circumspective understanding of other beings is dominated by technical and theoretical forms
of seeing. This also implies that "everydayness" itself incarnates the domination of a particular, historically rooted understanding. Commensurate
with its preparatory status, the analytic must first investigate the being of
Dasein in its metaphysical neutrality, beyond or exceeding its individuation
as an entity appearing in the world. The issue is complex because a certain
kind of *Vorhandenheit,* of independent being present-at-hand within the
world, *also* always belongs to Dasein—specifically to the Dasein of others,
and to one's own Dasein as being there for others, as *Mitdasein* (SZ, §26).
The issue is complex because this kind of presence-at-hand tends—"at first
and for the most part"—to remain embedded in or even subservient to
the readiness-to-hand governed by technical-teleological ends (just as when
the tool shows itself as broken). The being of the Other, or of oneself as
being for others, is not yet freed for the presence-at-hand appropriate to
it, for what Heidegger identifies as "a manner of 'presence-at-hand' *proper*
to Dasein" (SZ, 55). This kind of presence-at-hand proper to Dasein itself, its "facticity," is disclosed in attunement (*Befindlichkeit*), in which
Dasein is always already brought "before" itself, finds itself, and manifests
itself to others in its thrownness. The kind of primary or fundamental attunement whereby one is brought before oneself in the "thatness" of one's

---

[25] See 95–96 above.

being-in-the-world as a situated being there (Da-sein) is not an interiority, but a disclosedness "of world, *Mitdasein,* and existence." One also appears "before" others through such attunement. And yet, although the "fact" of Dasein's being "there" "stares it in the face with the inexorability of an enigma," the kind of "evidence" furnished by *Befindlichkeit* should not "be suppressed by measuring it against the apodictic certainty of a theoretical cognizing of something purely present-at-hand" (SZ, 136). The presence-at-hand proper to Dasein, rather, must first be freed from the tyranny of theoretical cognition in its scientific form.

Heidegger goes to extremes in §29 to resist this tyranny of theoretical cognition. The primary ontological uncovering of beings in the world is indeed accomplished by so-called "mere" moods; for "pure beholding or intuiting [*reines Anschauen*]" could never discover something threatening (possible "at any *Augenblick*": SZ, 142), for example. Yet presumably this does not exclude the possibility of our indeed "seeing" something threatening in a situation. Moods disclose our thrownness, not in a "looking at" it (*Hinblicken*—here apparently referring to a theoretical looking; but not all "looking at" is theoretical), but in a "turning toward or away"—in which we presumably also "see" or "catch sight of" something; the point is simply that this is not a "theoretical" apprehending. And it is only when measured by the idea and ideal of "an absolute cognition of the 'world' [*"Welt"-erkenntnis*]" that beings as they appear become reduced to a (Platonic) *mē on* (SZ, 138). We can indeed "see" beings themselves, as they show themselves in their properly worldly character, but not in the constancy or distantiation of the noninvolved, theoretical gaze:

> Precisely in our seeing the "world" in a nonconstant, flickering way in accordance with our moods the ready-to-hand shows itself in its specific worldly character, which is never the same from day to day. By looking at the world theoretically, we have already dimmed it down to the uniformity of what is purely present-at-hand, though admittedly this uniformity comprises a new abundance of things which can be discovered simply by determining them. (SZ, 138)

Heidegger here emphasizes the nonconstant temporality of our worldly seeing, contrasted with the constancy into which theoretical seeing seeks to place itself. Our involved, worldly seeing is more like catching sight of the flickering nature of things as they show themselves and withdraw, a catching sight of the turnings in the worldly presencing of things. Yet *theōria* too has its attunement, as Heidegger reminds us by reference to Aristotle:

> even the purest *theōria* has not left all attunement behind it;
> what remains as simply present-at-hand shows itself in its pure
> look [*Aussehen*] to our theoretical looking [*Hinsehen*] only if
> such *theōria* can let what is present-at-hand come toward it in
> its *tranquil* tarrying alongside ..., in *rhaistōnē* and *diagōgē* (cf.
> Aristotle, M, 982 b22ff.). (SZ, 138)

This tranquility, this *Ruhe* or restfulness, is thus essential and intrinsic
to theoretical contemplation; it is a particular kind of attunement in which
Dasein is brought before itself. But is it thereby authentically disclosed
to itself as such, in its most proper being? And if the worldly Dasein of
others is not properly or authentically disclosed by the "pure beholding"
of theoretical vision, what kind of seeing discloses others in their *proper
presence-at-hand*? Presumably, there are authentic modes of considerateness (*Rücksicht*) and forbearance (*Nachsicht*) (SZ, 123), grounded in an authentic transparency, care, and "solicitude," in which we can see the Dasein
of others, the being of others before us in their properly worldly presence-
at-hand. Although the question of such seeing is not explicitly analyzed
in *Being and Time*—in part because it becomes questionable whether the
being of Dasein has as yet been adequately disclosed in its originary character by the analytic itself—it will return later in another context. But it is
perhaps going too far at this stage to say—as Heidegger does—that "The
'that' of facticity can never come before us in a beholding" (SZ, 135). Or
at least this is true only if one equates beholding (*Anschauen*) in general
with theoretical seeing, and indeed in the specifically philosophical sense.[26]

The Time of the Augenblick

We have already noted that the themes of transparency, of open resolve,
of conscience, and of the *Augenblick* were all used in the *Sophist* course to
characterize various structural moments of *praxis* in Heidegger's analysis of
Book VI of the *Nicomachean Ethics*. To what extent does this early analysis
help to shed light on the same constellation of themes in *Being and Time*?
To what extent can Dasein's being, as thematized in *Being and Time*, be
understood as originary *praxis*, beyond the theory/praxis distinction? What
kind of "seeing" is implied by the *Augenblick* in the 1927 treatise, and what
is its specific temporality? In addressing these questions, let us begin with
a brief recapitulation of the earlier analysis of *praxis* in the 1924/25 *Sophist*
course.

In the *Sophist* course, Heidegger had already used the concept of "transparency" to analyze an intrinsic moment of *phronēsis*. While the particular

---

[26] See part 4 of the present study.

end of *praxis* has already been anticipated, chosen or projected in advance in each case, the concrete situation and the means toward achieving this end are initially concealed and must be uncovered so as to make the action itself transparent in its constitutive aspects (GA 19, 148). *Phronēsis* has the task of making an action transparent, via correct deliberation. The result of correct deliberation is "the *correct openness of resolve* [Entschlossenheit] as the transparency of the action.... The directional uncovering of the complete situation ends in an authentic openness of resolve for ..., in engaging" (GA 19, 150). Yet correct deliberation, as we have noted, is itself dependent upon the disclosure of the *eschaton,* of the concrete situation in its temporal particularity, which occurs as the "glance of the eye" or *Augenblick. Phronēsis,* whose essence lies in deliberative excellence (*euboulia*), is thus not only dependent upon the end projected (via *logos*), but also, and indeed primarily, upon the disclosure of the situation as that disclosure bears upon the approaching moment of action. In this sense, *phronēsis* is not a *hexis meta logou monon,* not a merely logical disposition; it is not merely an uncovering (*alētheuein*) that occurs via *logos.* Although *phronēsis* guides and directs all human action, it remains dependent upon something other than itself, namely, "the action itself" and is thus, unlike the *theōrein* of *sophia* (which is likewise not a mere *hexis*), not an independent form of disclosure (GA 19, 170). As Heidegger also puts it, *"Phronēsis* lies more in *praxis* than in the *logos"* (GA 19, 139). This also helps to clarify why Heidegger, earlier in his discussion, had identified *phronēsis* with conscience (*Gewissen*) and assigned to the latter the task of achieving transparency: *"Phronēsis* is nothing other than conscience set in motion [*das in Bewegung gesetzte Gewissen*], which makes an action transparent" (GA 19, 56). This statement occurs at the point where Heidegger first discusses Aristotle's brief justification for saying that *phronēsis* is not merely a logical disposition, because a purely logical or discursive potentiality can be forgotten or fall into concealment (*lēthē*) (NE, 1140 b28). A purely logical disposition or habit is one that can be repeated and learned (such as a *technē*), "whereas *phronēsis* is new on each occasion." "Conscience cannot be forgotten" (GA 19, 56). Our analysis of the role of the *Augenblick* in *phronēsis* suggests not only how to read this reference to conscience—and how not to read it—but also tells us something more about the *Augenblick* itself. It is clear that "conscience" here cannot mean conscience as experienced in the modern guise of subjectivity, where part of its role is the reinforcement of self-presence and permanence of self produced by various practices of repetition.[27] Rather the phenomenon of conscience in *phronēsis* is

---

[27] On the genealogy of modern conscience, see Michel Foucault's analyses of confession in *Histoire de la sexualité,* vol. 1 (Paris: Gallimard, 1976).

concerned with the unfolding disclosure (presencing) of the concrete situation *in and throughout* the entire process of *phronēsis,* from its beginning to
its end. Both situation and process are finite. In other words, "conscience"
here does not belong to an already existing subject; it does not refer to
the activity of an individual who "has" "conscience," but rather to the full
unfolding and accomplishment of *praxis* itself, where this unfolding is to be
understood as the coming into full (finite, concrete) presence of the finite
action itself. It is the *event of presencing* itself that cannot be forgotten,
for insofar as we are, we always *already* "stand in" this very event. To say
that the event of presencing (which Heidegger would later call *Ereignis*)
cannot be forgotten does not of course mean that it cannot become obscured as such an event. "Presumably," Heidegger notes, "one can let that
which conscience uncovers become hidden and ineffective, through *hēdonē*
and *lupē,* through [certain] passions. Conscience announces itself again and
again [or: conscience always returns, repeats itself, recurs: *Gewissen meldet
sich immer wieder*]." Conscience thus shows itself not as the activity of an
individual, but as the very process of becoming finite, of individuation as
finite individuation. *Praxis,* as radically finite and originary, shows itself
as a coming out of concealment, unfolding into presencing, returning back
into concealment.

   These remarks on conscience also indicate that the *Augenblick* or "glance
of the eye," as we have here preferred to translate it, is not to be understood as a "moment of time" in the sense of an "instant." Rather, it refers
to the unfolding disclosure of the presencing of a situation *in the duration
appropriate to it.* The *Augenblick* does not preclude, but indeed demands a
certain duration, albeit a finite one. The glance of the eye, while it may begin (or end) suddenly, as a sudden moment of appropriation or coming into
its own (in response to the sudden irruption into presence of something or
someone), has its own intrinsic duration and intensity.[28] This point is made

---

[28] The suddenness of such appropriation or expropriation is what was once understood
by the Greek *exaiphnēs,* a word that formerly stressed the originating moment of emergence, a coming into presence as though out of nothing (cf. Homer, *Illiad,* 17.738 and
21.14, where the word is associated with the sudden onset of a mighty fire, a sudden
igniting or flaring up, a coming into the light that brings its own illumination with it).
In GA 29/30, Heidegger indeed speaks of "flaring up" (*Aufflackern*) and "extinguishing"
(*Verlöschen*) as belonging to the momentary character of the *Augenblick* and its seldom-
ness (428). As we have noted, *exaiphnēs* is used in the *Nicomachean Ethics* with reference
to the time of action, the *kairos.* Kierkegaard sees Plato's *to exaiphnēs* as an inadequately
conceived forerunner to his conception of the *Augenblick,* noting "What we call the moment, Plato calls *to exaiphnēs....*" See *The Concept of Anxiety,* 87–88. Kierkegaard's
use of the term *Augenblick* (in Danish, *Øieblik*) is influenced by Schleiermacher, whose
translation of Plato's *Parmenides* (156d–e) renders *exaiphnēs* as *der Augenblick.* The
importance of Kierkegaard's analyses of anxiety and of the *Augenblick* is acknowledged
in *Being and Time* (see SZ, 190n. 1, 235n. 1; and [on the *Augenblick*], 338n. 1). Heidegger,

by Aristotle in his comments on the temporality appropriate to *phronēsis.*
The practical good has the temporal sense of the *kairos,* the appropriate
moment for action (NE, 1096 a26). This moment must be chosen with deliberation: in cases of war, it depends on strategy; in instances of disease, it is
to be determined by medicine (NE, 1096 a32). A certain degree of general,
even "technical" knowledge is thus necessarily in play and presupposed. Yet
in such cases, Aristotle insists, it is always necessary to consider what action
is appropriate to the moment (*tous prattontas ta pros ton kairon skopein*),
and for this reason ethics cannot be a matter of *technē* (NE, 1104 a9).
For in matters of *technē,* the end is fixed in advance, and precisely this
fixed character of the end (the form or *eidos*) means that a craft can be
taught. *Phronēsis* by contrast cannot be taught, but requires experience
of life. In *phronēsis* the particular end chosen in a *prohairesis* is radically
unstable: it is open to sudden modification as called for by the circumstances of the moment. The end of an action exists in accordance with
the occasion (*to de telos tēs praxeōs kata ton kairon estin*); an end is chosen (*hairetai*) at the time when it is done, that is, in the critical moment
of engagement, and therefore the terms *hekousion* and *akousion* (usually
misleadingly translated as "voluntary" and "involuntary") must be understood with reference to the time of action (*hote prattei*) (NE, 1110 a12f.).
An act may indeed have to be done "suddenly" (*exaiphnēs*) or instinc-
tively, in which case, although it may be chosen (*hairetai*) over another
possibility, it "cannot be said to be done in accordance with *prohairesis*"
(NE, 1111b 10). For *prohairesis* implies something chosen in advance, ahead
of time (i.e., of the time of action), something chosen with foresight and
thought (NE, 1112 a16). We see from this again why Heidegger asserts that

---

however, claims that Kierkegaard does not attain a satisfactory "existential interpretation" of the *Augenblick,* but remains wedded to the "ordinary concept" of time (338n. 1).
In the same note, Karl Jaspers' important discussion of the *Augenblick*—a discussion
that was surely pivotal for Heidegger, but which he altogether neglects in his 1919–
21 review of Jaspers' book (GA 9, 1ff.)—receives only a passing acknowledgement. See
Psychologie der Weltanschauungen, 2nd ed. (Berlin: Julius Springer, 1922), 108–17. In
the 1929/30 course *The Fundamental Concepts of Metaphysics: World, Finitude, Solitude,* Heidegger is much more forthright about the significance of Kierkegaard's analyses,
noting that "What we here designate as *Augenblick* is what was really comprehended for
the first time in philosophy by Kierkegaard—a comprehending with which the *possibility*
of a completely new epoch of philosophy has begun for the first time since antiquity"
(GA 29/30, 225). On the *Augenblick* in Heidegger and Kierkegaard, see Otto Pöggeler,
"Destruktion und Augenblick," in *Destruktion und Übersetzung,* 9–29; also Günter Wohlfart, *Der Augenblick* (Freiburg: Karl Alber Verlag, 1982). For an insightful discussion
of *exaiphnēs* and its relation to *kairos,* including an overview of relevant literature,
see Ruin, *Enigmatic Origins,* 178–84. Werner Beierwaltes, in " Ἐξαίφνης oder: Die
Paradoxie des Augenblicks," *Philosophisches Jahrbuch* 74/2 (1967): 271–83, provides a
detailed account of the significance of this term in Plato, Aristotle, and Kierkegaard (we
are grateful to Elizabeth Hoppe for bringing this essay to our attention).

phronēsis lies more in *praxis* than in the *logos*. Even the time of deliberation intrinsic to *phronēsis*—which time, Aristotle emphasizes, must be neither too short (it does not mean reacting quickly through presence of mind, *agchinoia,* nor having an intuitive instinct for the right moment, *eustochia:* NE, 1142 b3f.) nor too prolonged (NE, 1142 b26)—must receive its measure from the time of action. Thus, Heidegger notes, "Even the time [of deliberation] as such, whether one deliberates for a long time or for a short time, is not a distinctive feature of the *orthotēs* of *euboulia;* rather, everything depends on the time of action itself being an *agathon*" (GA 19, 155). The key point is that the actual end of an action, the means that are sought and discovered by deliberation, the time of deliberation itself, as well as the opportune moment of engagement, all depend upon what is called for by the concrete circumstances of the moment, as disclosed in the practical *aisthēsis* or *Augenblick.* This does not of course mean that they are dependent *only* on the circumstances of the moment (decision concerning the opportune moment, for example, in addition to certain general knowledge of what one is dealing with, also entails experience, as well as knowledge of the practical good), but they are *primarily* thus dependent. The thoughtful projection of the end and the *logos* of deliberation can only *respond* to what is given in the eschatological disclosure or presencing of the given situation. In the *praxis* of human existence, *logos* must in this sense respond to the finitude of being; no human *logos,* neither the *logos* of thought, nor that of a prior knowing or having seen, nor that of calculative deliberation (*technē*), can decide what happens in the moment. Yet the response, which participates in the way in which presencing unfolds, is itself—at least on Aristotle's argument—dependent also upon something not given within the situation: our understanding of a more primary good that has already been decided. This may either be a particular good (healing in the case of the doctor), or the good in itself that informs the actions of the *phronimos* and is accessible in its explicitness only to the philosopher whose *theōria* contemplates life (being) itself as such.

The various structural moments that Aristotle analyses here do not therefore constitute some detached theory of existence, but are latently present or at work in all their complexity in every situation of human action. We shall now try to explicate further some of this complexity by a comparative consideration of the *Augenblick* as interpreted in *Being and Time* and in Heidegger's Marburg and Freiburg lecture courses from 1924–30, and its earlier characterization in the particularly rich analysis of the 1922 treatise "Phenomenological Interpretations with Respect to Aristotle," to which we have already referred.

It is on account of the *duration* intrinsic to it that Heidegger in *Being and Time* characterizes the *Augenblick* as *held:*

To the anticipation that goes with resolute openness there belongs a presence in accordance with which an open decision discloses the situation. In resolute openness, presence is not only brought back from its dispersion into the objects of our most proximate concern, but is held within future and having-been. That *presence* [Gegenwart] which is held in temporality proper and which is thus itself authentic, we call the *Augenblick*. This term must be understood in the active sense as an ecstasis. It means the rapture of resolute openness [*die entschlossene Entrückung*] in which Dasein is carried away toward whatever possibilities and circumstances are encountered in the situation, but a rapture that is *held* in this resolute openness. The *Augenblick* is a phenomenon that *in principle* can *not* be clarified in terms of the *'now'*. (SZ, 338)[29]

In the anticipation of its own finitude and mortality, in its being ahead of itself in being toward death, Dasein achieves a certain *Selbstständigkeit,* a steadfastness of the self. This steadfastness is not to be understood as a constancy through or over different "moments" of time conceived as "now-points"; and the "self" in question does not refer to some entity or "I" that already exists independently of the present situation, but to the self as *praxis,* the self that is not *reducible* to an already existing individual (whether an empirical or transcendental self), but is rather the *individuation* (*Vereinzelung*) that occurs in and as the temporality of the practical situation.[30] This *Vereinzelung* Heidegger would subsequently describe as a *Verendlichung,* a becoming finite.[31] Such steadfastness does not mean being at a stand in the sense of having come to a standstill that is conceived in opposition to movement, but is precisely an *ec-stasis:* a being outside of any already achieved stand. Such being outside is not so much a stand as a *stance.*[32] It is the *"originary 'outside-itself' in and for itself,"*

---

[29] We have altered the standard translation somewhat; in particular, we have here rendered *die Gegenwart* as 'presence' rather than as 'the present', since the German has the sense of *Anwesenheit* and does not refer to a fully determinate, already existing moment. On the contrary, its indeterminacy is essential. Thus Heidegger goes on to highlight the more literal sense of the word by writing it as *Gegen-wart,* a 'waiting toward' that first lets things be encountered as present.

[30] See SZ, §64. Taminiaux, who insists that Dasein's individuation "is no longer the individuation of someone," goes too far in interpreting such individuation as "speculative" and as "purified of any belonging to appearances." (*La fille de Thrace et le penseur professionnel,* 178–79, 205.)

[31] See GA 29/30, 8.

[32] Heidegger would discuss this stance or *Haltung* more extensively in the second *Nietzsche* course, in the context of Nietzsche's thinking of the *Augenblick*. See in particular NI, 382–402, and our commentary in part 3.

originary temporality, the "*ekstatikon* pure and simple" (SZ, 329). And yet
this "outside itself," as stance, is so radical that it is not to be thought as
the being-outside of an already existing "self": ecstatic temporality "is not
in the first instance an entity that then subsequently steps out of *itself*."
It means a being "held" within future and having-been, a held "transport"
or "rapture" (*Entrückung*)—a *raptus,* as Heidegger elsewhere describes it
(GA 26, 265)—a stance that is a being held or possessed by the disclosure
that the *Augenblick* itself is. The *Augenblick,* as originary, ecstatic presence,
is a rapture held within a resolute openness in that, as Heidegger later put
it, it itself "is nothing other than the *look of open resolve* [der Blick der
Entschlossenheit], in which the full situation of an action opens itself and
is held open" (GA 29/30, 224). This ec-static stance of the *Augenblick* is a
transport, a rapture, a being held, a being possessed, thus almost like a kind
of trance—but *also* one in which "the entrancement of time" is "broken" or
shattered (GA 29/30, 226). The temporalizing of originary temporality is
such that, in temporalizing presence, it can entrance us in different ways; in
the latter context, that of the 1929/30 course, *The Fundamental Concepts
of Metaphysics: World, Finitude, Solitude,* the entrancement of time mentioned refers to the temporality of boredom as a disclosive attunement.

The different possible forms of entrancement or attunement correspond
to different ways in which we can exist in the presence of whatever is before us. The held ecstasis of the *Augenblick* does *not*—contrary to certain
prevalent readings[33]—entail a lack of being absorbed by something, but is
the way in which we are authentically affected by a being or field of beings
that fundamentally concerns us in our very existence, the presence of a
being or situation that we understand to be intimately bound up with our
own being, such that our own being is also at stake there. Such a situation
discloses not only *Dasein's* facticity—its being "bound up" with the being
of other beings in its "destiny" (SZ, 56)—in an originary (futural) manner;
it also takes the being of those other beings into Dasein's care in such a
way that in their being they are entrusted to Dasein for their safekeeping.
It is thus Dasein's very *being* that is held by something in being given over
to something in this way, and not our mere "attention." Although we often
speak of our attention being "taken" or "caught" by something—and here
we express the fact that it is the presence of the object itself that primarily gives rise to this event—we tend to interpret attention in a subjective
manner, as though our attention were something that existed prior to or
independently of the presence of things. Yet the phenomena of attention
and attentiveness do not require the positing of a "subject"; they are to be

---

[33] See Otto Pöggeler, *Der Denkweg Martin Heideggers,* 209–11; and Jacques Taminiaux, *Lectures de l'ontologie fondamentale,* 135.

thought temporally as the way in which Dasein is futurally open for the presencing of beings that have already affected it and that bear a certain significance (a worldly signification). When Dasein understands this future openness in an originary manner, that is, not merely in terms of possibilities of *beings,* but from out of the futural event of presencing itself, it stands in the *Augenblick* and lets beings be present in their worldly signification, thus first letting *world* properly be.

The held ecstasis of the *Augenblick* is thus fundamentally different from the way in which we are held, for example, in various degrees of boredom—a phenomenon that Heidegger would investigate in 1929/30 in terms of its intrinsic temporality.[34] In boredom, we are indeed *held,* yet in a strangely indeterminate manner, in a way that leaves us empty in our very being. Things themselves no longer fill us, no longer absorb us; we feel empty, unfulfilled, indifferent. Indeed, as Heidegger describes it, the experience of profound boredom, of being bored with beings as a whole, is a telling refusal on the part of beings themselves that calls us back to our proper vocation of "being there," toward the *Augenblick* in which we may experience the world as world—experience the fact that things call for us in their very being, that they need us to let them be. The temporality of boredom is thus also fundamentally different from, and yet an intimate counterpart of the temporality of curiosity, which Heidegger describes as "the most extreme counterphenomenon to the *Augenblick*" (SZ, 347). For curiosity is characterized by a nontarrying, by mere dispersion and distraction, by a restlessness and inability to dwell with whatever is there in any given situation:

> Curiosity is constituted by an unheld making-present which, merely making [things] present, thereby continually seeks to run away from the attending within which it is nevertheless "held" in the manner of being unheld. The present "springs forth" from its correlative attending, and does so in the emphatic sense of running away. The making-present that pertains to curiosity, in its "springing forth," is, however, so little given over to its "matter" that in attaining its vision it is also already looking away toward what comes next.... "Springing forth" is an ecstatic modification of attending such that the latter *springs after* making-present. (SZ, 347)

Curiosity, the desire for the new, continually seeks to make present the next newest thing, and is thus unable to dwell with what is present at any given moment. It is unable to let even possibilities for being concerned with

---

[34] See GA 29/30, part 1.

those beings that are present arise from out of those beings themselves. The presencing pertaining to curiosity is *unheld*—and yet, it is "held" in this very state of being unheld, held precisely by the constant possibility of something new. It "springs forth" from futural possibilities of concern in the sense that it is not held by such possibilities, but seeks to escape them. Attending (*Gewärtigen*), as the presencing of determinate possibilities of concern, begins to withdraw from these possibilities belonging to the presencing of worldly things. Our (futural) relation to the presence of things in the world seeks to withdraw from that very presence. The possibility of "the new," as conceived by curiosity, is the withdrawal of presence. The ecstatic modification that marks the temporalizing of such withdrawal thus implies a *closure* of presencing. Yet this closure of presencing is not identical to that which characterizes the *Augenblick,* even though it bears the trace of the latter. Rather, the ecstatic modification of "springing forth" characteristic of the temporality of curiosity is a closure and concealment of Dasein's very finitude, of the finitude of ecstatic temporality itself. In curiosity, Dasein flees its own finitude, its own being-toward-death (SZ, 348).[35]

The *Augenblick* as originary, ecstatic presence is not only *enclosed* within future and having-been (SZ, 328); as originary temporality, it is also radically finite in the sense in which such enclosure marks an intrinsic *closure*. This closure occurs as the temporalizing of the future, that is, in the way in which the temporalizing of temporality comes toward itself as presence, in the manner of presencing, of the temporalizing of the *Augenblick*. Such finitude, Heidegger remarks, does not primarily mean a cessation; Dasein does not merely "have" an end at which it ceases, but, in its being, as presencing, *"exists finitely"* (SZ, 329). The temporalizing of the originary future is:

> a coming toward oneself, toward *oneself,* existing as the un-surpassable possibility of nothingness. The ecstatic character of the originary future lies precisely in the fact that it closes our potentiality for being, that is, it is itself closed [*geschlossen*] and as such makes possible the open resolve of an existentiell understanding of nothingness. (SZ, 330)

This closure of the originary future exceeds the order of presencing in opening the possibility for a radical existentiell understanding of nothingness and of finitude, an existentiell understanding which *Being and Time* earlier thematized as the hearing of the voice of conscience. Such hearing is itself primarily futural: an opening for the presencing of the "voice" or

---

[35] Considered historically, in its specifically modern, technological form, curiosity thus becomes an increasingly active withdrawal from presence. See part 2 of the present study.

call, for *logos* itself (or for the promise of *logos*), but an opening that has also always already been closed, a finite opening for the presencing of a call that, in its finite coming, "comes from out of the silence of uncanniness and calls the Dasein that is called upon to be stilled back into the stillness of itself" (SZ, 296).[36]

In contrast to curiosity, which in the face of death (understood in an existential-ontological manner, as finitude and closure of presencing) takes flight from its own presencing into the promise of the new, Dasein in the *Augenblick* stands explicitly before its own finitude as the finitude of the factical situation into which it has been thrown. It anticipates this finitude in its authentic being-toward-death that casts it back upon its thrownness in disclosing the situation as a finite situation of action that Dasein can take upon itself in resolute openness. In the resolute openness of its anticipation, as the unfolding of the *Augenblick,* Dasein understands its potentiality for being in such a way that "it passes under the eyes of death [*dem Tod unter die Augen geht*], so as to entirely take on, in its thrownness, the being that it is" (SZ, 382). This passage under the eyes of death (from where do they look?) bestows upon Dasein the look of mortality;[37] it delivers Dasein over to the facticity of being in its particular, finite situation that offers finite possibilities for being-in-the-world, and in which it finds itself in its destiny with others. Such is Dasein's being for "its time"—a time shared as finitude, as the finitude of a world in which Dasein exists with other beings (SZ, 385).

Retrospect on the 1922 Treatise on Aristotle

This allusion to the inextricability of human vision and mortality reinvokes a theme that was broached at least as early as the 1922 treatise "Phenomenological Interpretations with Respect to Aristotle." There, anticipating his description of the *kairos* in terms of the *Augenblick* in the context of his discussion of the *Nicomachean Ethics,* Heidegger had formulated the issue even more strikingly. Factical life, he noted, occurs in such a way that its death is somehow always there for it, "stands in a certain perspective [*Sicht*] for it," if only in the manner of an evasive looking away. The point is not simply that death is somehow "seen" by life; rather, life itself first becomes visible as such, *as life,* and such visibility is first enabled, by the presence of the possibility of death. Yet insofar as death can be present in fundamentally different ways, this suggests that "life" and life are not

---

[36] We shall return to this uncanny stillness in part 4 of our study.
[37] Cf. part 4, "The Look of the Other."

always the same thing.[38] Only the life that takes hold of existence in such
a way as to take death into its care, only in the "care of existence" (where
caring is to be understood in the middle voice),[39] does life unfold its fullest
potentiality as life. "Death, insofar as it *is* in such a way [*Der so seiende
Tod*], gives life a perspective and constantly brings it before its ownmost
present and past ..." (PIA, 12). Here, death is not yet ontologized as a
"way of being" (as in *Being and Time*),[40] but is characterized as *seiend*, as
something that *is,* intrinsic to the unfolding of factical life. Yet by the time
we reach the context of Dasein's historicality in *Being and Time,* the ever
more pressing question that haunts the analytic is whether that death is
Dasein's *own.* Or whether—as that analytic increasingly suggests—Dasein
indeed undergoes appropriation, understanding itself with respect to its
potentiality for being under the eyes of death, but of a death that is *not*
its own.

    In the 1922 text, Heidegger ascribes the *Augenblick's* character of being
held to the epitactic operation of *phronēsis.* His interpretation first brings
out the peculiar temporality that culminates in the *kairos,* the temporality
that Book VI of Aristotle's *Nicomachean Ethics* had left unexplicated:

> The concrete interpretation shows how the being which is *kairos*
> constitutes itself in *phronēsis.* Solicitous conduct in action is al-
> ways concrete in the 'how' of its concernful dealings with the
> world. *Phronēsis* makes the situation of whoever is acting acces-
> sible in holding fast the *hou heneka,* the wherefore, in making
> available the 'toward what end', in apprehending the "now,"
> and in prefiguring the 'how'. It proceeds toward the *eschaton,*
> the most extreme point [*Äußerste*] in which the concrete situ-
> ation, seen in a determinate respect, culminates in each case.
> As discursive, solicitous, and deliberative, *phronēsis* is possible
> only because it is primarily an *aisthēsis,* an ultimately straight-
> forward overview of the moment [*Augenblick*]. As that being
> [*Seiende*] which becomes available and unveiled in the *alētheuein*
> of *phronēsis,* the *prakton* is something that exists as *not yet* such
> and such being [*Sein*]. As "not yet such and such," namely as the
> 'with which' of concern, it *is* at the same time *already* such and
> such, as the 'with which' of a concrete readiness to deal, a readi-
> ness whose constitutive illumination is provided by *phronēsis.*

---

[38] Thus Heidegger, in his later work, will emphasize the historical vocation and
determination of being-a-self, for example, in his claim that human beings, determined
as "rational animals," must first *become* mortals (VA, 171).

[39] PIA, 10 n. 1.

[40] See Division Two, chapter 1. This ontologization is returned to its existentiell
concretion via the analysis of "conscience" in chapter 2.

> The "not yet" and the "already" are to be understood in their
> "unity," that is, from out of an originary givenness for which the
> "not yet" and the "already" are determinate explicata. Deter-
> minate, because with them what constitutes the object is placed
> in a determinate aspect of movement. (PIA, 35–36)

Phronēsis "holds fast" the primary end or *hou heneka,* makes available
the particular, immediate end, apprehends the "now," and prefigures or
sketches out in advance the 'how' or means. Yet the discursive moments of
phronēsis are possible only because it is "primarily" practical *aisthēsis,* a
seeing of whatever is given in the moment. This seeing, as occuring within
phronēsis, proceeds toward the *eschaton,* the *kairos* of the moment at which
the concrete action begins. This action, the *prakton,* as disclosed within
phronēsis has at once not yet happened, in that it has yet to be achieved
concretely, and yet has already happened in the sense that it is already held
in readiness (as a determinate possibility) by the disclosive movement of
phronēsis. As a *hexis meta logou, phronēsis* holds an action at the ready, it
enables the (futural) coming into presence of an action which, as possible
at any moment, is already underway toward full concretion and already
lets the situation be seen in a determinate respect with regard to its possible unfolding, its possible "movement." "Movement" here is not to be
understood as movement in space, but as the coming into full presence of
a potentiality.

The action or *prakton* is constituted as this entire movement of disclosure that determines in a particular respect what is already being disclosed (coming to self-disclosure, showing itself) in the practical *nous* or
Augenblick. The ongoing disclosure that unfolds as the *Augenblick* of the
finite situation is "held" in its full disclosive movement, and this fullness
always already exceeds the determinate aspect in which it is oriented:

> The *alētheia praktikē* is nothing other than the full *Augenblick,*
> unveiled in each case, of factical life in the 'how' of its decisive
> readiness for dealing with itself, and it is so within a factical
> relation of concern with the world that is being encountered.
> *Phronēsis* is *epitactic,* it presents a being as the object of con-
> cern; it brings and holds within this aspect every determinacy of
> the *Augenblick:* the specific 'how', 'wherefore', 'to what extent',
> and 'why'. As epitactic illumination, it brings our dealings into
> the fundamental stance [*Grundhaltung*] of a readiness for …, a
> breaking-forth toward…. The goal of this 'toward', that which
> *is* in the manner of the *Augenblick,* stands within the aspect
> of significance for …, of possible concern, of that which is now

to be accomplished. *Phronēsis* is a seeing *kata to sumpheron
pros to telos* (1142 b32). Because it is the way in which the
full *Augenblick* is preserved, circumspection in its proper sense
holds the wherefore of action, its *archai,* in genuine preservation. The *archē* is what it is only in a concrete relatedness to
the *Augenblick,* it is there in being seen and being seized upon,
in the *Augenblick* and for it. (PIA, 36)

Circumspection, which is here defined less restrictively than in *Being
and Time,* and refers to the entire vision of *phronēsis* as oriented by deliberation, is here described as holding and preserving both *archai* of action
(the primary as well as the immediate goal) in their concrete relatedness
to the *Augenblick.* It thus also preserves or maintains the full *Augenblick*
itself whose disclosure is seen in a determinate respect. The *Augenblick* is
thus *preserved,* present within the circumspection of dispersion, as *Being
and Time* will conceive it. Yet deliberation, as we have noted, is dependent
upon what is already disclosed in the *Augenblick:* deliberative excellence,
as Heidegger remarks, "brings the 'how' of an appropriate and authentically goal-attaining going-to-work into circumspective vision from out of
the *Augenblick* itself" (PIA, 37).

In holding and maintaining every determinacy of the moment, *phronēsis*
as a *hexis* brings human existence as *praxis* into a certain stance (*Haltung*)
and thus brings human life to itself in a certain way. Yet this stance and
movement of disclosure in the *Augenblick* is radically unstable: *phronēsis*
understands the being of the *prakton* as that which can be otherwise at any
moment, and it maintains such being within the determinate possibility for
change in this or that respect. The movement intrinsic to human existence
as ongoing disclosure, as presencing and its unfolding in *phronēsis,* is by its
very nature incomplete; as a being underway and a seeking, *phronēsis* is
oriented toward something always yet to come. Yet this very fact, or more
precisely the way in which it is interpreted, results in what Heidegger sees
as a strange "doubling" within Aristotelian ontology:

In circumspection life is there in the concrete 'how' of something
'with which' we are dealing. The being of that 'with which' we
are dealing, however—and this is decisive—is not given a positive ontological characterization in these terms, but is characterized purely formally, as that which can also be otherwise,
something that is not necessarily or always as it is. This ontological characterization is accomplished by way of a *negative*
contrast to another, *proper* way of being. The latter, for its part
and in its fundamental character, is gained not by explicating

the being of human life as such, but in its categorial structure
arises from a particular *ontological radicalization, already accomplished, of what it means to be moved* [des Bewegtseienden].
That which is in being moved, together with the possible features of its structural meaning, is regarded in advance in terms
of the exemplary kind of movement belonging to *producing.*
Being means *being finished* [Fertigsein], that way of being in
which movement has attained its *end.* The being of life is seen
as intrinsically unfolding movement, and it exists in such movement when human life has come to its end with regard to its
ownmost possibility of movement, that of pure apprehending.
Such movement lies within the *hexis* of *sophia.* (PIA, 37–38)

The "dealing" or "going about" (*Umgang*) with . . . referred to at the beginning of this passage translates *praxis,* and its object is "human life itself,"
or as Heidegger had also expressed it, "the world" (PIA, 35). Aristotle's determination of *praxis,* Heidegger here indicates, does not understand *praxis*
originally enough, in the kind of movement proper to it. Aristotle does
indeed give an ontological determination of human existence as *praxis,* but
this determination is purely formal—and this because it is already oriented
by a prior understanding of being drawn from the sphere of *poiēsis* and
technē: being as being finished, being produced, being *formed,* that is, being
understood as the kind of being intrinsic to the product when productive
activity has come to a halt and the product has come to stand before us in
the form of its presence-at-hand.

As Heidegger indicates here, the being of human life for Aristotle finds
its proper end in the pure apprehending found in the *theōria* of *sophia.*
But this pure apprehending, the apprehending of pure actuality as "the
divine," as the constant presence of the world, Heidegger goes on to remark,
precisely turns away from human life as such (as *praxis*), in regarding such
life as primarily a way of being that can be otherwise at any moment. The
most proper possibility of human life as such is not fully human;[41] human
life achieves (sees) its most proper possibility only when it renounces its
immediate involvements and concerns, "only in the pure accomplishment
[*Zeitigung*] of *sophia.*" In this, human life comes to its own proper end—
not, as Heidegger emphasizes, in that its intrinsic movement ceases—but
precisely in *seeing itself as movement* and thus properly *being* movement:

Every movement, as *badisis eis*—being underway toward—by
its very meaning entails not yet having reached that toward
which it moves; it exists precisely as a proceeding toward its

---

[41] Cf. Nicholas Lobkowicz, *Theory and Practice,* 26ff.

end: learning, walking, house-building; in its being, walking is
in principle different from having walked: *heteron kai kinei kai
kekinēken* (M, 1048 b32). By contrast, having seen is simultaneous with seeing; someone has seen—has in sight—only insofar
as they are seeing right now, they have apprehended in their
very apprehending: *noei kai nenoēken* (ibid.). This state of motion is a way of being that preserves its accomplishment in accomplishing such preservation: *hama to auto* (ibid., 33; cf. M,
IX, 6). *Noēsis* alone as pure *theōrein* fulfills the highest idea
of pure motion.[42] The proper [*eigentliches*] being of man is accomplished in the pure achievement of *sophia* as an *untroubled
scholē* that has time, a tarrying alongside the *archai* of that
which always is in purely apprehending them. (PIA, 38–39)

What is striking about this discussion of *Metaphysics* Book IX is that
Heidegger omits to mention the entire paradox of what is and is not said by
Aristotle in this context. For the simultaneity of seeing and having seen is
here cited by Aristotle as the exemplary instance of *praxis*—of *praxis* at its
purest, pure *energeia,* as distinguished from *kinēsis.* This moment constitutes the most rigorous attempt on Aristotle's part to define *ontologically*
the essence of *praxis* as an end in itself, whereas elsewhere *praxis* is understood as the *kinēsis* of human life (EE, 1220 b27). But then what is at stake
where the removal or distancing of *sophia* from *phronēsis* is concerned is
not merely the increasing distancing of *theōria* from ethico-political *praxis,*
but a division within *praxis* itself whereby the theoretical life comes to be
favored over the remaining forms of *praxis* belonging to the political life,
and in such a way that the theoretical life itself comes to be obscured and
eventually forgotten altogether as a life, as itself a form of *praxis,* and especially of worldly *praxis.*[43] This division within *praxis,* in other words,
institutes the beginning of a historical divergence between the theoretical
and the practical, which are no longer seen as different kinds of *praxis* or
"ways of life," but as inherent within the very *being* of the human being.[44]
In the course of this divergence that becomes an inner dissension, *theōria*
increasingly withdraws into the *scholē* of the contemplative life. But it is
not only this concealment of *theōria* as a *praxis* in its own right that occurs
in such divergence.

What is most striking and most paradoxical is that Aristotle's text, precisely here where we find the most rigorous determination of *praxis,* gives

[42] Cf. the being of the prime, unmoved mover in *Metaphysics* Book XII.

[43] That *theōria* was itself originally understood as a *praxis,* indeed the highest, was
something Heidegger would frequently recall. See, for example, SDU, 11–12; VA, 48;
VS, 91; GA 55, 203.

[44] Cf. Lobkowicz, *Theory and Practice,* chapter 2.

no grounds whatsoever for preferring the vision of *theōria* over the vision
we find in *phronēsis*, or for that matter in rudimentary sense-perception.
Indeed, Aristotle does not mention *theōria* in this context, and Heidegger's
reading of *noei kai nenoēken* as referring to the *theōrein* of *sophia* is presumably informed by *Metaphysics* Book XII. But Aristotle's reference could
equally well apply to the practical *nous*. Indeed, Aristotle's text also attributes the simultaneity of seeing and having seen, as the strictest sense of
praxis, to *phronēsis: horai hama [kai heōrake], kai phronei [kai pephronēke]*
(M, 1048 b24), something that Heidegger conspicuously omits to mention.
Thus, even if, with Heidegger, we read the reference to *noein* as alluding
to the theoretical *nous* of *sophia*, *phronein* comprises no less of an end in
itself than does *theōrein*. Moreover, this mention of *phronein* seems to suggest that we find the authentic Aristotelian meaning of being not only in
moving away from *phronēsis* and remaining at a theoretical remove from it,
but that this sense of being might equally be found in the seeing intrinsic to
phronēsis itself. Might one speculate that Heidegger's neglecting to mention
the entire *practical* context of this point in *Metaphysics* Book IX could be
due to the very significance of this insight for his own germinating project
of reinscribing the *stasis* of vision (which, in the guise of pure presence,
had come to be aligned with the entire theoretical desire of philosophy)
back within the *Augenblick* of a *praxis* conceived more originarily? On the
other hand, *phronein* might of course here be taken in a less technical sense
(as "good understanding"). Whatever the case, it is paradoxical that this
key moment in the *Metaphysics* is not only the most ontological determination of *praxis* that we find in Aristotle;[45] it might just as well be said to
offer the *least* ontological determination of *praxis,* in the sense that it offers no basis for subordinating *praxis* to the *theōria* of *sophia*. Or rather, if
this determination of *praxis* is already a formal-ontological one, undertaken
from the perspective of *theōria*, it also provides precisely the grounds for
determining *theōria* itself as a *praxis*, albeit the highest, removed from the
"exoteric" *praxeis* of political life, withdrawn from the life of the *polis*.[46]
This "theoretical" determination of *praxis*, whereby "theory" becomes the
highest and truest (because "autotelic") *praxis*, conceals the concealment
and dependence on alterity intrinsic to the *praxis* of human life: it conceals
the finitude of the worldly horizon that holds human existence open for the
temporal disclosure of that which is truly new or other.

We shall not be able to unfold all the complexities of what is at issue
here at the present juncture. The key point is that only if *phronēsis* and
its intrinsic vision are regarded as in*complete*, as still underway toward ...,

---

[45] As Franco Volpi suggests. See *"Dasein* comme *praxis,"* 23.
[46] See P, 1325 b15f.; NE, X.

namely toward a future that is never fully disclosed—only then is there a basis for subordinating *phronēsis* to *sophia*. The practical *nous* of *phronēsis* can then be regarded as an incomplete form of *nous* and set off against the more perfected, more divine *nous* of *theōrein*. But a temporal consideration reveals that what occurs in such subordination is a subordination of the future proper (the horizon of *phronēsis*) to the future (the end and goal of motion) as *already* disclosed to vision, the future as that which has already come to presence and is held within presence, within the simultaneity of seeing and its object, and indeed within an increasingly "esoteric" seeing, withdrawn from the world.

If the simultaneity of seeing and having seen constitutes pure *praxis*—bringing the life of the human being whose highest capacity is *nous* into its highest possible completeness,[47] its highest actuality as its most proper being—then pure *theōria,* as one form of such seeing, is, as Heidegger's reading here suggests, nothing other than pure *praxis,* and the two cannot yet be distinguished on this basis. But we should again note that what occurs in the *energeia* of pure seeing is also a kind of *poiēsis.* Heidegger's translation suggests this by describing the state of motion (*Bewegtheit*) of this *energeia* as one that "preserves its accomplishment in accomplishing such preservation." "Accomplishment" here translates the German *Zeitigung,* which might also be rendered as "temporalizing" (it is the same term that Heidegger later uses, in *Being and Time,* to describe the temporalizing of ecstatic temporality), but which here carries more of its ordinary connotation of "maturation," or coming into maturity (thus, coming into that which a living being can most fully be). Vision unfolds into its ownmost fullness, the potentiality for seeing attains its ownmost perfection, precisely in the actuality of seeing, which is simultaneously and always already a having seen. But even in this accomplishment of its own proper perfection, such seeing remains, as Heidegger notes, a being-moved; as such it is intrinsically a *poiēsis,* an emergence and unfolding into its own proper end and finitude. In pure *theōrein,* Heidegger would later suggest in the *Sophist* lectures, we stand in the presence of an activity that brings itself to being (*poiein*) of its own accord, without any "practical" (kinetic) activity on the part of the human being (GA 19, 168f.). And this of course is why the activity of such pure *theōrein* is understood as *divine* activity, even though it requires that humans leave time for it, the *scholē* during which all other practical activities are interrupted.[48] By contrast with the kind of *stasis* or seizure

---

[47] See chapter 1. Note that Aristotle's consideration of the act of seeing as essentially complete or perfected (*teleia*) at any moment already regards this act from the perspective of the *eidos* of seeing, of what seeing essentially is as such (NE, 1174 a14f.).

[48] The *theōrein* of *epistēmē theōretikē* is the *end* of the seeking (*zētein*) of investigation, which seeking is itself a *praxis* in the very broad sense, having its end outside itself.

that occurs in such pure *theōrein*—the kind that had already taken possession of Socrates from time to time, interrupting his *logos* and his entire
worldly involvement—immersion in worldly projects cannot but appear as
mere dispersion and forgetting.

Augenblick and World

This overview of the 1922 analysis of *phronēsis* and its relation to *sophia*
in Aristotle not only helps, by virtue of the detailed examination of the
temporality and movedness (*Bewegtheit*) of *phronēsis* (something omitted
in the later analysis provided by the *Sophist* lectures), to shed light on
the temporality of the *Augenblick* in *Being and Time* and in the subsequent lectures of 1927–30. It also helps us to see the extent to which the
analyses of the *Augenblick* in *Being and Time* go beyond those of both
the 1922 treatise and the 1924/25 lectures, precisely in reintegrating the
phenomenon of *world*—which for Aristotle, or at least for subsequent Aristotelianism, comes to be increasingly displaced from everyday *praxis* into
the comparatively alienated and depoliticized realm of pure *theōria*—back
into the experience of originary *praxis*. In other words, these early analyses reinforce the extent to which *Being and Time* must be read as both
recovering and transforming the history of philosophy as the history of on-
totheology, and (even as the preparatory analytic of Dasein) demands to be
read repeatedly as a "destruction" of the history of ontology.[49] The transformative moves of the analytic are no less important than the recovery
and repetition of traditional ontological themes and interpretations.

   This transformative dimension of the analytic of Dasein can be seen, for
example, when we consider just *how* the phenomenon of world is retrieved
for Dasein conceived as originary *praxis*. If it were merely a case of retaining
a conception of world (i.e., beings as a whole) as actuality, as in Aristotle
or in the Aristotelian tradition, and of claiming that such actuality or presence is itself present in the *Augenblick* of *phronēsis*, and therefore does not
need to be made accessible via the purity of a detached *theōria*, such an
analysis would only entrench more firmly Aristotle's understanding of being
as the actuality or presence that can itself be present as such in and for
nous. Both the teleological conception of presence as completeness, and the
tendency to interpret being or actuality as a being or entity, would remain.
But Heidegger's analysis does not interpret world as the highest actuality
of beings as a whole; rather, the ecstatic analysis of the temporal disclosure

---

[49] In connection with the following discussions of the *Augenblick*, cf. the fine analysis
by Otto Pöggeler in "Destruktion und Augenblick." Unlike the earlier analysis in *Der
Denkweg Martin Heideggers*, this more recent analysis by Pöggeler no longer insists on
the "emptiness" of the *Augenblick* in *Being and Time*.

of world highlights the closure that first makes possible the presencing of
beings as a whole. World in its "nothingness" that collapses signification is
disclosed in the fundamental disposition of anxiety that brings Dasein back
upon its having-been, its thrownness, in its possible repeatability (SZ, 343).
Dasein, as being-in-the-world, is brought before the possibility of being able
to come back to the phenomenon of world (the presencing of beings as a
whole) as that which has already been, from out of its own futuricity. The
ecstatic presence of anxiety is a being *held* in the direction of this possibility, that is, primarily in the direction of having-been, and in this sense holds
Dasein ready for the possible actualizing of a decision. The ecstatic presence
temporalized in anxiety is to this extent different from the way in which the
presence of the *Augenblick* is held in a moment of decision: "Although the
presence pertaining to anxiety is *held*, it does not have the character of the
Augenblick that is temporalized in an open decision [*Entschluß*]. Anxiety
attunes us only in readiness for a *possible* decision" (SZ, 344). While the
presence that characterizes the *Augenblick* is a rapture that is held in the
direction of "worldly" possibilities, that is, "possibilities and circumstances
pertaining to concern" (SZ, 338), the presence belonging to anxiety is held
not toward any particular possible concerns of the moment, but toward
the world as such in its already having been, the disclosure of beings as a
whole, as a prerequisite for any particular intervention. But this is only to
say that the presence temporalized in anxiety is still futural and thereby
closed in advance; it is held toward the world as such *as possibility*, in the
dimension of possibility out of which any particular possibility can first
come to presence: "Anxiety springs from the *future* belonging to resolute
openness" (SZ, 344), that is, from the future proper. To say that it "springs
from" (*entspringt*) the originary future indicates that it is already closed,
but in this very closure Dasein is first able to come toward itself, come into
the *possibility* of the *Augenblick*. Anxiety, in disclosing the nonsignification
of the world, unveils the "impossibility" of Dasein understanding (projecting) itself in terms of a *particular* possibility of worldly concern (SZ, 343).
In bringing Dasein back to "the pure 'that' ['that it is'] of its ownmost,
individuated thrownness," it brings it back to the possibility of repeating
or retrieving such thrownness. And it "thereby *also* unveils the possibility
of an authentic potentiality for being that must come back to the thrown
'there' in a futural retrieval" (SZ, 343). Insofar as it is held toward the world
as such, as possibility, the presence pertaining to anxiety is also held within
"the most extreme not-yet," "possible at every *Augenblick*," held toward the
possibility of the impossibility of existing as such (as being-in-the-world);
in short, toward the *finitude* of existence as such (SZ, 258–67). Dasein's explicit retrieval of its having-been "responds" (*erwidert*) to "the possibility
of an existence that has been," and, as a responding in the *Augenblick,* is

simultaneously the "revocation" (*Widerruf*) of the "past" that is at work in the present day. Such explicit retrieval, unfolding in and out of the *Augenblick*, "neither abandons itself to the past, nor does it aim at progress" (SZ, 386). Unlike curiosity, it does not merely attend to "the next new thing" (*das nächste Neue*) in such a way as to already have forgotten "the old," but may be seen as a (self-)critical displacement and questioning of the present. As Heidegger puts it, it "undoes the present" that purports to be the present day (it is *eine Entgegenwärtigung des Heute*) and undermines the banalities of what 'one' does (SZ, 391).

If the way in which the presence of anxiety is held is not the same as that of the *Augenblick*, it is because the held presence of the *Augenblick* itself testifies to the more originary closure of a futural having-been, and is itself enclosed (as is all presencing) within these ecstases. Nevertheless, there is a profound and intimate connection between the presence of anxiety and that of the *Augenblick*. The *Augenblick*, as a held coming to presence and becoming finite, is already the way in which a *particular* possibility (the possibility of a particular *Entschluß* or decision) is held toward presencing for a possible actualization.[50] But the actualization or realization of a particular action does not entail that Dasein's existing in potentiality—in the realm of possibility that is always also indeterminate, never entirely determinate, never closed in the sense of being extinguished (as long as Dasein exists)—is thereby exhausted or at an end. The situation of action "cannot be calculated in advance," but "is disclosed only in a free resolve that is not determined beforehand, but is open for the possibility of being determined." The resolve belonging to decision "must be *held open* and free" for factical possibilities in each case. Resolve is certain of itself in the manner of its openness, as a *"holding oneself free for* the possibility of *taking back"* this very resolve, and this withdrawal is always factically necessary, as the modification of one's openness in accordance with the unfolding of a situation. Such resolutely open holding oneself free for taking back one's resolve is nothing other than "the authentic and resolute openness for retrieving itself," that is, for retrieving and maintaining this very resolve as such, as an openness for world (SZ, 307–08). The ecstatic presence characteristic of anxiety is precisely what *holds* the *Augenblick* in the indeterminacy of one's possibility. Thus, Heidegger indicates this intimate relation between the two by writing that the presence pertaining to anxiety "which is itself possible—and it alone—as the *Augenblick*, holds the *Augenblick at the ready* [auf dem Sprung]" (SZ, 344). The presence of anxiety, in other words, is intrinsic to the *Augenblick*; it testifies to the way in which the *Augenblick*

---

[50] The term *Entschluß* suggests this coming out of closure into disclosure in a moment of decision. See chapter 2, n. 26.

itself is held in a *suspension* of any full presence (or pure actuality). Resolute openness is not only nothing like an "act of the will" (even though one might ask whether *authentic* resolute openness does not imply a certain "will" to explicitly appropriate what one already is);[51] it would also, Heidegger emphasizes, be ontologically misunderstood were one to suppose that its actual reality depended on the "duration" of an "act" of resolve (SZ, 391). The temporalizing of anxiety comes to presence precisely as this repeated suspension of presence, the suspension that is the temporalizing of the *Augenblick* in which every determinate coming to presence is held suspended within an inevitable indeterminacy. "In resolute openness there lies an existentiell constancy [*Ständigkeit*] that, in accordance with its essence, has already anticipated any possible *Augenblick* that may spring from it" (SZ, 391). This does not mean that the factical content of a situation can be anticipated or seen in advance, but that the possibility of existing as the *Augenblick* at all is held and "preserved" as the finite freedom of existence for whatever can be encountered in a situation (SZ, 391). Likewise, the suspension of presence in the temporalizing of anxiety that holds the *Augenblick* at the ready does not of course imply that no actual decision can ever be made, or no particular action taken; on the contrary, it means only that such an action itself never escapes the realm of possibility, and thus also of ambiguity, that it remains held in a dimension of openness (so long as it is not "irretrievably" lost), even if that realm is no longer (merely) Dasein's own, but the realm of worldly possibility accessible to others.

As an indeterminate and open horizon of possibility that is nonetheless the futural closure of presencing as such, marking all presencing as finite, the way in which the phenomenon of world comes to be inscribed within Dasein as originary *praxis* is thus not a mere anthropomorphizing of the Aristotelian conception of the divine actuality of the *kosmos*. It is not to be aligned with the modern turn to subjectivity. Rather the very conception of world—a phenomenon which, Heidegger claimed provocatively in 1927, had "never yet been recognized in philosophy" (GA 24, 234), and which even Kant failed to see (SZ, 321)—is transformed, in keeping with the task of a transformation ("destruction") of the traditional meaning of being. This incursion of world, understood in terms of originary temporality, into Dasein's existing in the moment of *praxis* is highlighted more thematically after *Being and Time;* the following description of the *Augenblick* from the lecture course *The Basic Concepts of Phenomenology* expresses the point succinctly:

---

[51] Nevertheless, the will is certainly open to being interpreted in terms of *Entschlossenheit*. See EM, 16. See also chapter 5 below, on the Rectoral Address, and our comments on "The Origin of the Work of Art" in part 4.

In the *Augenblick* as an ecstasis, the Dasein that exists as openly
resolved is transported on each occasion into the factically determinate possibilities, circumstances, and contingencies of the
situation of its action. The *Augenblick* is that which, springing from resolute openness, first and solely has an eye [*Blick*]
for what comprises the situation of action. It is that mode of
existing in the resolute openness in which Dasein as being-in-
the-world holds and keeps its world in view [*seine Welt im Blick
hält und behält*]. (GA 24, 407–08)

Heidegger adds that authentic being with one another must also be primarily determined from out of the resolute openness of the individual. This
should not be taken to mean the individual "I" or an already individuated
self, but precisely the *individuation* that each Dasein can authentically be,
as the unfolding of originary *praxis* in which freedom occurs as finite closure:

Only from out of and in the individuation of resolute openness
is Dasein authentically free and open for the You. Being with
one another is not a tenacious empathizing of the I with the
You, arising from a common, concealed helplessness; rather, existing together and with one another is grounded in the genuine
individuation of the individual, an individuation determined by
a presencing in the sense of the *Augenblick*. Individuation does
not mean clinging obstinately to one's own private wishes, but
being free for the factical possibilities of existence in each instance. (GA 24, 408)

The same point is made in *Being and Time,* where Heidegger insists that
resolute openness, as authentic being-a-self, does not cut Dasein off from
its world, but "precisely brings the self into a concernful being involved
with the ready-to-hand on each occasion, and thrusts it into a solicitous
being with others" (SZ, 298). In resolute openness, Dasein becomes "free
for its world" and is brought into "the possibility of letting the others one is
with 'be' in the ownmost possibility of their being, by disclosing the latter
in a liberating solicitude that leaps ahead [*in der vorspringend-befreienden
Fürsorge*]." Such "leaping ahead" is the *same* leaping ahead into worldly
freedom (i.e., into the openness of the world) that is explicitly accomplished
in the anticipatory resolve that first opens Dasein for the finitude of its *own*
worldly being. "Authentic being with one another first springs from the
authentic being-a-self found in resolute openness ..." (SZ, 298). But such
being-a-self must be taken up and engaged in, or rather *as* the existing of
the individual on each occasion: "a common engagement [*Sicheinsetzen*] in

the same task is determined by the way one has taken hold of one's own Dasein" (SZ, 122).

These remarks reinforce the extent to which the temporality of the *Augenblick* concerns originary *praxis* in its full ethical and political character as a way of already being in a common world that is shared with others. Heidegger goes on to distance his understanding of the *Augenblick* from that of Kierkegaard (although he readily acknowledges the importance of Kierkegaard's genuine insight),[52] and to indicate that Aristotle had already seen the phenomenon of the *Augenblick* or *kairos* in Book VI of the *Nicomachean Ethics,* but had not explicated its specific temporality. While Aristotle did not fully explicate the time of *praxis* in relation to the time of the presence-at-hand of the world, the "now" (*nun*), Kierkegaard identified the ethical time of the *Augenblick* with an understanding of the moment as a "now," and from this constructed its paradoxical relation to eternity. Heidegger's rethinking of the temporality of *praxis* should thus also prompt us to rethink the time of the ethical and the political—a task that is only beginning to be undertaken today.[53]

---

[52] See also especially SZ, 338 n. 1 (also 190 n. 1 and 235 n. 1); and GA 29/30, 225–26.

[53] Among the work in this field, see Reiner Schürmann, *Heidegger on Being and Acting: From Principles to Anarchy* (Bloomington: Indiana University Press, 1987); Peg Birmingham, "The Time of the Political," *Graduate Faculty Philosophy Journal, New School for Social Research* 14/2–15/1 (1991): 25–45; also her essays "Logos and the Place of the Other," *Research in Phenomenology* 20 (1990): 34–54, and "Ever Respectfully Mine: Heidegger on Agency and Responsibility," in *Ethics and Danger,* ed. Arleen B. Dallery & Charles E. Scott (Albany: State University of New York Press, 1992), 109–82. Christopher Fynsk provides an insightful and penetrating analysis of *Mitsein* in his book *Heidegger: Thought and Historicity* (Ithaca: Cornell University Press, 1993), chapter 1.

Chapter 5

Theory and Praxis at the University: The Rectoral Address (1933)

The focus of the present study is not Heidegger's political actions and involvement with National Socialism in the 1930s, but the status of *theōria* and its relation to the *Augenblick* at different stages of his thought. Yet because the argument of the Rectoral Address, "The Self-Assertion of the German University" (1933), is articulated around the very concept of *theōria* and its relation to philosophy, the sciences, and political action, we must stop to examine its status in this text. In the present chapter, our remarks will concentrate on the clearly Aristotelian articulation of the *theōria/praxis* distinction and on its relation to the earlier role of this distinction in *Being and Time*. While commentators have frequently remarked on a Platonic tone (not to say Platonism) in the Rectoral Address that articulates the problematic and uncertain role of philosophy in relation to the *polis,* relatively little attention has been paid to the more Aristotelian side. Yet the conception and role of knowledge depicted in the course of the Address is more explicitly Aristotelian than Platonic, despite the fact that the Address ends with a citation from Plato's *Republic*.[1]

Before we turn to the text, a few words of caution and clarification may be in order. First, since no action or *praxis* is explainable solely on the grounds of thought (not even that of thought itself!), our purpose in these remarks cannot be to *explain* or account for Heidegger's "political

---

[1] Among the "Platonic" readings, see in particular Jacques Taminiaux, *Lectures de l'ontologie fondamentale,* and Günter Figal, *Heidegger: Zur Einführung,* 2nd ed. (Hamburg: Junius Verlag GmbH, 1996).

involvement" or complicities with National Socialism on the basis of this speech, however deplorable and unfortunate we may find those complicities to be. Heidegger's actions during the period of his rectorship, and in particular the assumption of the rectorship itself, were certainly "opportunistic," that is, a seizing of the opportunity of the moment, of the *Augenblick* or *kairos*. Our purpose here, however, can neither be to explain actions by thoughts, nor indeed to assess this speech on the basis of other actions. Nevertheless, the Rectoral Address may be read not only as indicative of Heidegger's thought of the period, but also as an action in its own right, and may be judged in accordance with the extent to which it remains responsible to the vocation of philosophizing in relation to political engagement. Our interest in the following comments is in the text of the Rectoral Address itself as a philosophical and also political statement in its own right, one that is relevant to the theme of the present study. We shall not attempt here to assess the speech in the light of Heidegger's other known political actions, nor to draw conclusions as to his ultimate and ulterior political intentions (which can never be known for certain in any case). Nor, finally, shall we attempt to integrate the Rectoral Address into a biography of the thinker's life. All of these ongoing tasks have already been taken up by others, and the literature is well-known. We shall, however, in this chapter try first to assess the Rectoral Address as a philosophical document, in relation to Heidegger's other philosophical writings, and second to draw certain conclusions with respect to the relation between philosophy and the political as conceived in this speech.

A thorough appraisal of the full context and situation of the Rectoral Address is not possible here; it would entail, among other things, a detailed examination of the political and cultural situation of the times in Germany, and of the predicaments of university education in that context. An appreciation of the situated context of Heidegger's thinking would also have to take into account the self-understanding of the German university system in that era, itself the result of an extended history of reflection by philosophers, political scientists, educationalists, and so on. One would also have to consider, in particular, Heidegger's own philosophical thinking on questions of freedom, education, and the relation of science to philosophy. None of this can be examined here beyond the immediate context; such issues would require an extended study in their own right. We shall address our comments, rather, to the precarious status of *theōria* in the Rectoral Address.

The inital tone and argument of the Rectoral Address are clear: what is at stake in the current situation is the "essence" of the German university (SDU, 9); this essence is *Wissenschaft,* "science" (SDU, 10); and the essence of science is philosophy: "All science is philosophy, whether it knows and wishes this—or not." As such, all science remains tied to the beginning (*Anfang*) of philosophy, to "the emergence of Greek philosophy" (SDU, 11). What is at stake is thus ultimately philosophy itself in its essence, philosophy itself as an originary *praxis:* not as "mere" philosophy, as opposed to the sciences or as a particular discipline that just happens to be found at the university, one discipline among others, but philosophizing as attentive to its own historically destined emergence, to its ongoing happening, and to its continual claim upon the community of this particular German university. Philosophy in this originary sense grounds the sciences not only as a historical ground that has been left behind, surpassed as no longer needed, or (more or less) forgotten by the majority of those who have a passion for science. It grounds the sciences as already claiming them in advance, as still giving rise to the very activity that science pursues—whether science acknowledges this or not. And this is why, as Heidegger stresses, "the beginning still *is*":

> But does not this beginning already lie two and a half thousand years behind us? Has not the progress of human activity also changed science? Certainly! The subsequent Christian-theological interpretation of the world, as well as the later mathematical-technical thinking of modernity, have temporally and substantively distanced science from its beginning. Yet the beginning itself is by no means thereby overcome, or even abolished. For granted that original Greek science [*Wissenschaft*] is something great, then the *beginning* of this great event remains what is *greatest* about it. The essence of science could not even become empty and eroded, as it is today, despite all its results and "international organizations," unless the greatness of the beginning *still* persisted. The beginning still *is*. It does not lie *behind us* as something that has long since been; rather, it stands *before* us. The beginning, as what is greatest, is what continues to come over everything in advance and thus is what has also already passed over and beyond us. The beginning has fallen into our future, it stands there in its distant prevailing upon us to retrieve its greatness. (SDU, 12–13)

As Heidegger indicates here, the "progress" of human activity may well have altered science, but not the *essence* of science, which, although empty and eroded, still prevails as a continual claim that has already swept up in its path, and continues to do so, those who have chosen to practice science. The beginning still holds sway inasmuch as science has claimed the passion of those who have chosen to pursue it, even though its claim transpires

at a "temporal and substantive [*sachlich*]" remove. Heidegger here names
Christian theology and modern mathematical-technical thinking (but notably, not Greek thought itself) as contributing to this present alienation.
Yet what exactly is the originary essence of *Wissenschaft?* What constitutes
the "greatness" (*Größe*), the power and might of its beginning?

The originary essence of *Wissenschaft* is certainly to be found in philosophy. But what is the latter itself, in its originary essence? Heidegger—quite
strikingly—does not in the first instance appeal to Plato or Aristotle to
highlight the originary essence of philosophy and science, but to Prometheus.
For Prometheus was, according to "an ancient report," the first philosopher. Heidegger cites from Aeschylus' *Prometheus* the statement, *"technē
d'anagkēs asthenestera makrōi,"* which he translates *"Wissen aber ist weit
unkräftiger denn Notwendigkeit,"* "Knowledge is much less powerful than
necessity." And this means, he elucidates, that "every knowing about things
remains exposed in advance to the supreme power of fate [*der Übermacht
des Schicksals*] and falls short before it" (SDU, 11). Nevertheless, Heidegger
adds, precisely on this account, knowledge (here *technē,* but in the Presocratic sense of a general know-how) must strive to assert itself in the face
of "the entire power of the concealment of beings," for only thus can it
encounter its actual limits.[2]

Now this "creative powerlessness [*Unkraft*] of knowing," Heidegger continues, might well be taken as the paradigm for an purely independent and
indeed self-oblivious knowing, interpreted as the "theoretical" attitude or
stance. Philosophical *theōria,* as we know, found its paradigm in *technē.*
But at this point one must ask, as Heidegger does: "What is *theōria* for the
Greeks?"[3]

---

[2] This appeal to *technē* does not seem to me to mark a fundamental shift from the
analysis of Dasein's authentic knowing in *Being and Time,* as Taminiaux has claimed. It
appears as such only if one already conceives of *praxis* in *Being and Time* in too narrow
a sense, opposed to *technē* and *poiēsis.* See Taminiaux, "The Origin of 'The Origin of
the Work of Art'," in *Reading Heidegger: Commemorations,* ed. J. Sallis (Bloomington:
Indiana University Press, 1993), 392–404. Nevertheless, the *Promethean* characterization
of *technē* certainly places the role of knowledge in a theatrical and tragic setting that
was, if not altogether absent, at least more muted and fragile in *Being and Time.*

[3] From here on in the text, Heidegger writes first *"Theorie"* and then *Theorie* (theory)
rather than θεωρία; likewise, he writes *Praxis* rather than πρᾶξις (although he retains
the Greek for *energeia,* and for the citation from Plato at the end of the Address).
At risk of reading too much into this, the shift might be taken to indicate that when
theōria (which, as noted, is also intrinsically a *poiēsis*) is accorded its due *as a praxis,*
the attempt to institute the rigid distinctions that would define the narrower, more
"technical" senses of these terms becomes problematic. If correct, this hypothesis would
also reflect the fragile status of the political in the Address, which we shall comment on
below. Robert Bernasconi has pointed out another place, in the "Letter on 'Humanism',"
where Heidegger writes *Theoria* rather than θεωρία, a move which Bernasconi interprets
as marking an important semantic shift, in this context protecting something of the

People say: A pure contemplating that remains bound only to what the issues in their fullness demand. Appealing to the Greeks, people say that this contemplative comportment is supposed to happen solely for its own sake. Yet this appeal is wrong. For on the one hand, "theory" does not occur for its own sake, but solely in a passion for remaining close to beings as such and under the urgency of their sway. On the other hand, however, the Greeks struggled precisely to comprehend and to accomplish this contemplative questioning as a, indeed as *the* supreme form of human *energeia*, of "being at work." They did not intend to assimilate praxis to theory, but the opposite: to understand theory itself as the highest actualization of genuine praxis. Science is not a "cultural asset" for the Greeks, but the innermost determinative center of the entire existence of their state and people [*des ganzen volklich-staatlichen Daseins*]. Nor is science for them a mere means of becoming conscious of their unconscious; rather, it is that power which maintains the perspicacity of their entire existence and encompasses it. (SDU, 11–12)

There is nothing here that conflicts in any way with Heidegger's reading of *theōria* in the 1924/25 *Sophist* course. Here, as in the earlier course, *theōria* is conceived ontologically (in accordance with Books VI and X of the *Nicomachean Ethics*) as the highest *energeia* of human existence, and thus as the highest *praxis*. *Theōria* is not an independent body of knowledge that could then be applied to "praxis"; rather, *theōria* is itself a *praxis*— indeed the highest—and all *praxis* has *theōria* as its intrinsic and innermost end. *Theōria* for Aristotle was thus a knowing whereby one comes to see one's own limits (albeit indirectly, through seeing the being of other worldly beings), the finitude of one's own being and what can be accomplished by it, thereby attaining a certain harmony with the world, coming to be "at one" with the world; it was conceived as the determinative basis of ethical and political life. As we have seen, such *theōria* does not at all preclude an openness to alterity and finitude (on the contrary, it first enables a genuine openness by its acknowledgement of limits), nor does it preclude engagement in political life. It remains attentive to the finitude of worldly existence by cultivating the ability to see beings in their being, as what and how they are and can be. It "remains close to beings as such and under the urgency of their sway [*Bedrängnis*]."

---

originary sense of *theōria* from the modern opposition between "theory" and "praxis." "It is theoria, not *theōria*," remarks Bernasconi, "which is so easily surpassed." See "The Fate of the Distinction between *Praxis* and *Poiesis*," in *Heidegger in Question*, 20.

An authentic understanding of this dependency on finitude and on what is finitely given in a situation was first explicitly developed by Heidegger in his analyses of historicality in *Being and Time*. As we have indicated in chapters 3 and 4, the analytic of Dasein clarifies the way in which all theoretical comportment is itself rooted in the being of Dasein as originary *praxis,* and that such *praxis* is itself seen in a genuine and authentic manner only in a "momentary" existing, an existing in and as the *Augenblick.* All *theōria* is intrinsically exposed to this finitude. In authentically taking up an explicit relation to its own mortality as that which always exceeds and surpasses it, Dasein comes to acknowledge its own finitude; it is thrust into the finitude of its own existence and given its ultimate goal, namely, its having to be (*Zu-sein*) as a finite being-in-the-world. It acknowledges the happening of its own being as fate (*Schicksal*), that is, as a finite existing that is primarily dependent upon the givenness of a factical and historical world. It "understands itself ... in the *supreme power* [Übermacht] of its own finite freedom, so as in such freedom, which only ever 'is' in having made a choice, to assume the *powerlessness* [Ohnmacht] of being abandoned to itself and to become perspicuous [*hellsichtig*] for the contingencies of the situation disclosed" (SZ, 384). The context makes it clear that this "supreme power" of its freedom does not *belong* to Dasein, as though Dasein were a subject that had freedom as a property at its disposal, but that such freedom occurs only in and through already having chosen, that is, only in and through one's own existence already having been decided in certain ways. In having chosen, one's existence has always already been abandoned to having (futurally) to be a having-been. One can come to be and have to be only from out of an already having been abandoned to a world, to a finite already-being-in-a-world. Such finite existing in a world is always already a being with others who have "found themselves" in the same world at the same time.[4] "If Dasein, as a fateful being-in-the-world, essentially exists in being with others, then its occurrence is an occurring with others and is determined as *destiny* [Geschick]. We thereby designate the occurrence of a community, of a people" (SZ, 384). Yet such existing in the same world at the same time is altogether fragile. Because Dasein exists only from out of a world that is always already a world of others, *there is, strictly speaking, no time that is simply Dasein's own:* my time is always already a time of others. The time of the world is always the time of the *Augenblick* in which a particular, finite Dasein "holds its world in view," holds itself open to a time and to a finitude that is not primarily its own, but that of a community and a historical world. In opening itself to a world, Dasein has always already closed itself off in advance from any possibility of a time that would be

---

[4] See the analysis of "world-time," SZ, 414ff.

exclusively its own. Its ownmost time is a time of being with others in a world that can never be exclusively its own. Heidegger thus writes that Dasein exists "in the manner of the *Augenblick* for 'its time'" (SZ, 385), thereby indicating that "its time" is always already the time of a worldly being with others. Dasein's time will always already have been a destiny. But it is important to see that such destiny does not at all preclude freedom. Quite to the contrary: Heidegger's analyses imply that *destiny in this sense first enables freedom*, as the freedom of being-in-a-world. To exist futurally, that is, freely, one must always already have been in a finite manner, and have been abandoned to a world. For there is no conceivable freedom that would not actually be a responding to a world that has already been given. It is only for modern subjectivity, unable to conceive freedom as anything other than self-determination (autonomy), and thus as a property of the will, that Heidegger's emphasis on "fate" and "destiny" seems intolerable (if not also unreadable). For modern subjectivity can conceive of destiny only as a blind fate, as the opposite of self-determination.

It is important to recall from *Being and Time* this emphasis on the superior power of fate and on the finitude of worldly freedom, and to note the pervasiveness of this theme throughout the Rectoral Address. For it is precisely this emphasis in the Address itself that precludes one understanding the relation between philosophy and the political in a purely Platonic sense. Science, as derived from the philosophical *theōria* of the Greeks, may well have been "the innermost determinative center of the entire existence of their state and people." But it did not determine political life directly, however much Platonism may encourage such an ideal. Aristotle's insight into the essence of the relative (but not absolute) independence of *praxis* from any "theoretical" idea of the good precisely restored to the *praxis* of ethical and political life a sense of its proper finitude and legitimacy. Yet it also thereby prepared the way for a severing of the theoretical from the political, such that each could come to be conceived and pursued as wholly independent ways of life—a possibility entirely alien to Aristotle's thought. For Aristotle, the theoretical and the political had rather to be maintained in an always tenuous and fragile interrelationship such that *theōria* indeed informed and guided *phronēsis,* yet only *indirectly,* by forming one's view of the world as a whole, and not by telling one what to do in a particular situation. Philosophical knowing, for Aristotle, was always fragile and exposed to worldly finitude in *praxis*. Yet on Heidegger's account, *theōria* was nevertheless for the Greeks "that power which maintains the perspicacity of their entire existence and encompasses it" (SDU, 11–12).

Yet insofar as *theōria* is itself a *praxis*, must it not itself be exposed, in its very genesis and accomplishment, to the very finitude of existence that manifests itself implicitly in and through Aristotle's analysis of ethical *praxis?* Must not the accomplishment and achievement (or work) of *theōria* itself be understood ultimately in terms of the finitude of being as presence that announces itself in the "moment" or *Augenblick,* and not in terms of an ultimate horizon of constant presence—as though this philosophical *theōria* were itself a permanent possibility of human existence that, until the philosophers came along, had just been waiting there to be discovered? Is not *theōria* itself, as one possible response to the finitude of being, something historical, something "destined"? Although Heidegger had not yet fully developed his thinking of the "history of being," which would attempt to articulate the way in which philosophical thought too was always already determined and destined as a response to the finitude of being or presence itself, the Rectoral Address is already clearly thinking in this direction. This emerges in the appeal to science and knowledge to open itself resolutely to the Greek beginning that is still at work in the contemporary happening of science, despite the erosion of its essence, that is, of its relation to the beginning. Such an erosion is thus the absence of any genuinely rooted *praxis* of science, of a *praxis* of theoretical contemplation that would know and acknowledge its enrootedness in and indebtedness to ethico-political existence. To cultivate such knowledge and acknowledgement, science would have to become philosophical. And this is precisely the *primary* and central demand of Heidegger's Rectoral Address.

The Rectoral Address is primarily a *philosophical* address. Certainly, it is *also* political—yet it concerns *directly* only the "politics" of the university and of the university community. The politics of the state and of the "people" (*Volk*) are for the most part addressed only indirectly and secondarily. This is clear already from a survey of the main themes: science, knowledge, philosophy, teachers and faculty, academic departments, and students. It is clear also from the title of the speech that its immediate concern is the university, and not the state, people, or nation.

Within this perspective, the nature of the political intervention that the Address makes is equally clear: what is sought and called for is *a defense of the essence of the university.* This essence, as we have indicated, is science, knowledge, philosophy. The political community of the university must direct itself toward this essence, must learn to *ground* this essence and thereby to assert (*behaupten*) itself. But how? Through questioning, through openness, through uncertainty—in short, by facing the *future.* But the latter itself, insofar as we practice science, is determined by the beginning of philosophy. This call to face a future that is also an essential finitude, indeed the very happening of finitude, is manifest throughout the Rectoral Address. Thus, just following his recollection of the Greek essence of the philosophical *theōria,* Heidegger characterizes science as "the assuming of a questioning stance [*das fragende Standhalten*] in the midst of beings as a whole as they constantly conceal themselves. This persistence, as an acting, knows of its impotence in the face of fate" (SDU, 12). Such impotence, again, does not mean a giving in to fate, but precisely the opposite: a facing up to it, developing a knowing resistance (*Trotz:* SDU, 11) to it, a knowing self-assertion in the face of finitude. It means recognition and acknowledgement of limits that first come to be seen and appreciated as limits through the practice of *theōria*—albeit now that of a transformed *theōria*. In the face of the "death of God," of the collapse of the medieval measure of the world, abandoning man to the sway of beings themselves, science is called before a transformation. It is called upon to open itself to its own originary essence, which is neither simply that of the Greek beginning— which was a tarrying and holding out (*Ausharren*) before beings (thus, a kind of pre- or proto-philosophical *theōria*)[5] attuned by wonder—nor primarily the task of finding definitive answers toward which questioning is merely a means (as occurred in the subsequent philosophical domination of *theōria* over the more preliminary, thus supposedly lesser and incomplete practice of questioning), but of letting "questioning itself become the highest form of knowing." The Greek beginning itself would thereby become transformed "into an entirely unprotected exposure to that which is concealed and uncertain, that is, worthy of question" (SDU, 13). The activity and practice of science and the quest of knowledge in the Western tradition would expose itself to its own finitude and uncertainty as a practice, expose itself to the question of the "spiritual mission" (*geistiger Auftrag:* SDU, 9) of the university that can help, indirectly, to mold the broader fate of the German people.

In this call for a defense and self-assertion of the essence of the university as the site of a community devoted to knowing and questioning it is, of course, as the title of the Address indicates, the essence of the *German* university that is at stake. But how is "the German" to be defined? The German essence of the university, as the above considerations imply, can be determined only from out of its belonging to the history of the Western world as philosophical and scientific. It can be determined and asserted only in relation to the Greek essence of philosophy and science, and in a questioning confrontation with that Greek beginning. There is, therefore, no simple nationalism being asserted in the Rectoral Address, but rather the demand to "place ourselves under the power of the *beginning*," so as to first assert ourselves in an encounter with that beginning. What is first of all demanded is the acknowledgement of the foreign in one's own, and of the necessity of asserting oneself in relation to others. This conception of community as first founded by confrontation with others—and here by

---

[5] We shall discuss this sense of *theōria* in part 4.

a knowing confrontation, a struggle of knowledge and of its essence (an essence that, as noted, will no longer be simply Greek)—runs right through the Rectoral Address at every level.

But what is it that the essence of the German university is to be defended against? Clearly, it is not a matter of defending it against the Greek beginning as such—since the essence of the German university is itself primarily defined by the spirit of the Greek beginning, the quest for knowledge in the form of *theōria*. If anything, the task is to regain a proximity to and knowledge of the Greek beginning, so as first to enable a genuine questioning of its essence. The essence of the German university must be defended, rather, against the corruption and erosion of its (primarily Greek) essence, against the erosion of the essence of science that marks its contemporary state. The corruption and erosion that characterize the present state of knowledge at the university and pose an ongoing threat to its essence threaten from two directions.

On the one hand, from within the university itself, in the alienation of the individual sciences from their originary rootedness in philosophy—a fragmentation and dispersion in the form of specialization, which Heidegger had identified several years earlier, in his inaugural Freiburg Address to the university community, "What is Metaphysics?" (1929). One result of this remoteness from its philosophical origins is that the activity of science seems to be something that is simply "there," a discipline that one enters just as one enters any other trade, business, or profession, without a sense of any broader responsibility or of the implications of one's actions. And yet, as the Rectoral Address recalls, "It is never absolutely necessary that science should be" (SDU, 10). Science is itself historically determined. And if we fail to attend to its own historical origins in human *praxis,* if we fail to acknowledge that, as rooted in human *praxis,* it has the nature of a decision and a responsibility, of a struggle against (and thereby acknowledgement of) contingency, "it remains a contingency that we happen into, or the tranquil comfort of an innocent [*gefahrlosen*] occupation serving to promote a mere progress in [accumulating] pieces of knowledge [*Kenntnissen*]" (SDU, 13). This characterization no doubt describes the way in which Heidegger viewed the state of the German university at that time.[6] And its validity is hardly restricted to the German university of that historical period. Against this passive acceptance and perpetuation of an existing system alienated from its roots, which is to say, from any genuine reflection (*Besinnung*) on the ultimate meaningful context of its activities (the world of a historical community and its limits), the Rectoral Address advocates

---

[6] It is what Heidegger in his 1945 retrospect characterizes as the "old" order. See "Das Rektorat 1933/34: Tatsachen und Gedanken," SDU, 22–23; cf. 19.

that we "ply ourselves [*uns fügen*] in resolute openness" to the "distant prevailing [*Verfügung*]" of the Greek beginning, so as to retrieve a sense of its greatness and let science become our "innermost necessity" (SDU, 13). The call to assume a stance of resolute openness (*Entschlossenheit*) toward necessity here is, once again, not at all a call to passive acceptance or resignation in the face of destiny, but the advocation of a stance of questioning and openness toward that beginning which already "stands" in our future. It is the call to cultivate an explicit, knowing, and questioning acknowledgement of that historical necessity which still prevails over our practice as a community determined by science, and to assume individual responsibility for that practice.

This first threat to the essence of knowledge as the essence of the university comes from within the university itself. As such a threat, it was clearly well established before 1933, and had already been attacked by Heidegger in the inaugural Freiburg Address of 1929. Nor was it anything peculiarly German, but a symptom of the direction taken by the scientific world generally. The situation could be changed only if a younger generation of academics could be encouraged and persuaded to challenge the old order in its very foundations. But for Heidegger clearly this meant nothing other than beginning to philosophize, undertaking a philosophical "renewal" or "grounding" of the sciences. Developing a sense of *Entschlossenheit* toward one's situation demands a philosophical attitude (even if philosophy of itself can never directly bring this about, since it also requires individual self-assertion and commitment).[7]

The second threat is not altogether unrelated to the first, since (up to a point, in its general import) it is really a product of the latter, albeit at a historical distance. This second threat, which nevertheless presented itself in a historically and politically very specific form in 1933, now came from outside the university, from the state. It was the National Socialist attempt to impose its conception of "political science," a conception which, in sum, was the demand that science (and thus the university) should serve *directly* the state and the people. But, despite assurances that the university could continue to administer itself, this demand meant in effect nothing other than the attempt to make science politically useful, to make it subservient to the present state and to political ends.[8] Heidegger's defense

---

[7] Cf. the later remarks that teachers and students must come to be "gripped" or "seized" (*ergriffen*) by the concept (*Begriff*) of science "and *remain* gripped by it" (SDU, 17).

[8] The National Socialist doctrine of "political science," as Heidegger expresses it in the 1945 retrospect "Tatsachen und Gedanken," was proclaimed in the form of a crude version of Nietzsche's conception of the essence of truth and knowledge (SDU, 28); crudely speaking, it meant "What is true is what is useful to the people [*Volk*]" (SDU, 30).

of the essence of the German university is directed just as much, if not more, against this doctrine of "political science," even though the National Socialist doctrine is not named directly, but only alluded to. Prior to his discussion of the philosophical and Greek essence of scientific knowledge, Heidegger thus states that:

> We will never experience the essence of science in its inner-most necessity so long as—talking about the "new concept of science"—we merely dispute the independence and presuppo-sitionless character of an all too contemporary science. This merely negative activity, which scarcely looks back beyond the recent decades, becomes the sheer semblance of a true concern with the essence of science. (SDU, 10)

The "new concept of science," of a science whose independence and self-grounding validity are to be questioned, alludes precisely to the National Socialist conception of "political science," and Heidegger's resistance is clear.[9] In the course of the Address, his discussion of science which at-tempts to retrieve its originary essence and the nature of a questioning confrontation with that essence develops a conception of science that op-poses itself to the National Socialist view with the emphatic words "*This* science is meant.... *This* originary concept of science ..." (SDU, 16–17). The resistance to the politicized conception of science is discernable not only in these remarks, however. It is developed philosophically in the analysis of the originary essence of science as *theōria.* Heidegger's entire argument here appears as a defense of the need to maintain a certain independence of *theōria,* and thus of the essence of science, from political "praxis" out-side the university.[10] Yet this independence is not that of an absolute or "pure" independence of a *theōria* which, having taken its paradigmatic ori-gins from *technē,* then becomes oblivious to its own responsibilities to the world (SDU, 11). "Theory," for the Greeks, "does not occur for its own sake, but solely in a passion for remaining close to beings as such and under the urgency of their sway" (SDU, 12). But this passion for remaining close to

---

[9] In "Tatsachen und Gedanken," Heidegger states that the Rectoral Address contains a "decisive refusal of the idea of 'political science' propagated by National Socialism.... The dismissal of the idea of 'political science' is, moreover, clearly expressed in the Address" (SDU, 28).

[10] In the appeal to philosophizing as a genuine and originary knowing that would ground the sciences by disclosing their own proper ground, there lies, as Heidegger was to express it later, a meditation on the sciences in their entirety through which the university would "through itself bring itself onto the ground of its own essence, a ground accessible only to the knowledge [*Wissen*] cultivated by [the university] itself, which is why its essence cannot be determined from elsewhere, from the 'political' [*aus der "Politik"*] or from any other establishment of its purpose [*Zwecksetzung*]" (SDU, 29).

beings as such (i.e., as beings, in their being: the *on hēi on*) requires precisely the maintaining of a "theoretical" distance from the immediacies of politico-technical "praxis" in the present. Only this distance, this suspension of "practical," political and technical ends, grants *theōria* the space within which to develop its insights. Thus, the Greeks "did not intend to assimilate praxis to theory, but the opposite: to understand theory itself as the highest actualization of genuine praxis." The essence of *theōria* is corrupted whenever it itself is interpreted in an overly restricted, "theoretical" manner, according to a means—ends schema borrowed from *technē*, whereby either theory becomes a means whose insights can be usefully applied to *praxis* (taken in a narrower or broader sense), or *praxis* is itself demoted and regarded as a lesser form of theory. In the former case, theory becomes a "cultural asset" or "mere means" (SDU, 12); in the latter, it becomes altogether remote from worldly concerns and responsibilities. In each case, *theōria* as itself a *praxis* in its own right is concealed.

Theōria, therefore, according to the Rectoral Address, must not be seen as an end in itself, *if* by that one means a self-serving end, an activity occurring "for the sake of itself," as Heidegger puts it. Yet nor, above all, should it be regarded as a mere means in service of the state or the "political"; and knowledge (*Wissen*), as the philosophical essence of science, "does not stand in the service of the professional vocations" (SDU, 16). As itself a *praxis,* indeed (as Aristotle was to discover) the highest *praxis* or *energeia* of human existence, *theōria* is an "end in itself" only in the sense in which all genuine *praxis* is an end in itself, that is, in the sense of being a *finite* activity of human beings, intrinsically complete and meaningful in itself and not first finding its end in some extrinsic product or work. As finite in this manner, *theōria* does not escape the "supreme power of fate." But the Greeks themselves, Heidegger notes, "struggled" to grasp "and to accomplish" this (SDU, 12). It took them three centuries "even to bring the *question* of what knowledge is onto the right ground and into a secure path" (SDU, 18). And so we too, he adds, should not expect to illuminate the essence of the German university, the essence of knowledge, in the current or coming semester.

That *theōria* should therefore not be regarded as a mere means in service to the state or to "technical" ends does not, however, mean that it is a "useless" activity, or one of lesser importance. It means only that *praxis,* whether directly political *praxis* or the *praxis* of *theōria* itself, is much too fragile and too finite an undertaking to be ordered within a technical, means—ends schema. Far from being insignificant, *theōria* or *Wissenschaft* was, as Heidegger recalls, for the Greeks "the innermost determinative center of the entire existence of their state and people . . . that power which maintains the perspicacity of their entire existence and encompasses it" (SDU, 12).

As the leading institution of science and knowledge, the German university too could become "the center of the most rigorous coming together in the highest service of the people in their state [*zum höchsten Dienst am Volke in seinem Staat*]" (SDU, 18). Yet precisely because it concerns gaining a perspective on existence as a whole, *theōria* in its fundamental, philosophical sense cannot and should not be put in the service of particular ends if it is to remain philosophical, that is, genuinely grounded and foundational. Above all, a *theōria* that is philosophically rooted should not be made subservient to *contemporary* political *praxis* or government. Knowledge, *theōria,* is indeed to provide "spiritual" or intellectual leadership for the wider community and the state, but such leadership can at best be indirect, mediated by way of the free activity and *praxis* of questioning. It entails the maintaining of a distance from the present, so that the philosopher must cease to be his or her own contemporary. The proper activity and *praxis* of the philosopher is oriented toward the future, toward an indeterminate future, always yet to be decided—toward the opening up and cultivating of possibilities.

This has important ramifications. It means, first, that philosophizing, when undertaken in this manner that retains a proximity to the Greek beginning, is indeed a "political" activity, but that its "political" implications and import are not immediately manifest or tangible, since they flow from a kind of Nietzschean *actio in distans.* A philosophical retrieval of the Greek beginning entails plying oneself to the "remote" or "distant" prevailing (*die ferne Verfügung*) of this beginning (SDU, 13, 16). Philosophy loses its importance, its proper political role, if it aims at immediate political "effect." But second, this also means that philosophizing itself, since it does not occur in a vacuum or without a community of its own, requires a certain protection from the present, from present-day interests, political, economic, and technical. Yet how is such protection to come about? Does it not entail that philosophy must *also* become engaged politically in the present, at least to a minimal extent? If the political community or state is to shield philosophizing from the forces and demands of immediate interests and pressures, it must first recognize and acknowledge what philosophizing is, its role, its potential, and its limits. But how can the *polis* come to recognize this if it is not led to such recognition by philosophy itself? Does this not require that philosophy assert itself in what it is, the *self-assertion* of philosophizing? And does it not require continual reminder in this respect (since the memory of the *polis* is short, and what has been established by history remains fragile)? On the other hand, if the need for such self-assertion becomes overwhelming, if philosophy becomes over-politicized, then philosophy itself in its most proper vocation risks suffocation. What is said here concerning philosophy ought to extend also to the activity of science and to the university as a whole. But this is, of course, no longer the case when science as a whole has already become subservient to technicity and to the technical, economic, and political demands of the present. In such a situation, the threat to philosophizing, as an activity grounded in free questioning alone (and perhaps having no other immediate justification), is grave.

Seen in such a light—and it is a light that has become only harsher today, even if one must immediately acknowledge that the particular forces that lay siege to the university today are not irreducibly the same as in the Germany of 1933, and that the light of today is certainly not that of the Third Reich—Heidegger's appeal for "The Self-Assertion of the German University" can be seen as a defense of philosophical and intellectual freedom, a defense grounded in a resolute openness of questioning bound to a responsibility toward the historical origins of Western thought, which is to say, a responsibility toward the future in its entire uncertainty and fragility. And it is in this and in this alone that the university, grounded in philosophizing, "serves" the broader community and its political direction. On this basis, we can well understand why this "supreme service" to the people and its state is, from the perspective of the contemporary political reality and of ordinary understanding, a rather dubious and unsettling service. A genuine will to question the essence of science, Heidegger emphasizes, "in the sense of the *assuming of a questioning, unprotected stance in the midst of the uncertainty of beings as a whole* . . . first creates for our people its world of innermost and outermost danger, that is, its truly *spiritual* [geistige] world." Such a "spiritual" or intellectual world means a world of knowing and resolute openness; for, Heidegger adds, "spirit is originarily attuned, knowing and resolute openness [*wissende Entschlossenheit*] toward the essence of being." Thus the community of teachers too must come to occupy "the most extreme outposts of danger amid the continual uncertainty of the world" (SDU, 14). The highest and most essential knowledge that the leading vocations of "statesman and teacher, doctor and judge, pastor and builder" call for, and to which they remain responsible (they "give rise to and administer" (*erwirken und verwalten*) such knowledge, as Heidegger puts it rhetorically, although, as noted, he states clearly that such knowledge "does not stand in the service of" these professional vocations), is itself "the most acute endangering of existence [*Dasein*] amid the supreme power [*Übermacht*] of beings" (SDU, 16). The essence of the German university, as an engaged community of scholars, being to create an extreme danger and uncertainty by a stance of open questioning, to open the intellectual leaders of the community to the questionability of the future—one can imagine how this was received by officials of the Party.

The Rectoral Address thus appears as a defense of the philosophical essence of the German university, a defense against internal conservatism and laisser-faire and, perhaps even more urgent, against external pressures from the state. It is not an attempt to have the philosophers rule the *polis,* in accordance with one prevalent reading of Plato's *Republic,* at least not if by that one understands that philosophers as such should have an immediate or direct political "effect" in the *polis,* or themselves occupy positions of political power. But this was a reading of the *Republic* that Heidegger had already dismissed.[11] The "politics" of the Rectoral Address are in this sense primarily confined to those of the German university; it is here that Heidegger's own direct political involvement plays itself out. The essence of the university is to be defended in its own proper essence, not asserted as the dominant political force in the state. And yet, as noted, the self-assertion of the German university, as a self-assertion of the philosophical essence of science and knowledge, entails that the university community itself assert itself against and in relation to the contemporary political pressures and demands coming from the state. The gesture of self-assertion on which the essence of the university depends is thus called for in the Address at three different levels: (1) at the level of the essence of *philosophizing* itself as a *praxis* of essential knowing whereby human beings assert themselves in the midst of the overwhelming power of beings as a whole; (2) in relation to the *state,* as the self-assertion of the *university community* of scholars; (3) *within* this self-assertion of the scholarly community, as first enabling it, the process of *mutual self-assertion among students and teachers* within the university.

Before briefly examining the three different levels at which self-assertion is advocated, let us note that the Rectoral Address speaks in all three of these directions at one and the same time. And this complexity also means that one should not read the Address as either purely philosophical or purely political, and that one must be sensitive to these different registers and to the way in which they are strategically articulated. Even if the content of the speech is primarily that of a philosophical argument, its rhetoric and style are thus not only philosophical, but also political, and directed at

---

[11] In the lecture course of winter semester 1931/32 on Plato's *Republic* and *Theaetetus,* Heidegger interprets the argument of the *Republic* as meaning that the guardians of human community in the *polis* must be philosophical human beings. This, he adds, does not mean that "philosophy professors are to become *Reichskanzlers,* but that philosophers are to be *phulakes,* guardians" (GA 34, 100). Those who govern the state should be philosophically guided. Ten years later, Heidegger would reiterate the point, while distancing the classical, "tragic" essence of the *polis* from both the Platonic and Aristotelian perspectives and from the National Socialist doctrine of the unconditional priority of the political. Although his characterization of the "historical uniqueness" of National Socialism is ambiguous, and presumably once more for essentially political reasons, his emphatic distancing of the greatness of the Greek *polis* from the contemporary concern with "the political" is clearly a critique not only of National Socialist "politics," but of the politics of modernity in its entirety. See GA 53, 105–06, 117–18.

political forces both within and outside of the university. Thus we find also the regimental style that has often been noted, as well as the less palatable rhetoric of "earth and blood," which, along with the talk of the march of the *Volk,* the will, *Kampf,* and fate, cannot be reduced to a purely philosophical register. Such ambiguity between philosophical content and the political style of the day is essential to the political pretensions of the Address. And although the philosophico-political resistance of the speech must have been evident to Party representatives (as Heidegger in "Tatsachen und Gedanken" claims it was), one can be fairly certain that neither they nor the rest of the audience would have been able to clearly discern the philosophical details of this resistance. The direction of Heidegger's persuasion is clear: an affirmation of the occasion and opportunity. But its reservations and hesitations, its tentative character, are no less evident—so much so that, as a *political* address, it could only be considered (as it apparently was by the Reichsminister Wacker, at least according to Heidegger's report) as absurd: a kind of "private" or apolitical National Socialism (SDU, 30–31). One does not give a political address couched in such heavily philosophical obscurities.

In the Rectoral Address, the theme of self-assertion is carried at all three levels by the philosophical conception of "struggle" (*Kampf*).[12] But one must be cautious about seeking to interpret the parameters of such struggle in terms of modern subjectivity, despite the fact that the rhetoric of the "will" and of self-legislation might seem to reinforce such an interpretation of self-assertion.[13] The concrete analyses of "struggle" at each of the

---

[12] In "Tatsachen und Gedanken," Heidegger insists that the notion of *Kampf* appealed to in the Address is that of Heraclitean *polemos* or *Auseinandersetzung.* Its essence lies in those who are engaged in such confrontational encounter first "exposing themselves to the other and thus showing themselves and coming to appear"; it lies "in *deiknunai,* showing and *poiein,* setting-forth: in Greek terms, setting something forth into the openness of its look [*in den offenen Anblick*]." The essential import of the reflection thus "goes back to the Greek *epistēmē,* and that means, to *alētheia*" (SDU, 28–29). For knowing, in the sense of *epistēmē,* is precisely this struggle with that which shows itself, the struggle to let it stand and bring it to stand before us in the openness of its look.

[13] The temptation to such readings is especially great since many commentators have proceeded from the outset with the intention of seeking in the Rectoral Address a philosophical "shortcoming" that would "explain" what is all too easily and reductively circumscribed as Heidegger's "political error." (If there was error—as Heidegger himself conceded there was—it was certainly not just a *single* error, but part of an entire nexus of actions undertaken within a complex and dynamic situational context.) Yet a close reading of the Rectoral Address shows that even what appears, at first sight, to be an explicitly Kantian formulation of autonomy ("To give oneself the law is supreme freedom": SDU, 15) is far from being the purely formal law of the Kantian will. The law of the freedom formulated here with regard to the student community, as Heidegger immediately specifies, finds its truth in the students first subjecting themselves to, and (through *Arbeitsdienst,* "labor service") participating in, a historical community existing

three levels named seems, rather, to forcefully resist a modern or subjective notion of self-assertion. (1) At the level of essential knowledge, as we have seen, the *praxis* of philosophizing must assume a questioning stance in the face of the self-concealment of beings as a whole, thereby acknowledging its own limits and first coming to itself, asserting itself, through such an encounter with other beings. The assertion of knowledge "itself" is an experience of the finitude of the *praxis* of philosophizing in the face of the finite self-disclosure of beings as a whole. The precondition of such a knowing experience is the openness of a questioning stance. Thus, the self-assertion of such knowing is this struggle in which "questioning itself becomes the highest form of knowing" (SDU, 13). "We choose the knowing struggle of those who question," asserts Heidegger, citing Clausewitz (SDU, 18). (2) Second, the relation of struggle between the university and the state is articulated by the resistance we have noted to any straightforward subservience of either one to the other. Without a recognition and acknowledgement of the finitude of the other, each is threatened in its essence. Each is bound by a responsibility to the other, but such responsibility can be open to the other only in and through mutual self-assertion. (3) Third, such self-assertion, as grounded in struggle, is most explicitly elucidated by Heidegger in relation to the issue of the university itself. The community of teachers and students is itself conceived as a community of struggle where each individual, asserting themselves through the openness of philosophical questioning, has already entered into a relation with others whose mutual, explicit, and knowing acknowledgement is based upon this common openness to a spiritual world. "All abilities of the will and of thought, all strengths of the heart, and all capacities of the body must be unfolded *through* struggle, be intensified *in* struggle, and remain preserved *as* struggle" (SDU, 18–19).

Nowhere here can self-assertion be conceived as an assertion of a priority of the self (of the individual, of the university, or of philosophy itself) over others. Furthermore, the relation to self is in no case grounded in knowledge alone, but in an acknowledgement of finitude and irreducibility. Nor, finally, can struggle or *Kampf* in any of these cases be conceived as the advocation of sheer aggression. The role of the university community as providing "spiritual legislation" to "the people" and to the state can at best be one of *Führung* as *leadership and guidance,* and not as command.[14]

---

as a political entity in the midst of other communities (thus requiring *Wehrdienst,* "military service") and having its existence at stake in being exposed to the questionability and fragility of a historical world (calling for guidance via *Wissensdienst,* ultimately via philosophical insight). In each case, an exposure to otherness precedes and binds the freedom of *Entschlossenheit.*

[14] Note that this is precisely the relation between *theōria* and ethico-political *praxis* as conceived by Aristotle: philosophy or *sophia* guides, but *phronēsis* gives the command.

What Heidegger states toward the end of the Address concerning leadership is pertinent not only for the "spiritual leadership" to be provided by the Rector within the university (SDU, 9), but for each of the three levels of struggle we have noted: "All leadership [*Führung*] must concede to its following [*Gefolgschaft*] its own independent force. But every following bears resistance within it. This essential opposition within leadership and following may neither be swept aside nor extinguished" (SDU, 18). Likewise, what he adds concerning "struggle" with respect to the body of teachers and students is relevant to each of the three levels: "Struggle alone holds open opposition and plants ...that fundamental attunement from out of which a self-limiting self-assertion empowers a resolutely open self-reflection to genuine self-administration" (SDU, 19). Thus conceived, self-assertion is precisely a *self-limiting* self-assertion, which does not mean that it first sets or posits its own limits, but that it acknowledges its own limits in the face of opposition and alterity. The "will" to a self-assertion of the German university as "the will to *Wissenschaft*" is not a will that originates its own activity, but one that is intrinsically bound to, and first arises through a historical community of others, a community guided by the Western tradition of knowledge: here, the German people (SDU, 10). The "will" at stake is a creative will which, through the will to essential knowing, participates historically in "creating" the "spiritual world" of a community. It thereby alerts us to the "most extreme danger" of community, the "continual uncertainty of the world" (SDU, 14).

Early in the Rectoral Address, Heidegger appealed to the university community to face a decisive question, a question calling for decision: "Is science to continue to *be* for us henceforth, or should we let it drive on toward its rapid end?" (SDU, 10). The Rectoral Address was an attempt to persuade the university community to ground the being of science and knowledge, and thereby its own being as a community of scholars, by opening itself to a philosophical questioning of being in the uncertainty and fragility of its historically rooted provenance. Heidegger's early recognition of the failure of this endeavor, if not yet of the necessity of this failure, was a recognition that the supposedly leading intellectuals of this particular Western community were unable or unwilling to open themselves to the question of "Western responsibility" (as Heidegger later put it) (SDU, 28). That is, they were unwilling or unable to question the activity of science itself as already determinative of their existence within the larger context of the Western world, and on this basis to mount a resistance to the political and intellectual pressures of the present. But this was not simply a lack of will or of ability on the part of the university community. Nor did Heidegger's failure leave only the recourse of letting science rush toward its own end in the sense of its own demise. For the end of science itself had already been overtaken by another end: that of modern technology, whose essence Heidegger had yet to fully recognize. In the 1945 "Tatsachen und Gedanken," Heidegger conceded precisely this:

> The case of the Rectorship of 1933/34, insignificant in itself, is presumably a symptom of the metaphysical predicament of the essence of science, which can no longer be affected by attempts at its renewal or halted from a transformation of its essence into pure technicity. I learned to recognize this only in the following years. (Cf. "The Grounding of the Modern World Picture by Metaphysics.") The Rectorship was an attempt to see in the "movement" that had come to power, over and above all its shortcomings and vulgarities, something far-reaching that could one day bring about a gathering with respect to the historical and Western essence of the German. In no way should it be denied that at that time I believed in such possibilities and to this end renounced the most proper vocation of thinking in favor of an intervention in office [*eines amtlichen Wirkens*]. In no way should what caused my own shortcomings in office be diminished. Yet such perspectives do not pinpoint what was essential in persuading me to assume office. (SDU, 39)

"What was essential" was a *philosophical* perspective on the historical determination of being in the Western world (which Heidegger here proceeds to specify in terms of the consummation of nihilism and the death of God). What Heidegger at the time of his political intervention had yet to fully recognize, however, was not only the already technological essence of modern science, but that to expect any decisive intervention to be achievable *philosophically* risks concealing the necessary distance of philosophizing from its own time, its own present. Philosophizing itself as a *praxis* is too fragile, all too finite an activity, for it to be capable on its own of determining or governing a present age—and particularly an age governed by the essence of technology. In his lecture course of 1934/35 on Hölderlin, Heidegger was to encounter in Hölderlin's poem "To the Germans" a timely reminder of the distance of essential thinking and poetizing from its own time, in the words with which he would later conclude the essay alluded to here (published as "The Age of the World Picture"):

Wohl ist enge begränzt unsere Lebenszeit,
Unserer Jahre Zahl sehen und zählen wir,
Doch die Jahre der Völker,
Sah ein sterbliches Auge sie?

Wenn die Seele dir auch über die eigne Zeit
Sich die sehnende schwingt, trauernd verweilst du
Dann am kalten Gestade
Bei den Deinen und kennst sie nie.

Our lifetime indeed is narrowly spanned,
We see and count the numbers of our years,
Yet the years of the peoples,
Did ever a mortal eye see them?

If your soul too beyond your own time
Transports you in its longing, mournfully you tarry
Then on the cold shores
Alongside your own and never know them.[15]

---

[15] Concluding verses of Hölderlin's poem "To the Germans" which provide the hinge
of Heidegger's first sustained interpretation of Hölderlin and the question of poetic time.
See GA 39, 49–50.

Part II

The Transformation of Theoria

We, late born, are no longer in a position to appreciate the significance of the fact that Plato ventures to use the word *eidos* for that which endures as present in each and every thing. (VA, 24)

What if *Ereignis*—no one knows when or how— became an *in-sight* [Ein-blick] whose lightning flash reached into that which is and is regarded as being? What if, through its turning in, *Ereignis* were to remove all that presences from mere orderability and return it to what is proper to it? (US, 264)

Chapter 6

Technovision: Modern Science and Technology

Our earlier examination of Heidegger's attempt to provide an existential or ontological account of the genesis of theoretical comportment, as opposed to the story of a "natural" genesis as narrated by Aristotle, led us to conclude that the radicalization of the grounds and foundations of ontology in the direction of ecstatic-horizonal temporality pointed repeatedly to the phenomena of absence, withdrawal of ground, and mortality. In particular, the Temporal analysis of being appeared unable to account for the emergence and establishment of the theoretical attitude as a new historical phenomenon. Indeed, the very attempt to provide an account or *logos* of the genesis of this new vision of things appears to remain ensconced within the theoretical attitude by virtue of its desire to explain, to account for, or to render "logical" grounds. This desire, we argued, was reflected in the conception of phenomenology as a *science* of being, with its accompanying ideal of theoretical transparency—an ideal stretching back, via the Cartesian insistence upon clarity, distinctness, and the immediate transparency of the *ego cogito, ergo sum,* to the Aristotelian interpretation of being as actuality (*energeia*) and Plato's vision of being as *idea.* All of which, according to Heidegger's interpretations, reflect an underlying desire for presence. Yet we also tried to show how those very phenomena marking the transgression of temporal horizons in the analytic of Dasein mean that the project of *Being and Time* cannot be confined to the guiding ideals of a theoretical enterprise. The radicality of the analysis of Dasein's ecstatic understanding of being is such as to explode any conception of Dasein as an already existing transcendental subject that would first project its own understanding of being in a projection that could be made theoretically

161

present to it in a relation of thematic, representational transparency. The ecstatic-temporal analysis of the very possibility of understanding being as presence shows that while being is indeed predominantly apprehended as presence, that presence is not the self-presence that marks the subjectivity of the historically specific, thinking subject (the *res cogitans*). Our being shows itself to be irreducible to the presence of thought or *cogitationes;* the "futural" projection of being exceeds the projective activity of any subject. This does not mean, as many readings of the later Heidegger would suggest, that Dasein or the essence of the human being is thereby reduced to a role of pure passivity in the face of what Heidegger calls a "destinal" unfolding of being, an unfolding in which it would not participate (according to such readings) except as passive or receptive, "subject" only as subjected to the "destinings" of being itself. Initially, it means only that the finitude of Dasein is more radical than any metaphysical or foundational account could contemplate.

In chapter 4 we tried to show how such finitude, which tends to be occluded by theoretical comportment insofar as the latter seeks the objectification of beings (positive science) or of being itself (philosophy as ontology, as metaphysics), is originarily manifest in Dasein as *praxis*. Heidegger's early work, animated in particular by a retrieval and radicalization of Aristotle, shows how this inevitable finitude of originary *praxis* permeates not only the *theōria* of the Aristotelian contemplation of being, but also the theoretical attitude and scientific aspirations of modern philosophy, most evident in Husserlian phenomenology and its rootedness in the primacy of pure intuition. This modern *theōria*, oriented toward noetic self-consciousness as transcendental subjectivity (Husserl) or as historical subjectivity (Hegel), is at once continuous with, and different from, the *theōria* of Aristotelian *epistēmē*, which was characterized by an "intuitive" beholding and apprehending of beings in their truth without any self-reflection on its own "method." Yet the primacy of method—the very need for which is itself a mark of the underlying insecurity, instability, and finitude of modern consciousness—comes to the fore not only in the phenomenological, scientific, and dialectical method found in modern philosophy wherever the latter withdraws from or brackets out the world in withdrawing into the absolute interiority of subjectivity (Heidegger's early phenomenology, as we have suggested, is a somewhat different case); it is also foundational for the contemporary, worldly reality of theoretical comportment as embodied in modern science and technology.

The insights that develop out of Heidegger's early phenomenology itself, coupled with his continued attempts to address and to intervene in the predicament of modern science at the university thus lead Heidegger, by the mid-1930s, to explicitly concede two essential points with regard to philosophical reflection on the essence of science. These points are made most succinctly in the *Beiträge zur Philosophie* (1936–38). First, concerning attempts to lay the ground or foundations of science, that is, to thematically and theoretically account for the activity of science as such, Heidegger concedes that:

> Every kind of theoretico-scientific (transcendental) attempt to lay the ground has become just as impossible as the attempt to "confer a meaning" that attributes to an already existing science (thus one that in its substantive essence cannot be altered) and to its activity the political purpose of serving the *Volk,* or any other anthropological purpose. These attempts at "grounding" have become impossible, because they already presuppose "science" [*"die Wissenschaft"*] and then merely provide it with a "ground" (that is no ground) and a meaning (that lacks meaningful reflection). (GA 65, 142)

Both the attempt at a theoretical-scientific or transcendental grounding of theoretical activity and the attempt to confer an extrinsic meaning or "ground" to scientific comportment have become impossible for the same fundamental reason: they both conceal the dimension of *praxis* in which theoretical activity is rooted. Philosophical questioning into the truth of being (*Seyn*) is thereby "excluded from the realm of action [*Handeln*]," from the realm of its own historicality (GA 65, 142). Heidegger here problematizes not only the Kantian and phenomenological transcendental attempts at grounding; the citation of "science" in the singular, in the absolute (*die* Wissenschaft) also implicates Hegel's *Wissenschaft* (as well, of course, as the contemporary appeal to science "itself" as such). Even the speculative self-knowledge of Hegel's historical Spirit would not attain the originary dimension of historicality; it would remain enclosed within a theoreticospeculative determination of thinking.

The second point made by Heidegger is indeed a correlate of this first concession:

> Meaningful reflection on *"die Wissenschaft"* ...must free this term from the historical indeterminacy of arbitrarily equating it with *epistēmē, scientia, science,* and must ascertain it with respect to the modern essence of *Wissenschaft.* (GA 65, 142)

The concept of science and of "theoretical comportment" must therefore also be freed from the historical indeterminacy with which these terms were used in Heidegger's own phenomenological analyses in *Being and Time.* As with the first point, Heidegger's critique is also a self-critique. Finally, a

third point that Heidegger adds in this context also relates to the experience of his own attempted confrontation with science: Modern science, as a
degenerate form and mere semblance of genuine *Wissen,* must be pursued
right into the institutional procedures and establishments that belong to its
essence, such as, he adds, the contemporary "university" (GA 65, 142–43).[1]

Thus far our inquiry has focused firstly on *theōria* in its Aristotelian
form, concentrating on its complex relation to *praxis,* and secondly, on
"theoretical comportment," the theoretical stance as analysed in *Being
and Time.* The analysis of theoretical comportment provided in *Being and
Time,* however, did not examine at any great length the deployment of such
comportment in its modern, scientific guise, but was content to provide a
preliminary sketch of the foundations of the scientific attitude, one that
could in principle apply either to the special sciences, or to phenomenology
itself still conceived in the Husserlian style as a "science of being." *Being
and Time,* rather, had the primary aim of demonstrating the rootedness of
theoretical comportment in the being of Dasein as care—which, we argued,
could be understood as *praxis* in an originary sense—and of tracing the
genesis of theory back to its problematic temporal horizons. These analyses
of *Being and Time* retain their validity inasmuch as theoretical seeing in
general has the primary sense of bringing something before us and letting it
lie before us in its (supposedly) pure presence. Yet such presence itself will
be modified in accordance with how the *comportment* underlying the theoretical attitude is modified, that is, in accordance with the way in which
theōria is integrated into *praxis* and interacts with *technē.* Not only do the
perspectives in which we see the object change depending on our interpretation (for example, are we seeing the object in terms of its fundamental
ontological features—substantiality, accidents, etc.—or are we seeing it as
something that is to be made into something else?); the *activity* of seeing
is also modified in accordance with the primary "projection" that determines it in advance. The activity of seeing and the perspectives it opens up
are subject to transformation, and such transformation means that *theōria*

---

[1] The word "university" is placed in quotation marks by Heidegger. The ensuing sections of the *Beiträge* provide an incisive critique of the contemporary essence of science
in terms of its institutions and procedures, while contentiously denying genuine philosophy any place or role at the modern university. Heidegger (in §75) emphasizes the
untimeliness of the attempt at reflection on the historical essence of science made in his
Rectoral Address, acknowledging the futility of any hope of "immediately" or directly
achieving a decisive intervention in the present. But this acknowledgement, far from leading Heidegger to seek refuge in an intensified preoccupation with antiquity, increasingly
remote from contemporary reality, precisely provokes a turn to examining the essence
of science in the present more closely and more attentively. Knowledge of the contemporary institutional and technological essence of science is a necessary "counterpart" to
knowledge of the historical essence of science. A radically historical, genealogical critique
of the present requires these "two ways" (GA 65, 144).

itself is intrinsically historical. The *theōria* of Aristotle is at once continuous with and yet different from the representational *theōria* of Cartesian science, which is different again from the technological transformation of representation.

The task of the present chapter is to investigate the transformation of *theōria* that has issued in the modern "theory of the real" propounded by representational thinking in its technological mutation. Modern science and technology are not related to one another as "theory" and "praxis"; technology is not just the "practical application" of a "scientific theory" of reality. Rather, Heidegger's analyses argue that modern science and technology share a pervasive, unitary trait that he terms *Gestell*, "enframing." The present chapter tries to make visible this unitary trait as a highly specific and peculiar transformation of the desire to see. From the perspective of Heidegger's early meditations, it can be seen that this phenomenon is nothing other than a particular configuration and transformation of *theōria, praxis,* and *technē:* as a form of knowledge, it embodies a specific kind of *theōria;* as desire, it embodies the being underway toward ...that characterizes human *praxis* (only now directed toward the infinite, impossible goal of the "will to will"); as productive, it is a highly regulated form of *technē.* What we shall try to make manifest here is the specific dynamic of desire that this configuration as a whole presents. In addition, we hope to show that Heidegger's apparent focus on the third of these moments, on technology as a specific form of revealing or *technē,* does not contribute to the "oblivion of *praxis,*" as some have charged.[2] Rather, by emphasizing the *conformity* of human activity to the "will to will"—a conformity that (among other things) erases any essential plurality—Heidegger's analyses show how technology itself points toward the finitude of originary *praxis* as that which is refused or concealed.

In addition to examining the intrinsic dynamic of technology as a modern transformation of the desire to see, the present chapter also argues against certain prevalent readings of Heidegger's interpretation of technology as the culmination (*Vollendung*) of metaphysics, namely, those readings that regard metaphysics, and by extension technology, as embodying the desire for presence. Paradoxically, as we shall show—and this is the very paradox of technology itself—modern technology is nothing other than a desire for absence (albeit a highly specific configuration thereof), a withdrawal from the temporality of the world and its finitude. The problem or paradox of technology is not a desire for presence, but its very flight from any worldly presence.

---

[2] See Dana Villa, *Arendt and Heidegger,* chapter 7.

The Age of the World Picture

The 1938 lecture published as "The Age of the World Picture"[3] and originally delivered under the title "The Grounding of the Modern World Picture
by Metaphysics"[4] attempts to understand the metaphysical grounds that
enable the emergence of the distinctive epoch of modernity. In metaphysics,
Heidegger claims, there occurs both a reflection (*Besinnung*) on the essence
of beings, and a decision (*Entscheidung*) concerning the essence of truth.
Metaphysics reflects upon and grounds that which truly is. In projecting
beings in their ground and truth, in stipulating what things truly are and
how they are to be, metaphysical reflection determines the being of beings in advance and thereby also marks *time;* it determines a certain time:
the time of an era, of an epoch or age, the time during which beings will
be understood in this particular way. Metaphysical reflection attempts to
determine time itself:

> Metaphysics grounds an era in providing it with the ground of
> its essential configuration by way of a particular interpretation
> of beings and through a particular conception of truth. This
> ground governs and permeates all appearances that distinguish
> the era. (H, 69)

Through sufficient reflection on the phenomena of the era, Heidegger asserts, we must come to know and recognize this underlying ground.

Heidegger lists several characteristic manifestations of the contemporary
era, but limits his essay to inquiring into the essence of modern science, with
the intent of discovering its metaphysical ground and thereby the essence
of modernity. Modern science is characterized by exactitude, and as such
is something fundamentally different from medieval *doctrina* and *scientia,*
but also from Greek *epistēmē*. More precisely, Heidegger claims that these
are "essentially" different, different in essence. This should not be taken
to mean that there is no connection between, say, Greek *epistēmē* and
modern science.[5] Initially, it is merely a precaution, intended to resist the
temptation to claim that modern science is more "correct" or "precise" than
Greek *epistēmē*. It is meant to guard against our habit "of comparing the
new science with the old solely in terms of degree, from the point of view of
progress" (H, 71). In other words, there is a resistance on Heidegger's part
to understanding modern science in terms of any explanatory or causal
model of history that would simply explain the emergence and current

---

[3] *Die Zeit des Weltbildes,* literally "The Time of the World Picture."

[4] *Die Begründung des neuzeitlichen Weltbildes durch die Metaphysik.* Referred to at
SDU, 39: see our concluding remarks in chapter 5.

[5] See GA 65, §76, no. 1.

dominance of the modern in terms of the past, or that would encourage definitive qualitative or quantitative judgments on the present with regard to the past, or on the past from the perspective of the present.

Heidegger follows this caution with an assertion: "The essence of what we today call science is research." And in what does the essence of research consist? "In the fact that cognitive knowledge [*das Erkennen*] establishes itself as a way of proceeding [*als Vorgehen*] within some realm of beings, in nature or in history" (H, 71). Research thus refers not to a kind of knowledge as such, but to the fact *that* a particular kind of knowledge—cognitive knowledge, *Erkennen*—becomes the primary manner of human comportment toward what is, the primary way in which human beings "proceed" or move forward among beings. Heidegger explains that "procedure" here does not refer primarily to method or methodology; the latter is possible only within a realm of beings that already lie open or manifest before us. Rather, by "procedure" Heidegger is referring to this more fundamental "opening up" of a particular realm in a particular way. With respect to nature, for example, such procedure occurs in a determinate, prior projection (*Entwurf*) of a fundamental outline or framework (*Grundriß*) of natural processes. It is this projection that also prefigures the way in which cognitive procedure must bind itself to the realm of beings thus opened up. In other words, a prior understanding of what and how particular regions of beings are must guide the way in which our knowledge has to proceed in approaching such beings. This "approach" or "binding" is prior to the concrete methodological procedures of discovery; it constitutes the specific *rigor* of research, whose modern character is exactitude.

Heidegger elucidates this further by recourse to the Greek conception of the mathematical, *ta mathēmata,* which in a key respect provided the model for modern mathematical science. For the Greeks, the mathematical is to be taken in the broad sense, as referring to that which is always already familiar and known about beings in advance. Number is merely one instance of the mathematical, but does not exhaust it. A profound continuity is manifest between the Greek interpretation of mathematical knowledge and modern science, in that something is posited in advance as already known. Such positing or projecting in advance constitutes the basis or ground upon which the concrete investigations of modern scientific research can proceed. Heidegger illustrates this using the example of modern mathematical physics:

> If, therefore, physics takes shape explicitly as something mathematical, this means that, in an especially pronounced way, through it and for it something is stipulated in advance as what is already known. That stipulating has to do with nothing

less than the plan or projection of that which must henceforth, for the sought-after knowledge of nature, *be* nature: the self-contained system of motion of units of mass related spatio-temporally. (H, 72)

This prior stipulation is the projection of the fundamental framework in terms of which every natural process is seen in such a way as to be fitted into it in advance, so that it first becomes visible in terms of such a perspective. Thus, the fundamental and grounding procedure to be found in research is not simply the fact that beings are discovered, or that scientific research is a process of discovery (for all human comportment is, in Heidegger's view, a kind of discovery, an uncovering of beings, in which process human beings can be active to a greater or lesser extent); rather, the fundamental "procedure" at stake is the particular *way* in which beings are approached in advance, projected in respect of their ontological domain which constitutes or stipulates what and how they are, their very being.

The phenomenon of projection and the rigor pertaining to it together constitute the first essential element of research. A second essential element is methodological procedure (*Verfahren*), in which projection and rigor are unfolded. With the aim of achieving objective results and facts, methodology proceeds in terms of rules and laws, explanation, investigation, and experiment. A third fundamental feature of modern science is industriousness (*Betrieb*), through which the sciences become institutionalized and increasingly specialized. Together, the phenomena of projection and rigor, methodology, and industriousness "constitute the essence of modern science, transform it into research." (H, 80)

Yet does projection then comprise the ultimate grounding procedure of research that enables us to understand its essence or unitary trait, leading us to the essence of modernity? Such projection not only precedes, but is also already part of, a process of differentiation, unfolding itself in unison with industriousness and methodological procedure. The "opening up" that occurs in the projection of specific domains of beings does not yet let us understand what such opening up is as a phenomenon in its historical uniqueness: it does not yet let us understand what is historically distinctive about such an event. The essence of research does not consist in the explicit projection of particular domains that are understood in advance. Rather it consists primarily "in cognitive knowledge establishing itself as a way of proceeding. . . ." In other words, it is the specific way in which discovery is itself understood or "projected" in advance that constitutes the fundamental "opening up" at the basis of modern scientific research. An attempt to comprehend the essence of research must therefore address the question of the essence of knowledge and its role in the era of modernity.

Having diverted the inquiry into an examination of the unfolding and differentiation of research, Heidegger's essay now returns to its primary focus, namely, to inquire into the metaphysical ground of modern science. This entails inquiring into the configuration of knowledge (*Erkennen*) that first grounds research: "What conception of beings, and what concept of truth, ground the fact that science becomes research?" (H, 80). The answer, in short, is truth conceived as representation (*vor-stellen*), in which beings are objectified and secured in their objectivity for the human being as knowing subject.[6] Science (as a form of knowledge that can be traced back to Aristotelian *epistēmē*) can *become* research, argues Heidegger, only when the essence of truth has been transformed into certainty of representation—a move that can first be identified in Descartes' *Meditations on First Philosophy* as an inquiry that radically transforms the Aristotelian conception of *prōtē philosophia.*

If science as research is an *essential* phenomenon of modernity, then whatever constitutes the metaphysical ground of research must, "beforehand and far in advance," determine the essence of modernity (H, 80). The essence of modernity, Heidegger notes, is often regarded as a liberation of human knowledge from the medieval doctrines of scholasticism, a self-liberation of the human being as subject. The human being's becoming subject and the attendant rise of individualism, however, go hand in hand with a growing objectivism in which the objectivity of world events seems ever farther removed from any individual viewpoint, or indeed any possibility of meaningful intervention on the part of the individual subject. Heidegger claims that what is essential in this interplay and reciprocal conditioning of subjectivity and objectivity goes back to "events more profound" (H, 81). What is essential is not a liberation, but a *transformation* of the human essence. To think through the transformation of human beings into "subjects" (from the Latin *subiectum*), Heidegger asks us to consider the notion of *subject* as a translation of the Greek *hupokeimenon*, meaning "that which lies before, that which, as ground, gathers everything upon itself" (H, 81). This meaning of "subject" has no necessary or intrinsic connection to human beings. By contrast, when human beings become subjects, they assume the role of *subiectum:* they become those beings upon which all other entities are grounded in their being and truth. Humans become the "relational center" of beings as such.

Yet what underlies such a transformation? How is it possible? Heidegger does not attempt to pose the question in this explanatory manner, but asks: "In what does this transformation manifest itself? What, accordingly, is the

---

[6] The German *vorstellen,* particularly when hyphenated, suggests the literal sense of setting or placing something before us.

essence of the modern age?" (H, 81). Heidegger characterizes the modern era
as the age of the "world picture" (*Weltbild*), where "world" refers to beings
as a whole in relation to their ground, and "picture" means, not a copy
or imitation, but the way in which the world is set before us as something
familiar and ready to be acted upon. The "world picture" comprises the
modern configuration of the being of beings:

> Hence world picture, understood essentially, does not mean a
> picture of the world, but the world conceived and grasped as
> a picture. Beings as a whole are now taken in such a way that
> they first are beings if and only if they are set up by humans,
> who represent and produce them.[7] Wherever we have the world
> picture, an essential decision takes place regarding beings as a
> whole. The being of beings is sought and found in the repre-
> sentedness [*Vorgestelltheit*] of beings. (H, 82–83)

The underlying interpretation of the being of beings as representedness
is thoroughly characteristic of the modern era. So much so, Heidegger insists, that it is wholly misleading to speak of a medieval or ancient "world
picture." Previous eras did not have a world picture at all, since beings as a
whole were not understood as objectively set before the subjectivity of the
human subject for human representation. Heidegger briefly contrasts the
modern understanding of the being of beings with that of the Middle Ages
and of Presocratic antiquity. In the medieval period, beings are understood
as *ens creatum,* created by God, and allotted their being in terms of the
extent of their correspondence (*analogia entis*) to the creator. The interpretation of beings in Greek antiquity is "even more remote" from that
of modernity. Parmenides' fragment *to gar auto noein estin te kai einai*
(usually translated "for thinking and being are the same") has nothing to
do with thinking understood as the subjective representation of beings as
objects. Heidegger comments:

> This statement of Parmenides means: The apprehending of be-
> ings belongs to being, because it is demanded and determined
> by being. That which is, is that which arises and opens itself,
> that which, as something presencing, comes upon the human
> being as someone who presences, that is, comes upon the one
> who opens himself to whatever is presencing in apprehending it.
> Beings do not come to be through human beings first looking
> upon them in the sense of a representing that has the charac-
> ter of subjective perception. Rather the human being is the one

---

[7] "...durch den vorstellend-herstellenden Menschen gestellt": literally, "set in place
by the human being who sets them before him and sets them forth."

who is looked upon by beings, the one who is gathered—by that which opens itself—toward presencing in its vicinity [*der vom Seienden Angeschaute, von dem Sichöffnenden auf das Anwesen bei ihm Versammelte*]. To be looked upon by beings, to be drawn into their openness, held within it and thus borne along by it, to be driven about by their oppositions and marked by their discordance: such is the essence of human beings in the great age of the Greeks. . . . The Greek human being *is* as the apprehender of beings, which is why the world cannot become picture in the age of the Greeks. (H, 83–84)

Where the world becomes picture, by contrast, human beings "enter the scene." No longer primarily spectators looked upon by the spectacle itself, they seek to control and decide the drama, to control the destiny of their own actions. They become the ones who look at, contemplate, and inspect beings in forcing beings to present themselves to humans as the ground and center of the world. Representing beings as picture means relating them back to human beings, *making them present* in precisely this way. It is not simply the human being that becomes central here, however, at least not if by human being we mean an entity or individual subject. Rather, it is this particular form of *relationality* that becomes, as Heidegger puts it, the definitive or "normative" realm that provides the measure for the modern understanding of the being of beings. The modern human being does not simply understand him- or herself as an existing "I," but as an already existing field of presence for every possible making-present of beings. It is this total identification of ourselves with the measure of being itself—understood as presence—this relationality of making things present before us, setting things before us and holding them in place in their presencing as objects, that constitutes the essence of the modern human being as subjectivity or "subjectity," as Heidegger elsewhere puts it, in order to emphasize that the essence of subjectivity has no intrinsic or necessary connection to understanding oneself as "I" or ego.[8] In an Appendix to the essay, Heidegger contrasts the modern human being as the "measure" of beings with the sense in which the human being is to be understood as measure in Protagoras' saying that man is the measure of all things.[9] The essence of knowledge as representation in the modern era is fundamentally different from the knowledge or *eidenai* of which Protagoras speaks. Heidegger here translates *eidenai* as "apprehending" and as "knowing" (*Wissen*), adding that for the Greeks this means "being 'faced' by something" (*etwas zu "Gesicht" bekommen*), beholding the face of things (H, 97). For Protagoras,

---

[8] See NII, 450ff.; also Appendix 9 to "The Age of the World Picture."
[9] See Appendix 8.

the human being is "measure" in the sense that each individual comprises
a limited field of possible presencing—temporally limited by his or her tarrying for a while (*Verweilen*) in a particular situation—a field within which
beings can come to presence and show themselves for human apprehension.
Modern representation, by contrast, is marked precisely by a de-restriction
of the particular situatedness of human presencing:

> It is one thing to preserve the sphere of unconcealment, limited
> at any given time, through the apprehending of what is present
> (man as *metron*). It is another to proceed into the unlimited
> realm of possible objectification, through the calculative reck-
> oning of what is accessible to everyone and binding for all as
> representable. (H, 98)

In *Being and Time,* we have already seen Heidegger remark on this
de-restriction or decontextualization (*Entschränkung*) as a key moment in
the genesis of scientific-theoretical comportment, a moment in which the
contextual place and situatedness of things comes to be "overlooked," in
which place becomes an indifferent "world-point," and human apprehending shifts into an objectivizing thematization of the totality of whatever
can be made present as objectively present-at-hand (SZ, 361ff.).[10] In the
1925 course *Prolegomena to the History of the Concept of Time,* the modification from circumspection to the theoretical, thematizing look (a distancing *looking at* something) is characterized as "the attempt on the part
of Dasein no longer to be in its nearest environment" (GA 20, 266). Yet
the other side of Dasein's attempt no longer to be in its own vicinity, in
the vicinity of its surrounding world, is the attempt—manifest in modern telecommunications—to make present whatever is remote: a veritable
frenzy for nearness:

> Today, a concert in London is near for whoever owns a radio. Via
> the radio, modern Dasein accomplishes an appresentation of its
> environment, an appresentation that is not yet fully surveyable
> in its meaning for Dasein, a peculiar extension of the process of
> bringing the world nearer. Viewed more accurately, nearness is
> nothing other than a distinctive remove of distance [*Entfernung*]
> that is available in this particular temporality. All the increases
> in velocity, which we go along with today more or less freely and
> compulsively, involve the overcoming of distances. This peculiar
> overcoming of distances is, in its ontological structure (and this
> is to be understood without any value-judgment), a frenzy for

---

[10] See chapter 3 of the present study.

nearness [*eine Tollheit auf Nähe*] which in its being is grounded
in Dasein itself. (GA 20, 312)[11]

The "frenzy for nearness," Heidegger indicates, is to be understood as a
fleeing of time from itself in which it nevertheless remains itself as a specific
possibility of presence. The frenzy for nearness ultimately manifests nothing other than the temporal structure of falling that characterizes Dasein's
curiosity: the fleeing of presence from its own finitude, from its own time,
from any tarrying in Dasein's immediate presence. This temporal dynamic
illustrates well the ambiguity conveyed by the German word *Entfernung,*
which can mean distancing, but also the removal of distance: in bringing
the world nearer, Dasein becomes increasingly removed from itself, from its
own immediate and finite presence. This derestrictive, decontextualizing
move via modern telecommunications into tele-presentation is also, in its
very essence, inseparable from the vision of a world-community: decontextualization is an opening up of what can be re-presented, that is, presented
or referred back to world-subjectivity "as accessible to everyone and binding for all." In other words, as Heidegger himself will later remark, modern
science is intrinsically, that is, essentially political (VS, 96–97).
     This contrasting of Presocratic apprehending (*noein*) with the modern
transformation of *theōria* into representation provides a suitable backdrop
against which we shall now try to examine more incisively some of these
key features of modern science. We shall do so with reference to several
of Heidegger's later writings on this theme, while making no claim to any
comprehensive treatment of these later essays. Our remarks, rather, restrict
themselves to the more immediate context of the present study: the modern
transformation of *theōria.*

The Contemplation of the Real

What kind of "seeing" characterizes modern scientific "theorizing"? As
noted, the essence of modern science concerns a form of cognitive knowledge
(*Erkennen*) in which the erstwhile apprehending (*noein*) of the presencing
of beings has been transformed into a more aggressive, "contemplative"
inspection of beings. For Parmenides and Protagoras, human beings are
"looked upon by beings"; in modernity, human beings do the looking, they
are the active, aggressive inspectors of everything that is. The Platonic interpretation of being as *idea* and the Aristotelian understanding of *theōrein*
as pure *energeia* are intermediate stages in the process of this transformation. Plato's doctrine of ideas has as its consequence that what truly *is* is no

---

[11] Cf. SZ, 105; also G, 17.

longer to be found in the immediacy of that which presences and is apprehended by human beings in each specific, concrete situation. What truly is,
beings in their truth, becomes displaced to the realm of the nonsensible, the
ideas, which nevertheless are claimed to determine and give rise to whatever presences in the way that it presences. Thus, Heidegger notes in "The
Age of the World Picture," "the fact that Plato determines the beingness of
beings as *eidos* (outward appearance, view) is the presupposition, destined
far in advance and long prevailing indirectly in concealment, for the world's
having to become picture" (H, 84). Aristotle's "science" or *epistēmē*, as yet
far removed from research or science in the modern sense, was based upon
the claim that the forms are present in, and determinative of the presencing
(*energeia*) of things themselves; its "experimentation" (*empeiria*) remained
primarily "an observing of things themselves," in order to discover the (initially concealed) rules governing the ways in which things appear, and to
do so starting from the ways in which things show themselves. Heidegger
stresses that modern research and experimentation, by contrast, begin by
projecting a law (or nexus of laws), and only then proceed to investigate, via
experiment, to what extent beings can be challenged or made to conform
to such laws (H, 74).

In the modern configuration of knowledge an incisive kind of panopticism remains paramount. Heidegger traces some of the transformations
of ancient *theōrein* into modern "theory" in his 1953 essay "Science and
Reflection." Expounding the thesis that modern science is "the theory of
the real," Heidegger remarks that the origins of the word "theory," the
Greek noun *theōria* and the verb *theōrein,* are words that have "an exalted
and mysterious meaning":

> The verb *theōrein* grew out of the amalgamation of two root
> words: *thea* and *horaō. Thea* (cf. theater) is the outward look,
> the aspect in which something shows itself, the visual appear-
> ance in which it proffers itself. Plato names this aspect, in which
> whatever is present shows what it is, the *eidos.* To have seen
> this aspect, *eidenai,* is to know [*Dieses Aussehen gesehen haben,*
> eidenai, *ist Wissen*]. The second root word in *theōrein, horaō,*
> means: to look at something attentively, to take in its appear-
> ance, to look at it closely. Thus we see that *theōrein* is *thean*
> *horan:* to look attentively upon the outward appearance wherein
> that which presences becomes visible, and through such vision
> to tarry alongside it in seeing. (VA, 48)

Pointing toward the importance of the *eidenai* of the *eidos* for Platonic
and Aristotelian thought, Heidegger's condensed discussion of the history

of *theōria* here simultaneously points back toward a more ancient "exalted and mysterious" sense of seeing conveyed by the word *theōria*. This more ancient sense concerned a tarrying in the presence of the look of something as it shows itself, a tarrying not yet determined as the more active, "perspectival" seeing of modern subjectivity. In the "Letter on 'Humanism'" (1946) Heidegger had characterized this later transformation as an abandonment of a more originary look and approach of things, of a being in touch and in contact with other beings in a manner that comes to be foreclosed by modern subjectivity:

> The clearing itself . . ., within the destiny of being in metaphysics, first grants that view in terms of which whatever is present touches and moves the human being who is present to it, so that human beings themselves can first touch upon being (*thigein*, Aristotle, *Met.* IX 10) in apprehending it (*noein*). Such a view first draws a perspect [*Hin-sicht*] toward it. It abandons itself to such a perspect when apprehending has become a setting-forth-before-itself in the *perceptio* of the *res cogitans* taken as the *subiectum* of *eertitudo*. (W, 163)

The reference to Book IX, chapter 10 of Aristotle's *Metaphysics* points to a more original apprehending of being, a pure *noein* that remains preserved in Aristotle as a straightforward, prediscursive apprehending of something in its self-showing. Such apprehending is "true" by its very event; its truth is not yet dependent upon apophantic disclosure in the *logos*. It is thus also prior to the Platonic-Aristotelian determination of truth in terms of the *eidos* (itself understood as *logos*), which is only ever something that has been seen, and not the original event of self-disclosure. Aristotle's discussion of this pure *noein* in *Metaphysics* Book IX (which, along with Book VI of the *Nicomachean Ethics*, was for Heidegger one of Aristotle's most important texts) retains an echo of a more ancient sense of *theōrein*.

In the 1953 essay, Heidegger chooses not to pursue the further characterization of *theōrein* in its disclosure of *archai* and *aitiai*, its sighting of "grounds," "causes," and "principles," but refers us to Book VI of Aristotle's *Nicomachean Ethics*. He points back instead to the more ancient sense of *theōrein* (an analysis of which we shall reserve for part 4), and looks ahead to a later moment in the history of knowing qua seeing.

This later moment concerns a further transformation subsequent to the emergence of epistemic *theōrein* in Plato and Aristotle. The transformation concerns the translation of Greek *theōrein* into the Latin *contemplatio*.[12]

---

[12] Regarding this translation, and the role played by Christianity in the semantic shifts of *contemplatio*, see especially Franz Boll, "Vita Contemplativa," *Sitzungsberichte der Heidelberger Akademie der Wissenschaften* (Heidelberg, 1920), 6–7 and 25ff.

With respect to this translation, Heidegger elucidates the accompanying
shift in meaning:

> The Romans translate *theōrein* by *contemplari*, *theōria* by *con-*
> *templatio*. This translation, which issues from the spirit of the
> Roman language, that is, from Roman existence, makes what
> is essential in what the Greek words say vanish at a stroke. For
> *contemplari* means: to partition something off into a separate
> sector and enclose it therein. *Templum* is the Greek *temenos*,
> which has its origin in an entirely different experience from that
> out of which *theōrein* originates. *Temnein* means: to cut, to
> divide. That which is uncuttable is the *atmēton*, *a-tomon*, the
> atom. (VA, 50)

Thus, the advent of modern "atomic theory" and its products is prefigured and prepared by this transformation of vision into an incisive and
determinative inspecting that seeks its clarity in the installation of clear-
cut boundaries, divisions, and delimitations. The development of this kind
of seeing is decisive for the subsequent transformation of modern scientific
objectivity into technological orderability, in which everything can be set
in "its" place: in a place cut off from everything around it, decontextualized from everything actual, and whose only relational context is its being
kept and held in place for possible actualization within the field of technological ordering, which we shall examine more closely in a moment. Yet
the uncanny thing about the incisiveness of contemplative vision is that it
can never stop cutting, not even when it reaches the supposedly "uncut-
table" atom.

Hand in hand with the incisiveness of the modern scientific vision, with
its penetrating into ever smaller divisions—and ever greater division: for
the process of division itself is incessant- coeval with its expansion into
ever darker realms, there belongs a second feature: the well-documented
expansiveness of its panopticism, its overarching gaze upon everything,
its surveying and establishing of the entire "world-picture."[13] Heidegger
reminds us of this in recalling the significance of the Latin *templum:*

> The Latin *templum* means originally a sector carved out in the
> heavens and on the earth, the cardinal point, the region of the
> heavens marked out by the path of the sun. It is within this
> region that the diviners make their observations in order to
> determine the future from the flight, cries, and eating habits

---

[13] For a graphic illustration of some of the concrete consequences of a vision that is at
once incisive and panoptic, see Michel Foucault's *Surveiller et punir* (Paris: Gallimard,
1975).

of the birds (cf. Ernout-Meillet, *Dictionnaire étymologique de la langue latine* [3], 1951, 1202: *contemplari* is derived from *templum*, that is, from [the name of] the *place which can be seen* from any point, and from which any *point can be seen.* The ancients called this place a *templum*).[14] (VA, 50)

Templum thus has the sense of a region cut out between the heavens and the earth, establishing a panoptic site from which every other point can be seen. Yet it is also a place that can be seen from any point: a prophetic note indeed if we consider that the site of panoptic vision is, in modernity, a site that also gathers and serves as a focus for each and every human being: the site of representation itself. Likewise, the reference to the *templum* as a site from which the future can be determined or established is no less prophetic; for, as we shall shortly consider, modern *theōria* is essentially constituted by a distinctive projection of the future.

Heidegger's account of this transformation of vision that is itself a translation should not be taken as any kind of "causal" or explanatory claim. Such a transformation is far from being straightforward or perspicuous. For one thing, the Latin translation of *theōria* by *contemplatio* is not simply due to the Romans. It is a move already prepared in Greek thought itself: for what is the Platonic-Aristotelian beginning of philosophy if not the attempt to delimit things as such in what they are? What manifests itself already in the Socratic dialogues if not the power of division amid the desire to oversee? Moreover, the Greek word *theōria* does not simply disappear in this translation. It remains a word in its own right. It is a question, therefore, of a certain shift in meaning, a reinterpretation of *theōria* by association with *contemplatio*. *Theōria* turns into and becomes *contemplatio:*

> In the *theōria* that has become *contemplatio* there comes to the fore the impulse, already in part prepared within Greek thinking, of an incisive, compartmentalizing inspecting. A type of encroaching advance by successive interrelated steps toward that which is to be grasped by the eye makes itself normative in cognitive knowing. But even now the *vita contemplativa* continues to be distinguished from the *vita activa.* (VA, 50–51)[15]

The medieval distinction between the *vita contemplativa* and the *vita activa* derives, of course, from the Aristotelian distinction between the *bios theōrētikos* and the *bios politikos,* although the Aristotelian proximity between these two moments of *praxis* has now been eclipsed. In the medieval

---

[14] The Latin reads: contemplari dictum est a templo, i.e. loco qui ab omni *parte aspici,* vel ex quo omnis *pars videri* potest, quem antiqui templum nominabant.

[15] On "turnings" as the very issue of translation, see GA 53, §12.

period, notes Heidegger, this distinction becomes that of the contemplative-monastic life as opposed to the worldly active one. Thus, even when the supposedly "detached" observation, uninvolved in any real "activity" (a misunderstanding of the theory/praxis relation to begin with) becomes a highly active advancing and proceeding, the illusion persists that such theoretical-contemplative activity is "mere" theory, disengaged from the realm of "praxis."

Cognitive knowledge thus remains the normative site of a vision that will rapidly develop into modern science. At this point of "Science and Reflection," Heidegger appeals to another translation—the modern German translation of *contemplatio* by *Betrachten*—in order to illuminate a second prominent feature of contemporary science.

Grasping Things

A second key moment of modern theory concerns precisely the characteristic activity of *encroaching advance* or procedure (*Vorgehen*). The essence of science as research, according to "The Age of the World Picture," consists in knowledge establishing itself as a manner of proceeding within a particular realm of beings. In "Science and Reflection," Heidegger draws attention to this moment via his discussion of the German *Betrachten*, "contemplation," which derives from the root *trachten* (from the Latin *tractare*, to manipulate, work over). The verb *trachten* means to strive or aim for something: as Heidegger elaborates, "to work one's way *toward* something, to entrap it in order to secure it" (VA, 51). Procedure, moving forward and toward something, is intrinsic to the work of the searching *contemplatio*, the modern theorizing of "the real":

> Science sets upon [*stellt*] the real. It orders it into place to the end that at any given time the real will exhibit itself as an interacting network, that is, in surveyable series of related causes. The real thus becomes surveyable and capable of being pursued in its (con)sequences [*in seinen Folgen verfolgbar*]. The real becomes secured in its objectness. From this there result fields of objects that scientific contemplation can entrap after its fashion. Such entrapping representation, which secures everything in that objectness which is thus capable of being pursued or followed out, is the fundamental characteristic of the representing through which modern science corresponds to the real. (VA, 52)

The surveying *contemplatio* which seeks to set things in their place (*stellen*) is a reaching out, an ongoing activity that seeks to set things in place and hold them in place, "entrap" them (*nachstellen*) and secure them (*sicherstellen*), thus holding them in place before us for representation (*vorstellen*). Such representation is thus itself never finally secured, it is never secure and ultimately never can be, but exists and is sustained only as an ongoing, forward-reaching activity. This activity of pursuit, the reaching out and attempting to get a hold on things, to keep them held in place, manifests itself as a process of grasping and manipulation at work in the modern, contemplative *theōrein*. Modern science, remarks Heidegger, "in the sense of a contemplation that strives after things [*Be-trachten*], is a working over of the real that grasps at it in an uncanny manner" (VA, 52). The German for grasping here, *eingreifen,* suggests more precisely a grasping that intervenes and reaches into what is real or actual.

The characteristic pursuit intrinsic to modern science necessitates that its own way of proceeding be secured by recourse to method. "Because modern science is theory in the sense described, for this reason in all its contemplation [*Betrachten*] the manner of its striving-after [*Trachten*], that is, the manner of its entrapping-securing procedure, that is, its method, has decisive priority." The importance of the priority of method was already understood by Nietzsche ("It is not the victory of *science* that marks our nineteenth century, but the victory of scientific method over science"),[16] and announced in advance in the title of Descartes' seminal *Discourse on Method* (1637). Indeed, it is the transformation of the traditional question guiding metaphysics, the question "What are beings?," into the search for method as a means whereby humans can secure an unconditionally certain truth for themselves that marks the beginning of modernity, of the new era (or "new time," as the German *Neuzeit* literally says) of inquiry. "This transformation," Heidegger notes elsewhere, "*is* the beginning of a new thinking whereby the era becomes a new one and the subsequent epoch becomes modernity" (NII, 142). Method cautiously projects the path of prospective pursuit along the lines of what is measurable, and in terms of the measure already known and projected as known in advance: mathematical knowledge. In other words, the pursuit of science proceeds as calculation. Calculation keeps the pursuit on the "right" path, prescribes its directionality in advance, sets up an expectation, looks out for itself in advance. It seeks to let its entire activity be regulated (not to say programmed) in advance by the projections of its calculations, and herein lies its intrinsically "technical" manner of proceeding. Because the end is in fact already known and projected as such, the work of pursuit cannot but "work" in the sense of proceeding as an ongoing process of securing "results" that in turn

---

[16] *Der Wille zur Macht,* §466. Cited (in slightly altered form) by Heidegger in a letter from 1966 to Eugen Fink, now published as an Appendix to GA 29/30.

become the basis for further pursuit. When we say that science "works," we
mean in effect that its results correspond to, and function in terms of, what
we have already projected in advance. "Everything works [or functions:
Es funktioniert alles]," remarks Heidegger in the *Der Spiegel* interview,
"That is precisely what is uncanny...."[17] Yet this uncanniness at once announces itself in and withdraws from the claws of calculative thinking in
its all-consuming character. In the "Postscript to 'What is Metaphysics?'"
(1943), Heidegger had expressed the point in the following way:

> Calculative thinking compels itself into a compulsion [*Zwang*]
> to master everything on the basis of the consequential correct-
> ness of its procedure. It is unable to foresee that everything
> calculable by calculation—prior to the sum-totals and products
> that it produces by calculation in each case—is already a whole,
> a whole whose unity indeed belongs to the incalculable that
> withdraws itself and its uncanniness from the claws [*Griffen*] of
> calculation. (W, 104–05)

By its very nature, therefore, science is also violence, one particular form
of war, of *polemos:* a relentless, ongoing act of aggressivity toward beings as
a whole. Heidegger had already alluded to the inherent aggressivity of such
pursuit in "The Age of the World Picture," most succinctly in Appendix 9,
when comparing the ancient apprehending of beings to the modern form of
representation that attempts to ground itself in Descartes' *Meditations:*

> Representing is no longer a self-revealing for ..., but is a laying
> hold and grasping of ... [*das Ergreifen und Begreifen von*]. It
> is not that which presences that prevails; rather, assault [*der
> Angriff*] rules. Representation is now, in keeping with its new
> freedom, a proceeding or going forth from out of itself into the
> sphere, first to be made secure, of that which is secured. That
> which is, beings, are no longer that which presences; rather, they
> are that which, in representation, is first set over and against us
> [*das im Vorstellen erst entgegen Gestellte*], that which stands
> over and against us and has the character of an object. Rep-
> resentation is a making something stand over and against us,
> an objectifying that proceeds and masters [*vor-gehende, meis-
> ternde Ver-gegen-ständlichung*]. (H, 100)

Assault, laying our hands on things, holds sway in the work of this
supremely energized pursuit. Assault rules. Its relentless energy and ener-
gizing, which we shall examine in a moment, are indissociable from the "new

---

[17] *Der Spiegel,* 31 May 1976, 206.

freedom" mentioned here, a freedom not simply of human beings, but one that pertains to the activity of representation itself: a liberation of world-vision from the things and the "life" going on around it in its immediate vicinity, a liberation for this venturing forth in pursuit. *Angriff*, attack, is intrinsic to the entire venture of grasping, of *greifen* and its cognates—a verb that can mean both physical grasping with the hands, and comprehending, grasping with the invisible hand of the "mind"—in short, to the adventure of the concept and of conceptual thinking as a desire to appropriate.[18] In stark contrast to modern thinking, Heidegger notes elsewhere, the Greeks did not have concepts (*Begriffe*):

> In grasping [*Be-greifen*] there lies a way of comportment that is a taking-into-possession. The Greek *horismos,* by contrast, embraces in a manner strong yet tender whatever our vision takes into view; it does not grasp. (VS, 137)

Do we today, we moderns of the age of science and technology, "have a grip" on things? In our own grasping at beings as a whole, in our own attempt to lay hold upon world-totality, do we grasp what is going on in the momentous rise, not to say explosion, of science and technology? Do we grasp what is going on in this very activity as such? Or are we not rather in the grip of science and technology, veritably possessed by a process that, in itself, in its essence as a "process," has become unsurveyable for us, unforeseeable in its consequences, so that we simply give ourselves over to the supposed "security" of being involved in this self-securing process?

Are we losing our grip on technology? Is it getting out of our control? Are we losing our hold on the overall picture amid the accelerating dispersion and specialization of sciences and technologies? Far from it—or so it seems. In the face of such dispersion, technology, which has by now wholly absorbed the activity of science, finds itself challenged to make a new attempt at control, a new attempt at securing an overview of the entire process. An ultimate attempt, as we shall see, an attempt which, according to Heidegger, has the character of a finality both menacing and promissory. Before examining this attempt, however, we must set more clearly into relief another aspect of the phenomenon of pursuit.

Making Progress: The Future of Science

Pursuit, as indicated, is an *ongoing* activity, it has the character of *advancing toward,* proceeding, moving on, and thus turning away from the presence of whatever is given as present in any given instance. The so-called

---

[18] Cf. "On the Question of Being," W, 230.

"advances" of science are a direct result of its own fundamental activity
of advancing. Such advance is regulated as pursuit. The pursuit of modern
science is not a tentative reaching out in various directions whose discoveries would lead to reassessment and revision of the very nature or grounds
of the initial activity of pursuit. Rather the nature of the pursuit is knowingly posited or projected in such a way from the outset that in itself it
must remain secure, and it secures its own security as a process via method.
The pursuit is regulated and controlled with respect to its directionality;
fundamentally, it pursues a singular direction. It advances toward the future, the new, characterizing its own movement as *progress*. Science "makes
progress." And in our era, one must, above all, be seen to be progressive.
This trait, which is a fundamental, that is, pervasive, unifying, and quite
decisive trait of modern science and technology, is not at all straightforward. It takes us back, in effect, to the question with which our inquiry
began: the desire to see as a desire for the new, as *Neugier*. But what form,
configuration, or constellation of this desire does it comprise?

    What do we see, if we stop to look around us at the world today?, asks
Heidegger in a 1973 seminar:

> What, in truth, do we see? What rules today, in determining
> the actual reality of the entire earth?
>
> The *force of progression* [Progressionszwang].[19] This force of
> progression conditions a compulsion to produce [*Produktions-
> zwang*], which is coupled with a compulsion aiming at ever new
> needs. And the compulsion that aims at ever new needs is of
> such a kind that everything that is compellingly new has also
> just as immediately become old and been surpassed, suppressed
> in turn by whatever is "even newer," and so forth. (VS, 125–26)

    The desire for the new compels us, irresistibly and compulsively, toward
the even newer, testifying to a seemingly irrepressible curiosity. For once
achieved and produced, the new that we have attained has always already
become old. It has ceased to be "the new." The so-called "new" is never,
and never can be, new enough. Even before it is conceived, the new has been

---

[19]More accurately, a force that aims at or "compels" progression and progress. The
German *Zwang* appears throughout the following discussions; it is used in various registers, and we shall translate it variously according to context. *Zwang* is also the Marxist
term for 'force,' as in 'forces of production'; it can also mean a 'compulsion' in the psy-
choanalytic sense, for example; or it may mean 'constraint' in the sense of something
restrictive or constricting. The overall sense is thus that of something that compels in one
way or another, a force that is 'irresistible.' Heidegger indicates elsewhere that *Ge-stell*,
by which he designates the essence of technology, is meant to think the "ontological
determination" of *Zwang* (VS, 129).

inserted into an integral system of infinite substitutability. Contemporary existence itself becomes a process of replaceability, in which every entity can be replaced, in essence and in principle (i.e., with respect to its role in the process as process), by every other. Where every being can take the place (*Stelle*) of every other, can essentially *represent* every other in the sense of this ongoing substitution: such is the situation of contemporary industrial, consumerist society. As Heidegger remarks, for something to *be* today means for it to be replaceable:

> Today, to be is to be replaceable [*Sein ist heute Ersetzbarsein*]. The very idea of a "repair" has become an "uneconomical" thought. To every item of consumption there essentially belongs the fact that it *has already* been consumed and thus calls for replacement. Here we find one of the forms in which whatever is traditional, that which can be passed on from generation to generation, is disappearing before us. (VS, 107)

Being, as infinite replaceability and substitutability, thus manifests itself in the characteristic restlessness of modern technological society, its extreme haste to pursue the new. This by now almost desperate rush, in which we feel stressed and pressed ("pressed for time," as we say, usually because we no longer have time to engage with those around us), itself seems to be undergoing an extreme acceleration today, an acceleration that we can hardly fail to notice, and which perhaps ought to worry us—if only we had time to worry about it, if only we weren't so pressed. This pursuit of the new—are we getting more desperate because we can't seem to attain it?—is oriented exclusively toward a distinctive projection of the future, to the exclusion of the past and of tradition.[20] Not just whatever is traditional, but the very power of tradition, is fading and disappearing "before us," before our very eyes—if only we could see it. The suppression of whatever has just been attained, its immediate relegation to the realm of what is old and "dated," outdated and surpassed, has always already occurred in our compulsive desire for the even newer:

> In particular, what happens through the oppressiveness of this occurrence is the break with every possibility of tradition [*Über-lieferung*]. What has been can no longer be present—except in the form of that which has been *surpassed* and consequently is not taken into consideration at all. (VS, 126)

---

[20] On this and related issues, see David Wood, *The Deconstruction of Time* (New Jersey: Humanities Press, 1989), in particular part 4, chapter 6, "The Philosophy of the Future."

Yet this exclusion of tradition is not limited to the consumer realm of the fashion industry, bent on the next newest thing. It is part and parcel of a dynamic of desire intrinsic to the activity of modern science itself as representation. The claim regarding the break with tradition cannot simply be countered by pointing out that there has never been more interest in, or more intensive pursuit of history. For the "tradition" and history in question refer to a past that remains essentially inaccessible to natural and human sciences alike. Precisely as sciences, they remain entirely within the said exclusion. As Heidegger comments elsewhere, with respect to anthropology:

> No era has known so much and such a variety of things about the human being as the present era. No era has presented its knowledge of human beings in such a vivid and captivating way as the present era. No era has hitherto been able to offer this knowledge so rapidly and readily as the present era. Yet no era has known less concerning what the human being is than the present era. In no era has the human being become so worthy of question as in our own. (KPM, 203)

What is problematic in the modern human sciences is that they reduce the human being to an object of representation. The sciences remain within the process of the objectifying representation of their object, making it present before us as something standing over and against us, something thus "available" like any other object of representation. What is so problematic about the scientific or historiographical presentation of history is precisely its conception of what has been as that which is past, the view that historiography itself is the study of "the past."[21] For even if this past is regarded as "contributing" to our own present, it is only as something already surpassed, a series of events that we are somehow already beyond. The past that is thus made present before us, presented as "history," is thereby not only cut off from any living relation to the present; it is also precisely cut off from the very process of objectifying making-present that constitutes it as a possible object of scientific investigation in the first place. In the *Beiträge zur Philosophie*, Heidegger thus writes that the interpretive perspective upon the past assumed by historiography "is only ever the reflection of the contemporary history in which the historian stands, yet which *he* precisely cannot know historically, but can only explain historiographically in the end" (GA 65, 152). Historical science does not stop or

---

[21] We use "historiography" or "historical science" to translate *Historie*, reserving "history" to render *Geschichte*. On Heidegger's account, the "history of being" is more originary than historiography since it first brings us into a particular way of being historical. Historiographical presentation, by contrast, is only one possible way of presenting history, one possible relation to the historical occurrence of being.

attend to its attained "results" in terms of their implications for the historicality of its own activity, but continues to "research." It "attends" to its results only in the interests of the new, that is, only within the parameters of the ongoing scientific activity itself. The ongoing activity of science itself is profoundly ahistorical in the sense that this activity fails to recognize itself as both constitutive of and constituted by history. It is constitutive in the sense of constituting or participating in the way in which history itself occurs (or fails to occur) in the modern era of representation. "Constitutive" here, however, does not mean determinative, since this would entail science's being independent of a history that it would first decide. Precisely this is not the case. The making-present that is distinctive of modern science is, as an activity, equally co-constituted by a temporality and a history that it itself does not know or understand. For all human understanding, before it engages in a present or in any activity of making-present in whatever way, already participates in an arrival of presencing, and thus in an archaic past, that comes from beyond the presence of the present.

When Heidegger therefore states that what has been can no longer be present except as something surpassed, "what has been" does not refer primarily to an object or entity, to a being that has been made present and as such is now already "past"; for such beings (the "new" that, once attained, is already "old") are marked precisely by the fact that they *can* be made present, that they are held in readiness for this very possibility of being made present at will, whether as still "useful" objects, or as "interesting" "historical" objects (antiques, historical "documents," museum pieces, etc.). "What has been" refers, rather, primarily to that which precisely cannot now become present in its truly historical import, namely the "tradition," because, insofar as it is present at all, it has already been demoted in advance to the level of an object of representation. The "tradition" here must be thought in terms of the "history of being," that is, in terms of the event of presencing as it addresses us, in language and in thought, from an archaic or historical realm that exceeds the field of presence. This address—as a "sending" or "destining" (*Geschick*) of being as presencing—happens in coming from beyond us and in calling upon us to respond to presencing in a particular way: today, in the manner of the representation of beings. The focus on the re-presentation of beings, their presentation at the site of representation (i.e., modern "man" as subjectivity) closes off the very activity of representation from its more originary site, the clearing as the happening or arrival of presencing, of the site where the advent of destining—such as the activity of representation itself—occurs, the site of its emergence.

The modern transformation of *theōria* that issues in the science of historiography thus transforms the original sense of the Greek *historia* that

Heidegger elsewhere finds to be related to the root of the Latin *videre* (to see). *Historia,* on this account, originally had the sense of "bringing into view" (GA 54, 165). But this did not mean a historiographical presentation of "the past." The Greeks, Heidegger notes in the *Beiträge,* were not historiographers (they were *unhistorisch*), since "their *historein* turned toward what was present and at hand, and not to what was past as such." Nevertheless, "The Greeks were historical [*geschichtlich*], so originarily that history itself had to remain concealed from them, that is, did not become the essential ground that gave shape to their 'Dasein'" (GA 65, 508). *Historein* was a letting oneself be looked upon and claimed by the address of that which presents itself and thus continues to be present, all the more powerfully and memorably by its having been. In calling past words and deeds into the present, it called the present into the past. Present and past were not separated, but belonged together in the overwhelming presence of their enduring and remaining, in the steadfastness of their presencing.[22] That which had been was not past (in the sense of surpassed or bygone, *vergangen*), but overwhelmingly present; and it was not past because the Greeks had no sense of "the future" in the modern manner. They thus had no historiography. They were turned toward the presence of the present. A sign of this is the fact that there was no *research* aimed at uncovering the past, but simply a recounting of whatever great and noble deeds had been seen to have happened. Yet it is not because they did not have the modern sense of future that their own historicality was concealed from them (since such historicality is also precisely what is concealed in and through modern science—and herein lies the paradoxical proximity of the modern era to what is refused in the Greek beginning), but because their thinking did not respond to presence itself in a historical manner. If the essence of historicality lies in a binding relation to what has been, such that what has been (now seen as lying beyond the present) is regarded as determinative in advance of one's present and future, then the historicality of the Greeks (precisely concealed from them in the philosophical beginning) itself begins when *theōria* turns into a seeing beyond the present, a seeing of that which already is and has been and as such is determinative of the presence of the present.[23] Thereby, the philosophical *theōria* becomes determinative of the human relation to that which endures, in place of the *historein* and even the pre-philosophical *theōrein* (most notably in Greek theater) of the "works" of *praxis* and *poiēsis.* What came to "presence" in the Greek philosophical *logos* as thus refused inaugurated Western historicality, which remains

---

[22] Such was the sense of the Greek *aei.* See GA 65, 507.

[23] On Greek *historia* and its relation to the philosophical beginning, see Hannah Arendt, "The Concept of History," in *Between Past and Future,* 41–90. See also her essay "What is Authority?" in the same volume.

henceforth destined to retrieve, in a non-dialectical manner, what was re-fused in the Greek beginning. Such retrieval does not, however, mean a factical return to the Greeks, nor does it mean a return "only in thought." It means a transformation of the overwhelming presence of the Greek be-ginning (which, in a destinal manner, continues to determine the modern age) and thus the beginning of another beginning.

For its part, the modern presentation of history occurs not so much via the historical sciences, but via technologized science. It occurs precisely at a distance from events themselves, via tele-presentation: tele-vision, tele-text, tele-phone, and radio (originally an abbreviation for radiotelegraphy). Thus, Heidegger comments in "The Anaximander Fragment":

> All historiography calculates that which is coming on the basis of its images of the past which are determined by the present. Historiography is the constant destruction of the future and of our historical relation to the advent of destining. Historicism has today not only not been overcome, but only now is it entering the stage of its dissemination and securement. The technolog-ical organisation of world publicity by radio and by the press, which already lags behind, is the real form of our domination by historicism. (H, 301)

And what is it that the tele-reportage of history thrives upon? What gives it its compelling character? What makes a television program "com-pulsory viewing," as we say? What compulsion compels the "compulsive viewer," the television "addict," if not the desire for the new? It is no acci-dent that the very program that advertises itself as "The News" often has the highest viewing figures. One must follow and have seen "the news" in order to "be in the picture."

There is the paradox: The "future" of science, mirrored in the public face of world-representation, is the past and will always have been the past: the future, once discovered, will always already have been surpassed and will appear only as such. The only future that *remains* is the ongoing activity of representational research and presentation, the endlessly self-perpetuating activity that is its own end.

The Transformation of Presence: From Science to Technology

In order to better understand this entire phenomenon, we must consider more closely the peculiar temporality to which the scientific-technological desire for the new testifies. Just following his characterization of being as substitutability or replaceability, Heidegger remarks:

> With respect to *time,* the result of this feature is *actuality.* Duration is no longer the constancy of what has been handed down, but rather the ever new of relentless change. (VS, 107)

The duration of that which endures throughout this phenomenon is "the ever new of relentless change." Relentless and incessant, this constant and continual change is the mark of contemporary being in the era of substitutability. What occurs in this is nothing other than a circulatory exchange, and what is exchanged is not merely goods and entities, but being as actuality. Consumer society in this respect exhibits the same dynamic as modern technological science.

The advent of full-blown technology, its thorough appropriation of science, corresponds to a transformation in the way presencing itself is understood. Science now becomes almost entirely subservient to the essence of technology, to the technological configuration of presencing. Technological presence no longer means simply the objectivity of objects, their standing before us and being set before the gaze of representational thinking. Yet nor does such representational thinking simply disappear. Rather representational thinking (*Vorstellen*) is itself maintained yet transformed in being taken up into orderability (*Bestellbarkeit*). Heidegger elucidates this in the important essay "On the Question of Determining the Matter of Thinking," first presented as a speech in 1965:

> That which is present is no longer encountered nor lingers [*verweilt*] in the form of objects. It dissolves into stock [*Bestände*], which must be capable of being made, delivered, and replaced at any time for particular purposes. Such stock is required from one instance to another in accordance with particular plans. As such, it is set in place [*gestellt*] with a view to its suitability. Such stock has no constancy [*Beständigkeit*] in the sense of a constant, unchanged presence. The manner in which stock presences is orderability [*Bestellbarkeit*], distinguished by the possibility of the inconstant ever new and improved, without prospect of the best. (BSD, 11)

The setting-in-place granted by representational thinking is maintained (and in this sense technological thinking remains thoroughly representational), but it is now inserted into a system of exchange in which it is no longer simply objects in the constancy of their presence that are set in place. What is set in place, rather, is the *presencing* of objects, as a presencing that has in each instance always already been foreclosed, cut off as merely one possible actuality, one possible temporal moment that is always already past. The inconstancy of such presencing, its being merely a moment within the system of the regulated exchange and alternation of presencing, is what marks it as different from mere objectivity. Heidegger, in the above citation, refers to the *possibility* of the inconstant ever new as what is distinctive about orderability: it is not ordering as such, but the ability to order that is decisive here. The German *Bestellen* has the double sense of setting things in order and commanding (as when we "order" something from a catalog).

To understand this, we must ask what form of actuality or presence is involved in such exchange and circulation. What is at stake in the infinite process of substitutability is not so much the exchange of presence as it is the exchange and circulation of presencing, where the latter is understood as a making-present of objects that can be ordered and set in place as "standing reserve" or "stock" (*Bestand*). This making-present, in its technological form, is indeed directed toward the presence of whatever can be present, that is, of "objects," but it is a making-present that in no way distinguishes objects from their possible presence. It is important to stress the element of the possible here: The presencing or making-present at stake, the making-present of "objects" or stock that *can* be present at any moment, is itself held, that is, ordered and organized, within a realm of *potentiality* (which is to say, power) in which it is not the actuality or actual presence of objects before us that is decisive. What is decisive, rather, is that such actuality itself, the stable presence or stability of the object that stands before us, hardly matters anymore; what is decisive is that such actuality is held at bay as only ever a possible actuality, inserted into the ordered network of all possible presencing. The actual presencing of something *as presence* matters so little that it is not allowed to encroach too insistently upon us. Claimed by technological presencing, we no longer tarry alongside the look of something or someone, lingering in such presencing, but have always already looked away toward another possible presence, in a "seeing" that cuts off the encroachment of actuality itself. It is the orderability of whatever can be present as stock or "standing reserve," setting it in its place (*Stelle*) and securing that place (*sicherstellen*) within a unified and unifying (i.e., gathering) network or system (*Ge-stell*) that constitutes the technological regulation and ordering (*Bestellen*) of presencing. This network is a system of the regulative circulation and exchange of presencing; its concrete form, as Heidegger insists in "On the Question of Determining the Matter of Thinking," is cybernetics, the installation of the computer network. The chain of cognates built around *Stelle,* "place," emphasizes the centrality of a conception of *placing:* setting things in place, holding them in place, ordering them into place, securing their place within a system of placement where everything has its place. But this "placing" and delimiting of everything within the system entails precisely a *displacement* from the immediate field of presencing or actuality.

It is presumably no accident that the dynamic of the technological system of presencing bears a resemblance to the temporality of curiosity that Heidegger had outlined in his earlier work, although it is also different in certain decisive respects. In curiosity, we recall, Dasein manifests a desire to escape its own proximity and the vicinity of things around it, to direct itself, in its displacement (*Entfernung*), toward a "distant and foreign world"; it manifests a seeking to disown its being alongside the ready-to-hand in seeking "merely" to have seen, a "non-tarrying" (*Unverweilen*) and restlessness amid the excitment and excitation caused by the "ever new"; a constant distraction and dispersion into new possibilities and a "never dwelling anywhere," a being "everywhere and nowhere." Curiosity itself was described as "a new way of being pertaining to everyday Dasein" (SZ, 173).

We have already examined in chapter 4 something of the temporality of curiosity as described in *Being and Time*. In the 1925 course, *Prolegomena to the History of the Concept of Time,* Heidegger had already given a preliminary analysis of the temporality of curiosity in terms that closely parallel those of his remarks on the temporality of technology, and that can help us to examine that temporality more incisively. There he remarked that curiosity, in the desire "merely to have seen," is not concerned with a binding or thematic presence:

> The end [*Worumwillen*] of curiosity is not any determinate presence, but rather the possibility of a constant exchange of presence [*des ständigen Wechsels der Präsenz*]. In other words, the non-tarrying that pertains to curiosity is fundamentally concerned with not having to intervene [*zugreifen*] and with merely being entertained by the world.... the presence of whatever is to be seen by the concern of curiosity is constantly exchanged in accordance with its essence, because curiosity itself is concerned with precisely this exchange. (GA 20, 382–83)

The German *Wechsel* implies change in the sense of exchange or alternation, as distinct from alteration or change as *Veränderung*. The end of curiosity, that for the sake of which it is undertaken as an activity, is not any determinate presence at all, but "the possibility of a constant exchange of presence." The desire for the new is enacted on the basis of a prior projection, an understanding that has posited the end of desire in advance, and that regulates and determines its entire activity. Unlike the temporality of curiosity, however, which seeks to flee the finitude of its own being-in-the-world, that of modern technology in its final transformation is involved in a peculiar appropriation of such finitude, one that nevertheless remains largely concealed as such. Modern technology, far from being concerned with "not having to intervene and with merely being entertained by the world," is, as we have noted, a supreme form of intervention that seeks to *take hold* of actuality. And in order to do so, technology must precisely maintain actuality in the realm of possibility, of a possible future that is its own. Curiosity as "entertainment"—a contemporary phenomenon no less overwhelming than technological grasping—is what remains when such intervention relinquishes its claim upon the individual, leaving merely this nonappropriative, "unheld making-present" that is nevertheless "held," precisely by a desire for "the new" that fundamentally does not concern it as its own—the entertainment side of contemporary everydayness.[24]

This comparison helps us understand what is distinctive about technological comportment as an *ongoing* activity, dependent upon the distinctive projection of a future that can be its own. In this final epochal transformation, the desire that once gave rise to Western philosophy and science remains the desire to see and to have seen, but no longer as the desire to stand in the presence of things themselves. Technologized, this desire withdraws from the actuality of things themselves, concerning itself with actuality only insofar as the latter can be produced and secured within the system of the possible—the self-securing system of possibility that the technological operation itself is. But what, then, is the future of technology? What is the end that drives and motivates its desire? Technological making-present is not a futural projection that, like that of curiosity, desires its possibilities merely as something actual, no longer attending to the originary approach of things.[25] As we have argued, it does not ultimately seek anything actual at all, but seeks rather nothing less than *possible actuality or actualities*. In the era of full-blown or consummate technology, there is, strictly speaking, nothing actual anymore.

There is no actuality anymore: Such is the startling, somewhat uncanny meaning of being in the epoch of technology. Actuality or "reality" is everywhere virtual. "Virtual reality" is not merely some epiphenomenon or contained by-product of technology; rather, the whole of our reality is becoming virtual reality. Of course, presence as such is always in a sense virtual (namely, in the sense that it is never fully constituted, never pure presence). But the specific virtualization of presence that occurs via technology is a

---

[24] Cf. the intervention of worldly involvement with the ready-to-hand and the form of "tarrying" alongside the world in the attitude of pure *theōrein* discussed in chapter 3.

[25] Curiosity, Heidegger noted in *Being and Time*, "does not attend to a *possibility,* but in its desire merely craves this possibility as something actual" (SZ, 347).

product of the technological intervention; it concerns our strange inability to tarry in the presencing of things as they show themselves, as they come to presence in and of themselves. We no longer *attend* to the things around us, no longer "let them be" things. Dasein's attempt to escape from its own vicinity, the attempt of the present to escape or "spring away" from its own proper future and having been (SZ, 348), is complete. And it has attained its completion and end (i.e., its ultimate possibility) in the name of an appropriation of itself as an escape and flight from presence. But the attainment (the virtual attainment) of this end does not in itself grant an insight into this end as such. Before considering this end more closely, we must first bring out, in all too cursory fashion, some further traits of scientific and technological desire.

The Collapse of Causality

The desire to see at the heart of modern technological knowledge is thus far from being that of "pure" method, of a disinvolved or disengaged *theōria*. Rather, such desire is fundamentally engaged in the ongoing, forward-driving, busy activity of setting everything in order. Its highly engaged vision, far from being "disinterested" in the name of pure, scientific objectivity or scientific truth, is that of a supremely productive process. It is a vision engaged in production, thus in a form of *technē*. In the busied activity of this productive seeing, a sense of the finitude of human presencing, and all sense of *praxis*, seem to be lost. Yet is this in fact the case? What is the relation between this universalized technological desire and human finitude? Before we can address this question satisfactorily, we must first examine more closely the *productive* part of the technological operation. In what sense is the essence of technology a form of *technē?*

The conventional view of technology understands it as a means in the service of ends, and as an activity undertaken by human beings. In the essay "The Question Concerning Technology," Heidegger argues against this instrumental and anthropological conception of technology. The instrumental view of technology is "correct," indeed "uncannily" so, and to such an extent that it determines all human endeavors to master and control technology. The instrumental view is correct in the sense of prevalent and dominant, such that it prevails throughout the technological era. Yet that which is correct does not necessarily reveal what is essentially occurring amid the prevalence of this view. It does not necessarily reveal the "essence" of technology. Heidegger undertakes to examine this essence by considering the conception of *causality* underlying the instrumental view. According to the classical Aristotelian doctrine of causality, there are four

causes: material, formal, final, and efficient.[26] The efficient cause has come
to be interpreted as the human maker or producer—in modernity, as the
"subject" who masters all making and producing, as well as all means.
Heidegger notes that this one cause is today determinative for our conception of causality in general:

> The *causa efficiens,* merely one among the four causes, deter-
> mines and provides the measure for all causality. This goes so
> far that we no longer even count the *causa finalis,* finality, as
> belonging to causality. (VA, 12)

The final cause is the goal or end, the *telos* or "purpose" for the sake of
which an activity (whether production or *praxis*) is undertaken. The end
must be projected and understood in advance, prefiguring the activity in
such a way as to determine and regulate the path that the activity follows in
its execution. In the case of producing a chair, for example, the maker must
know in advance that the chair is something for sitting on; the projected
goal of "sitting" determines in advance every step of making a chair. In this
sense, it causes the chair to appear as it does. With respect to technology
itself, however, to the movement of technological desire as a whole, we have
seen that there is, precisely, no end. The end of technology is absent, and
this absence secures its very possibility as an infinitely ongoing activity.[27]
More precisely, the end or future of technology is projected in advance in
such a way as to be absent, to be essentially unattainable. The absence of
the final cause here implies that if technology itself is a means, it is a means
to nothing—to nothing other than or beyond the endless self-perpetuation
of itself, the eternal recurrence of the Same. Heidegger suspects that the
absence of finality in the contemporary understanding of causality is merely
a counterpart of the dominance of the efficient cause, that is, of the notion
of the human being as producer. For, as he points out with reference to
the "efficient cause," Aristotle's doctrine "neither knows the cause that is
named by this term, nor uses a Greek word that would correspond to it"
(VA, 13). The notion of "efficiency," of "effecting" and producing an effect,
in fact emerges via a translation of Greek thought into Latin, a translation
that prepares far in advance for the subsequent modern emergence of the
"efficiency," "efficacy," and putting plans "into effect" that we recognize as
keywords in the rhetoric of modern technology. The Latin *causa efficiens*
translates the Greek *archē tēs kinēseōs,* the point of departure from which

---

[26] See Aristotle, *Physics* Book II, 194 b16ff.

[27] Even if we presume the end to be human happiness or well-being, the "good life,"
it is in the infinite self-perpetuation of the productive process that this "end" is to be
found.

motion begins, the source of movement. Heidegger's essay, via its analysis of
causality, attempts to question precisely the modern view that it is "man"
or human beings who are the origin of motion, that it is humans who initiate
everything, that it is their very being or existence that sets itself in motion
and is thus able to control and regulate itself in an infinite self-deferral of
presencing. Thus, Heidegger asks: "But suppose that causality, for its part,
is veiled in darkness with respect to what it is?... From where is the causal
character of the four causes determined in a unitary way, such that they
belong together?" (VA, 12). Heidegger initially attempts to understand the
essence of fourfold causality in terms of the German *verschulden,* being
responsible for something. The material, the form, and the end or purpose
are each in part responsible for the eventual product. Yet what role is
played by the fourth cause in Heidegger's example (taken from Aristotle's
Physics), namely, the silversmith who produces a sacrificial vessel? His role,
Heidegger indicates, is primarily not that of an active agent who "effects"
something, but is in the first instance one of gathering:

> The silversmith deliberates and gathers the three aforemen-
> tioned ways of being responsible. To deliberate [*Überlegen*] is in
> Greek *legein, logos. Legein* is rooted in *apophainesthai,* bringing
> into appearance. The silversmith is co-responsible [*mitschuld*]
> as that from whence the bringing forth of the sacrificial vessel
> and its resting upon itself take and retain their first point of
> departure. (VA, 13)

Verschulden is Heidegger's translation of *aition,* "cause," which we may
render—with certain qualifications[28]—as "responsibility" in the sense of
being responsible for something. The silversmith is "cause" in the sense of
being "co-responsible," in part responsible; he plays the part of that site
in which the remaining causes are "gathered" and in which they come to
appear by way of the *logos.* The silversmith, the *archē tēs kinēseōs,* himself
properly is "that [site] from whence" the bringing forth of the sacrificial
vessel takes its point of departure. Yet it is not only the bringing forth
that has its point of departure here, but also the way in which the vessel
"rests upon itself," that is, the way in which it comes to assume its boundary (*peras*) and instantiated form (*morphē*) so as first to be itself as this
particular thing, and not something else. And this in turn entails that the
bringing forth of productive making is also, and always already, a letting-
be, a letting presence that meets and needs resistance, and is indeed the

---

[28] As William Lovitt explains in his translation of the essay, *verschulden* has a wide
range of meanings including "to be indebted, to owe, to be guilty, to be responsible for
or to, to cause." See QT, 7 n. 5.

very encounter with resistance itself—with a resistance that is primarily neither "spatial" in the ordinary sense, nor substantive.

In order to understand the role of the craftsperson more precisely, Heidegger examines the four ways in which being responsible for something occurs with respect to that which they are responsible for. "Responsible," Heidegger cautions, is not to be understood either moralistically or in terms of "effecting." The four ways of being responsible for are together responsible for the product that lies ready before us. But not only this. Heidegger emphasizes, rather, that what lies ready before us does so as present, and that it is *presencing* that is thereby transformed in bringing something forth or producing it:

> Lying before and lying ready (*hupokeisthai*) characterize the presencing of something that is present. The four ways of being responsible bring something into its appearing. They let it come forth into presencing [*An-wesen*]. They set it free to that place and so start it on its way, namely into its complete arrival. Being responsible has the fundamental trait of this starting something on its way [*An-lassen*] into arrival. (VA, 14)[29]

The pivotal employment of the verb *lassen*, "letting," in this citation attempts to articulate the absence of any simple origin from which the activity of production would begin. The four "causes," all of which are responsible for the product, and which are gathered in the deliberation of the craftsperson, are gathered not merely in the final concrete product itself, but rather in the coming into presence of the product. The four "causes" let the presence of the product arrive. They thus let a transformation of presencing occur. This "letting" is, in the German *lassen*, not merely indecidable with respect to passive or active voice, as is often noted. It also a *leaving*: a leaving in the sense of a freeing, a setting-free of the work. The work or product is left to come into its own, to arrive in its own presencing, and indeed in such a way that the craftsperson must already have left, that is, withdrawn from such presencing in advance, so as to let the work presence freely of its own accord. Such leaving, however, is not a mere passivity, no more than is the "letting" involved. Heidegger now appeals to the word *Ver-an-lassen* to convey the sense of activity entailed in letting something come into presencing. *Ver-an-lassen* has the sense of letting something be occasioned, letting it be brought about. Heidegger uses this term to designate the *essence* of "causality" as thought by the Greeks in the word *aitia*, which only later came to be translated as "cause."

---

[29] For a discussion of the sense of *An-lassen*, see QT, 9 n. 8.

Each of the four manners of letting something be occasioned is brought together with each of the others in the coming into presence of the work. The four are brought together, gathered into a unity in being gathered into the singular presencing of a singular work.[30] Together, the four "let that which is not yet present arrive into presencing. A bringing thus prevails through their unity, a bringing that brings what presences to appear." Translating a sentence from Plato's *Symposium* at 205b, Heidegger identifies the occasioning of something as *poiēsis*, "bringing forth":

> Every occasion [*Veranlassung, aitia*] for whatever passes over and goes forth into presencing from out of that which is not presencing is *poiēsis*, is bringing-forth [*Her-vor-bringen*]. (VA, 15)

The term *poiēsis*, Heidegger emphasizes, is to be understood in a broad sense. It is not restricted to making or craftsmanship, but also refers to what occurs in all artistic and poetic bringing-forth, as well as what occurs in nature (*phusis*). Indeed, "*phusis* is even *poiēsis* in the highest sense." And this is so because whatever presences in the manner of *phusis* is an irruption (*Aufbruch*) that occurs of its own accord, within the realm of that which presences of itself. Whatever comes to presence in the manner of *technē*, by contrast, has need of another; it has its "irruption" in and through another being, the craftsperson or artist. Again, Heidegger's use of the word "irruption" here avoids any reference to a simple origin that would reinvoke the notion of a *causa efficiens*. Such reference to a single origin is elided not only in the case of human *poiēsis*, but also in the case of natural *poiēsis*, suggesting that the presencing that occurs in other living beings likewise has no simple origin.

If Heidegger takes such care with language and translation in order to think *poiēsis*—and particularly that which occurs by way of human production—otherwise than in terms of a simple origin, it is in part in order to show that making or producing, as a transformation of presencing, need not be thought in terms of modern subjectivity as the determined action of the will. The will, the modern determination of human causality, is the modern word for being as activity, for the way in which presencing itself occurs. The Greeks, although a supremely active people, had no conception of the will or subject of action in the sense of self-legislating, "free" causality. Neither the will nor the subject is necessary for there to be human *praxis*. The essence of freedom, Heidegger will note later in the essay,

---

[30] According to Heidegger's reading of Aristotle in the 1931 course on *Metaphysics* Book IX, 1–3 (GA 33), such being gathered into presencing is the essence of what Aristotle thinks as *energeia*. See also "On the Essence and Concept of Φύσις in Aristotle's *Physics* B, 1" (W, 309–71).

"is *originarily* not associated with the will nor even with the causality of human willing" (VA, 28). The decisive Kantian determination of the modern will as that freedom that seeks freedom as its own in submitting itself to the *logos* of the moral law is nothing other than a historical prefiguring of the attempt of presencing to secure itself in the endless and deferred production of itself.[31]

Heidegger's approach in this essay on technology thus attempts to emphasize the moment of coming to presence, of coming into unconcealment from out of concealment, that occurs in all *poiēsis*. Where human beings intervene in such *poiēsis* in the case of producing a work, whether a work of technology, of artisanship, or of art, what is at stake remains a form of bringing-forth or revealing (*Entbergen*): that form of revealing that is referred to in the Greek word *technē*. Technology, coming from the Greek words *technē* and *logos*, has to do with the *logos*—the language and the rule—of that kind of bringing-forth that entails human intervention. As such, the essence of technology is fundamentally a manner of revealing and bringing something forth into the field of presencing. Heidegger notes that in Plato *technē* is associated with *epistēmē*, and that both refer to "knowing [*Erkennen*] in the broadest sense." Knowing discloses something and is thus itself (like all seeing and apprehending) a kind of revealing, a way of letting things presence. In Book VI of Aristotle's *Nicomachean Ethics*, these two kinds of knowing (*technē* and *epistēmē*) are, as we have seen, distinguished according to what it is that they reveal or "disclose" in each case. Whereas *technē* is concerned with knowledge of that which does not bring itself forth, that is, with knowledge of human-produced artifacts whose coming into presence follows no constant law, Aristotelian *epistēmē* is concerned with that which appears and comes to presence in an unchanging manner, in accordance with constant laws. Heidegger does not provide a detailed analysis of this divergence here in "The Question Concerning Technology," but his mention of it invites our attention. If *epistēmē* becomes modern science (via a long series of subtle transformations, of course), it is nevertheless *technē*, according to Heidegger's interpretation, that in essence (i.e., from the beginning, far in advance, from its very emergence) thoroughly governs the unfolding of science. The sighting of the *eidos*, of the "aspect" in which things are seen to show themselves in their constancy for Aristotelian *epistēmē*, is itself a moment extracted from *technē*. But in *technē*, the *eidos* is not at all simply read off from things as they lie before us; rather, it belongs to a power granted to humans to foresee—within certain limits—and thus to regulate the presencing of things in advance,

---

[31] Cf. here Heidegger's remarks in Appendix 9 of "The Age of the World Picture" concerning Descartes' role in grounding the newly-found human freedom as a self-securing freedom.

to impose on the material presencing of things a particular form. Thus, when in modernity human beings free themselves to become the relational center of beings as a whole, it is not surprising that this human power over presencing should seek to constantly establish and confirm itself, to "prove itself." The priority of *technē* in its modern guise is manifest precisely in the fact that technologized science is fundamentally no longer concerned with establishing truths about nature or about things themselves as they show themselves in their constancy. It is not primarily concerned with things themselves at all, nor is it concerned with the ascertaining of immutable laws of nature by observation. Rather, as we have noted, modern, technologized science is concerned primarily, if not exclusively, with the production of presencing and of the law of presencing, in short, with the self-production of the law.[32]

In its modern ascendancy over Aristotelian *epistēmē* and even modern science, *technē* itself undergoes transformation. The transformation of *technē* becomes visible in its specifically modern character whenever we consider the kind of revealing that occurs in technology. Technology itself is "a manner of revealing," and not simply the application of an instrument or means lying ready-to-hand. The Greek *technē* "belongs to bringing-forth, to *poiēsis;* it is something poietic [*etwas Poietisches*]." Yet what is the nature of technological revealing? Is it too not a *poiēsis,* a bringing-forth? According to Heidegger, no. The production and revealing that occurs in technology, Heidegger stresses, "does not unfold into a bringing-forth in the sense of *poiēsis.*" It is as though something about technological revealing precluded or foreclosed its being a revealing in the sense of bringing-forth. Every bringing-forth, Heidegger insists, is grounded in revealing (VA, 16). But the opposite does not hold: not every revealing is a bringing-forth (*Her-vor-bringen*). In contrast to bringing-forth in the sense of *poiēsis,* technology is a revealing that occurs by way of challenging forth (*Her-ausfordern*). Such challenging challenges nature to supply "energies" that can be stored; it "sets" nature in place and sets upon it in setting it in order. And it does so in the manner of a strange double gesture, a doubling carried in the German text by an ambiguity in the word *fördern,* which can mean both to extract, and to further or promote:

---

[32] Kant's meditation on the essence of human freedom, in the *Grounding for the Metaphysics of Morals* and the *Critique of Practical Reason,* is thus the most complete anticipation in the history of philosophy of the fundamental law of presencing in the essence of technology—of that law which Heidegger will think as *Gestell.* See "Overcoming Metaphysics" XXI, where Heidegger himself describes the modern technological "will to will" as the "consummation [*Vollendung*] of that essence of the will that announced itself in Kant's concept of practical reason as pure willing" (VA, 85). See also our comments on this in the next section.

> The setting-upon that challenges forth the energies of nature is a *Fördern* in a double sense. It extracts [*fördert*], in disclosing and setting-forth. Such extracting, however, has in advance the set intent of furthering [*fördern*] something else, that is, of driving forward toward maximum yield at minimum expense. (VA, 19)

This double sense is not merely a word-play. It describes the singular yet doubled gesture that is intrinsic to the technological operation of revealing: on the one hand transforming material presence in a movement of disclosure, yet on the other hand denying the very presencing of materiality as an *actual* presencing, already ("in advance") looking toward another possible disclosure of presencing which, of course, like all presence, has in advance been set within the tension of the possible, held as possible presencing, and as thus held maintains the very potential that the technological operation itself is. The technological operation is maintained within the tension of the possible that it "sets" in unknowingly seeking to actualize itself as pure potentiality. The expenditure of effort on the part of this operation should be minimal (the less encounter necessary with actuality, the better); its yield maximal, in the sense of setting in place and storing the greatest potential. In the suppressed negativity intrinsic to the very moment of this doubling there resides the ghost of the technological operation.

Technological revealing as an ongoing challenging does not merely abandon that which it has revealed in order to move onto something new; it does not merely flee its own having-been (the having-been of its own presencing), as does the "natural" or ontic curiosity that seeks or believes that it seeks the presence of things themselves. The technological desire, as we have noted, is concerned precisely with the *moment of presencing* itself, and not primarily with things. The moment of having-been that belongs to the process must be secured as part of that temporal span or tension within which the process secures *itself,* controls itself in securing the power to freely dispose over itself within an economy of the proper. Such self-securing reveals the "concealed energies" of nature (and not only of nature) and secures them within a self-regulating field of possible presencing. The fundamental feature of technological desire is its desire for self: for self-regulation and self-control, self-security in self-legislation. Within this system, the securing of having-been occurs as a *storing.* We need only think of the contemporary self-perfecting of the computer network as a self-regulating system of the circulation of stored information. The computer network is not merely an illuminating example in this respect; it is the most perfect imaginable form of self-securing technological revealing, in which energies are stored mathematically, ready to hand for possible deployment, for example, in the self-piloting of a missile, or in the self-controlling movement of an airplane on autopilot, in which the only remaining contingencies are reduced to the possible "disturbance factor" of the "human element," the proverbial "finger on the button," or else are an "act of God" or of "nature." Heidegger describes concisely how technological revealing secures itself within a self-regulating network that relies on storage:

> The revealing that rules throughout modern technology has the character of a setting-upon, in the sense of a challenging-forth. Such challenging happens in that the energy that is concealed in nature is opened up, what has been disclosed is transformed, what has been transformed is stored, what has been stored is in turn distributed, and what has been distributed is switched about ever anew. Disclosing, transforming, storing, distributing, and switching about are ways of revealing. Yet this revealing never simply comes to an end. Nor does it run off into the indeterminate. This revealing reveals for itself its own, manifoldly interlocking paths by regulating them. This regulating [Steuerung] is itself everywhere made secure. Regulating and securing even become the chief traits of such challenging revealing. (VA, 20)

Whatever is revealed, set and held in place in this way, exists as "stock" or "standing reserve," Bestand. This term, Heidegger notes, does not merely refer to "supply"; rather "it characterizes nothing less than the way in which everything presences," namely everything affected by technological revealing (VA, 20). Insofar as human beings understand themselves only in terms of the desire instituted in this system of presencing—insofar as human beings already experience the "challenge" of challenging nature in this way—they themselves are subject to, set upon and ordered by this desire to see everything in terms of this order of presencing. Human beings too, indeed "more originarily" than nature, come to appear as Bestand, as "human material," or "human resources" as our administrative systems put it.

Within the technological system, both natural and human "resources" are integrated into a system of information within which they are ordered in terms of calculated availability. Such a system, Heidegger notes, is determined by a transformed causality:

> It [i.e., such causality] now displays neither the character of letting something be occasioned in bringing it forth, nor the nature of the causa efficiens, nor indeed that of the causa formalis. Presumably, causality will collapse into a reporting [Melden]— a reporting challenged forth—of standing reserves that must be secured either simultaneously or in sequence. (VA, 26–27)

The "causality" determining the system of technological revealing is neither that of the Greek *poiēsis,* nor that of a *causa efficiens,* a human agent or "subject" who effects something, nor even that of a *causa formalis* in which a material object is produced in accordance with its *eidos.* If causality collapses, it occurs in that all "natural causality" now becomes entirely subsumed under the causality of freedom, except that the latter no longer belongs to the subjectivity of the individual will, but to the absolute subjectivity of the "will to will." Technological causality is not primarily in the control of human beings as individual subjects. It regulates itself in such a way that the individual, embodied human being is but a substitutable element or "cog in the machine," infinitely replaceable within the system that controls human beings in controlling itself. Any productive activity undertaken is not "caused" by the individual human will, but destined by the "will to will" of the system itself, to which each individual has already subjected themselves in inserting themselves into the system. But technological causality is not primarily concerned with the production of material goods in accordance with their *eidos* either. It is concerned primarily with the regulated production of presencing. It is presencing that is called upon and challenged to "report itself" (*sich melden*) in a manner calculable in advance. The verb *melden* carries the sense of an instantaneous or momentary appearing in which someone or something "announces" their presence, like the momentary blip on the radar screen of air traffic control. Heidegger elsewhere explains that this "reporting" is to be understood in the sense that the systematic theories of contemporary physics, although they are not entirely "invented," do not provide a *description* of nature. Rather they are constrained to only ever giving "news reports," *Nachrichten* (the word is also that used for the television "news" programs), concerning nature.[33] These "news reports" no longer describe nature in accordance with its intrinsic aspects, but are "oriented exclusively toward the calculability of their object. To the extent that there is any description here, it is not concerned with bringing the outward appearance [*Aussehen*] of an object before our eyes, but limits itself to establishing [*festzustellen*] something of nature in a mathematical formula that presents [*darstellt*] a law of motion" (VS, 95). Whereas Greek *theōria* moves toward an ontological description of nature, "contemporary theory, by contrast, relinquishes any ontological tendency." Modern experimental theory, as Heidegger emphasizes with reference to Bohr and Heisenberg, is purely methodological and no longer has any ontological significance (VS, 93–95).[34]

---

[33] On *Nachrichten* as "an as yet scarcely comprehended phenomenon of the present" see GA 45, 134.

[34] See also BSD, 8; and SD, 65.

The End of Technology

In "The Question Concerning Technology," Heidegger makes it quite clear
that the word "essence" (*Wesen*) in the phrase "the essence of technology"
is not at all to be understood in the metaphysical sense of *essentia,* namely,
substantive being or whatness. The word *Wesen,* rather, is to be understood in the verbal and temporal sense of enduring (*währen*), and is to be
thought in terms of presencing (*Anwesen*). This is in deliberate contrast
to the traditional philosophical equation of "essence" with the nonsensible
eidos, the idea or primary form that tells us the universal genus, the *logos*
that in modern representation becomes the "concept." Heidegger recalls
that a certain enduring is indeed also thought by Socrates and Plato when
they think the enduring essence of something as *eidos* and *idea.* They understand such enduring, however, in the sense of a permanent perduring and
remaining (*das Fortwährende, aei on*) that is distinguished from the particular, transitory appearing of form in its material instantiations. "Yet,"
Heidegger writes, "in no way can it ever be established that that which
endures should reside solely in what Plato thinks as the *idea,* Aristotle
as *to ti ēn einai* (that which any particular thing has always been), or
what metaphysics in the most diverse interpretations thinks as *essentia*"
(VA, 35). "The Question Concerning Technology" thus invites us to take
leave of the traditional sense of essence that opposes it to the temporal,
to the transitory, and to the particular. Or rather—and here is something
"astonishing"—technology itself extends this invitation:

> The *Ge-stell,* as a destining of revealing, is thus indeed the
> essence of technology, but never in the sense of genus or *essentia.*
> If we pay heed to this, then we are struck by something astonish-
> ing: It is technology that demands of us that we think in another
> sense that which is usually understood by "essence." (VA, 34)

Why is this so? To say that there is no "essence" of technology in the
classical sense might be taken as implying that there are only particular
"technologies," specific instantiations of technological processes. Yet this
would still imply that there is something like a concept of what technology
is in general, by which we could then first recognize these various instances.
This conclusion would merely be an inversion that would remain subject
to the same logic of the concept. Presumably, if there is something about
technology itself, about the "essence" of technology, that resists this logic
of the concept, then it must lie in the essence of technology "as a destining of revealing." *Ge-stell,* as this destining, must be something other than
the mere application of a general idea or concept. It must entail something

other than *technē* as it has been classically, that is, philosophically understood, namely as the application of a prior idea or concept to a material reality. This "something other," we shall suggest, points in the direction of an originary finitude of presencing. Indeed, if Heidegger's claim here is sustainable, technology itself must point in this direction. But how?

If the "essence," now understood as the essential enduring and prevailing of technology, is nothing other than a particular transformation of desire inseparable from human activity, this nevertheless does not at all mean that such desire is primarily subject to the control of the human will and willpower. For the "will" in its modern guise (for which the Kantian conception of freedom as autonomy remains paradigmatic) is only another name for subjectivity as a particular relation to presencing. The will that unfolds into technological desire is a sublation of finite Kantian autonomy into the absolute subjectivity of the "will to will" that subjects this relation and law of freedom to the *technē* of a production of presencing, one that strives to produce *itself* (self-presencing) in and through its production of the presencing of objects or "standing reserve." Thus Heidegger writes, in the collection of remarks published as "Overcoming Metaphysics":

> The will is already in itself the accomplishing of striving [*Vollzug des Strebens*] as the actualizing of whatever is striven after, in which process the latter is specifically known and consciously posited in the concept, that is, as something represented in general. To the will there belongs consciousness.... The goal-lessness, namely the essential goal-lessness of the unconditional will to will, is the consummation [*Vollendung*] of the essence of the will that announced itself in Kant's concept of practical reason as pure will. The latter wills itself, and as the will it is being. This is why, with regard to content, the pure will and its law are formal. The pure will as form is the sole content of itself. (VA, 84–85)

The formality of the law that emerges here corresponds to the logical organisation of *existentia* whose priority (goal) is self-regulation, and which invades and permeates the presence of material content (*essentia*) while simultaneously denying and withdrawing its own investment. The movement of such simultaneous withdrawal and investment sustains the economy of technological desire.

Yet how can the will produce itself? It cannot, after all, first bring itself *ex nihilo* into being. It produces "itself" only secondarily, only indirectly, in and through the detour of the infinitely ongoing activity of producing the presencing of beings, of making them present in the manner of its ongoing, representational challenging forth and ordering. In so doing, however, this very activity maintains "itself" in the element of a continual absence, a pervasive nothingness or *nihil* that is the absence of any determinate presence or actuality of beings. Being, in its technological configuration as infinite substitutability, is this very *nihil* in which the presencing of actuality is suspended. This is why, with regard to the desire documented in this transformation of *technē*, the desire of the "will to will," Heidegger can describe technology as "the organisation of lack":

> The exploitation of all materials, including "human" raw material, for the technological production of the unconditional possibility of a production of everything is, in a concealed manner, determined by the complete emptiness in which beings, the material of what is actual, hang suspended. This emptiness must be filled out. Yet since the emptiness of being, especially when it cannot be experienced as such, can never be filled out with a fullness of beings, the only remaining way of evading it is the unceasing establishing of beings with respect to the constant possibility of ordering as the form in which goalless activity is secured. From this perspective, because it is unknowingly drawn toward the emptiness of being, technology is the organisation of lack. (VA, 91)

The goallessness intrinsic to technological desire is not, however, perspicuous to it. Such desire, in the form of the will to will, remains blind to its own lack; it cannot even see this nothingness as its own, let alone assume an appropriate response to it. Yet the goallessness of the technological operation does not mean that it has no goal whatsoever. It means, rather, that goallessness—the impossibility of arrival—is itself the goal. It means that "the will has forced the impossible upon the possible as its goal" (VA, 95). The possible, which here refers not to a particular possibility that might be actualized, but to the future proper, the source of possibility as such, has become the impossible, that is, that whose presencing is refused, because infinitely deferred: the impossible future. The impossible future is the projection of "the new" as goal: not of this or that particular new thing or product, but of the new as such, of that future which, although *as future* it can never be actualized, is posited *as though* it could arrive. The impossible is thereby (hypothetically or virtually) made possible; the possible, the future, becomes the impossible; the impossible itself becomes omnipresent. Thus projected as the only goal or final cause of the consummate subjectivity of the will to will, the impossible constitutes the end that has claimed technological desire in advance, enabling its infinite self-deferral and self-perpetuation. What is thus unknowingly appropriated along with and as the very basis of this self-like activity of the will to will is precisely nothing: "the will to will can will nothing other than a void nothingness over and against which it asserts itself, without being able to know its own consummate nothingness" (VA, 69). The activity of the will to will is literally nothing apart from the presencing and presence of the products it produces. Technological existence, the technological "operation," dwells in this uncanny nothingness.[35]

In the present context, we are using the term "technological desire" to designate a dominant human response to the phenomenon of technology. Such technological desire, which indeed makes way for the "will to will," is itself only a response to the essence of technology. Once again, Heidegger's primary concern in "The Question Concerning Technology" is directed toward the *essence* of technology, in the sense of "essence" we have indicated, and not toward technology itself. This is another way of saying that "technology" is not *primarily* about things, products, or instruments, nor even about the human use of such technological products, but rather concerns a demand that is made upon human beings to respond to being (to presencing) in the manner of a very specific revealing. Similarly, with respect to what Heidegger calls "the danger," he states unequivocally that "It is not technology that is the danger.... The essence of technology ...is the danger" (VA, 31–32). The "essence" of technology concerns not the independent being of things as such, but our more primordial human relation to the kind of presence in which things first show themselves as such, reveal themselves in a particular way. The "danger," as the essence of technology, is being itself, that is, the presencing of a historical world that places a demand upon human beings to respond to presence (to being) in a particular way. *Ge-stell,* as the "essence" of technology, is thus primarily a *demand:*

> We now name that demand [*Anspruch*] which challenges and gathers human beings to order as standing reserve that which reveals itself—the *Ge-stell.* (VA, 23)

Human beings are "gathered" (*versammelt*) by *Ge-stell* into a particular form of activity insofar as this demand "concentrates human beings on setting to order the actual as standing reserve" (VA, 23). Insofar as human beings understand themselves only in terms of the demand of *Ge-stell* that challenges them to reveal beings in the manner of ordering them into standing reserve, human beings too, as technological desire increasingly asserts

---

[35] In the *Beiträge zur Philosophie,* Heidegger thus identifies this goallessness with supreme nihilism: "the real nihilism: one is unwilling to concede this goal-lessness.... the greatest nihilism, an organized closing one's eyes to the goal-lessness of human beings" (GA 65, 139).

itself, expanding to planetary dimensions, come to understand themselves and other human beings in virtually the same terms. And yet, Heidegger emphasizes, human beings can never become "mere" standing reserve, precisely because they are challenged or claimed "more originarily" than other beings (VA, 22).[36] Humans are never reducible to the independent being of "things," and yet this is not, as in Kant, because the essence of "personhood" or of being human lies in the independence of autonomy. It is, Heidegger writes, because technological revealing does not occur "somewhere beyond all human activity." But, he adds, "neither does it occur only *in* man, nor authoritatively *through* him" (VA, 27). Technological revealing does not occur only "in" man, conceived as a sphere of subjectivity that stands over and against the world; nor does it occur authoritatively (*maßgebend*) through human beings, in the sense that human beings do not first provide or disclose the measure (*Maß*) of such revealing. For all human revealing, as human activity, is already in every case a response to presencing, to "an event of unconcealment that has already occurred" (VA, 22).

Yet it is not only this event, the event-like character of finite presencing, that has always already occurred, earlier than any human response. The event of unconcealment itself is a calling: it "calls forth [*hervorruft*] the human being" into particular ways of revealing. In order to understand the way in which technological revealing occurs "not beyond" us and yet not exclusively in or through us, we must examine how the essence of technology occurs as a call, as a historically rooted claim or demand. We must learn "to be astonished at that which is coming in its earliness." This means "the endeavor to think through in a still more originary manner that which was originally thought," namely, in the Greek beginning. For the proto-technical Platonic-Aristotelian thinking of being as *eidos* and of our relation to being as a *theōrein* of the *eidos*—as that which can be brought forth into presence—still claims and determines the activity of modern technological revealing. The Greek beginning in this sense continues to be our destiny, determining our present and our future.

---

[36] Cf. the reference in *Being and Time* to the Greek reduction of *pragmata* to "mere" things on account of the proto-technical, theoretical understanding of beings in terms of their *eidos* (discussed in chapter 3 above). As the Greek, "eidetic" understanding of things unfolds into modern subjectivity, the presence-at-hand in which things show themselves becomes transformed from understanding such presence in terms of the *eidos* into the objectivity of what is set (*gestellt*) before the representational activity of a subject. Such activity, however, is further transformed when the setting-before of representation becomes subservient to a setting-before of that which is (always yet) to be produced, namely, the presencing of beings as *Bestand*. In this final transformation, theoretical activity—which has never been able to see or set before it its own activity as such—finds the confirmation of its power only in and through the presence of its products, of its "technical" achievements.

Heidegger calls "destiny" (*Geschick*) the primary demand or claim that brings human beings onto a particular path or into a particular way of revealing:

> To bring onto a path: in our language, this means *to send* [schicken]. We name that sending that gathers and that first brings human beings onto a path of revealing, *destiny* [Geschick]. From this the essence of all history is determined. (VA, 28)

"History" (*Geschichte*), Heidegger reminds us, does not mean here the science of historiography (*Historie*), nor only the accomplishment of human activity, although it is indeed also that. Presumably *Geschichte* also entails a certain kind of *Historie,* not conceived as a "science" of inquiry into past events, but as a "writing," a narrating and relating of deeds and words accomplished but no longer purely present.[37] History in the sense of *Geschichte* is to be understood, rather, in terms of our responding— thoughtfully, in action—to a demand that issues from an already existing world. To be dependent, in the first instance, upon the claims of a world is to be subjected, always already, to destiny. Human activity or action "first becomes historical as something destinal" (VA, 28).

In the realm of human activity, all revealing happens as a destiny, notes Heidegger, insofar as what is revealed is not simply produced by humans, nor something that is purely under the control of human subjectivity. Human activity occurs as a response (for the most part concealed) not only to an originary finitude of presencing, but also to the particular way in which, at any given moment, such presencing always already calls upon us to respond in one manner or another. "Destiny" in the broadest sense refers simply to this call or claim, which is always inseparable from the finite and singular event of presencing in each instance. In a narrower sense, "destiny" may refer to a primary and more general demand that claims not just a particular individual in this or that situation, but human beings generally in a particular historical era or epoch (such as the primary metaphysical projection that grounds the modern age of the "world picture" and becomes transformed into the destiny that demands modern technological revealing). It is this narrower sense that is Heidegger's main concern in "The Question Concerning Technology." Wherever they find themselves, human

---

[37] Cf. "The Anaximander Fragment," where Heidegger asks: "Yet can we represent or present the earliness of a world era in any other way than by means of historiography? Perhaps historiography [*Historie*] remains for us an uncircumventable means of presenting the historical [*des Geschichtlichen*]. But this does not at all mean that historiography, taken on its own, is capable of bringing about, within the realm of history, a relation that would adequately reach the historical" (H, 301).

beings are always already called upon, "addressed," by the presencing of what is unconcealed:

> The event of such unconcealment has already happened [*sich ereignet*] wherever it calls human beings forth into those ways of revealing that come to be assigned to them. When human beings in their own way reveal that which is present within the realm of unconcealment, then they simply respond to the address [*Zuspruch*] of unconcealment, even where they are in conflict with it. (VA, 22)

Yet the human response to the claims of unconcealment is never causally predetermined. The term "destiny" thus does not mean that the human being is purely passive or "unfree":

> The unconcealment of that which is always proceeds upon a particular path of revealing. The human being is always pervaded by a destiny of revealing. But such destiny is never some force of fate [*das Verhängnis eines Zwanges*]. For the human being indeed first becomes free insofar as he belongs to the realm of such destiny and so becomes a listener, but never a slave.
>
> The essence of freedom is *originarily* not an attribute of the will, nor even of the causality of human willing. (VA, 28)

Heidegger here takes leave not only of the vulgar concept of freedom as "doing whatever we wish," but also of the Kantian concept of freedom as causality of the will bound by the law of autonomy. Human beings are not in themselves the "cause" of their actions. Human actions have no simple "cause" or origin in this sense, but are always an-archic.[38] As anarchic in the sense of having no simple cause or *archē,* they nevertheless remain originary, that is, they participate in bringing to the fore something new, unforeseeable, something that would not otherwise have come into being. The human being, according to Heidegger, first becomes free in belonging to the realm of "destiny." Freedom, he goes on to say, indeed *is* the realm of destiny (VA, 29). This does not say that freedom *is* destiny, but that freedom and destiny are not opposed to one another. Only where there is destiny can there be freedom, and vice versa. Yet freedom does not first make destiny possible. Freedom does not come first; it is not in itself an origin. Indeed, freedom is neither an attribute nor a property of human beings: it is not an exclusively human phenomenon. "Freedom prevails over what is

---

[38] On the anarchic in Heidegger, see Reiner Schürmann, *Heidegger on Being and Acting: From Principles to Anarchy.*

free in the sense of cleared [*des Gelichteten*], that is, revealed" (VA, 28–29). All that has been revealed is thus free: it belongs within freedom, within the clearing as the site of presencing. Yet such freedom does not simply prevail in the sense of a secure "given," a "fact," as it were. Rather, "Freedom is that which conceals in clearing" (*das lichtend Verbergende:* VA, 29); it is an event of finitude which, in closing presence, first holds us open, freeing us in advance for a further claim of presencing to which we must respond. And in this we have no choice. *Already* belonging to such a claim, we are destined to respond to presence—not in a predetermined way, but always in a particular way, always in one way or another, precisely because of the finitude of presencing. Freedom, as an event, thus occurs and comes to pass in the *realm* of destiny. But in what way do human beings enter and belong to this realm of freedom? Heidegger writes that the human being "first comes to be free insofar as he belongs [*gehört*] to the realm of destiny and so becomes a listener [*Hörender*], but never a slave [*Höriger*]." Such belonging is a dwelling in proximity to destiny, a dwelling whereby we come to be listeners, come to be open for the address and call of presencing, of un-concealment, in any given instance. This coming to be (thus, a *poiēsis*) is not a human activity, but the happening of the originary future—an event of origination that occurs in and through human beings, certainly, but only insofar as they already belong historically to a world, only insofar as they have always already given themselves (their presence) over to a having-been, and thus to the possibility of a future. In belonging to the realm of destiny, in listening to its claim—in letting ourselves be claimed by it—we first come to be free. In other words, an originary letting whose primary moment is a "passivity" (a primary, nonexplicit affirmation of mortality) is prior to any possibility of free human action or activity, prior also to the possibility of resistance. Freedom, on Heidegger's account, is an *event* of concealing and clearing which, as an event, remains "concealed and ever self-concealing ... the mystery" (VA, 29).

The dominant sway of modern technology, according to Heidegger's interpretation, is such that it closes human beings off from experiencing this originary event of freedom. Technological desire has in advance already closed itself off from the finitude of its own occurrence, that is, from itself as originarily rooted in the primarily responsive happening of finite human *praxis*. Representing itself as originarily and infinitely active, the will claims its own infinite being only at the expense of finitude. The end of technology, as the impossible future of the infinite striving and self-representation of the will to will, proves to be the impossibility of any end. Yet the pervasive dominance and increasing prevalence of the demand of *Ge-stell* that has claimed technological revealing in advance not only thereby closes off the originary event of freedom; it also precisely *tends to manifest this event as what is concealed,* that is, to manifest it in its very essence, as a self-concealing event of un-concealment. Technology in its essence, as a demand, tends to bring to the fore the originary and finite character of revealing. The end of technology, by the very extremity of its claim, shows itself as the im-possible. Why is this so? How, through the demand of the essence of technology itself, can technology's end come to be seen as end?

The Turning of Presence at the End of Technology

In "The Turning" Heidegger writes:

> But we do not yet hear, we whose hearing and seeing is fading under the domination of technology via radio and film. The constellation of being is the refusal [*Verweigerung*] of world as the desecration of the thing. Refusal is not nothing; it is the highest mystery of being within the domination of *Gestell.* (TK, 46)

Radio and film bring the tele-presentation of the new, they bring what is coming. But they thereby close off as such the dimension of that very coming, the clearing of presencing that occurs as an event of un-concealment. They close off as such the realm of the destiny or demand that calls for the technological disclosure of beings, thereby closing human beings off from the realm of originary freedom as such. The originary finitude of presencing is refused in the domination of technological revealing, oriented as it is toward "the new." Such refusal conceals from human beings the originary event (*Ereignis*) of world, the happening of world as an event of finitude. The constellation, or specific technological configuration of revealing and concealing thereby also refuses any experience of "the thing" in its properly worldly character; it refuses any experience that would not already have demoted the presencing of things to the realm of technological orderability.

This refusal is a concealment specific to *Gestell* as the "essence" of technology, a concealment that Heidegger describes as the "supreme danger." The danger is not technology, but the "essence" of technology, *Gestell* "as a destiny of revealing" (VA, 29), as the specific demand that gives rise to and sustains technological desire. The danger lies in the particular way in which this demand "conceals not only a previous way of revealing, namely, bringing to the fore; rather, it conceals revealing as such, and thereby that wherein the event of unconcealment, that is, truth, happens" (VA, 31). This leads humans to the brink of the possibility of "pursuing and engaging with only that which is revealed in ordering, and of taking from here all measure" (VA, 29). This concealment of the event of originary finitude as such is a failure to see and to hear the demand of technology in its "essence," the demand that has claimed technological desire as such, and is thereby a failure to encounter ourselves in our essence, in our own originary belonging to the finitude of the world. In the era of technological revealing, it indeed seems as though (in Heisenberg's words) we everywhere encounter only ourselves; it seems as though everything we encounter is a mere human construct. Yet this only indicates, remarks Heidegger, that we nowhere encounter ourselves in our "essence," that is, in our belonging to the realm of "destiny," in the freedom of our originary finitude:

> The human being stands so decisively in the draught of the challenging belonging to *Gestell* that he fails to apprehend this as a demand, that he overlooks himself as the one who is claimed and thereby also fails to hear any way in which he ek-sists out of his essence within the realm of an address and thus *never can* encounter only himself. (VA, 31)

To come to see ourselves as those who are claimed, to hear ourselves as those addressed, to encounter ourselves in our "essence," is thus anything but to encounter only ourselves. It entails entering explicitly into an ec-static relation to that which has claimed us, coming to exist knowingly in the realm of an originary finitude. And this entails our first taking "an adequate look" at what *Gestell,* as the "essence" of technology, is as a demand of revealing (VA, 32); it entails coming to see and "to catch sight of [*erblicken*] that which essentially comes to presence [*das Wesende*] in technology, instead of merely staring at what is technological" (VA, 36). Yet according to "The Question Concerning Technology," technology itself— not the essence of technology, but technology itself, the technological, in its very concealing of its own essence—calls upon us to think that very "essence." Heidegger's analysis suggests that it is the claim of the event of un-concealment *as such an event* that beckons us in the happening of technology. The refusal of the happening of world is "not nothing," but rather is itself "the highest mystery of being within the domination of *Ge-stell.*"

This claim of the event of un-concealment itself addresses us, it turns toward us in and through technology. The demand of presencing itself takes another turn—and yet such a turning does not happen without us, without the participation of human beings. It requires that we become open: "When we open ourselves explicitly to the *essence* of technology, we find ourselves unexpectedly taken into a claim that frees us" (VA, 29).

Such opening occurs as questioning. It entails that we come to question what technology is (the traditional question of essence). But in order for us to do so, technology itself must first have become worthy of question for us: it must have become worthy of question with respect to what it itself *conceals,* namely, what it, technology itself, is. This very claim upon us to question it comes from the being of technology, from technology itself as it presents itself to us, in its happening. Technology itself thus opens us to its "essence," to the concealment of finitude, and thereby frees us even as it claims us, bringing us into the realm of freedom, the realm of "destiny." Technology itself in its pervasiveness can free us explicitly to experience its demand as such.

In "The Turning," Heidegger describes how the claim of technological presencing may turn toward human beings in such a way as to grant them explicit insight into such presencing, thereby letting them catch sight of the event of finitude as that which technological desire otherwise conceals. In the specific configuration of technological desire, being itself, as the order-ability of *Gestell,* is "the danger," inasmuch as it threatens to let all beings (including human beings) presence only as standing reserve, subjected in advance to technological organization and planning. The essence of human beings as *praxis,* a *praxis* that is in each case so singular and finite that it essentially cannot be planned "technically," is thereby also concealed, re-fused. Such refusal is a refusal of world, of the finitude of presencing out of which "things" and other human beings, as "mortals," may come to pres-ence together. This refusal of originary finitude is a flight from presence that entails decontextualization, a diminishing responsiveness to whatever presences in the finitude of its given situation. The essence of technology, being itself under the rule of the technological demand concealed in the will to will, is the danger that precisely conceals itself "*as* the danger" (TK, 37).

Catching sight of the danger as danger entails that human beings attend to the dominant claim that calls upon them to respond to presencing in the manner of technological ordering. Such attentiveness—which demands that before asking "what ought we to do?" we must stop to ask "how must we think?"—itself occurs as a *thinking.* But the thinking called for is not that of a free-floating, theoretical contemplation that seeks to determine, in advance and independently of a given situation, what our ethical response should be; the required thinking, rather, responds to a necessity ("how *must* we think?") of another order. Originary thinking is not a *theōrein* that contemplates and dictates in advance the grounds of ethical *praxis.* Originary thinking is itself an acting. Such acting, furthermore, is equally a *poiēsis,* the preparation, bringing about, or "building" of a site:

> For thinking is authentic action, if to act means to lend a hand
> to the essence of being. This means: to prepare (build) for the
> essence of being in the midst of beings that site into which it
> brings itself and its essence to language. Language first gives
> all will to deliberate its paths and ways. Without language, all

activity lacks any dimension in which it could turn to action and take effect. . . . Language is the originary dimension within which the human essence is first able to respond to being and its claim at all, and in its response to belong to being. *This originary response,* expressly carried through, *is thinking.* (TK, 40)[39]

Thinking, as an originary responsiveness to the claim that presencing makes upon us in any given situation, is, in its very accomplishment, a doing, an acting. It lends being (presencing) a hand in first bringing the presence of beings to the fore in a particular way. This bringing to the fore is a *poiēsis,* a letting presence from out of or by way of a responsiveness to the claim that a particular situation makes on us. It is, as responsiveness, a coming to hear the claim or "destiny" by way of which the presencing (being) of a situation already calls upon us, thereby bringing itself to language in and through our very listening. But the presencing of a situation calls upon us in the finitude of the event of that very presencing and its call; our response is itself always already a call of finitude, a call that calls for decision. Decision is not the result of free-floating deliberation that surveys the situation from a distance; rather, deliberation as response is always already closure, is itself always already decision, and such closure is itself origination, the bringing of presence to the fore in a finite way. Yet thinking—the thinking of the thinker or "philosopher"—as authentic action, as an originary responsiveness to this very event, also thereby lets presencing be seen in its very finitude. This is what thinking "does," its quiet action and accomplishment. It brings the finitude of presencing itself to the fore as finitude, thus "preparing" or "building" a "site" in the midst of beings where being itself, as presencing, can *come* to language. The "essence" of the human being is to be the one who, in building, can come to inhabit this site in attending to it, in tending to it and in waiting upon it. The essence of the human being "is to be the one who waits, who waits upon the essence of being in thoughtfully tending to it. Only if the human being, as the shepherd of being, waits upon the truth [unconcealment] of being can he await a coming of the destiny of being, without falling into the mere will to know" (TK, 41). Attending to this site is thus something quite other than the traditional will to know, the desire to see which, increasingly distancing itself from its finite situatedness in the midst of beings, culminates in the "destiny" of modern technology.

The particular "destiny" of modern technology can thus be understood as the increasingly universal dominance of a primary claim or demand made upon human beings to respond to presencing in the manner of ordering.

---

[39] Cf. the beginning of the "Letter on 'Humanism'," W, 145–46.

This claim threatens to subjugate, to refuse and conceal, all other possible claims or demands. The concealment of this danger as danger is, we have argued, the concealment of the event of finitude (freedom) as such. Were human beings to come to see the danger as danger, this would not entail the elimination of technology, but simply seeing *Gestell* as what it is, in its specific relation to finitude. Such a seeing would be a thoughtful attentiveness to what is refused in *Gestell* as such. It would also be a *transformation* in the "destiny" or claim of being as presencing. Such transformation would occur as a knowing relation to concealment, that is, as a thoughtful relating to the appropriative event (*Ereignis*) of presencing itself as finite in each case. But this thoughtful responsiveness would itself be a response to a turning of presence, to a turning whereby presencing itself is destined to us in a different and yet related way. Such turnings in the destiny of presencing itself, however, do not follow any laws of causality. They precisely resist any scientific or calculative predictability, and this because they occur in an event of originary finitude that engages human responsiveness and responsibility. In the case of our present dominant world-destiny, that of modern technology, the turning in question indeed transpires as a kind of "recovery" (*Verwindung*) of the as yet concealed truth of technology. "But the recovery in a destiny of being, here and now, the recovery in *Gestell*, in each case occurs in the event of the arrival of another destiny, one that can neither be calculated in advance in a logical or historiographical manner, nor constructed metaphysically as the result of a process of history" (TK, 38–39).

Such a turning occurs without mediation (in a dialectical-historical or causal sense). At the beginning of the essay Heidegger remarks that "What is destined in each case proceeds intrinsically toward a distinctive *Augenblick* that sends it into another destiny, whereby, however, it does not simply become submerged and lost" (TK, 37–38). The appearance of the *Augenblick* in this context is not fortuitous: it locates the historical turnings of presencing in a site of human responsiveness that occurs in such a way as to be held open for the possibility of hearing and response, for an event (*Ereignis*) of language.[40] With respect to the history of being, the *Augenblick* is nothing less than the site of the epochal turnings of presencing: it is that site in which the emergence of a new world, or of a new openness of world, first occurs and comes to presence, a site in which historical human beings are called upon to respond to the presencing of a world in an new and unforeseeable way.[41]

---

[40] On the *Augenblick* in relation to the *Ereignis* of language (discussed in *Unterwegs zur Sprache*), see Günter Wohlfart, *Der Augenblick*, 113–60.

[41] Compare the conjoining of *Augenblick* and contemporary, world-historical destiny in the "Letter on 'Humanism'," W, 176, 182–84.

In the epoch of technology, coming to see the danger as danger, that is, coming to see the essence of technology as such, occurs insofar as that danger, the concealment of the event, itself turns toward human beings and looks them in the face, as it were. In such turning, it comes to presence, comes into un-concealment. The concealed event of un-concealment itself, no longer concealed as such, comes to presence as such an event, provoking the thoughtful response of human beings. But this turning will be revealed not only to the philosopher who, at the consummation of metaphysics, asks concerning the "essence" of technology, even though it cannot occur without thought. It will occur, presumably, simply in and through the increasing progression of technological revealing. Will not human beings come to be increasingly less "held," spellbound, fascinated, by the ever-more punctual nature of technological presencing? Will they not become increasingly left empty, indeed increasingly bored by the constant orientation toward "the new" in technological consumerism that drives them to infinite distraction without abode? In the 1929/30 course *The Fundamental Concepts of Metaphysics: World, Finitude, Solitude,* Heidegger had already asked whether a profound boredom is not indeed the supressed fundamental attunement of the modern age—an attunement that, once genuinely awakened and experienced as such, would impel us toward the "extremity" of the *Augenblick* of authentic action and its own resolute openness, and before this toward an authentic knowing of the phenomenon of the *Augenblick* itself.[42] In the *Beiträge zur Philosophie,* profound boredom is explicitly identified as the concealed destination of modern science (GA 65, 157).

Heidegger's thesis concerns the issue of presencing itself as such presencing manifests and/or conceals itself *in the midst of beings themselves,* now reduced to standing reserve. In the age of mass television and computer technology, what comes to the fore more evidently than the event of presencing as such, lodged within sequences of increasingly disconnected events of sudden appearing and disappearing, events of un-concealment that simply "announce themselves" without any underlying coherence and without any end in sight? Will not technology bring about, that is, manifest its own end *as such,* become at once increasingly transparent in what it is, and yet increasingly obscure as to its provenance? Will not technology itself become increasingly visible *as a demand,* namely, the demand upon human beings to respond to presence in the manner of the will to will? Would this not be a turning in the very nature of the claim that the essence of technology makes upon us? Would not such a turning call for thinking?

Such a turning, writes Heidegger, can occur only "suddenly," in an "unmediated" manner, in a sudden event in which the "essence" of being as

---

[42] See GA 29/30, §§31–38.

Gestell is cleared. It occurs "in a flash," as an *Ereignis,* a finite and appropriative event of presencing:

> *Blitzen* [to flash], in terms both of the derivation of the word
> and the issue it names, means to look or glance [*blicken*]. In
> the look and as look, coming to presence enters into its own
> illuminating. Moving through the element of its illuminating,
> the look retrieves that which it catches sight of into its looking.
> Looking, however, simultaneously preserves, in its illuminating,
> the concealed darkness of its provenance as that which has not
> been cleared. The in-turning of the flash of the truth of being
> is insight [*Einblick*]. (TK, 43)

This sudden vision is a vision that brings its own illumination with it:
the happening of presencing as an event of clearing that first lets beings
be seen in their presencing. But it is equally a vision of concealment, a
look that looks from out of concealment, a look of concealment—a glance
that preserves within it "the concealed darkness of its provenance." What
is it that this look of concealment catches sight of? The look as "insight"
alludes to the title "Insight into That Which Is," the title of the lecture
series in which "The Turning" was the concluding lecture. But this insight,
Heidegger now explains, does not refer to the human activity of looking
or seeing:

> From the first and almost to the last it has seemed as though
> "insight into that which is" meant only a look that we human
> beings of our own accord cast into that which is. That which is
> is usually taken to be beings. For it is of beings that we assert
> "is." Yet now everything has turned around. Insight does not
> name any discerning look that we take at beings. Insight as
> in-flashing is the *Ereignis* of the constellation of the turning
> within the essence of being itself, specifically in the epoch of
> *Gestell.* (TK, 44)

In representing the thing as a mere being and setting it into orderability, the essence of technology conceals not only "the nearness of world
that nears us in the thing." It conceals this very concealment as such. And
yet, amid all the dissimulation that characterizes technological presencing, writes Heidegger, the "illuminating look" (*Lichtblick*) of world lights
up, "clears itself."[43] "Although veiled, *Gestell* still remains look, and not
some blind destiny in the sense of a completely ordained fate" (TK, 44–45).

---

[43] The term *Lichtblick* appears to be taken from Schelling. Cf. GA 29/30, 529, and
the 1936 course published as *Schellings Abhandlung über das Wesen der menschlichen*

The "look" of world is not simply our apprehending the presencing of beings as a whole as already present before us, but a vision (a self-showing
or manifestation) of the concealment that is at play, at work, in all such
presencing—in the face of beings themselves. This look as the "glance" or
"flash" of world is the "truth" or un-concealment of being, as a "play" of
presencing and concealment, "the worlding of the world as the mirror-play
of heavens and earth, mortals and gods." "Worlding" means the finite happening of the presencing of beings as a whole as a happening of originary
finitude. Such happening, as an *Ereignis* or event of finitude, is, Heidegger
writes, *eignende Eräugnis:* the disclosive event of a glance that brings beings
into their own, into what is appropriate to them.[44]
    This vision of un-concealment, of the concealed event of world, does not
happen without human beings. Yet nor are human beings the originators of
this vision. They are, rather, those who are caught sight of in such insight:

> When the event of insight occurs [*Wenn Einblick sich ereignet*],
> then humans are the ones who are struck, in their essence, by
> the flash of being. Humans are those who are looked upon in
> such insight.

> Only when the human essence, as that which is looked upon in
> the insight of this event, renounces human self-will [*Eigensinn*]
> and projects itself away from itself toward that insight, can the
> human being in his essence respond to the claim of this insight.
> In such responding the human being is gathered into his own
> [*ge-eignet*] in such a way that, within the safeguarded element of
> world, he may, as the mortal, look toward the divine. (TK, 45)

Freiheit (1809) (SA). See also the 1931/32 course on Plato, where the term is used to
designate the essence of freedom, as the clearing of a projection of being (*Seinsentwurf*)
to which one binds oneself in advance: "The essence of freedom is, in short, a *Lichtblick:*
letting a light emerge for oneself in advance and binding oneself to such a light." Through
such emergence and binding, beings come to be seen in a particular light: such is, for
example, the projection of nature that enables modern science (GA 34, 60f.).
    [44] On *Ereignis* as *Eräugnis*, see *Identität und Differenz*, where Heidegger states:
"Er-eignen heißt ursprünglich: er-äugnen, d.h. erblicken, im Blicken zu sich rufen, an-
eignen" (ID, 24–25). Heidegger also here notes the untranslatability of the word *Ereignis*,
which names something "singular" (*einzig*). According to these remarks, *Ereignis* means
"catching sight of . . . , calling to oneself in looking, appropriating as one's own" (see also
US, 258, 260, 264; and VA, 95). However, as the present context helps to clarify, such
"looking" and "catching sight of" do not refer to a purely human activity (cf. Ruin,
Enigmatic Origins, 202 n. 64). "Looking" here cannot simply or primarily be thought
in terms of the activity of the eye as such. Rather, it is things themselves that call to us
in looking at us, in "catching our eye," in showing themselves in their very withdrawal
(*Enteignis*), thus (appropriatively, via the essence of language) coming into their own
being (*Ereignis*). See Ruin, 199–207 for some more general remarks on the *Augenblick*
and *Ereignis*.

Only in responding to this claim of the presencing or look of concealment can human beings come to be gathered into their own, come to find their own proper abode in the presencing of world. In such response, human beings first *come to be* mortals. Coming to dwell in such an abode is presumably to be contrasted with the epochal turning of being described here in all its "suddenness" (such suddenness suggesting the unforeseen moment of *exaiphnēs* that marks the finitude of the *Augenblick*);[45] it is not something that can simply be achieved once and for all. It entails, rather, learning to dwell in this very coming, in the properly finite element of the *Augenblick*. Such a learning, presumably, as preparation and building, would be the most proper action of originary thinking.

---

[45] On *exaiphnēs*, see our remarks in chapter 4, 116–17n. 28.

Part III

The Threshold of Representation: The Augenblick in Heidegger's Reading of Nietzsche

In Nietzsche's fundamental metaphysical position ...there occurs the greatest and most profound gathering, that is, consummation [*Vollendung*] of all essential metaphysical positions in Western philosophy since Plato and in the light of Platonism. (NI, 469)

...Thus it is advisable for you to postpone reading Nietzsche for a while and to first study Aristotle for ten or fifteen years. (WD, 70)

Chapter 7

Vision and the Enigma

In a transformation already prepared in Greek philosophy (but also only prepared, and by no means necessary), *theōria* in modernity thus becomes world-representational thinking, a "seeing" that occupies an imagined third-person, spectatorial position from which it sees everything and to which it relates everything back: the "Archimedean point," as Hannah Arendt calls it.[1] The imagined identification with this Archimedean vantage point levels out the time of the world into a series of homogenously ordered "now"-points, thereby eclipsing the originary time of the world, the time of the *Augenblick* as the time of originary action. In modern representation, the spectator stands and acts at a contemplative remove from the world as a whole, which he or she represents as "picture." This distance, which is quite other than the distance intrinsic to the being of the self in originary *praxis,* is precisely a concealment of one's own involvement as a finite, acting being who is addressed by and always already entangled with the presencing of the world. It entails an alienation, not from an already existing, hypostatized "true self" or self-presence, but from one's own finite worldliness and embodiment as a site of the possibility of originary *praxis.* The "alienation" in question is the concealment not of an original presence or self-presence, but precisely of the absence that pervades and attends all finite action.

This contrast between the stance of modern representation and the stance of what we have been calling originary *praxis,* understood in terms of the specific seeing intrinsic to each, is highlighted in Heidegger's 1937 course on Nietzsche's thought of the eternal recurrence of the same. This thought, and Heidegger's interpretation of it, is of crucial significance for our theme, because it announces the critical limit of modern representational thinking in making visible that which representation is unable to think, and which

---

[1] See *The Human Condition* (Chicago: The University of Chicago Press, 1958), §36ff.

it must exclude in order to be able to constitute itself as such, namely, the finitude of originary *praxis*. Our remarks here restrict themselves to a renewed consideration of the *Augenblick* and its temporality; we shall not attempt to address the wider context of Heidegger's reading.[2]

The relevant part, for our purposes, of Heidegger's interpretation is found in his reading of the eternal return as presented in *Thus Spake Zarathustra,* and specifically in the section entitled "On the Vision and the Enigma." The enigma in question, notes Heidegger, concerns the concealment of beings as a whole, as the "vision" (*Gesicht*) of "the most solitary one," the vision that becomes visible only in what Nietzsche calls our "supreme solitude."[3] The enigma itself is presented by Zarathustra as he narrates the story of his ascent up a mountainside, accompanied by a dwarf, the "spirit of gravity," who rests on his shoulder. In the course of his ascent Zarathustra confronts the dwarf, who drags him downward, with an invitation to think his "most abyssal thought." The confrontation occurs at a gateway, which bears the inscription *"Augenblick."* In the gateway, two long avenues meet, one leading forward, the other leading back. The two avenues, one the image of the past, the other the image of the future, run counter to one another; each leads in an infinite direction, into eternity. The gateway and its two avenues thus present an image of time, seen from the *Augenblick,* from the "now." The image as a whole brings the enigma into view, albeit not yet *as* an enigma. A process of questioning first lets what is seen, this "vision," become visible as the enigma that it ultimately is—but only for the one who remains open to it in the manner of a critical questioning.

In the story, questioning proceeds in two phases. Zarathustra begins by interrogating the dwarf, who is described as one who is "curious" (*der Neugierige*). In his curiosity, the dwarf sits on a rock in front of Zarathustra, where he has a vantage point on what is going on. Zarathustra first asks the dwarf whether, if one were to proceed along one of these avenues, one avenue would ever meet the other; or whether, instead, the two avenues run counter to one another eternally. The dwarf's response is that "everything straight lies"; that "All truth is curved; time itself is a circle." The dwarf's answer implies, as Heidegger clarifies it, that the two avenues meet in some remote infinity, unsurveyable by us; that time thus constitutes a homogenous, uninterrupted path; and that the moment or "now"-point thus returns infinitely, eternally as the same, as an ever-identical point on this

---

[2] The following interpretation was first presented as part of a seminar on the history of contemporary thought at DePaul University in the Spring of 1996. It is dedicated to the students who participated in that class.

[3] We here follow Heidegger's account at NI, 289ff. For a discussion of solitude, see NI, 275–76, 300–01, and 302–18; also GA 29/30, §§2–3 and §§39–40.

path, a segment on the perimeter, as it were, of this imagined great "circle" of time.

Zarathustra, however, is dissatisfied with the dwarf's "contemptuous" response; he initiates a second phase of questioning in the following manner:

> "Behold," I continued, "behold this *Augenblick!* From this gateway *Augenblick* a long avenue runs eternally *backward:* behind us lies an eternity.
>
> Must not whatever *can* run its course with respect to all things already have run this avenue once before? Must not whatever *can* occur with respect to all things already once have occurred, be done, have run its course?"

This question asks us to consider the relation between the finitude of things and the supposed infinity of time. In an infinite time, all finite things and events, which need only a finite time in order to occur, must already have occurred. Not only must "all things," beings as a whole in their actuality, already have occurred; all things with respect to their *possibility,* as Zarathustra emphasizes, the *future* of all finite things, would already have to be exhausted in an infinite time. Were time infinite, there would be no possibility of anything new being disclosed: there would be no future.

Yet what is decisive in the thinking of this thought, in this vision of beings as a whole, is the perspective in which it is to be thought. What is decisive is the way in which beings as a whole stand in relation to the thinker himself, the way in which the thinker relates to what is seen in the vision opened up by this thought. Heidegger draws attention to the way in which this second phase of questioning opens, namely with the injunction "Behold this *Augenblick!*" The entire vision, he notes, "is to be pondered anew from the perspective of the *Augenblick* and in relation to the *Augenblick.*" Zarathustra's questioning continues in drawing our attention away from what might easily be envisaged as simply standing before us—all things in their course—toward the seeing itself, toward the *Augenblick* as the moment of vision in which and from out of which beings as a whole are seen:

> "And if everything has already been there: what do you, dwarf, think of this *Augenblick?* Must not this gateway too already— have been there?
>
> And are not all things knotted tight together in such a way that this *Augenblick* draws after it *all* that is to come? And *therefore*—itself as well?..."

And this slow spider creeping in the moonlight, and this moonlight itself, and I and you in the gateway ...—must we not all
already have been there?"

The second phase of questioning unfolds and culminates in such a way
that the dwarf offers no response; he disappears from the scene. And this, as
Heidegger remarks, because new conditions of understanding are brought
into play, conditions that the dwarf is unable or unwilling to entertain.
These new conditions entail that questioning now proceed starting from
the *Augenblick;* it "demands taking up a position of one's own within the
Augenblick itself, that is, within time and its temporality" (NI, 297).

What does it mean to assume such a position or stance? In his commentary on a later section of *Thus Spake Zarathustra,* "The Convalescent,"
Heidegger returns to this question. The dwarf, he remarks, makes things too
easy for himself in his initial response. He regards the place where the two
paths meet, if they meet, in a purely formal manner, as an empty infinity or
"eternity," far removed from himself. The *Augenblick* thus appears as the
point where "everything recurs in a sequential process of sheer alternation
that levels out everything as it passes through the gateway" (NI, 311). The
dwarf sees time itself as a sequential and perpetual process that passes from
a not-yet-now to the now, and from there into a no-longer-now. According
to this schema, the two avenues of past and future merely pursue one another sequentially—and so on for all eternity; how, then, are they supposed
to "collide head-on," as Zarathustra puts it? "And yet," notes Heidegger:

there is a collision. To be sure, it is there only for one who
does not remain a spectator [*Zuschauer*], but who *himself is* the
Augenblick, who acts futurally and in so doing does not discard
the past, but rather simultaneously takes it up and affirms it....
To see the *Augenblick* means: to stand in it. But the dwarf keeps
to the outside, perches on the periphery. (NI, 311–12)

The dwarf remains a mere spectator, observing things from the outside.
In his attitude of "curiosity," he shares with all representational thinking—
which merely posits all beings before itself as objects of observation—a
fundamental *indifference* toward beings as a whole in their presencing, and,
as a correlate, a fundamental indifference toward his own being, toward
his own place and stance as participating in such presencing, as a stance
in the midst of beings as a whole, and not simply standing over against
them at a "theoretical," representational remove. For, as Heidegger later
notes, "the principle characteristic of the curious is that, fundamentally and
from the outset, nothing of that which they are curious about concerns or
affects them; all curiosity thrives on this essential indifference" (NI, 338).

Such indifference (*Gleichgültigkeit*), in which everything is experienced as being ultimately of equal (*gleich*) worth (*Gültigkeit*), in which "everything is the same [*gleich*]," in which "nothing is worthwhile," is also the essential trait of what Nietzsche diagnoses as nihilism: with the (apparent) abolition of the suprasensuous world, the world of the sensuous appears without intrinsic value or worth. Thought in this way, the eternal recurrence of the same (*die ewige Wiederkunft des Gleichen*) appears as a formulation of the most extreme nihilism.[4]

Heidegger's analysis emphasizes the divergence between, on the one side, the mere spectator who embodies "habitual acquaintance and observation" (*Kennen und Zuschauen*), and on the other side "proper knowing" (*eigentliches Wissen*) (NI, 310). Proper or authentic knowing corresponds here to philosophical *sophia,* which is a knowledge of world, of the being of beings as a whole, and of one's own place as an acting and thinking being in the midst of such beings. The insight of such knowing first lets us see (without guarantees or certainty, since it is not calculative), that is, weigh up, what seems appropriate in the finite situation of action. Our habitual acquaintance and "knowledge" of things levels out good and evil, indeed acknowledging "death, departure, and disintegration," "all destruction and everything negative, adverse, and supremely evil," yet it does so only with the comforting reassurance that things will change and get better again in the course of time. In this way, notes Heidegger, everything gets continually leveled out. "This leveling out makes everything indifferent; conflict becomes leveled down into mere alternation; and in this manner one has a comforting formula for the whole and maintains oneself outside of every decision" (NI, 310–11). Such a stance obtains when the eternal return of the same is "known" only as a ditty, in a dwarf-like manner where the words have no recoil upon the existence of the one repeating them, for they too in their essential import have in advance been reduced to the level of a representation. Such a stance fails to let the thought that is to be thought here weigh as "the greatest burden" upon our actions.[5]

By contrast to such an observer, to think the thought of eternal recurrence in the manner invited by Zarathustra's second phase of questioning means, as Heidegger puts it, *to be the Augenblick.* "To see the *Augenblick* means: to stand in it." But this vision and its stance are fundamentally different from the seeing and stance of the dwarf. Rather than standing at a distance from what is to be thought, picturing it in a representational manner, standing in the *Augenblick* means "taking up a position of one's own within the *Augenblick,* that is, within time and its temporality."

---

[4] *Der Wille zur Macht,* §55.
[5] *Die Fröhliche Wissenschaft,* §341.

In taking up such a stance, one becomes the *Augenblick* itself; and such a stance is simultaneously an "acting." One acts futurally, into the future, in the sense that "what will come to be is precisely a matter for decision" (NI, 312). By contrast with the dwarf, with the representative of the "everyday," for whom every day is ultimately the same, to be the *Augenblick* is to acknowledge and explicitly assume the stance that one already is, as a stance that stands into the possible, in acknowledging and assuming the decisive moment of one's own finite temporality—decisive with respect to the being of beings as a whole, with respect to the way in which the presencing of a world occurs. In explicitly assuming such a stance, one comes to stand in a new way between the necessary (what one has been) and the possible (what one can come to be), explicitly entering the ec-stasis of originary temporality. The dwarf, by contrast, understands himself and the being of all other beings as eternally the same: he posits beings as a whole in such a way as to set himself outside the time of the world. From the outside vantage point proffered by such a stance, time indeed appears like a series of indifferent now-points. The dwarf fundamentally knows nothing of himself as a being whose very being is temporal, who thus has the intrinsic possibility of explicitly assuming his own being as that of a finite stance whose thought and actions participate in transforming the presencing of the world. As Heidegger later puts it, to represent beings in the manner of the outside spectator is like forgetting to include oneself in the being of the world:

> Merely to represent to oneself that he or she is a progression of processes and is, as it were, forged as a link in a chain of circumstances that enter on the scene time after time in an endlessly circling monotony—merely to represent oneself in such a way is to be absent from oneself [*nicht bei sich selbst*], not to be as the very being that inherently belongs within the whole of beings. To represent the human being in this way means to forget altogether to take him into account as a self; it is like someone who undertakes to count the number of people who are present but forgets to count himself. To represent human beings in this manner means to calculate everything extrinsically, as though one could slip stealthily outside of beings and take up a stance outside it all. (NI, 398–99)

To "stand in" the *Augenblick* means not only not having the stance of a mere, uninvolved spectator, however. It is also not to be understood as standing "in" the *Augenblick* as though the gateway *Augenblick* were a mere framework, represented as a kind of spatio-temporal container. This is also to say that assuming an appropriate stance (namely, appropriate to what is to be thought here, appropriate to the way in which the thought is depicted, which is itself determined by that which is to be thought in this poetic telling) entails the explicit engagement of a moment of excess that essentially cannot be depicted, set before us in an image or picture, or reduced to the content of what is poetically presented in the text. The stance called for entails transposing oneself into the *Augenblick* in such a way as "to be the *Augenblick*" oneself, which is why Heidegger insists from the outset that seeing and taking hold of the enigma as such require a "leap" (*Sprung*), a transition that is fundamentally different from the moves of deductive or calculative thinking (NI, 289-90). To "stand in" the *Augenblick* in the sense of being the *Augenblick* is not to be determinately situated at a fixed point, but to be ec-static in a peculiarly finite and yet indeterminate manner.[6]

In order to adequately understand the nature of the "stance" in question, we must first look more closely, albeit briefly, at the temporality of the *Augenblick* itself. As we can already see, Heidegger's account of this temporality closely parallels the analysis given in *Being and Time*. It should go without saying that we cannot here exhaust, or even approach the entire wealth of what invites our attention in Heidegger's interpretation. For reasons of economy, we must restrict our remarks to a few essential pointers.

Heidegger emphasizes that the thought of eternal return thinks the way in which beings as a whole are. For a thinking that thinks from out of the *Augenblick,* the phenomenon designated "beings as a whole" (*das Seiende im Ganzen*) is not to be conceived as some kind of represented totality (the world as picture) or aggregate of beings. It refers, rather, to the way in which everything (world) presences in and as the *Augenblick,* which also means, finitely. The *Augenblick* is the moment of the presencing of beings as a whole, but only for someone whose very being *is* the *Augenblick.* Yet what does it mean to "be" the *Augenblick?* Does one oneself become the presencing of all other beings? In a certain way, indeed—but not in the sense that one would become other beings in the manner of coinciding with, dissolving into, or becoming identical with their being, conceived metaphysically as the independent being of things subsisting as independently present-at-hand. To understand this requires that one experience thoughtfully the fact that being does not belong to beings as their own, as their property, or as something they "have," just as my own being is not something I possess,

---

[6] Cf. the way in which, in *Being and Time,* the temporality of anxiety is said to hold the *Augenblick* in the indeterminacy of its ownmost possibility, "at the ready" (*auf dem Sprung*). The temporality of this very holding is thus that of a leap that must be explicitly retrieved and enacted as such in genuine knowing. For a discussion, see chapter 4 above; also our analysis of "The Origin of the Work of Art" in chapter 8.

but on the contrary that which always already possesses me. To stand in the *Augenblick,* to be held in ec-stasis, to exist as a finite presencing—which also means, as a being that has the possibility of action—essentially entails not being able to be oneself in the manner of self-coincidence. It means existing as the "there," as the indeterminate, nonlocalizable spatio-temporal site where beings can show themselves in their presencing. The *Augenblick* names the site of the presencing of beings as such and as a whole, it names the "there" where all that "is" in whatever way can show itself and "be."

What is decisive in thinking the eternal return is that everything that now is, and is thus already present, *has already been "there"* (da), and yet does not presence without us: "... and I and you in the gateway ...— must we not all already have been there [*dagewesen sein*]?" In hearing this invitation, in letting this thought claim and "tower over" us, as Heidegger puts it,[7] we undergo an *experience.* We are carried elsewhere than where we might otherwise have thought ourselves to be in understanding ourselves only in the manner of representational thinking. In this thinking of the *Augenblick* we experience the fact that insofar as we ourselves "are," we are those who have already been there. And yet this entails that our originary being does not lie in our already being present—as though we, as a self in each case, were merely something present—but precisely in our being futural. Such an experience is the insight that the proper being of those who have already been there (those who presence in the manner of being-in-the-world) lies in their futuricity. This futuricity is not simply ours, as though it were our property, but one to which we have already been delivered over, one that has always already been given us as a gift, always already claimed us. It is our openness for the being and presencing of a world.

We are now able to understand more precisely the nature of the collision between past and future that is said to occur in the *Augenblick.* The collision concerns the coming together of future and having-been in this originary sense, and not the temporal moments of the everyday, dwarf-like concept of time. Heidegger emphasizes a number of points regarding this collision and coming together (NI, 312ff.):

(1) That which is to come is "precisely a matter for decision," for the *Augenblick* itself is the site of all decision, the site of possible freedom (the latter understood as ethico-political freedom in the *worldly* sense, but not as the possession of human freedom conceived as a property of the will or as autonomy).

(2) The point of collision is a point of *closure:* The ring of eternal return is not closed in some remote infinity, but "has its unbroken closure [*Zusammenschluß*] in the *Augenblick* as the center of the conflict; that which

---

[7] The German is *überwachsen,* more literally, to "grow over" (NI, 297).

recurs—if it recurs—is decided by the *Augenblick* and the force with which the *Augenblick* can cope with whatever in it collides with that which is counterstriving." "Closure" here implies two things. First, it implies the coming together, and thus belonging together in an "unbroken" manner, of future and having-been. "Unbroken" here does not mean that there is no possibility of interruption, and thus of action, but only that there is no possible future that could constitute an absolute break with what has been. That which has yet to come can only be a taking up and transforming of what already has been and is thus given. Second, however, "closure" suggests that this collision and coming together occurs as an event of finitude and as the necessity of decision. These two senses of closure are not mutually contradictory: we have already examined how the radical finitude of presencing is itself the phenomenon of the originary future, thus a making way for the possibility of anything continuing to come to presence within the realm of unconcealment.[8] The "continuity" at issue here is not like the spatial continuity of an unbroken line; it is, rather, that continuity between "birth" and "death," between origination and finitude, that Heidegger in *Being and Time* had analyzed as the temporal stretching (*Erstreckung*) that constitutes the constancy—the stance and steadfastness—of the self (*Selbstständigkeit*).[9] The necessity of decision, of giving up one possible decision in favor of another, Heidegger noted, "does not interrupt" the constancy of existence, "but precisely preserves it in the manner of the *Augenblick*" (SZ, 391).

(3) This closure, as finitude and continuity, is thus nothing other than the held time of the *Augenblick,* the peculiar *stasis* of ecstasis that ruptures representational time. Hence Heidegger writes that "Here," namely, in the collision of future and past, "the *Augenblick* comes to itself." This "coming" of the *Augenblick* presupposes an originary closure that opens the possibility of the new, the possibility of a recovery or recurrence, of a coming again (*Wiederkunft*) of presencing as dis-closure.[10]

(4) These hints allow us to understand better what is meant by the "eternity" of the "eternal return." Heidegger writes: "This is what is most grave and proper to the doctrine of eternal return: namely, that eternity *is* in the *Augenblick,* that the *Augenblick* is not a fleeting 'now,' not an instant of time whizzing by a spectator, but the collision of future and past." Clearly "eternity" here does not mean the atemporal, but rather the

---

[8] See chapter 4, 131–34.

[9] See SZ, §§64, 75, 79; also GA 24, 381–82.

[10] In *Being and Time,* Heidegger had discussed the originary phenomenon of the future (*Zukunft*) as "that coming [*Kunft*] in which Dasein comes toward itself [*auf sich zukommt*] in its ownmost possibility of being" (SZ, 325). See our remarks on the temporality of anxiety in chapter 4, 132–34.

duration appropriate to the *Augenblick* itself: it means that which endures, that which recurs and thus remains. What properly remains is not that which is present (beings as such), but the *Augenblick* itself as the site of presencing, of the presencing of whatever is and can be present, the presencing of beings as a whole. The being of beings as a whole, the originary presencing of world, is, as it were, in this sense laden or pregnant with "eternity." That which now *is* as a whole is only insofar as it has the occasion and opportunity to recur, to return into presencing.[11]

(5) What recurs as the same (*das Gleiche*) in the eternal recurrence? "Answer: that which will be in the next *Augenblick*" (NI, 398). This refers, therefore, not to beings in the first instance, but to being, to presencing as the presencing of beings, to beings as a whole in their presencing. "The eternal return of the becoming of world as a whole must be a recurrence of the same" (NI, 370). Being itself returns as presencing in each moment—and yet such presencing, as the presencing *of beings,* is never separable from *what* comes to be in the *Augenblick.* Whether the moment returns as a purely formal sameness, or whether it is transformed in its very returning, is also itself precisely a matter for decision: it depends on the stance adopted by *the thinker* toward beings as a whole in their presencing; it depends on the *way* in which the thinker relates to beings as a whole. "The matter will be decided in your *moments* [*Augenblicken*] and there alone; it will be decided on the basis of what you yourself hold concerning beings, and what sort of stance you adopt in their midst ..." (NI, 398). "The decisive condition ... is you *yourself*—the way in which you attain yourself ... and come to freedom" (NI, 400).[12]

---

[11] Whether this time of recurrence may be thought of as the intrinsic power of the "will to power"—intrinsic to the being of beings themselves—is a problem we cannot address here. The "will to power," when thought in its metaphysical import, formulates philosophically what Heidegger has identified as the "will to will" at work in modern technology. To the extent that (as Heidegger argues) the "will to power" thinks the essence or whatness of beings as a whole, and the eternal return thinks their existence or *existentia,* their way of being, the eternal return and the will to power think the Same and must be thought together as the fundamental metaphysical articulation of the being of beings as a whole. Yet while the "will to power," like the eternal return, formulates the most extreme nihilism, it is the thought of eternal return that manifests the ambiguity of this extremity and, in thinking the temporality of recurrence in relation to the thinker, points toward the overcoming of nihilism. In this respect, cf. the temporal analyses of "profound boredom" and its emptiness in GA 29/30; also Heidegger's theses on nihilism in "Overcoming Metaphysics" (VA, 67–95).

[12] Note that Heidegger here refers to Aristotle's *Physics* Book IV, chapters 10-14, where Aristotle discusses the interval between two times or "nows" not only in terms of the "eternal" (*aei*), but in relation to continuity or stretching, and to the "ecstatic" (*ekstatikon*) and "sudden" (*exaiphnēs*) nature of change. The "now" not only holds time together in its apparent continuity (*sunecheia*), but is also a limit (*peras*), and as such is both *archē* and *telos*. Both Heidegger's thinking of ecstatic temporality and Nietzsche's

(6) What sort of stance is called for by the thought of the eternal return? Heidegger's interpretation emphasizes throughout that the thought of eternal return is not to be conceived as a "theoretical" thought that has a "practical" application and a "poetical" depiction. Rather, in the experience of this thought, these three determinations of being (correlate with the Greek *theōria, praxis,* and *poiēsis*) belong together in such an originary manner that they cannot be separated. Thinking the thought of eternal return demands a thinking ahead or *anticipatory* thinking—"and that is thinking proper" (NI, 398)—namely, a thinking that explicitly anticipates the presencing of beings as a whole, of world in its coming to be. But it also means thinking one's own *participatory* involvement (as a being that is open to world) in such presencing; it entails thinking one's own relation as thinker to the presencing of world. What is to be thought in this thought, namely, "the world as a whole and the thinking of the thinker," cannot be separated from one another; *what* is being thought (the presencing of beings as a whole, which includes the thought itself as something that also "is") is not to be separated from the *how* of thinking, the way in which it is being thought (NI, 380–82). "The thought itself *is* only when those who are *thinking—are.* The latter are accordingly more than, and something other than, mere *instances of what is thought*" (NI, 413). Only if the thought of eternal return is leveled out and reduced to a general "theory" does the thinker, as a particular being, become a specific instance of a general concept, a concept that can then be "applied" in particular "practical" cases. But this erases precisely the ethical or protoethical singularity of the thinker as existing in the *Augenblick.* Just as in ethical *praxis* what is to be done cannot be decided on the basis of the application of a general concept that one "has" in advance, so too what is to be thought here cannot be known beforehand in the manner of a "theory." On the contrary: the thought of the eternal return demands that the thinker "enter into the accomplishment [*Vollzug*] of the thinking, and be determined simultaneously, and not after the event, from out of what is to be thought.... a 'practical' application of the thought is impossible, because it has always already become superfluous in the *Augenblick* in which the thought comes to be thought" (NI, 382). The *way* of thinking called for by this thought demands thinking from out of the *Augenblick,* which is to say, "transposing oneself into the temporality of independent action and decision." "In this thought, *what* is to be thought recoils upon the thinker through the *way* in which it is to be thought, thus compelling the thinker. Yet it does

---

thinking of the *Augenblick* draw these reflections on time back from a theoretical perspective into the time of action, emphasizing the decisive participation of the being of the self in the phenomenon of origination, that is, in the finitude that in both Aristotle's *Physics* and in Nietzsche is thought as "eternity."

so solely so as to draw the thinker into what is to be thought. To think eternity demands thinking the *Augenblick,* that is, transposing oneself into the *Augenblick* of being-a-self" (NI, 446–47). Seen from the *Augenblick* that oneself *is,* originary thinking is an acting, and originary action is a thinking, in each case finite and unique.

The decisive criterion in thinking the thought of eternal return is thus the *Augenblick* itself, and that means, notes Heidegger, "the kind of stance [*Haltung*] from out of which and in which the eternal return of the same demands to be thought, the way in which this thinking itself comes to be" (NI, 318). The thinking itself comes into being—this means that the thinking in question here is not only thoughtful and protoethical, but is also a poietic unfolding. Heidegger discusses the stance that is called for by this thought in his remarks on the thought as a "belief," that is, a "holding to be true." The relation of the thinker to the thought is a holding to be true, a holding oneself in the true, "and thus a holding oneself in the double sense of having a hold [*Halt*] and preserving a stance [*Haltung*]. Such holding oneself is determined by what is posited as true" (NI, 386). More precisely, it is determined by the kind of truth-claim made upon the thinker by the thought, that is, here by the *way* in which what is to be thought is disclosed so as to draw the thinker into this disclosure in its very unfolding. Holding oneself in the true and assuming a stance will in this case be all the more genuine "the more originarily they are determined from out of the stance, and the less exclusively they are determined only by the hold...." What is at stake in having, or rather, *being* such a stance is the assuming of a certain self-steadfastness (*Selb-ständigkeit:* NI, 387). But this does not mean that the thinker has an independent "position" outside of and beyond the thought. Rather, the stance in question arises only *in* and *as* the singular relatedness to what is to be thought here, that is, the way in which the thinker in his or her being is simultaneously drawn into the being of what is to be thought. What needs to be emphasized is that "holding oneself in this thought is itself co-essential for its being true, ...the hold is determined from out of the stance" (NI, 392). As the thinking of *this* thought, the stance is itself nothing other than our *response* to the specific *claim* that this thought makes upon us as it is being thought. The response is not separable from the claim, but co-determined by it. The uniqueness of this thought consists in the fact that its truth-claim is not that of an independent or purely "logical" truth which one could judge from an independent position or perspective, but rather a truth of disclosure, of the disclosure of that *being* into which the thinker is simultaneously drawn in his or her thinking it: namely, the being of beings as a whole, or world. The truth-claim of this thought does presuppose that there are beings there who can think it; but this does not entail that it thereby becomes "dependent" upon an already existing, individual "subject," for one first comes to be who one will have been in and through one's response to this claim. The claim—which in this way calls forth a *poiēsis* of one's being-a-self—thus presupposes only that the one who can think is the one who is open to the possibility of the presencing of a world. This possibility itself unfolds through finite disclosure by way of thinking, that is, as finite response to the presencing of thought. The being of the thinker consists in being the finitude of such response, which is the finitude of presencing itself—not only of the presencing of thought, however, but of *world*. Originary thinking is a response not only to thought (or to the history of philosophy), but to the presencing of world.

"Stance" (*Haltung*) here refers therefore not to some "theoretical" position (a position taken up and occupied on the basis of some supposedly independent and universal truth), but to the coming into being of a finite response: a coming into being that, in such *poiēsis,* is *held* in the dis-closure of the *Augenblick,* and that has been claimed by what is to be thought in this thought. And that is: the coming into being of a world, together with the thought itself as belonging to that world. The coming into being (*poiēsis*) of the thinking of this thought is itself a finite coming into being, a coming into being that is thus also a coming into finitude, a coming to pass of finitude.

The thinking of the eternal return of the same is thus a responding to— and as such a participation in—the poietic essence of language, to language as "the originary and emergent sounding [*Aufklingen*] of the truth of a world" (NI, 364). Just as the distinction between "theory" and "praxis" is inappropriate to the configuration of this thought (i.e., to the way in which "the *manifestness* of beings as a whole is structured into beings themselves, in such a way that the latter first show and configure themselves as such"), so too the distinction between "theoretical" and "poetical" fails to capture the essence of the thought of eternal return. All philosophical thinking, notes Heidegger, is intrinsically poietical (*dichterisch*) (NI, 329; cf. 428ff.). This is in keeping with the intrinsic finitude of the stance called for in the thinking of this thought, namely, the way in which the stance is not determined solely or exclusively by the "hold," that is, by what *has been* thought, but participates in the coming into being of the thought and of what is disclosed in and through it. Existing in the manner of a responsiveness to this thought is at once a knowing occurrence of finitude, that is, of freedom ("We are free only in coming to be free" [NI, 400]), and a transformation of that which has already been, of that which has been given us (*das Mitgegebene*). The thinking of this thought is creative in that it imparts and communicates new possibilities, brings new possibilities into being: "Creating imparts and communicates a new being [*Sein*] to those

234 THE GLANCE OF THE EYE

beings that already are." And as such, genuine creating is farthest from the danger of "being an end in itself" (NI, 389). As creative, the thinking of the eternal return is a "liberating transfiguration" of that which is *becoming* as that which is coming to *be*. Thus, Heidegger notes, the two fundamental responses to the guiding question of philosophy, the question "What are beings as such?," are thought together in this thought: "that which becomes is in its *coming to be* and *being becoming* in creating." Thus understood, creating, as a creating over and beyond that which is, and thus over and beyond oneself too, is "most intrinsically this: standing in the *Augenblick* of decision, in which *Augenblick* that which has already been and has been given us is raised up and carried over into what has been cast before us as our given task, and is thereby preserved" (NI, 465–67).[13]

(7) The nature of the stance entailed by the thinking of the eternal return of the same has not yet been fully understood, however, in our grasping the equiprimordiality of thinking, acting, and creating as intrinsic to this stance. It should be emphasized once more that the "thinking" at stake here is the highest and most profound kind of thought: a *philosophical* thinking of the being of beings as such and as a whole. Only in relation to *this* thinking of the thought will acting and creating be appropriately configured. Yet such thinking does not come about in a day, let alone in a "moment." When Heidegger remarks that the thought of eternal return thinks beings in such a way "that from out of beings as a whole there comes a constant call upon us of whether we merely want to drift with the tide of things, or whether we wish to be creators," he adds that this means in the first instance "whether we desire the means and conditions by which we might again *become* creators" (NI, 437). The word "again" indicates here that this "we" is a historical "we," that of Western humankind, and not the individual self. We must first *become* creators—and no less thinkers and actors—and this "becoming" is not brought about by the (momentary) thinking of the thought itself. Presumably, however, a first thinking of this thought, the initial incomprehensibility of which we are called upon to think here, can be a spur for such becoming. Zarathustra's becoming—itself poetized as tragedy—begins, Heidegger emphasizes, with his "downgoing,"

---

[13] "Cast before us as our given task" here translates *das vorentworfene Aufgegebene;* clearly, this cannot refer to a task that *we* project in advance (in the calculative manner of something planned by a "subject"), but alludes to the primary "projection of being" (*Entwurf des Seins*), that is, of world, to which our thinking responds in the anticipatory manner of "a leap" that "executes, assists, and accomplishes" that projection (NI, 392). The terms *das Aufgegebene* and *das Mitgegebene* cited above are taken from Hölderlin, for whom *das Aufgegebene*—what is given us as a task, thus as the future—is "the free use of one's own." See Heidegger's 1934/35 course on Hölderlin (GA 39, especially §24b, which also refers to Nietzsche) for a discussion of these terms. On preservation, cf. "The Origin of the Work of Art" (H, 54ff.), and our comments in chapter 8.

with his experience of the *Augenblick* itself as a downgoing and transition (*Untergang* and *Übergang*), with his "exposure to the supreme possibilities of being and becoming" (NI, 301–02). The thinking of this thought of itself demands that we must first grow equal to it, that the thought at first "grow over" and tower over us.

Incorporation (*Einverleibung*) is thus essential to the thinking of the thought of eternal return, to Zarathustra's "convalescence," in which his downgoing reaches its end in such a way as to first properly understand itself as transition. Until the thought has been incorporated, Heidegger remarks, it has not truly been thought (NI, 302–03). What is meant by incorporation?

> That which is incorporated is that which makes the body—our bodying forth—steadfast and secure; it is also that with which we have come to terms, that which determines us in the future, it is the juice from which we draw our energies. To incorporate the thought here means to accomplish [*vollziehen*] the thinking of the thought in such a way that right from the start it comes to be our fundamental posture toward beings as a whole and as such pervades every single thought in advance. Only when the thought has become the fundamental stance [*Grundhaltung*] of all our thinking has it been appropriated and taken into the body as its essence demands. (NI, 331–32)

The thinking of this thought must itself *become* a fundamental stance, an enduring disposition that comes to pervade all our thinking, acting, and creating in advance. And this takes time, it comes to be only with time: with the time of repetition and of decision, the time of the *Augenblick* itself. It can come about only with the explicit affirmation on the part of the thinker him- or herself: a second affirmation of an affirmation that has already occurred, a second affirmation that affirms the time of the *Augenblick* in explicitly incorporating it into one's being, that is, into one's becoming.

This incorporation of the thought, however, affirming it in such a way as to let it bring about a decisive change and transformation in one's own stance, entails something more: namely, coming to understand one's own becoming as intrinsically *historical,* in short, an affirmation of *history.* For our own presencing in each case, as we have seen, is nothing other than a responsiveness and responsibility to the claim of that which has already been. In other words, the nature of the claim of language and of thought, its coming to be as the responsiveness of the thinker, is always a coming to be of that which has already been and which, in its return, approaches us as a matter for decision. To incorporate this thought entails not only cultivating and preserving a stance; such cultivation and preservation themselves occur as a critical confrontation (*Auseinandersetzung*) with history as it addresses us, placing us in question, giving us the possibility, but also the necessity and the responsibility of decision.[14] The decision called for by the thinking of this thought of eternal return is thus at once thoughtful in the sense of originarily philosophical (it concerns the way in which beings as a whole will return), practical (it co-determines my stance and place in the midst of beings), and poietical (the being of beings as a whole and of myself as attuned in their midst unfolds as a coming-into-presence, a *poiēsis* that calls upon me to participate, that thus calls me into presencing).

The thinking of the eternal return is thus not only a standing in the *Augenblick* of decision, a constant deciding concerning my own being as originary ethical *praxis;* the thinking of the *Augenblick* is also decisive in being intrinsically a confrontation with history and with a historical world, a decision concerning what will return, what will be able to return, what is to be preserved as something yet to come, if and when it comes. "The thought not only has to be thought in each instance from out of the creative *Augenblick* of decision in a given individual but, as a thought that belongs to life itself, it is a *historical decision*—a *crisis*" (NI, 415). To stand in the *Augenblick* is to be called to decision in affirming, taking on, confronting, and, as a being that comes to stand in the possibility of action, creatively and thoughtfully transforming the history that constantly approaches us. It is to see the *Augenblick* in the light of history, and history in the light of the *Augenblick,* of the moment of presencing of a world. The thought of the eternal recurrence of the same thus intrinsically calls for a thoughtful and philosophical confrontation with nihilism, that is, with the history of metaphysics or Platonism which determines being and becoming in such a way as to culminate in the most extreme nihilism, the judgment "everything is the same." As the confrontation with nihilism, Nietzsche's thought of eternal return is an "epochal" event (*Ereignis*) that itself comes to be inserted into "the newly-created sphere of beings as a whole" (NI, 402). It interrupts and transforms history hitherto, it "brings another history." The epochal significance of Nietzsche's thought marks it as not just another event "within" history; rather, what it means to be historical is itself transformed. "It is not merely that another series of happenstances unfolds; what becomes other is the kind of happening, acting, and creating.

---

[14] On *Auseinandersetzung* in Nietzsche and Heidegger, see our essay "Traces of Discordance: Heidegger—Nietzsche," in *Nietzsche: A Critical Reader,* ed. P. Sedgwick (Cambridge, MA: Blackwell, 1995), 171–202; also Rodolphe Gasché, "Towards an Ethics of 'Auseinandersetzung'," in *Enlightenments,* ed. H. Kunneman & H. de Vries (Kampen, the Netherlands: Kok Pharos Publishing House, 1993), 121–40.

The color, the look [*Anblick*], the appearance [*Aussehen*], the presencing of things—being is transformed" (NI, 395). The seeing of things in terms of their Platonic-Aristotelian *eidos,* together with all the transformations that such seeing undergoes (culminating in the removed spectatorship of modern technovision) is itself transformed in and through the vision that the *Augenblick* itself is. This transformation of being itself is ambiguous: as a transformation of the entire history of being as the history of metaphysics, the history of the oblivion of being, it comes at and as the end of that history and yet exceeds it in inaugurating an other kind of "history," another possible response to the destinal happening of presencing.

***

Heidegger's 1937 reading of Nietzsche's thought of eternal return, together with the 1936/37 meditation on the will to power as art, undoubtedly contributed to the shift in his understanding of the *Augenblick* as not only, nor even primarily, the originary site of Dasein's being as being held in a finite, ecstatic presencing, but rather as the site of the event of presencing as the presencing of a historical world. The nature of this shift is traced most explicitly in the *Beiträge zur Philosophie* of 1936–38. The site of the *Augenblick* remains the site of the proper selfhood of the human being (GA 65, 52), but such being-a-self, which is intrinsically historical, is first temporalized in response to the call (*Zuruf*) of a world, a response that is our "momentary [*augenblickliche*] relation to this *Ereignis*" (GA 65, 31). In the *Beiträge,* much of the language describing the *Augenblick* is clearly Nietzschean. Thus, writing of Dasein as the fundamental happening of future history, Heidegger notes: "This happening springs from *Ereignis* and becomes the site of a possible *Augenblick* [mögliche Augenblicksstätte] for the decision concerning man—his history or *Ungeschichte* as that site's transition unto downgoing" (GA 65, 32).[15] Yet Heidegger's reading of the *Augenblick* in Nietzsche also raises the question of whether Nietzsche's most abyssal thought, despite its transitional and epochal character, leads him to rethink the originary temporality of presencing as such, to think presencing itself as historical. Does Nietzsche's thought remain entangled in a struggle with the metaphysical opposition of being and becoming, and in a thinking determined by a kind of representational remnant, concerned with ultimate "facts"? In his later essay "Nihilism as determined by the history of being" (1944/46), Heidegger begins with a thought-provoking claim concerning the limits of Nietzsche's thinking of the *Augenblick*—limits that perhaps

---

[15] The word *Ungeschichte* suggests not merely "non-history" but a monstrous history, an enormity.

resonate in the shock undergone by Zarathustra at the very moment he thinks the thought of eternal return:

> Neither the acknowledgement of beings as the most elementary issue and fact [*Tat-Sache*] (as will to power) leads Nietzsche to a thinking of being as such, . . . nor does the thought of the "eternal return of the same" become a spur to ponder eternity as the *Augenblick* from out of the suddenness of presencing that has cleared or to ponder return as a manner of presencing or to ponder both in terms of their essential provenance from originary "time." (NII, 335)

Part IV
Originary Theoria

Life . . . is like a festival: just as some come to the festival to compete, some to ply their trade, but the best people come as spectators [*theatai*], so in life the slavish men go hunting for fame or gain, the philosophers for truth. (Pythagoras, cited by Diogenes Laertius)

Seeing something and expressly catching sight of what is seen are not the same thing. Catching sight of [*Er-blicken*] here means: looking into that which properly looks at us from out of what is seen—that is, looks at us in terms of what is most proper to it. We see a great deal and catch sight of very little. Even when we have caught sight of what is seen, we are seldom capable of sustaining the look of what has been caught sight of and of holding it in view. For truly retaining something entails, for mortals, an ever new, that is, ever more originary appropriation. (SG, 85)

Chapter 8

In the Presence of the Sensible: Vision and Ecstasis

If in modernity *theōria* becomes world representation for the subjectivity of the subject, this representational thinking, as we have shown, is not over-come but merely consolidated in its final transformation that submits it to the planned production of presencing. But this kind of spectation, which ex-hibits essential traits of the temporality of curiosity—ever oriented already toward the new (toward the new that, for technology, is always *its* new, the new it has already projected in advance and for itself), never able to dwell in the immediate presencing of the sensible, always withdrawn from the present in pursuit of the future that can be produced—this transformation of *theōria* is not merely the occlusion of seeing *oneself* in the manner of the immediate involvements of *praxis* (of seeing oneself addressed, for example, by the primary claim of technology). It is also an inability to see *other beings* in their proper dignity and worthiness: an inability to tarry and dwell in the company of other worldly beings, seeing them for what they are, as they show and conceal themselves. Yet such was precisely the originary meaning of *theōria,* prior to its philosophical transformation. Traces of this more original sense of *theōria* are indeed still found in Plato and Aristotle, even though it became increasingly obscured in the course of the ascendancy of seeing things exclusively in terms of their *eidos.*

This fourth and final part of our study seeks to gain a more profound appreciation of our theme thus far in attempting to situate the *theōria* of philosophy, science, and technology in the perspective of this more ancient, pre-philosophical sense of *theōria* and the kind of seeing it presupposes. An appreciation of the originary sense of a *theōria* attentive to the presencing of other beings in their worldly immediacy also helps to recall a sense of

the ethical and of *praxis* that is not yet seen in tension or opposition with
the "theoretical"—a tension that seems to impose itself upon contemporary
reflections on the ethical with a profound yet enigmatic inexorability. This
more ancient sense of a pre-philosophical *theōria* also informs, as we shall
discover, Heidegger's attempt to think *technē* beyond its philosophical and
scientific restriction. Throughout the following reflections, we try to indicate that this pre- or proto-philosophical *theōria* and the kind of seeing
implied by it are not simply opposed to its philosophical transformation,
but manifest both continuities and differences. These continuities and disjunctions, we shall argue, help to illuminate what is distinctive about the
beginnings of Greek philosophy and science.

   We begin this final part with a retrospective assessment of the complex
relations implied in the desire to see as it manifests itself in philosophy,
science, and curiosity. Drawing on the work of Hans-Georg Gadamer and
Nicholas Lobkowicz, these brief reflections serve to recall part of the theological history that plays a role in the complex genealogy of this desire.
In the second section, we turn to several of Heidegger's texts that suggest
how, via Aristotle and Christianity, a pre-philosophical sense of divinity
associated with ancient *theōria* and still found in the Presocratics becomes
distanced from the presencing of the sensible through the philosophical appropriation of *theōria*. Before attempting to read more closely this theme of
a more ancient and divine seeing in Heidegger, we then attempt, in section
three, to provide an overview of the more important connotations of ancient
theōria by turning to the work of Hannelore Rausch, Hans-Georg Gadamer,
and other scholars. The final sections of the study turn back to examine
several of Heidegger's later texts in the light of these insights, beginning
with the 1936 essay "The Origin of the Work of Art." The *Parmenides*
lecture course of 1942/43 and "The Anaximander Fragment" of 1946 help
to illuminate further what we have sought to understand as the ecstasis of
vision in Heidegger's thought and its relation to the presence of the sensible.

Theoria in Retrospect: Philosophy, Science, and Curiosity

If we pause to consider the trajectory our present study has taken with
respect to the initially proposed tripartite delimitation of the desire to see,
a complex picture begins to emerge. In part 1, we concentrated our analyses on the emergence and development of the *philosophical* desire to see,
all the while maintaining its intricate tension to our vision of the sensible
essential to the disclosure of the practical situation of action. There is a
profound affinity between philosophical and practical vision (in its most

excellent or virtuous sense, that of *phronēsis*) in that their ultimate end
is the same. "The same" here means a fundamental relatedness and belonging together that allows for originary difference, allowing each to be
its own unique *praxis*. But this sameness of their ultimate end shows itself only to someone who has already seen it, who thus knows it in the
most complete, most perfect sense: the one who knows it best, because he
knows the highest good. The good and the true coincide in the sameness
of this ultimate end of philosophical and practical wisdom, of *sophia* and
phronēsis. For only one who has seen the highest good in the whole of nature or the *kosmos* (the First Philosopher as "theologian") can act well,
that is, honorably and nobly in a manner attuned to *eudaimonia,* in the
affairs of ethical and political life and thus be a person of practical wisdom.
All *praxis* points beyond itself toward something that transcends or exceeds
it, but this ultimate end is, as it were, excentric to *praxis,* not actualized in
any particular action as such. Indeed, *praxis* can be an end in itself only if
it does not aim primarily at any particular end, but at the highest good as
a whole for human beings. Although virtuous *praxis* is a "means" toward
this ultimate end (*pros to telos to haplōs:* NE, 1142 b30), this end does
not *determine* in advance what the appropriate action should be on any
given occasion. The particular action chosen is mediated via deliberation,
which weighs up the best action to take in the light of the moment and
in view of its knowledge of the ultimate good. Likewise, the practical vision intrinsic to *phronēsis* is not merely a sensible seeing of the particular
givens of a situation with respect to a particular end desired; rather, as
Heidegger's analyses show, the "glance of the eye" also already sees something else, something nonsensible: the finitude of its own presencing. And
it can see this very finitude that marks it as the accomplishment of a *praxis*
only because, in turn, it has already seen what transcends it: the presencing of the world as a whole, the vision of which is the ultimate end of the
philosophical striving. Only from out of such having seen the world in its
presencing can the finitude of the particular, of one's own being and that
of others, be acknowledged and that which is fitting to each be seen in the
concretion of ethical *praxis*. Only a vision of this harmony of the *kosmos,*
of the unity and belonging together of the presencing of beings as a whole,
precisely in their respective finitude, provides a fitting measure for ethical
action (which of course requires mutual recognition and acknowledgement)
among human beings, that is, among those beings whose distinctive way of
being is *praxis*. Such seeing thus itself creates (actualizes and brings to the
fore) the possibility of community in and for human existence, but precisely
as a possibility, indeed one that, on account of the finitude of human *praxis,*
must continuously be striven for. But, since the human being is not divine,
and can only strive for what is most divine, such a vision must itself be

actualized *in* finite, individualized *praxis*. It is in this sense that Heidegger argues, as we saw at the end of chapter 4, that authentic community must be primarily determined from out of the individuation of *praxis*. This does not mean that one first constructs an entity called "community" starting from already existing individuals, but rather that community can come to exist only in and through finite, individuated *praxis* that in each case knows itself to belong to a possible whole.

Yet it is not only in the sameness of their ultimate end that we find an affinity between philosophical and practical vision. Although we are considering two extremes (the actualization of two possibilities) of one and the same phenomenon, of *"nous* in its most extreme concretion and *nous* in the most extreme *katholou,* in its most universal universality,"[1] as Heidegger put it—a seeing directed primarily toward the sensible particularity of the practical situation, and a seeing directed primarily toward the whole of the world that transcends that particularity—vision is in each case a kind of ecstasis, an attentiveness that is held by and dwells on its object. The practical "glance of the eye," as we discussed in chapter 4, is a held rapture, an ecstasis in which Dasein is held open for whatever is encountered in the situation. But the ancient Greek *theōria* was also precisely such a rapture, a dwelling with its respective objects, whether the beings studied by the special sciences, or the heavens and their stars, the ultimate horizon of the world that held the attention of *sophia*.

Such dwelling and tarrying in proximity to phenomena themselves is in marked contrast to the first form of the desire to see which we identified at the outset of our inquiry: the desire for the new, the desire *only* to have seen that characterizes curiosity according to Heidegger's analyses in *Being and Time*. By contrast to this phenomenon of everyday disclosure, we noted, the philosophical desire is a desire to tarry in the presence of its object: to have seen, and in having seen, first to see more clearly, more appropriately, more fittingly. Yet our analyses in part 2 have shown that this strange inability to tarry that marks the temporality of curiosity is found not only in our everyday distractions, but precisely in the world-dominating, modern transformation of *theōria:* in the modern scientific seeing of things that is fundamentally subservient to the technological transformation of presencing. This corresponds to the strange circumstance that modern science, as Heidegger put it, no longer has any ontological significance, that is, it no longer plays any truth-disclosive role with regard to that which already is. Its "truths" are truths concerning solely that which can come to be in accordance with the will to will: that which "works" (functions).

---

[1] Note that *katholou* comes from *kata* and *holon,* and thus suggests the meaning "with respect to the whole." See GA 19, 78ff.

Indeed, not only the desire to "know" at work in modern science, but also that of philosophy itself (as a modern institutional practice) is no longer able to resist the same subservience to technological presencing: no longer a seeing of the being of things themselves in their historically situated existence, philosophy today has largely become the desire for novelty in the form of an ongoing production of the new. What happens through this ultimate, technological transformation of presencing is the alienation (or closure) of historical existence from itself. That which has been—the *claims* of that history that still claims us precisely in science and technology—can no longer be heard except as that which is already surpassed. In this way, modern technological ordering perpetuates its own blindness to itself. Yet how could the Greek *theōria,* originally a dwelling with things as they show themselves in their presencing, become the very inability to dwell, a seeing increasingly withdrawn from the presence of the world, oriented toward "the future"?

A few hints must suffice here. In his important essay "In Praise of Theory," Hans-Georg Gadamer reminds us that the desire to see, even as the desire to see the sensible, did not have the pejorative sense of curiosity for the Greeks (GW 4, 37ff.). As we noted in our introductory chapter, the desire to see can acquire this pejorative connotation only when a veritable gap opens between the sensible and the nonsensible, only when truth is no longer a truth belonging to and inherent in the sensible world. But this gap that reduces the seeing of the sensible to a desire *merely* to see is not yet present in Aristotle's schema of the various stages of seeing that culminate in the *theōria* of *sophia.* For these stages are unfolded as degrees of intensity, completeness, and appropriateness of disclosure in our attentiveness to worldly beings. Because our seeing is itself a *praxis* and thus resists teleological determination, there is no determinative hierarchy among these various levels of seeing. They may be compared to one another with regard to their completeness, but one does not determine the other in advance. *Theōria* does not already determine our *aisthēsis* of the sensible such that the latter would be merely an inferior level of the former. *Aisthēsis* itself, as Heidegger had noted in the 1924/25 course, is a *kurion* in its own right, an independent power (GA 19, 92). The gap that makes way for teleological hierarchization opens up only with the Christianizing of Greek thought,[2] when worldly divinity (in both its pantheistic and monotheistic forms) is replaced by the monotheistic, non-worldly God of Christianity. The world is seen and projected as *one* homogenous world, from the perspective of a single, supersensible truth and origin beyond the world—a

---

[2] Cf., for example, the status of *theōria* in Plotinus (*Ennead* III, 8). For an analysis of *theōria* in Plotinus, see R. Arnou, *Theoria et Praxis* (Paris: Libraire Félix Alcan, 1921).

schema that also pretends to survey the world in its entirety, occluding and homogenizing the radical finitude of worldly origins, the unforeseeable and unsurveyable multiplicity and plurality of human *praxeis*. *Theōria* becomes the *vita contemplativa*, turned toward God and opposed to the *vita activa*, to participation in worldly affairs. To the extent that the world has a place in *contemplatio*, notes Gadamer, "it is nothing but a mirror, a *speculum* of God: *contemplatio* is at the same time *speculatio*" (GW 4, 40).

This turn, however, as Gadamer goes on to note, not only turns the "theoretical passion" of human beings away from the world and toward God, it also announces "a revaluation of the elementary thirst for knowledge that Aristotle could appeal to in all innocence: the desire for knowledge becomes *Neugier, curiositas.*" This revaluation that comes to regard all desire for worldly knowledge as curiosity, as a dangerous distraction from divine contemplation, is nowhere more evident than in Augustine's polemic against the "lust of the eyes": to regard the desire to know as curiosity represents, as Gadamer puts it, "an extraordinary provocation to human nature. Behind it lies a radical devaluation of the visible world" (GW 4, 41).

This radical turn, this revaluation and devaluation that would later be diagnosed with such acuity by Nietzsche, not only demotes all worldly knowledge to the status of mere curiosity; it does so in transforming the very meaning of the word *curiositas*. Gadamer's commentary on this is especially insightful:

> Once again, words tell us an entire history. That the new is always ambivalent and can be received in contrasting ways is evident. Yet it is significant that the pejorative sense of the new is scarcely encountered among the Greeks with their thirst for knowledge. Even the Latin equivalent, *curiositas*, does not initially carry any negative tone: it is derived from *cura*, care and respectful attentiveness [*rühmliche Sorgfalt*]. Even though *curiosus* could have the pejorative sense of the curious [*des Neu-gierigen*] in this basically rustic language, and although careful looking ahead means concernfully warding off anything new that is undesired and can come from the future, the emphasis still lies on care [*Sorge*] and careful provision, and precisely not on the "craving" [*Gier*] for something new. The anti-gnostic front adopted by Ambrose and Augustine first definitively establishes the meaning of *curiositas* in its negative sense. (GW 4, 41)[3]

---

[3] For an overview of the complex history of *curiositas*, see Hans Blumenberg, *Die Legitimität der Neuzeit* (Frankfurt: Suhrkamp, 1996), part 3. See also the review by Gadamer (GW 4, 52ff.).

Augustine's discussion of the *concupiscentia oculorum* alludes to the *epithumia tōn ophthalmōn* inveighed against in the First Letter of John.[4] Augustine's polemic against the concupiscence of the eyes targets not only the desire for spectacle that clings to the immediate objects offered to our visual sense, leading to the "empty besottment" (*vanus hebesco*) that distracts us from contemplation of the divine (this desire, this "disease," he reminds us, extends not merely to the pleasurable or beautiful, as in the case of the other senses, but desires even to see the "torn carcass" that strikes horror into us);[5] the same "curious desire" also "masks itself under the title of knowledge and learning" (*nomine cognitionis et scientiae palliata*).[6] Hence, by the same disease "men also proceed to investigate the operations of that nature which is not before our eyes, which it does them no good to know, and yet men desire to know for the sake of knowing."[7]

Yet why is the *theōria* of modern science, oriented as it is toward the truths of this world and not toward divine contemplation—why is this *theōria* not an abiding with beings in their truth? Why does it bear already, in anticipation of its eventual manifest subservience to technological presencing, the temporal structure of curiosity? The answer, as we saw in part 2, has to do with the concept of *world* that claims modern science. The advent of the new science in the seventeenth century constitutes, as Gadamer puts it, "a veritable explosion" of the geocentric and theocentric medieval understanding of the world, an event that "also alters the theoretical ideal of life." The force of this explosion manifests itself in the fact that "science becomes research" (GW 4, 42).

---

[4] I. John 2.16.

[5] Cf. Plato, *Republic*, 439e–440a. For a detailed discussion by Heidegger of the *concupiscentia oculorum* and its relation to *voluptas* as a *concupiscentia carnis*, see GA 60, §§13–14.

[6] It is primarily Greek *epistēmē* and learning that is under attack here: the Latin *pallium* refers specifically to a *Grecian* cloak or mantle.

[7] *Confessions*, Book X, chapter XXXV. On the denigration of the desire to see in Ambrose, see in particular *De bono mortis*, a sermon that Augustine may well have heard. Cf. especially 7.28: *coditie lucrum quaerimus, et nullus cupiditati modus ponitur. non satiabitur inquit oculus videndo nec auris auditu.... cupimus cotidie scire nova, et quid est ipsa scientia nisi cotidiani doloris abiectio? omnia quae sunt iam fuerunt et nihil sub sole est novum, sed omnia vanitas.* "Daily we seek gain, and no limit is put to our desire. *The eye,* Scripture says, *will not be satisfied with seeing, nor the ear with hearing....* We daily seek to know new things, and what is this knowledge except the repudiation of daily grief? Everything that is now has already been, *and nothing is new under the sun, but all is vanity.*" (Cf. Ecclesiastes, 1.8–10 and 2.17.) Or again, 11.49: *videmus inquit nunc per speculum in aenigmate, tunc autiem faciem ad faciem.* "Scripture says: *we see now through a mirror in a confused manner, but then face to face.*" (Cf. I. Corinthians, 13.12.) Note also the discussion of the deception of the senses (3.10), and the warning to men not to let their eyes be captivated by the sight of women (9.40).

As Heidegger points out in "The Age of the World Picture," this occurs because the new world emerging from the medieval period posits itself explicitly as new (H, 84–85). This formulation, however, is inadequate, since it implies that the new world somehow already exists. But what is at stake is precisely the historical emergence of this "new world." And what is decisive here is that this emergence, as the transformation of an already existing, medieval world, occurs as the response to a particular claim. If the advent of modernity marks a new beginning, it is nevertheless not absolutely new in the sense of a beginning *ex nihilo*. The liberation of human beings from the truth of Church doctrine certainly appears as a liberation for something new, but it coincides, first with a transformation of the essence of human beings into *subiectum*, into "man" as the new ground of the world. The liberation in question is a liberation of humans from the truth of salvation *for themselves*, for *self*-freedom (H, 81). Second, however, and decisively, this transformation that occurs as the liberation *for* what is properly new is itself only the response to a primary *claim* that is made upon human beings in the very happening of this event of freedom. The human claim (the claim made by man as subject) to a fundamental ground of truth as the freedom of self-certainty first arises as a response to this more primary historical claim. For this liberation, Heidegger notes:

> still frees itself, without knowing it, from being bound by the truth of revelation in which the salvation of the human soul is made certain and secured for human beings. Hence liberation *from* the revelational certainty of salvation had to be intrinsically a liberation *for* a certainty in which man makes secure for himself what is true as what is known in his own knowing. (H, 99)

The liberation from Church doctrine was certainly understood as a liberation for something new, yet was still conceived as liberation for a new truth, which, moreover, had to continue to offer certainty. Explicitly posited as new, and yet uncertain; as nonsensible, and thus not immediately given, but something to be discovered; as the future, and yet the great unknown; finally, as a truth of *logos*—truth appeared as something concealed that could be secured only via the ongoing procedure of a knowledge constantly reverting to and securing itself in and through its relentless interrogation of beings as a whole (i.e., of this new world) for representational reason. The fragility and finitude of individuated human *praxis* was unable to sustain itself in the sensible presencing of the only world that remained (with all its concealments) in the face of the imminent collapse of Church authority. So habituated by centuries of Christianity to its primary dependence on a concealed truth of *logos,* Western European existence was no longer able (and had already for centuries been unable) "to be looked at by beings, to be drawn into and held within their openness, and thus to be borne along by them, to be driven about by their oppositions and marked by their discordance," in the manner that, according to Heidegger, was "the essence of human beings in the great age of the Greeks" (H, 83–84). Yet what Nietzsche so penetratingly diagnoses as this degeneration of Western European existence does not first begin in Christianity; or rather, its origins are not so straightforward. They are announced already (albeit still ambiguously) in Plato (cf. H, 84) and then Aristotle, and particularly in early and medieval Aristotelianism, in the increasingly formal identification of the *eidos* with *logos,* whereby the individuated, finite *seeing* of the *eidos,* the inseparability of its presencing from the finite *praxis* of living existence, becomes occluded. The site of vision, as a site of finite embodiment, becomes increasingly concealed.

According to our reading of Heidegger's analyses of vision in modern science and technology, the repercussions of this concealment of living *praxis* come increasingly to the fore as the technological essence of modern science becomes the dominant and all-pervasive world reality. For the modern projection of *theōria* was already in essence technological, concerned with the *production* of its own truths, explicitly posited as the new, in a self-referential, self-confirming, and self-grounding manner. These truths had to manifest themselves, their own power, *in* the sensible; they could no longer be mere grounds of belief or faith in a purely nonsensible truth, a supersensible reality. Hence the priority of the "experiment" from the very beginnings of the new science.[8] This also entailed that *theōria*—which in the Aristotelian *epistēmē* had no "practical" "applicability," but remained an attentiveness and dwelling in proximity to the sensible world as it showed itself in its most constant presencing—was required continually to demonstrate and justify its discoveries in a tangible manner that could be universally confirmed by everyone.

The demand that speculation become "useful," subservient to "practical" ends, and in general to the task of mastering nature is most famously formulated in the sixth and final part of Descartes' *Discourse on Method.* Descartes writes of the possibility of attaining knowledge that is "most useful" in life, expressing the hope that "instead of the speculative philosophy taught in the Schools, a practical philosophy can be found by which, knowing the power and the effects of fire, water, air, the stars, the heavens, and all the other bodies that surround us, as distinctly as we know the various

---

[8] On the experiment, see Heidegger's *Beiträge zur Philosophie* (GA 65), §§77–80. See also Patricia Glazebrook, "Heidegger's Philosophy of Science," Ph.D. dissertation, University of Toronto, 1994.

trades of our craftsmen, we might put them in the same way to all the uses
for which they are appropriate, and thereby make ourselves, as it were,
masters and possessors of Nature."[9]

The need for theoretical knowledge to be deployed in the service of
a *technē*, equated with the "practical," could not be more clearly stated.
Theōria is no longer to be conceived as an end in itself, a straightforward apprehending and observing of the *kosmos* and of nature, but must become
a means whereby human beings can "make" (*rendre*) themselves master
over nature—as though this very mastery could itself be produced or fab-
ricated through the new knowledge. Yet the same call was made already
some thirty years earlier in Francis Bacon's *Novum Organum,* which praised
"fruits and works" as being "as it were sponsors and sureties for the truth
of philosophies."[10] As with Descartes, Bacon's work too thus contains the
demand to begin anew from the very foundations.[11] Yet quite apart from
these philosophical formulations that no doubt reflected the shifting historical roles of artisan and bourgeois life—ways of life that had been changing
markedly since the thirteenth century—one has to note also the increasing instability of the presumed theoretical "truths" of Church doctrine,
"truths" that found themselves increasingly challenged by new theories in
physics and astronomy.[12]

What emerges all too conspicuously from these developments, in short,
is the demand upon theory to prove itself in "practice" by tangibly and visi-
bly *producing* its truths. The *work* of truth becomes all-important. *Theōria*
from now on subserves such work; *praxis* in the genuine and originary sense
has long since been eclipsed, especially the Aristotelian conception of *theōria*
as itself the highest *praxis*. The consequences of this transformation are
hinted at by Gadamer in the aforementioned study. That science becomes
research, remarks Gadamer, signifies something new in two respects. First:

> 'Science itself' becomes an anonymous quantity. The individual
> researcher is not the man in whom 'science itself' has its form
> and actuality—he is one of the many whose research results
> indeed contribute to science, yet in the same moment surpass

---

[9] René Descartes, *Discours de la méthode* (Paris: Garnier-Flammarion, 1966), sixième
partie, 84.

[10] Francis Bacon, *The New Organon,* ed. F. H. Anderson (Indianapolis: Bobbs-Merrill,
1960), LXXIII.

[11] Cf. the discussion by Nicholas Lobkowicz, *Theory and Practice,* 89. Chapter 7 of
Lobkowicz' study contains a general overview of some of the most important historical
and philosophical developments of this period. Lobkowicz locates what may well be "the
first modern articulation of the notion and ideal of historical progress" even earlier,
toward the end of the sixteenth century, in the work of Louis Le Roy (103–04).

[12] See Lobkowicz, *Theory and Practice,* chapter 8.

what was previously held to be 'true'. 'Science itself' dissolves
into continual self-surpassing. It is no longer *doctrina,* in which
one knows, teaches, and learns the true. (GW 4, 42)

Second, however, this entails that "it becomes the vast enterprise of
penetrating into unfamiliar realms, an enterprise that receives neither a
human nor a divine command to stop" (GW 4, 42). In the ongoing process
of infinite discovery, of infinite penetration, neither gods nor humans have
staying power, neither are afforded a veritable abode or dwelling place. And
precisely because of its fundamental insecurity, the path of modern science
has to be that of the constantly self-securing certainty of human reason.
Since, moreover, this certainty has to be that of the human being as such,
it must be universally available to any- (and every-) one at any (and every)
time and in any (and every) place. Thus, the method that secures the activity and path of modern science in its investigation of nature must become
that of mathematical truth, precisely because it is the most empty and formal, just as the *ego cogito* of Descartes can ground the subjectivity of the
modern subject because it knowingly represents and posits the most empty,
formal, and universal truth of thinking. In the modern science of nature, as
Gadamer expresses it, "the concern is no longer the speculative contemplation of divine creation in the fullness of its sensible forms in which God's
wisdom could be honored; rather, in mathematical abstraction laws are revealed that are concealed from the senses." Yet the researcher still pursues
"the never ultimately attainable goal of understanding the book of nature
penned by God's finger," thereby betraying his or her continued belief in
an underlying, concealed truth and *logos* of nature itself (GW 4, 42).

Gadamer's remarks on the anonymity and absence of any dwelling place
that characterize the ongoing, universalizing activity of modern science
serve to highlight what is increasingly concealed and refused by that activity, namely, the possibility of finite abode, of cultivating through philosophical insight and experience an enduring disposition or *hexis,* not only
utterly singular and finite in its actualizations, but attentive to the finite:
the possibility of an *ēthos* of finite *praxis* that would offer an abode for
practical and ethical life. To be virtuous, such an *ēthos* must be attuned
by the insight of a philosophical (or proto-philosophical) *theōrein,* oriented
toward the whole of one's worldly being and from there able to see and to
judge what is fitting on each occasion, able to temporalize an ethical stance
that would be responsive in an originary yet finite manner to the situation
of action. Through his readings of the Greeks, we shall suggest, Heidegger's
interpretation of the philosophical *theōrein* displaces its implicit orientation
toward beings in their most constant or recurrent presence (an orientation
that in Aristotle culminates in the ultimate unity or being of the *kosmos*

being identified with the presence of an entity, the heavens) into a vision of the concealment and finitude intrinsic to the presencing of all beings.

Theoria and Divinity: The Philosophical Turn

Our preceding reflections indicate clearly enough that the historical genesis of the *theōrein* found in modern science and technology has its roots not simply in the emergence of the philosophical *theōria* in Greek thought, but in the complex history of the way in which this emergence is bound up with various transformations in the experience of the divine. The Christian appropriation of Greek thought is only part of this complex history, for Greek philosophy itself already transformed a more ancient experience of the sacred, one which, as we shall examine shortly, was connected with a pre-philosophical sense of *theōria* found throughout the classical age.

In the *Sophist* course of 1924/25, Heidegger had himself alluded to this originary sense of *theōria*, albeit only in passing and by way of a cautionary remark. *Theōrein,* he there recalled, derives from *theōros,* the "spectator" at the Greek games and festivals, the public celebrations. The word *theōros* is a composite of *thea,* look or view, and *horaō,* seeing. *Thea* as look or view refers not to a subjective, nor even to a human "activity," but to a view understood as the outward appearance or "look" that something presents in showing itself in its distinctiveness; it has, Heidegger notes, "a similar meaning to *eidos*" (GA 19, 62–63). Heidegger chooses not to pursue any further the semantic history of the word *theōros,* in which "seeing" is "expressed twice" (thus, the view that something offers when one stands in view of it), but he does add the following cautionary remark:

> We cannot present the semantic history of this expression in any greater detail here. We should point out only that during the period directly preceding Plotinus, ... *theōria* came to be interpreted in such a way that it was said that in *theō-* there lies the root *theion, theos; theōrein* means: looking upon the divine. This is one specific Greek etymology, as provided, for example, by Alexander of Aphrodisias. We are here concerned with a reinterpretation, one that has its grounds in certain of Aristotle's accounts, yet does not identify the proper sense of the word. *Theōria* is translated into Latin as *speculatio,* which means pure contemplation [*das reine Betrachten*]; "speculative" thus means the same as "theoretical." The word *theōria* then came to play a major role in theology, where it is opposed to *allēgoria: theōria* is that kind of contemplation that identifies historiographical facts just as they are, prior to any *allēgoria;*

theōria becomes identical to *historia*. Finally it becomes identical to biblical theology and theology pure and simple. The fact that the translation of *theōria, theologia speculativa,* later represents precisely the opposite to exegetical theology is one of those peculiar contingencies that occur from time to time in the history of a meaning. (GA 19, 63)

Heidegger's caution here concerns not the association of *theōria* with the divine per se, but with the specific late-Christian interpretation of the divine under the influence of Aristotelian philosophy.[13] Heidegger does not pursue further in this context what is implied in the proper or more original sense of *theōria* and in the subsequent transformations in its meaning, but returns to his analysis of Aristotle, for whom *sophia* constitutes the supreme fulfilment of *theōrein*.

Nevertheless, Heidegger in this early context broaches a theme that would be taken up again in his later work. His passing remarks point to an issue of great contention among philologists ancient and modern, namely, whether the first part of the word *theōros* derives, as Heidegger here suggests, from *thea,* "look," or from *theos,* "God." Heidegger's derivation agrees with that of most modern etymologists; the majority of ancient etymologists, by contrast, associate the first part of the word with *theos.*[14] Heidegger himself remarks in this context that—as we ourselves have noted—the association of *theōria* with the divine is certainly found in Aristotle (as it is also in Plato). The question thus remains of how to properly interpret this association with the divine. Heidegger's comments here on the Christian interpretation of *theōria* identify one of the most prominent features that comes increasingly to the fore in the history of this word: pure, disinvolved contemplation, a pure seeing and apprehending of things as they are, of the true "facts." Of course, this is not just a result of the Christian interpretation of Greek thought; it is also a feature we see emerging already in Plato and Aristotle, with the increasing tendency to separate divine *nous* from human *dianoia* and thus from the human *logos*—the same separation that tends to remove human *theōrein* from direct involvement in sensuous immediacy and to institute the distinction between the *bios theōrētikos* and

---

[13] For the etymology provided by Alexander of Aphrodisias, see his commentary on Book I of the *Prior Analytics* (Wallies: 3, 20): to gar theōrein kai ap' autou tou onomatos dēlon hōs esti peri tēn tōn theiōn opsin te kai gnōsin; sēmainei gar to horan ta theia: "It is clear from its very name that theorizing ... means seeing what is divine." The same etymological connection with *theos* is found in Plutarch, *De Musica,* 27; and Philodemus, *De Musica,* 23.8ff.

[14] For an overview of modern and ancient etymologies, see Hannelore Rausch, *Theoria: Von Ihrer Sakralen zur Philosophischen Bedeutung* (München: Wilhelm Fink Verlag, 1982), 13–17.

bios politikos, a distinction that (via Plotinus and early Roman thought) becomes a veritable separation of ways of life in the opposition between the *vita contemplativa* and the *vita activa.*

In Heidegger's analysis of Aristotle in the *Sophist* course, his reading followed this *tendency* toward a separation of the *bios theōrētikos* from the life of *phronēsis.* This reading, we suggested, should not be taken as Heidegger's last word on Aristotle, so to speak, but is a reading in the light of the history of ontology, a history that founds itself on this very separation. Heidegger reads Aristotle with an eye to the philosophical tradition, but his reading identifies, albeit tacitly and in a preparatory way, what is problematic about this traditional reading, namely, the all-pervasiveness of an implicit understanding of being as sheer presence. This understanding has as its consequence a concealment of presence as such (of its event-like character, as presencing), in the tendency to interpret presence—specifically, the supreme presence of *nous,* that is, the "divine" (the *theion*)—precisely as a being, as an entity, this being the interpretation that comes to sanction the aforementioned separation. If, by contrast, our own reading of Heidegger's analysis attended to the inseparability (in the sense of the fundamental relatedness of their ultimate ends) of the *theōrein* of *sophia* and of the practical *aisthēsis,* then this also had the strategic purpose of showing that *theōrein* in Aristotle (namely, that of *sophia*), by virtue of its relevance to the practical *nous* of the *phronimos,* still bears the trace of an earlier sense of worldly involvement in the sensuous. Men like Pericles, Aristotle notes, are said to be *phronimous* precisely because they can engage in *theōrein,* in "seeing" what is good, for themselves and for other human beings (NE, 1140 b8).[15] Similarly, Aeschines in his speech *On the Embassy* exhorts his fellow citizens to view their ambassadors in the light of the "crisis" in which they served (*theōrein pros ton kairon*) (80). In its earlier sense, *theōria* precisely did not mean a pure, disinvolved contemplating, being a mere "onlooker" or "spectator" in the modern sense of having a disengaged, "objective" view of things. The problematic that opposes the "actor" to the "spectator" is in this regard a thoroughly modern one, first enabled by a representational perspective.[16] Being present as a spectator at a theatrical event such as an ancient Greek tragedy did not mean that one was able, from a neutral and objective distance, to survey as a picture the totality of events portrayed (the unfolding of destiny in the actions of humans, gods, and their world) and thereby to comprehend the meaning of the tragedy. On the contrary, the meaning of

---

[15] On this citation of Pericles as an exemplary *phronimos,* see Pierre Aubenque, *La prudence chez Aristote,* 51ff.

[16] See Richard J. Bernstein, "Judging—the Actor and the Spectator," in *Philosophical Profiles* (Philadelphia: University of Pennsylvania Press, 1986), 221–37.

the tragedy remains in essence incomprehensible to any "mere spectator." The accomplishment of theatrical presentation was rather to involve the spectator in the "action," to draw him or her into a knowing (seeing) relationship to a world that now became manifest as exceeding or transcending his or her individual actions.[17] The classical Greek "theatrical" and tragic view of the world was precisely such that it could not be reduced to a merely pictured or represented totality of meaning. Ancient *theōria* entailed, on the contrary, an involved participation in the disclosure of other beings, a seeing oneself as addressed, invited, called upon to disclose oneself in response, if only in the manner of reticence and awe. As such, ancient *theōria* not only had fundamental ethical and political significance; it was also inextricably associated with experience of the divine and sacred presence of other beings.

But what exactly is the divine (*to theion*) in the pre-philosophical experience of the Greeks, and how has this pre-philosophical sense been transformed by the time of Aristotle? Philosophy is defined early on by Heidegger as the knowledge or "science" (*Wissenschaft, epistēmē*)—that is, the "theory" or contemplation (*theōrein*)—both of beings as such and of beings as a whole. It has a twofold character. Heidegger of course takes this twofold concept of philosophy from Aristotle's *Metaphysics,* where First Philosophy is characterized as the investigation of the *on hēi on*—what came to be called ontology—and as *theologikē:* knowledge of *to theion,* the divine.[18] Yet what is meant by the divine here? For Aristotle, it is that which is supreme and most exalted in all things (*timiōtaton*), that which comes first in First Philosophy. As early as 1928, in *The Metaphysical Foundations of Logic,* Heidegger identifies the divine with the "almighty" in the sense of the supremely powerful (*das Übermächtige*), the overwhelming (*das Überwältigende*) as that which "captivates" us, in a word, *world:*

> *to theion* means: beings pure and simple—the heavens: that
> which encompasses and overwhelms us, that amongst which and
> into which we are thrown, that by which we are captivated and
> which befalls us, the almighty. *Theologein* is an observing of the
> *kosmos.* . . . (GA 26, 13)

Heidegger here appeals once again to Book VI of the *Nicomachean Ethics,* where Aristotle, discussing the difference between *sophia* and *phronēsis,* recalls what people say of Anaxagoras and Thales: that they are

---

[17] This point is made clearly enough in Aristotle's *Poetics.* On the *theōria* of Greek tragic theater, see our essay "A 'Scarcely Pondered Word'. The Place of Tragedy: Heidegger, Aristotle, Sophocles," in *Philosophy and Tragedy,* ed. M. de Beistegui & S. Sparks (London: Routledge, forthcoming).

[18] On Heidegger's account of the twofold character of philosophy, see Robert Bernasconi, "'The Double Concept of Philosophy' and the Place of Ethics in *Being and Time,*" in *Heidegger in Question,* chapter 2.

wise (although they do not show *phronēsis*) because they "have an eye for
what is *peritta*—the inhabitual; for what is *thaumasta*—that which arouses
our wonder and astonishment; for what is *chalepa*—difficult; for what is
daimonia—that which constantly befalls human beings and concerns them
in the last resort and as a whole" (GA 26, 14; NE, 1141 b3ff.).[19] Those
who are said to be wise "have an eye for" such things, as Heidegger here
renders the Greek *eidenai*. Their *theōrein* is a beholding above all of the
visible heavens, as that which most arouses wonder and astonishment in
lying "beyond" and yet touching the earth-bound existence of mortal human beings, that whose very existence lies beyond mere human comprehension, yet whose presence constitutes the ultimate horizon within which
human existence is lived and finds its own meaning. Thus, as Aristotle elsewhere recounts, when Anaxagoras was asked for what end one should choose
to come into existence rather than not, he is reported to have answered,
"For the sake of contemplating [*theōrēsai*] the heavens and the whole order
of the universe."[20]

Aristotle's point in alluding to these first philosophers in the context of
his *Ethics,* however, is to emphasize the remoteness of their *sophia* from
the realm of human affairs and of *phronēsis*. On account not only of being
bound by the need to procure the necessities of life, but also, and for
Aristotle more importantly, because of its dependence upon the existence
of other human beings and their opinions within one and the same world,
human existence cannot for the most part afford the leisure to tarry contemplatively in the presence of the "eternal," of that which is most constantly
(*aei*) present and beyond the human realm. Or at least, one should not de-
vote oneself exclusively to that most noble of ends, if one is to acknowledge
one's existence as ultimately human, even though an appreciation of the
ultimate sameness of the one world shared by human beings, whatever their
individual differences, remains for Aristotle an indispensible precondition
of political community informed by *phronēsis*. Nevertheless, in the realm
of the visible as such, there are, it seems, only differences. For Aristotle,
theōria is not restricted to "the most visible of those divine things of which
the *kosmos* is composed" (NE, 1141 b1), but must behold the very divinity
and ground of these divine manifestations (i.e., of the celestial bodies) in
each case. It must contemplate what is most eternal (*aidia*) in these eternal manifestations, "the causes [*aitia*] of what is visible of things divine"
(M, 1026 a17)—the eternal forms of the circular movements of the heav-
enly bodies—as well as the highest good in the whole of nature, the prime,
unmoved mover that first imparts these eternal motions as such. This first

---

[19] Cf. *Metaphysics*, Book I, chapters 1 and 2.
[20] *Eudemian Ethics,* 1216 a14. Cf. *Protreptikos,* b18–20, where Pythagoras is also
mentioned.

mover is what is most divine: it is the eternal activity (*energeia*) of *nous* as that which first lets the eternal movements of the visible heavens be manifest as such, as constantly the same, but which is itself invisible. Eternally at work in the *kosmos,* it is present to human beings only in the act of human *theōrein,* and most fully present only when such contemplation contemplates the oneness produced in and through its being at work in us.[21] Human *theōrein* is in this sense part of the "immortal" activity of the oneness of the *kosmos:* it is our possibility of "immortalizing" (*athanatizein*). Aristotle's God, as that which is most divine and most "is," is conceived as that which, as an object of love (*hōs erōmenon:* M, 1072 b4), ultimately moves the human desire to see, and does so in such way as to "activate" the potentiality of *nous* in us, the *theōrein* that first lets beings be in the relative constancy of their presence. Although this supreme being is invisible as such, and even uncontaminated (*amigēs*)[22] in the sense that it does not itself become any of the visible things, Aristotle's divinity is nevertheless not independent of the world, but constantly "at work" in it as that which lets all things be in their belonging together in the being of one world. "For everything is ordered together with respect to One" (M, 1074 a17). It is that for the sake of which everything ultimately is, that with a view to which we can ultimately judge a life to be "good" (M, 982 b5f.).

As in 1924/25, Heidegger's 1928 appeal to Aristotle's testimony concerning the pre-philosophical "eye" for divine things does not stop to investigate this pre- or proto-philosophical sense of divine vision. Rather, Heidegger again follows Aristotle in translating this experience of the divine into the end of a concerted striving that requires human beings to look beyond what is immediately given in the realm of the sensible, to look toward the most constant and permanent aspects of beings: that which arouses astonishment is interpreted as that which "constantly presses us toward new questions"; it is subsumed into the concernful striving of *philosophia* that makes *prōtē philosophia* into the *epistēmē zētoumenē,* "the sought-after science" (*die gesuchte Wissenschaft*), the knowledge pertaining to our proper understanding of being. This knowledge can indeed never become our secure possession, but must be "sought anew each time" (GA 26, 13–14). The search for this knowledge is the striving of *philo-sophia:*

> It belongs to the essence of this science that it must be sought after. There is such knowing only if a search for and propensity toward it is alive, an inclination behind which there is a concerned effort, a desire. This knowledge is a voluntary leaning toward an original understanding: *philo-sophia.* . . . (GA 26, 14)

---

[21] *Metaphysics,* Book XII. Cf. DA, 430 a10ff.
[22] DA, 429 a15f.; 430 a18.

Yet this understanding of philosophy and its desire, Heidegger notes, is also in keeping with Aristotle's remark that *sophia* can be understood as an *aretē technēs*, as "an exceptional free disposition of knowing what one is about"—as a standing over and against things (*vor-stehen*, the literal sense of *epistēmē*), overseeing the possibilities of things (i.e., seeing them in advance of their full presencing, as in the artisan's seeing the *eidos*), seeing through them in attaining transparency (GA 26, 14).[23] It is already symptomatic of what, in the "Letter on 'Humanism'," Heidegger would later call the "technical" appropriation of thinking, as a prior orientation toward the *eidos*, that of a *theōrein* separated out from the moments of worldly *praxis* and *poiēsis*. Yet the ambiguity noted in our introductory chapter remains: Wonder or astonishment, if it indeed stands at the origin of philosophy, nevertheless also already exceeds it; it can never be entirely subsumed within the philosophical desire as conceived by Aristotle and brought to completion by Hegel. That *eidenai* that has an eye for the divine perhaps once referred to a vision that was not yet the desire to see that marks the beginning and end of philosophy.

Yet what is decisive in the critical turn taken by the Greek thinking of being toward the end of the classical age, in what Heidegger calls the "end of the great beginning" of Greek philosophy, namely, the philosophy of Plato and Aristotle (EM, 137), is not the fact that philosophical seeing turns toward the *eidos* as such, but the particular interpretation that the *eidos* itself undergoes. The nature of this turn in the understanding of *eidos* is not fully explicated by Heidegger until the 1935 course *Introduction to Metaphysics,* where an interpretation of the Presocratic philosophers Heraclitus and Parmenides, and of the tragedies of Sophocles, first opens up a more profound appreciation of the change that has taken place, of a change that enables nothing less than the scission or separation of being from thinking and the subsequent domination of being by *logos*. The same meditation also complicates the apparent insertion, in §36 of *Being and Time,* of Parmenides' statement that "being and apprehending are the same" into an uninterrupted continuity with the history of philosophy from Aristotle to Hegel (see the beginning of chapter 2 above). For Parmenides' *noein,* Heidegger now argues, is not at all properly conceived as a human activity or mode of comportment (as in Aristotle—although here too, as we have noted, it still retains the trace of its "divine" origins), but as an event (*Geschehnis*) in the self-disclosure of being whereby human beings themselves first come into being as historical. It is not at all a human property, but on the contrary an event that "has the human being" (EM, 108). Only when being itself comes to be understood as *eidos* and *idea,* and thereby

---

[23] Cf. NE, 1141 a12.

as something "had" or possessed by man (*ousia;* cf. EM, 138), does seeing, apprehending, "thinking" come to be conceived as a human activity.

The *eidos* or *idea* means the view or aspect that something visible presents, the look or face of something. The look of something is that in and through which it presents itself to us and thus *stands* in place before us. And this look of beings belongs originarily to *phusis* itself, to the being of beings as emergence, as appearing and shining-forth, as presencing. "This standing is the constant steadfastness [*Ständigkeit*] of that which has emerged of its own accord, of *phusis*" (EM, 138). As such, the *eidos* is not something that could be circumvented; in its originary belonging to *phusis,* it does not at all seem to entail a distancing or falling away from the experience of being as self-emergent appearing that belongs to the Greek beginning. Heidegger indeed concedes that "it cannot be denied that the interpretation of being as *idea* arises from the fundamental experience of being as *phusis*. It is, as we may say, a necessary consequence of the essence of being as *emergent appearing and shining*" (EM, 139). And yet, the Platonic-Aristotelian primacy of the *eidos* nevertheless constitutes a falling away or concealment of the originary Greek experience of being as *phusis:*

> Yet what if that which is an essential *consequence* is raised to the status of the essence itself and thus comes to occupy the place of the essence—what then? Then a falling away is there, one that must for its part produce peculiar consequences. And so it indeed happened. It is not the fact that *phusis* was characterized as *idea,* but that the *idea* comes to be the sole and authoritative interpretation of being that is decisive." (EM, 139)

What is entailed in this falling away? The *eidos* or *idea* as the look or face (*Gesicht*) that presents itself does so for human apprehending only insofar as it has *already* come to a stand, only insofar as it has already come to presence within the orbit of such apprehending. The look as *eidos* is that which has been seen in having already been sighted: it is *das Gesichtete.* Yet as such, it is only the consequence of self-emergent appearing, not that appearing as such. Certainly, Heidegger notes, something that has been sighted belongs to seeing; "but it does not follow from this that having been sighted [*die Gesichtetheit*], as such, should or could alone determine the presencing of what has been sighted" (EM, 140). What thus occurs in the interpretation of the *eidos* as the sole essence of being is the separating out of that which has been sighted, or seen, from its self-emergent coming into presence as such. In and through this critical separation, the *eidos* becomes increasingly isolated from the site of its appearance in beings themselves; it is set over and against the self-emergent appearing of beings, which (in yet a "further misinterpretation") comes to be interpreted as mere appearing, opposed to that which truly is. The originary "truth" of *phusis* becomes *homoiōsis* and *mimēsis*, "correctness of seeing," of an apprehending that must orient itself in advance toward the *idea* conceived as a *logos* in conflict with appearing (*phusis*).

We cannot here recall the entire wealth of Heidegger's 1935 interpretation. In the present context, it is sufficient to indicate the importance of the insights formulated in this 1935 course for Heidegger's subsequent work, and in particular for the 1936 essay "The Origin of the Work of Art." For what comes to be concealed in and through the ascendancy of the *eidos* in its Platonic-Aristotelian interpretation is, as Heidegger here expresses it, nothing less than the originary worldly character of *phusis: "phainesthai,* coming into appearance in the great sense of the epiphany of a world." "World turns away" (EM, 48). The increasing focus on that which has already appeared and been sighted becomes a growing disregard for the originary appearing and approach, the coming and advent of beings themselves in their singular radiance and shining and in the situated belonging together of their worldly being. *Phainesthai,* in the sense of the epiphany of a world, "now becomes the demonstrable visibility of present-at-hand things. The eye, seeing, which in its originary beholding once brought about its project in looking into the prevailing of things, brought forth its work in looking into such prevailing, now becomes a mere regarding and inspecting and staring. The look of things is now merely the optical." In "The Origin of the Work of Art," Heidegger attempts to describe precisely the epiphany of world, in its relation to *phusis,* that is brought forth in the great work of art in and through the "project" of a poietic seeing. This epiphany of a world that occurs in and through the work of art, as we shall see, is also an experience of the divine and of divinity that is not yet that of onto-theology.

The 1936 essay on the origin of the work of art not only brings to language the establishment of the great work of art as opening up the epiphany of a historical world. It also approaches the human encounter with such a work in terms of a seeing that is not yet that of the Platonic-Aristotelian apprehending of the *eidos* removed from its originary appearing. It approaches a more originary sense of *theōria* as an attentive tarrying with that which is present in the epiphany of its enigmatic shining. Such is the appropriate comportment of knowledge called for in order to receive and preserve (*bewahren*) the great work of art in its truth or unconcealment. This comportment, which we shall examine below, is nevertheless not made explicit as *theōria* in the 1936 essay.

The first published essay of Heidegger to broach this originary sense of *theōria* appears to be "Science and Reflection" (1953), to which we have already referred in part 2. That essay indeed begins by recollecting a theme from "The Origin of the Work of Art," namely, that the essence of art lies not in its being merely a cultural phenomenon, to be lined up alongside science, but consists in its being "a consecration and a shelter in which what is actual bestows anew on each occasion its hitherto concealed splendor [*Glanz*] upon human beings, so that in its luminance they may see more purely and hear more clearly what addresses itself to their essence" (VA, 41). As Heidegger had already expressed it in a course that predates the essay on the origin of the work of art, the 1931/32 course on Plato's *Republic* and *Theaetetus,* the essence of art lies in the way in which the artist, by virtue of his "essential eye for the possible," "brings to the work the concealed possibilities of beings, and thereby first opens the eyes of human beings for what actually is, for that realm in which they blindly go about their business" (GA 34, 102). Yet it is not in connection with art, but via a discussion of modern science as "the theory of the real" that Heidegger now approaches the ancient meaning of *theōria.* He does so, however, only after clarifying that the actuality of the real, in German, *die Wirklichkeit des Wirklichen,* demands to be thought historically in terms of the *work,* of the German *Werk* and the Greek *ergon.* The actuality of the real, in Aristotelian terms the *energeia* of the *ergon,* is historically determined as the lying and holding itself before us, in the intrinsic completion (*entelecheia*) of its presencing, of that which has been brought forth into presencing (*An-wesen*). The *wesen* in *An-wesen*—the essential presence in presencing—means "enduring" (*währen*), "remaining" (VA, 45–46). Yet such enduring is inadequately thought as the constant presence of the *eidos* or *idea.*

In turning to "theory" and to *theōria,* as we may recall from part 2, "Science and Reflection" alludes to "an exalted and mysterious meaning" pertaining to the words *theōria* and *theōrein.* In the earlier context, we remarked that the initial interpretation offered of *theōrein,* tracing it to the same double root of *thea* and *horaō,* and relating it to *eidenai,* to knowingor *Wissen* as "having seen" the *eidos* of something, both pointed forward to the Platonic-Aristotelian interpretation of seeing, and pointed back to a more ancient kind of vision. *Theōrein,* Heidegger concludes from his initial discussion, "is *thean horan:* to look attentively upon the outward appearance wherein that which presences becomes visible, and through such vision to tarry alongside it in seeing" (VA, 48). Just as this determination of *theōria* can be seen to point both forward and back, so too Heidegger points to the undecidability that seems to attend the status of the *bios theōrētikos* in Greek thought (presumably, Aristotle is primarily intended here). On the one hand, the *bios theōrētikos* is distinguished from the *bios praktikos,* which Heidegger glosses as "the way of life that devotes itself to doing and making"—thus indicating the predominantly broad sense in which *praxis* is thereby understood. On the other hand, as his 1924 reading of Aristotle had already insisted, the "way of life of the beholder" is also the supreme form of activity (*das höchste Tun*). *Theōria* is in itself, and not first by way of some additional utility that attaches to it, "the consummate form of human existence" (VA, 48). Yet this supremacy of *theōria* as the activity that brings human existence into its own proper end and completion, Heidegger now suggests, may well derive from a more ancient sense of *theōria*. "For *theōria* is our pure relation to those views proffered by whatever presences, those views which, through their shining [*Scheinen*], concern and affect human beings in bringing the presence of the gods to shine [*indem sie die Gegenwart der Götter be-scheinen*]" (VA, 48–49).

This characterization of *theōria,* in which we encounter a reference to "the presence of the gods," does not yet describe the Aristotelian transformation of *theōrein,* its ability to "bring before our apprehending ... the *archai* and *aitiai* of whatever presences." To understand this earlier sense of *theōria* entails hearing something else, something earlier, letting the Greek word *theōria* speak to us in another way:

> Bound up with the supremacy accorded *theōria* within the Greek *bios* is the fact that the Greeks, who in a unique way thought from out of their language, that is, received from it their existence, might have heard something else in the word *theōria.* When differently stressed, the two root words *thea* and *oraō* can read: *theā* and *ōra*. *Theā* is the goddess. It is as goddess that *Alētheia,* the unconcealment from out of which and in which that which presences presences, appears to the early thinker Parmenides. We translate *alētheia* by the Latin word *veritas* and by our German word *Wahrheit*. (VA, 49)

This attempt to hear a Presocratic sense of the divine in *theōria* had in fact already been undertaken by Heidegger a decade before, in a 1942/43 course on Parmenides, to which we shall turn shortly. In "Science and Reflection," Heidegger goes on to relate vision in the early sense of *theōria* to a kind of *respect,* to a vision that pays heed:

> The Greek word *ōra* means the respect [*Rücksicht*] that we have, the honor and esteem that we bestow. If we now think the word *theōria* in terms of the meanings just cited, then *theōria* is a reverent paying heed to the unconcealment of what presences. Theory in the ancient, that is, early, and by no means obsolete sense is the *beholding that watches over truth* [das hütende Schauen der Wahrheit]. Our Old High German word *wara* (whence *wahr,*

wahren, and Wahrheit) goes back to the same root as the Greek
horaō, ōra: wora. (VA, 49)

Theōria, interpreted as a protective, respectful beholding of the unconcealment of whatever presences, here corresponds to one essential moment
of what Heidegger, in "The Question Concerning Technology" from the
same year, identifies as "the highest dignity of the human essence," namely
to protect (hüten) the unconcealment of all beings, "and before this in each
case the concealment" of all that presences upon this Earth. In "Science
and Reflection," we see unconcealment itself, alētheia, referred to the Par-
menidean goddess, to theā, and thus to the divine radiance of whatever
presences by way of its look. Equally significantly, the German word for
"truth," Wahrheit, is traced back to ōra, to a seeing that is a respectful beholding of the unconcealment of whatever presences. Theōria and alētheia,
Heidegger here indicates, may be understood in terms of an experience of
the sensuous presencing of beings themselves in their un-concealment, an
experience not yet referred to the Platonic-Aristotelian determinations of
the eidos.

The Theoria of the Ancients

Before examining more closely the specific kind of seeing that the ancient
theōria implied, we must give a brief overview of the various connotations
of theōros, from which the word derives. Hannelore Rausch in her important study of the ancient theōria recalls that the word theōros could have
five different, though related meanings: 1) Someone seeking advice from an
oracle; 2) the envoy to a festival; 3) someone who announces a festival; 4) an
official with local authority; 5) a beholder (Zuschauer).[24] In each of these
meanings, a relation to the divine is expressed, a relation that calls for a
particular ethical stance on the part of human beings. The disclosure of the
divine and its relation to the human are also always bound to a particular
place and time, and thus imply in each case the experience of a singular and
finite event. In the first case, that of someone seeking advice from an oracle
(the oldest recorded meaning, first found in Theognis, in Sophocles, and

---

[24] Rausch, Theoria: Von Ihrer Sakralen zur Philosophischen Bedeutung, 12. Rausch's
work brings together the philological and philosophical insights of a number of more detailed studies concerned with the original meanings of theōria. See in particular: Hermann
Koller, "Theoros und Theoria," Glotta, vol. 36 (1958): 273–86; Franz Boll, "Vita Contemplativa," 3–34; and Otfrid Becker, Plotin und das Problem der geistigen Aneignung
(Berlin: De Gruyter, 1940). The study by Götz Redlow, Theoria (Berlin: Veb Deutscher
Verlag der Wissenschaften, 1966), also contains many significant insights, but analyses
the genesis of theōria from the modern perspective of subjectivity and consciousness.

in Euripides, but also later, for example in Demosthenes),[25] the disclosure occurs at a sacred place, and is mediated via a priestess, whose language is not that of the everyday. In such disclosure, notes Rausch, "The human being experiences his being bound to an absolute measure, to which he must respond accordingly in his stance. Through the interpretation of what is proclaimed he receives a directive that obligates him in his action."[26] In the second and closely related third meanings, the *theōroi* are official envoys sent on behalf of one community or town to participate in festive activities (sacrifices, dances, games) in another town. They are representatives of their home town in a foreign community; their role is always that of mediation between two communities, between the home town and the foreign: "in all instances of official theory, travel to another place is entailed. Change of place is always connected with theory and with the *theōroi*."[27] As we shall see, this circumstance is significant for the subsequent development of the word *theōria*. The verb *theōrein* in this context means to send someone to a festival in the official capacity of *theōros;* a *theōria* designated the mission of ambassadors sent in this official capacity. This second meaning of *theōros* is the most prevalent; we find it widely documented in the early historians Herodotus and Thucydides, but also much later in Polybius, in Demosthenes, and indeed in Plato and Aristotle.[28] But it is important to understand that the *theōros* in this capacity was not at all a mere observer or spectator in the sense of someone who merely looks on from the outside, without any involvement. On the contrary: *theōrein* in this sense, as Rausch stresses, "entails an extremely active participation, and in this connection never means 'going to a festival as a spectator [*Zuschauer*]'."[29] *Theōrein* was an act of sharing something in common, of encountering, maintaining, and transforming the limits of one's own community through the encounter with the foreign, through the mutual respect of otherness. This very encounter transpired through the mediation of a shared experience of the divine as transcending the limits of human self-identity, but thereby precisely making those limits visible as such. This experience of the divine was certainly a *seeing*, but in the sense of a genuine participation.[30] "The form of manifestation of this divine is the festival, which is bound to a particular time and a particular place, and whose significance is expressed through

---

[25] Theognis, 805ff.; Sophocles, *Oedipus Tyrannus,* 114, and *Oedipus at Colonus,* 413; Euripides, *Hippolytos,* 792, 807; Demosthenes, *Meidias,* XXI, 53.

[26] Rausch, 21.

[27] Ibid., 23; cited from Koller, 278.

[28] Herodotus, VIII, 26; I, 59; Thucydides, III, 104; VI, 16, 2; VIII, 10, 1; Polybius, 28, 16, 4; Demosthenes, *Meidias,* XXI, 115; Plato, *Phaedo,* 58bff.; Aristotle, *The Athenian Constitution,* LVI, 3. The earliest allusion may be in Pindar: see Koller, 277.

[29] Rausch, 22; Koller, 277.

[30] Cf. Becker, 64.

the sending of *theōroi*. The divine, moreover, appears as something that founds community, that connects those towns that are celebrating by way of peace, friendship, and common cult."[31] The same connotations of community, order, and the divine are present in the fourth meaning of *theōroi* as town officials who oversaw and enforced the observance of laws—for example, as one document indicates, of the decree that no one may harvest when the priest sets off for the sacred realm.[32] These *theōroi*, Rausch concludes, "oversee the observance of a law, a law in which time plays a special role and through which, with regard to the sacred, a binding order is created."[33] Finally, the fifth meaning of *theōros* in the ancient sense—that of a *Zuschauer* as a beholder, onlooker, or spectator—is found documented in Aeschylus and Euripides.[34] Yet in these instances too the seeing referred to is always a very specific kind of seeing, namely, a seeing of the divine, and this in an ambiguous sense: the god may be either the one looking, or the one looked upon.

Surveying the range of these diverse meanings in which the sacred appears as the dominant and unifying connotation, Rausch seeks to understand the apparent association between seeing and the divine, between *theos* and *thea,* not in terms of etymological speculation, but on the basis of the underlying context of all these usages, which refer to the phenomenon of divine epiphany. The appearance of the divine as an event finds its proper context in the phenomenon of the festival that emerges as central in the most prevalent meaning of *theōros,* that of an envoy present at a festival.[35] The festival marks a special, yet recurrent time, a sacred time distinguished from the profane time of the "everyday" in which human beings become so absorbed that they risk losing themselves, their proper singularity, altogether.[36] The time of the festival is distinguished by a distinctive

---

[31] Rausch, 24.

[32] Inscription of Paros, cited by Rausch, 26.

[33] Ibid.

[34] In Aeschylus' *Prometheus Bound,* Prometheus greets the approach of the daughters of Oceanus with the following words: "Hath there come to this crag at the confines of the world someone to stare upon my sufferings (*ponōn emōn theōros*)—or with what intent? Behold me (*horate*), an ill-fated god ..." (116ff.); later, he addresses Oceanus: "So then thou too hast come to stare (*epoptēs*) upon my sufferings ... to gaze upon (*theōrēsōn*) my state and join thy grief to my distress? Behold a spectacle (*theama*)— me here ..." (298–304; cited in the translation by H. Weir Smyth [Cambridge, MA: Harvard University press, 1988]). In Euripides' *Ion,* the god looks upon his own festival by night: "I fear the much-sung god (*theon*), when the night watchman will see him as beholder (*theōron*) of the torchlight procession among a sea of dance on the sixth day of the great Eleusinia ..." (1074–77).

[35] It may be significant that the Greek word for festival, *heortē,* appears to contain the same root *wor* that modern etymology finds in *theōria.* Cf. Becker, 64 n. 1.

[36] Cf. Rausch, 28–29.

presence: that of the divine. Citing a hymn to Apollo by Callimachus,[37] Rausch notes that the festive experience of the divine entails a readiness for and openness to the approaching event of the god's coming to presence. The epiphany of the god occurs as an *event of seeing* that not only requires a prior readiness on the part of human beings, but also transforms what is thus looked upon by the god:

> [The god] shows himself and is seen. "Not to all, but only to the noble does Apollo show himself. To see him is to be exalted; not to see him is to be abased. Archer, we shall see you, and shall never be abased." This seeing of the god has a transformative character. It elevates the human being and is the measure of his value (great, slight). To be noble, thus to have a particular human stance, a particular ethos, is a precondition of seeing.... Yet even he who is noble first receives his proper rank in the epiphany of the god.[38]

It is clear that the event of this disclosure, this seeing of the god, is twofold: neither simply human nor purely divine. On the one hand, a prior human disposition is required, an openness toward the divine, a readiness for this seeing. On the other hand, this openness first receives its specific character, as openness for *the divine* (for *this* divinity, here and now—in this singular "here and now" that will be marked by the event of the holy), only because it is already called by the divinity, by the approach of the god.[39] It is primarily the god who looks, for no human openness can bring about (*poiein*) the disclosure of the divine if the latter does not appear of its own accord (as *phusis*). The human "vision" of the divine is a seeing in the sense

---

[37] In translation, the hymn reads:

> How Apollo's laurel bough quivers,
> his whole temple quivers! Back, back, you sinners!
> Phoebus is knocking at the door with shapely foot.
> Don't you see? The palm from Delos gently swayed
> all of a sudden, the swan in the sky is melodiously chanting.
> Push yourselves back, O bolts on the door,
> open yourselves, O keys! Already the god dwells nearby.
> And you servants, ready yourselves for song and dance.
> Not to all, but only to the noble does Apollo show himself.
> To see him is to be exalted; not to see him is to be abased.
> Archer, we shall see you, and shall never be abased.

Translation adapted in part from John Ferguson, *Callimachus* (Boston: Twayne Publishers, 1980), 111–12.

[38] Rausch, 31.

[39] Cf. Heidegger's remarks on the opening lines of Hölderlin's hymn "The Ister," which poetizes the river Danube as a "demigod," neither purely human nor purely divine (GA 53, 5–9).

of being looked upon. This vision, as Rausch indicates, is transformative in the sense that it elevates the human being into what is beyond him, thus first bestowing upon him his proper measure, letting him be seen in his proper limits, whether great or slight. Yet it is transformative not only of human beings, but also of beings as a whole: "It also seizes things and nature in their visibility, in their sensuous perceptibility in general....."[40] The event of divine disclosure thus denotes a beginning, an irruption into profane time, coincident with the "moment" of creation of the world: it is the event of the *poiēsis* of beings as a whole, as *phusis*.[41]

Thought in terms of the issue of divine disclosure embodied most tangibly in the phenomenon of the festival, the close connection between the *theōros* as envoy to a festival and as someone who is witness to a "spectacular" event, who beholds and is looked upon by the divine, is thus concretely indicated by Rausch's account.[42] In the Greek festival, she concludes, "this situation of *thea,* of a beholding, to which gods and humans come together, is repeated time and again."[43] This concrete connection between festivity and spectacle helps to explain the shift that the word *theōria* undergoes, such that in Plato and Aristotle it assumes the primary sense of seeing or beholding, yet a seeing that, in its highest instances, invariably continues to be associated with divinity. Yet other factors also play a role in this semantic shift. In particular, the circumstance we noted above, namely, the fact that travel, journeying, change of place, the encounter with the foreign are always entailed in the ancient meaning of *theōria* is also significant. For *theōria* is thereby associated not only with participation in a festive event disclosing the spectacle of the divine; it is associated also with *experiencing,* with knowing in the sense of having seen many things—things strange and foreign, unusual and astonishing, extraordinary and divine. This connotation we find already in Herodotus, who provides a report of Anacharsis "visiting or seeing many parts of the earth in his capacity as *theōros*" (*gēn pollēn theōrēsas*).[44] More telling still with respect to the shift in meaning of *theōria* is Herodotus' account of the journey of Solon, where *theōria* is

---

[40] Rausch, 32.

[41] Ibid., 36–37.

[42] Even when, in Aristotle, the *theōros* assumes a more political, rather than sacred role, the theme of witnessing remains important—specifically, of witnessing something or someone *present,* a present event. Thus, in Book I of the *Rhetoric,* Aristotle characterizes the *theōros* as one kind of hearer, the one who discerns and witnesses the presence of the speaker, while the other kinds of hearer are concerned with judging (forensically) the past or (deliberatively) the future (1358 b2f.). It is significant that this connection between the *theōros* and presence is explicitly made by Aristotle, since the time at issue again pertains to past, present, or future actions, that is, to human *praxis,* and not merely to the time of "nature" as thematized in the *Physics.*

[43] Rausch, 34.

[44] Herodotus, IV, 76, 2ff. For a discussion of this passage, see Rausch, 41–43.

explicitly associated with *sophia,* with worldly knowledge. Three excerpts
from the account are particularly suggestive:[45]

> To the rich and flourishing city of Sardis there came among
> others all the wise from Greece who lived at this time, among
> them Solon from Athens as well, who at their bidding had given
> the Athenians laws, and who left the country for ten years; he
> removed himself under the pretext of a *theōria,* so that he would
> not be forced to repeal any of the laws that he had laid down.[46]

> For this reason and on account of a *theōria* Solon left the coun-
> try and came to Amasis in Egypt as well as to Croesus at
> Sardis.[47]

> "Guestfriend from Athens," Croesus addressed him, "many sto-
> ries have already come to us about you, concerning your wisdom
> and your travels, since as a friend of wisdom you have investi-
> gated many lands on account of *theōria.*"[48]

Here the travels of Solon the *theōros* are closely associated with his wisdom (*sophia*); he is addressed as a "friend of wisdom" (*hōs philosopheōn*).
In Herodotus' account the official, political motive for Solon's journeys is
prominent; in a later account given by Aristotle in *The Athenian Constitution,* however, the *theōria* is also depicted as having private motivation:

> For the purpose of trade and also for *theōria* Solon undertook
> a journey to Egypt, and declared that he would not return for
> ten years; for he did not consider that it was right to remain
> there and to explain the laws, but believed that everyone should
> carry out their provisions for himself.[49]

In Aristotle's account, Solon's journeys are undertaken not only for the
purposes of a *theōria,* but also for trade (*emporia*). The association of
theōria with wisdom is not mentioned. These factors may suggest that
the original political significance of *theōria* is by Aristotle's time already
receding. In both accounts, moreover, any direct association with the sacred
mission of a *theōria* is absent.[50]

---

[45] The following translations essentially follow the German rendition by Rausch. See
Rausch, 43–44.

[46] Herodotus, I, 29.

[47] Ibid., I, 30.

[48] Ibid.

[49] *The Athenian Constitution,* XI, 1.

[50] For a discussion of some of the differing interpretations of these passages, see Rausch,
43–47. Rausch also cites and comments on the rich passage from Book XII of Plato's
Laws (950 d4–951 c4), in which diverse meanings of the pre-philosophical sense of *theōria*
are interwoven (Rausch, 48ff.).

These brief reflections on the sense of originary *theōria* may suggest that
Aristotle's dismissal of *empeiria* as true wisdom or *sophia* at the beginning
of the *Metaphysics* marks an increasing domestication of the foreign: *theōria*
turns inward, as it were, toward the domesticated other, the One that is
always and universally accessible, toward the monotheistic divine that always already governs the experiential relation to the other, to the foreign.
It is thus perhaps unsurprising that, compared to the practical life of the
bios politikos pursued by the many, the *bios theōrētikos* should appear,
as Aristotle puts it, as "the life of a foreigner" (*to xenikos*).[51] Empirical
or experiential knowledge no longer provides the measure of *sophia;* true
knowledge is knowledge of the universally knowable, closest to us, that lets
us know, always and in advance, what the other will be (what Heidegger
calls the "technical" interpretation of thinking). Only in one case does experience retain its primacy and uncircumventability: the case of *phronēsis,*
which (as ethico-political knowledge) entails precisely the openness to otherness, to the foreign at any moment, and which itself is possible only for
one who is already experienced, "well traveled" in the world and in life. The
practical *nous* operative in *phronēsis,* in other words, embodies precisely
this originary sense of *theōrein: phronēsis* in this sense demands a certain
theōrein. This is perhaps reflected in the fact that in Book IX of the *Nicomachean Ethics,* Aristotle indeed uses *theōrein* to describe the relationship
we may have to the being and actions of our friends. *Theōrein* here, as
always, refers to our ability to apprehend (and thereby witness) the being
of that which is other than ourselves: we are better able, notes Aristotle,
"to observe [*theōrein*] our neighbors' actions [*tous pelas ...praxeis*] than
our own"; and, insofar as the attainment (*energeia*) of true *eudaimonia*
must itself come into being ("since it is not like a piece of property that
we possess all the time"), and this entails the *theōrein* of good actions as a
way of contemplating and coming to know what is good, we cannot attain
eudaimonia without the presence and company of friends whose actions
are good (NE, 1169 b28ff.).[52] *Theōrein,* with its intrinsically ethical import, thus cannot come about through solitary activity. It is in seeing the
actions of others who act well, by dwelling in the company of friends whose
actions are good, that I come to see the kind of being that I myself may
strive for (yet never fully attain, except perhaps, if I am fortunate, at the
end of a lifetime, in the eyes of others). This point is made again in Book II
of the *Magna Moralia,* where Aristotle notes that, since direct contemplation of oneself is impossible, it is impossible to see and have seen oneself

---

[51] *Politics,* 1324 a15.

[52] For an illuminating discussion of this passage in relation to Heidegger—a discussion
to which we are indebted—see Walter Brogan, "Heidegger and Aristotle: Dasein and the
Question of Practical Life."

(*to hauton eidenai*) without another who is a friend. Thus, he concludes,
he who is free or self-governing (*autarchēs*) will need friendship in order
to know himself.[53] All of this indicates clearly that the ontological understanding of the being of the self as *praxis* which is developed in Books VI
and X of the *Nicomachean Ethics,* and which appears to argue that *theōria*
is ultimately a solitary, free, and independent activity, makes sense only
insofar as this solitary activity first arises, and remains a genuine possibility of human existence, only within a political context of being with others
each of whom are equally free in their being. The continuity and solitariness
of *theōrein* as the highest way of relating to being (to the worldly being
of beings as a whole) should thus, in its intrinsic import, properly be understood *ontologically* (as finitude and individuation of one's freedom), and
not as an ontic isolation of the individual from others. Furthermore, this
ontological relation to self is not originary, but only indirect: it first comes
about only in and through an exposure to the being of others. It is precisely because, at root, I can never *theōrein,* or discern contemplatively, my
own being (which as such is always already other than it has been) that the
philosophical insight provided by the *theōria* of *sophia* can only ever inform
phronēsis in an *indirect* and mediated manner. The ultimate good of human
existence or of a human life as a whole—the *meaning* of human presence
in the world as such—can never be purely present or immediately "seen"
amid the finite temporality of one's being. The unfolding meaning or story
of a life as a whole can be seen only by others, and only retrospectively,
whence the ethico-political significance of the *theōria* of Greek tragedy. The
momentary being of the self in its finite temporality has nevertheless always
already been seen or caught sight of, apprehended (however implicitly) in a
certain transparency in and through our being in a world with others, and
this "seeing" is the accomplishment of *theōrein.*[54] For Heidegger, Aristotle's

---

[53] *Magna Moralia,* 1213 a14ff.

[54] Thus, what tends to come to the fore in a way of life devoted exclusively to being
with others (the *bios politikos*) is the tendency to understand one's own being, and that
of others, solely in terms of the *eidos* of that which has already presented itself within the
world (including accomplished actions); the originary being of oneself and of others, as always already existing futurally, becomes occluded. (Cf. Heidegger's descriptions in *Being
and Time* and in the Marburg courses of how the being of one's own Dasein comes to be
interpreted in an ontologically reductive manner via a "reflecting back" [*Rückstrahlung*]
upon oneself of the being of other beings within the world. SZ, 15–16; see also GA 24,
§15b.) The practice of philosophizing, by contrast, helps to maintain an insight into the
originary openness of human existence as protoethical, in its finitude and singularity,
by first letting us see the essence of *praxis* as that which resists reduction to the *eidos.*
An appropriate relation between the *nous* at work in *phronēsis* and that of *sophia,*
as understood by Aristotle, thus entails the maintaining of a delicate balance between
having-been and future: the *nous* of *theōrein* is "present" or *at work* in *phronēsis* not in
the manner of a direct and immediate presence, but in the manner of a having-been, a

greatness lies in his insight into the finitude of practical *nous*—an insight that is most prominent in the *Nicomachean Ethics*—and this despite the tendency for it to become overshadowed by a *theōrein* increasingly conceived as independent. Whence the ambiguity in our earlier reading of Heidegger's reading of Aristotle: the *theōrein* required by *phronēsis* is indeed an *experiencing* of presencing as such (of the presencing of the practical situation in and through which others disclose themselves as *praxis*), but this presencing is inappropriately interpreted as an independent and omni*present* presence (or "being at work," *energeia*) of *nous*, as the ever-sameness of an existing *entity*, the *theion* as first mover. Heidegger's attentiveness to the finitude of presence directs us to understand that all *theōrein* is ultimately rooted in the finitude of *praxis*; in other words, that the only *theōrein* possible always already lies within a practical *nous*, even if the finitude of the latter can come to be concealed as such—as happened precisely in the emergence of Greek philosophy.

What else can be said of the specific kind of seeing implied in the ancient *theōria?* We remarked earlier that, as with the "glance of the eye" of practical *aisthēsis*, such *theōria* is also an ecstasis, a rapture in which we are held open for, and dwell in proximity to the beings that are present in a given situation. This ecstatic dwelling entails participation in a common world, in an openness of beings that may be shared with others, that is, in an openness to the finite, event-like character of presencing that exceeds determination by *logos*. In his aforementioned essay "In Praise of Theory," Hans-Georg Gadamer, recalling the ancient connotations of *theōria* as "observing the stellar constellations, being a spectator, for example, at a theatrical play, or participating in a mission sent to a festival," emphasizes the participatory nature of *theōria* as a "being-there":

> *Theōria* is not so much the individual, momentary [*augenblick-liche*] act, but rather a stance, a stand and state of being in which one holds oneself [*eine Haltung, ein Stand und Zustand, in dem man sich hält*]. It means 'being-there' [*Dabei-Sein*] in the felicitous double sense of this term, which means not only presence, but also the fact that whoever is present is 'fully there'. Such is a participator in a ritual undertaking or ceremony when he becomes absorbed therein in his participation, and this also

having-seen that continues to affect one's present and futural deliberations. At work in an existence guided by *phronēsis* is the *en-ergeia* of a *nous* that has not yet become what it has (potentially) always already been. When interpreted as a priority of *energeia* over *dunamis*, however, this is indicative of the tendency to understand potentiality, origination, coming-into-being (*phusis, phainesthai*) starting from the already given presence of the world, and is thus, for Heidegger, a reductive, "metaphysical" understanding of being. It tends to occlude the *poietic* origins of *praxis*.

always entails that one is participating with others or possible others in the same event. (GW 4, 48)

Gadamer's remarks here help us to clarify and ponder further the participatory character of the ancient *theōria*. He ascribes to ancient *theōria* precisely the crucial element of stance, *Haltung*, that we have repeatedly identified as characterizing the disclosive temporality of the *Augenblick* as a protoethical, practical vision. But this stance, this ec-stasis of *theōria*, he emphasizes, is in itself, intrinsically, a participation which has the sense of absorption (*Aufgehen*), of being entirely "there," that is, of being fully given over to whatever is unfolding. *Dabei-Sein* does not mean mere physical presence. The sense of "being-there" invoked by Gadamer can be readily conveyed by recalling its privative mode, that is, what we mean when we say that someone is "not fully there" in the sense of being distracted, being "lost in thought," as we also put it. Such a person is physically present, but not altogether "there." He or she is absent, "away," removed from being fully present to what is going on.[55] Yet "being there" is not to be understood as a comportment of subjectivity. Participation here has the sense of being delivered over to whatever is unfolding, to events in their disclosure, of an attentiveness that is *held* by beings themselves as they appear and conceal themselves. It means a dwelling in the sense of "dwelling on" something, tarrying with it, maintaining oneself in its presencing, *leaving time* for it, giving one's time to the presencing of other beings in the world. It means precisely the opposite of self-presence in the sense of a preoccupation with the presence of thought, whether in the Greek sense of the philosophical *theōrein*, or in the intensified sense of modern subjectivity.

These remarks of Gadamer thus indicate that, in considering the ancient *theōria*, participation should not simply be understood as a kind of "physical involvement," as doing something with someone else. Rather, the primary element of participation is a *world*, a world insofar as it is shared by a certain community as the medium of their common existence. Ancient *theōria* is participatory by its very disclosiveness; and such participation requires neither the actual presence of others (of other human beings) on a particular occasion, nor a "mixing in and doing things together." One participates by one's very ability to respond to presencing, which responsiveness unfolds concretely in every case via *logos*, through language and

---

[55] The same illustration is used by Heidegger to clarify what, among other things, is entailed in his understanding of the *Da* of *Da-sein*. See GA 29/30, 91–99. The term *Aufgehen*, absorption, is of course used also in *Being and Time* to characterize Dasein's everyday fallenness, in which its own finitude is concealed from it. While Heidegger cautions that such "absorption" is nothing negative, Gadamer's use of the term is more unequivocally positive.

thought, through binding oneself to a particular linguistic community and to certain interpretations of the world and of the beings found in it.

In *Truth and Method* Gadamer explains in greater detail this sense of ancient *theōrein* as participation, focusing precisely on its ecstatic character. While we cannot here exhaust the wealth of Gadamer's interpretation (an interpretation that acknowledges its evident debt to Heidegger), nor relate it explicitly to his own analyses of *phronēsis,* it may be helpful to turn to some of his key points by way of conclusion.

In his analysis of the temporality of the aesthetic, Gadamer highlights the similarity and continuity between the phenomenon of the festival and that of a theatrical play in terms of the participation of those who are present. This essential continuity is suggested to him by the original meaning of *theōria.* The spectator of a theatrical play is present precisely in the manner of "being there" (*Dabeisein*):

> Being there means more than mere co-presence with something else that is there at the same time. Being there means participation [*Teilhabe*]. Whoever was there at something knows full well what was really going on. It is only in a derivative manner that *Dabeisein* also comes to mean a mode of subjective comportment, a 'being fully with it' [*das Bei-der-Sache-sein*]. Observing [*Zuschauen*] is thus a genuine manner of participation. We may recall the concept of sacred communion that underlies the original Greek concept of *theōria.* It is well known that *theōros* means somone who participates in a legation sent to a festival. Those who participate in such a mission have no other qualification or role than to be there [*dabei zu sein*]. The *theōros* is thus a spectator [*Zuschauer*] in the proper sense of the word, someone who participates in a festive act by being there, and thereby acquires the legitimacy of his sacred distinction, for example, his inviolability. (GW 1, 129)

While Gadamer emphasizes the association of *theōria* with seeing, observing, and spectating, the references to the most prominent sense of *theōros* cited by Rausch make it evident that the participation of the *theōros* in a festival was very much an active involvement, albeit one in which the visible, the epiphany of the divine, plays an integral role. Yet Gadamer's point is not that ancient *theōria* meant observing as opposed to being involved; rather, his purpose is to show that observing or seeing should not be taken in a narrow sense opposed to participation. As we remarked earlier, the very notion of the *mere* spectator is a thoroughly modern one. The *theōros* participates in and through his seeing, just as he sees in and through his participation; his participation is participation in a *world* of ethico-religious *praxis*—a world in which visual and "aesthetic" disclosure, in the presence of others in a public realm, constitutes the general and primary meaning of being.[56] Seeing in the sense of "being there" is no less of a concrete involvement, a *praxis*, than is a so-called "physical" involvement. Indeed, one might well choose to translate *Dabeisein* as "being involved," and we have seen Gadamer himself describe its meaning as "absorption." "Being there" must be understood in the sense of participation in *disclosure,* in the presencing of whatever is transpiring and "holds" one's attention; it is a precondition of the modern distinction between "active" and "passive" involvement. The "being there" that characterizes the *theōros* is not, therefore, that of a mere spectator who looks on or spectates without getting involved. Nonetheless, there is a certain *primary* passivity in such "being there," a "passivity" that exceeds the active/passive distinction in the modern and now customary sense. This originary passivity is what is at stake in Gadamer's insistence that although "being there" does mean being fully given over to something—knowing in the sense of having seen and witnessed what is really going on—this is not to be understood as a merely active and "subjective" presence of mind, so to speak. As Gadamer goes on to indicate, this does not, of course, preclude that something of the originary sense of *theōria* is carried over into Greek philosophy, and indeed into modernity:

> In the same way, Greek metaphysics still conceives of the essence of *theōria* and *nous* as a pure being there in the presence of what truly is, and even in our eyes the capacity of being able to comport oneself theoretically is defined by the ability to forget one's own ends in relating to something. *Theōria* is not primarily to be thought as a comportment of subjectivity, as a self-determining on the part of the subject, but in terms of that which it beholds. *Theōria* is genuine participation, not a doing, but a being acted upon (*pathos*), namely, a being torn away and absorbed by the look of something. (GW 1, 129–30)

Ancient *theōria* is precisely this ability to forget one's own ends in opening oneself for the look of another being, in leaving time for a genuine

[56] In this regard, see Gadamer's discussion of how the apparent distinction between the being of the actor in a theatrical play and the being of the spectator of such a play is fundamentally overcome or sublated when one appreciates the primacy of this "theatrical" sense of being (GW 1, 114–16). We may recall also the familiar characterization of the whole of the Homeric world as a *theatron,* a "theater," "a place of spectacle for divine spectators," as Rausch puts it (Rausch, 34ff.). On the *theōria* of Greek tragic theater, see our essay "A 'Scarcely Pondered Word'. The Place of Tragedy: Heidegger, Aristotle, Sophocles."

encounter with the look of the other. In giving oneself over to the presencing of the other's look in the midst of a world to which one is always
already exposed, one thereby leaves one's own time, exits from a time that
would be determinable as one's own, thus entering the time of a world that
transcends one's own being. *Theōria* in this sense is a tarrying in the presencing of another worldly being, a tarrying in which the pursuit of one's
own ends is interrupted. Yet as Gadamer indicates, the source of this interruption is not primarily oneself, but the address of the other's look that
calls us into a worldly dwelling with other beings. This primary "passivity"
is attested by those visual phenomena that produce an extreme fascination
and absorption in us, and over which we often seem to have little control, or
can tear ourselves away from only with difficulty—television being the most
obvious modern example. Significantly enough, it is the moving image that
seems most to absorb us, that calls us into dwelling and remaining with it,
precisely because what most fascinates us is the promise of more, that is,
those images that bear within their very presencing the promise of more,
the unstable presencing that points to an unknown future.

It is here that Gadamer's remarks on the temporality of the aesthetic
as participation rejoin the concern of our own study with the temporality
of curiosity. Gadamer writes:

> There is evidently an essential difference between the spectator
> who gives himself over entirely to the play of art, and the desire
> to see that characterizes mere curiosity. It is characteristic of
> curiosity also to be carried away, so to speak, by what it sees, to
> entirely forget itself in what it sees and not be able to tear itself
> free from it. But what is distinctive of the object of curiosity
> is that it fundamentally does not concern or affect one. It has
> no meaning for whoever is observing it. There is nothing in
> the object that he could genuinely come back to so as to collect
> himself therein. For here it is the formal quality of newness, that
> is, of abstract alterity, that grounds the attraction of the image.
> This is manifest in the fact that the dialectical counterpart of
> such attraction is a becoming bored, a dulling. By contrast, that
> which presents itself to a spectator as the play of art does not
> exhaust itself in our merely being torn away in the moment,
> but entails a claim to duration and the duration of a claim.
> (GW 1, 131)[57]

---

[57] Cf. our remarks in chapter 4 on the relation of the temporality of curiosity to that
of boredom (121).

The phenomenon of the new as the object of curiosity is here appropriately characterized as "abstract alterity," abstract otherness or difference that has a merely "momentary" attractiveness. As in the above citation from "In Praise of Theory," it should be clear that the word "moment" or *Augenblick* is here used by Gadamer in a more conventional sense of transitoriness that is precisely opposed to the duration that the *Augenblick* entails for Heidegger. What Gadamer seeks to understand as the claim to duration and as a "gathering" of one's own being, as a participatory being held in which one is fully "there" in the sense of being open to and for the look of the other is the same phenomenon that Heidegger in his own work seeks to understand as the temporality of the *Augenblick*. The attraction, the attractiveness and attractive power of the image that comprises the object of curiosity is the power of a claim that one knows in advance to be merely transitory; indeed, transitoriness constitutes the very power of this attraction, the power of a future that can become present, but only in such a way as to have withdrawn already into the future of a further promise, the promise of abstract alterity. The claim that issues from the work of art in a genuine aesthetic experience (artworks are of course not immune to becoming objects of curiosity), by contrast, carries us away in a different kind of transport which Gadamer characterizes as an "ecstatic self-forgottenness" that responds to the "full presence," that is, the enduring claim of the work. The authentic being of the work of art is *Gleichzeitigkeit*, "simultaneity," not in the sense of the co-existence of a subject and an object posited in advance as separated, but in the sense of the "total mediation" that is the very immediacy of the work in its presencing. This sense of "simultaneity," which is said to "constitute the essence of 'being there' [*Dabeisein*]," corresponds, in effect, to the Aristotelian insight into the *hama* of seeing and having seen, although Gadamer himself does not draw this parallel here.[58]

What is meant by "ecstatic self-forgottenness" here? We have seen that for both Heidegger and Gadamer, curiosity is itself a kind of ecstasis, a being held and carried away in a distinctive kind of temporality. In *Being and Time* Heidegger even characterizes the temporality of curiosity in terms of Dasein's self-forgetting, its fleeing before its own finitude, while Gadamer in *Truth and Method* depicts genuine and authentic aesthetic experience as a self-oblivion or self-forgottenness, as a distinctive kind of absorption. Yet, as we noted just now with respect to their differing usage of the word *Augenblick,* the two accounts are not at all incongruous. In discussing self-forgottenness as characterizing not the being of the artwork, but the being of the spectator, Gadamer relates it to the Platonic insight into ecstasis:

---

[58] Gadamer instead compares the *Gleichzeitigkeit* in question to Kierkegaard's theological conception, and to the claim of faith in Lutheran theology. See GW 1, 131–33.

> Being there [*Dabeisein*] ...has the character of being-outside-
> oneself [*Außersichsein*]. Plato in the *Phaedrus* already portrayed
> the lack of understanding shown by rational analysis in mistak-
> ing the ecstasis of being-outside-oneself by regarding it as a mere
> negation of being "together" [or "collected": *des Beisichseins*],
> and thus as a kind of derangement. In truth, being-outside-
> oneself is the positive possibility of being fully there in the pres-
> ence of something [*ganz bei etwas dabei zu sein*]. Such being
> there has the character of self-forgottenness. It constitutes the
> essence of the spectator to be given over, in self-oblivion, to
> what he sees. Self-forgottenness is here anything but a priva-
> tive condition. It arises from a full turning toward the matter in
> question, something that the spectator accomplishes as his own
> positive achievement. (GW 1, 131)

The spectator must already have been addressed by the image that calls
for his or her attentiveness: herein lies a first kind of passivity, in that the
spectator as such does not first create the image. But even the turning
toward the image or spectacle that the spectator "actively" accomplishes
entails, as its precondition, another more profound and less determinable
kind of "passivity": in turning oneself (one's attention) toward something,
one must, in so doing, *let* oneself be turned. By no degree or kind of active or "self-conscious" striving can one forget oneself in the kind of self-
oblivion that advenes when one is absorbed by something. One must first
have agreed, in an affirmation, to abandon oneself to the presencing of the
image itself; and such abandon is the very accomplishment of being fully
there, an accomplishment produced or brought about in and through us, by
virtue of our primary (yet for the most part concealed) affirmation of the
presencing of the image, of the look of the other being. Gadamer thus goes
on to characterize self-oblivion in terms of the aesthetic distance implicit
in such transport and necessary for the intrinsic continuity and duration of
participation:

> The one apprehending is directed into an absolute distance that
> refuses him any purposive practical involvement. This distance
> is an aesthetic distance in the authentic sense. It signifies the
> removal that is necessary for seeing, and that makes possible
> an authentic and multidimensional participation in whatever
> is presenting itself before one. To the ecstatic self-oblivion of
> the spectator there thus corresponds his continuity with him-
> self. The continuity of sense is demanded of him by precisely
> that wherein he loses himself as a spectator. It is the truth of

his own world, of the religious and ethical world in which he
lives, that presents itself before him and in which he recognizes
himself. Just as parousia, absolute presence, characterized the
mode of being of aesthetic being, and the artwork is nevertheless
the same wherever it enters such presence, so too the absolute
moment [Augenblick] in which the spectator stands is at once
self-oblivion and mediation with himself. That which tears him
away from everything simultaneously gives him back the whole
of his being. (GW 1, 133)

It should be clear from the context that the "full presence" and "self-
continuity" referred to are not to be understood in the metaphysical sense
of presence, self-presence, or presence of thinking to itself as criticized by
Heidegger. The "full presence" referred to in this context is the sensuous
presencing of the work of art in its aesthetic play; the "self-continuity" is
precisely not a self-absorption in which one closes oneself off from the presencing of the sensuously given other, but the maintaining of an openness,
the openness of a dwelling that, for an appropriate time, can be filled, yet
never saturated, by the look of another being. It is, as Gadamer expresses
it, the "absolute Augenblick" ("absolute" in the sense of nonmediated by
purposeful involvements or ends) in which one has left time for the presencing of the work—the word Augenblick here being used in a sense that
is closer to Heidegger's.

In "self-oblivion" or self-forgottenness, therefore, the "self" in question
is not a transcendental self, nor an already existing self that comes to be
"forgotten" in a lapse of human remembering. Rather, it is one's own bodily
presencing that is, so to speak, stilled: it withdraws into a stillness, into the
bodily composure, the gatheredness (Sammlung) and fundamental stance
(Haltung) that in one way or another always already inhabits it, in which
it always already "stands" (even in curiosity, Heidegger noted, Dasein is
already "held").[59] In theōrein as a tarrying in the presencing of other beings
that presence in their outward appearance or look, this stillness is itself
present, albeit mostly in a concealed manner. It presences as the ecstasis
of being-outside-oneself in "being there," as that which infinitely exceeds
every end. This theōrein is an originary praxis: it is the praxis, the response,
that is called for in this specific situation where what is demanded is an
attentiveness to the presencing of the other as a visible presence within the
world. In the stillness of this seeing of the other, what is called for is not in
the first instance a movement (kinēsis) of one's own body, but a theōrein
that corresponds to the highest sense of embodied praxis, one that is also
precisely present in and throughout all self-movement. This also means that

---

[59] See our analysis in chapter 4 (121–22).

stillness here should not be understood as absence or negation of movement:
on the contrary, it can be the highest gatheredness of movement, supreme
"movedness."[60]

***

Our retrospect on philosophy, science, and curiosity, and our discussion
of the ancient, pre-philosophical connotations of *theōria* provide us with a
better understanding of what has been our theme thus far. Yet they also
furnish us with a suitable perspective from which to approach, by way of
conclusion, some readings of vision in the later Heidegger that invoke these
pre-philosophical resonances. Our own commentaries here are of necessity
highly selective; they restrict themselves to a few contexts that have a
special bearing on our interests in this study.

"To Things Their Look ... ": The Origin of the Work of Art

Earlier, in chapter 6, we concluded our account of Heidegger's essay "The
Turning" with some remarks on his discussion of human beings coming
into their own, that is, first coming to be mortals, in being "looked upon"
by world in the disclosive event of its un-concealment. Such an experience
of world may well be prepared and even invited by technology itself as it
increasingly unfolds its own infinite expansion, paradoxically thereby manifesting its own end and calling for the thoughtful response of human beings
to its "essence." Yet how is this look of world supposed to occur concretely?
And why is this look a look of the divine, a divine vision? Is there a more
originary kind of seeing, a vision that would occur beyond the philosophical, that is, "technical" appropriation of seeing that draws sensuous vision
into the nonsensible presencing of the idea, distancing it from the sensuous
and the sensible? To approach the possibility of a more originary seeing, of
a *theōria* excentric to the history of philosophy, would presumably entail an
interpretation of *technē* beyond its philosophical appropriation, the appropriation foretold most clearly in Plato's *Republic*, where the "true," politically permissible *technē* is distinguished and distanced from its dangerous
and "mimetic" sense. A distinction is prepared between the "ideational"
technē that brings forth items of utility, useful for the *polis* and controllable
in their production, and the *technē* of art, of the artistic bringing forth that,
from the perspective of the idea, is "merely" mimetic and thus dangerous,
concealing the underlying "truth" of presencing. But what would it mean

---

[60] On this point, see Heidegger's essay "On the Essence and Concept of Φύσις in
Aristotle's *Physics* B, 1" (W, 353ff.).

to interpret *techne* beyond its philosophical appropriation? What kind of "rehabilitation" of *techne* as artistic *poiesis* is entailed? Does Heidegger's interpretation of *techne* as poietic bringing-forth and occasioning also imply a reinterpretation of the sensuous beyond its metaphysical reduction? And does this interpretation invite a renewed meditation on the human body, on the sensuous presencing and bodying forth of the body of the "mortal" as the site of a distinctive *poiesis?*

For a preliminary answer to some of these questions, we must return to consider the conclusion of "The Question Concerning Technology." Toward the end of that essay, Heidegger recalls the following:

> There was once a time when not only technology bore the name *techne*. Once that revealing which brings truth forth into the radiance of what shines in appearing was also called *techne*.

> There was once a time when the bringing-forth of the true into the beautiful was also called *techne*. *Techne* referred also to the *poiesis* of the fine arts.

> In Greece, at the beginning of the destiny of the West, the arts soared to the supreme heights of the revealing granted them. They brought the presence of the gods, brought to radiance the dialogue between divine and human destiny. (VA, 38)

Art was referred to as *techne* because it too is a revealing, a bringing-forth and to the fore, a mode of *poiesis*, of the "poietic" (*das Dichterische*). The poietic, understood as a revealing, brings something to the fore amid the materiality of appearance. It "brings the true into the radiance of what Plato in the *Phaedrus* calls *to ekphanestaton*, that which shines forth most purely" (VA, 39). Yet for Plato the true stands in a discordance with the sensuous; Plato's thought is already the beginning of the decline of the "supreme heights" of Greek art.[61]

In his 1936 essay "The Origin of the Work of Art," Heidegger had attempted to interpret the being of the work of art beyond the sensuous-nonsensuous discordance that Plato's thought inaugurates. Art and the beautiful cannot be thought adequately in terms of their distance from the idea or truth. But nor, for that matter, are they to be understood by contrast with the practical or the good. Heidegger makes this especially clear in his epilogue to the essay. If art is to be understood as the happening of "truth" in the work, such "truth" is to be understood as the unconcealment of beings as such, as the "event" (*Sichereignen*) of sensuous presencing: the truth referred to, Heidegger notes, "is not equivalent

---

[61] Cf. the closing sections of the 1936/37 lecture course "The Will to Power as Art," NI, 189ff.

to what one is familiar with under this term and attributes to cognitive knowledge and science [*Erkennen und Wissenschaft*] as a quality to be distinguished from the beautiful and the good, which serve as names for the values of nontheoretical comportment" (H, 67).

The traditional categories of the true, the good, and the beautiful correspond to the traditional, and for Heidegger reductive philosophical delimitations between *theōria* (seen in the narrower sense as the ground of *epistēmē*, of cognitive knowledge or science), *praxis*, and (non-useful) *poiēsis*. The good and the beautiful are accordingly seen as "nontheoretical," and, as a correlate, *theōria*, together with non-useful *poiēsis*, is regarded as "nonpractical." *Praxis* and *poiēsis* in general, as bringing-forth amid the sensuous, are seen in contrast to the "mere," disinvolved contemplation or *theōrein* of the pure forms of beings. Yet in this assertion of the apparent autonomy or independence of *theōria*, the originary rootedness of *theōria*, *praxis*, and *poiēsis* in the unitary and worldly being of Dasein is increasingly concealed, as we already indicated in our reflections on *Being and Time* and the Marburg lectures.[62] The more thinking is seen as an independent activity of deliberation in service to doing and making, the more thinking taken in itself comes to be regarded as a purely theoretical comportment, as a *theōria* severed from *praxis* and *poiēsis*, as Heidegger points out in the 'Letter on 'Humanism'" (W, 146). The "truth" of being-in-the-world is henceforth seen only in the light of theoretical, practical, or "technical" perspectives, all of which attest to the primacy of the theoretical remove from worldly involvements. In this light, the work of art appears either as a merely mimetic and intrinsically useless residue by comparison with the true *theōrein* of ideas and with the useful production of *technē;* or (as in the great systems of German Idealism), it indeed appears as the original site that unifies the theoretical, practical, and technical interests of reason—but only in retrospect, only as a supplement whereby the established distinctions of reason are precisely maintained (or *aufgehoben*) and once again legitimated from the foundational and primary perspective of pure intuition (*Anschauung*), the pure beholding of *nous* mediated by the *logos* of conceptual reason. Precisely because of its retrospective and supplemental role, the work of art is thus unable to bring about any transformation of the fundamental configuration of reason that marks the first beginning of Western-philosophical thought, the configuration that begins with the transformation of *theōria* itself. The work of art has itself not yet been freed for the possibility of its being an origin, of its being a beginning.

In "The Origin of the Work of Art," "truth" is understood as the historical event of unconcealment (*alētheia*) as it occurs in the great work of

---

[62] See chapters 3 and 4 in part 1, above.

art, in the midst of the sensuous itself. "Historical" here does not mean happening "within" history, but refers to the kind of event that first opens, initiates, and "founds" a subsequent history. Such an event marks an origin, the origination and coming into being of something new; it is an event of disclosure, of *poiēsis*. In the work of art such an event is "set" into the work, that is, established in a sensuous being, it is brought to a "stand." A disclosive and originary event itself attains a certain constancy in the work. "The being of beings enters into the constancy of its shining" (H, 25). The work of art thereby first *opens up* and reveals the being of beings (H, 28). But this does not mean that it reveals only the being or presencing of the particular being that a particular artwork is; it does not mean that an artwork simply shows itself in its own being, as what it is. The great work of art opens up the being of beings as a whole, it first opens up a *world* for human beings. The openness of beings as such is first brought to a stand, as this or that particular configuration of openness, as this or that particular historical world, and indeed *needs* to be brought to such a stand "in order to be what it is, namely, *this* openness" (H, 49).[63] Consider Heidegger's initial description of a Greek temple:

> A building, a Greek temple, is not a depiction of something. It simply stands there in the midst of the rock-cleft valley. The building encloses the figure of the god, and in this concealment lets it stand out into the holy precinct through the open portico. By means of the temple, the god is present in the temple. This presencing of the god is in itself the opening out and delimitation of the precinct as a holy precinct. (H, 30–31)

The temple building is not the depiction of an already existing form or meaning. This artwork is not simply the result of imparting a form to already existing "matter." Enigmatically, it encloses and contains the divine, the god that presences, in its very concealment, in and through the work.[64] The enigmatic presencing of the god certainly gives this particular building its distinctive being: it makes this building what it is, namely a temple, a place of the presencing of the holy; it configures the way in which, as this particular temple, it extends and delimits the spatiality belonging to it. Yet this is not all:

> The temple and its precinct, however, do not fade away into the indeterminate. It is the temple-work that first articulates and

---

[63] The *Reclam* edition italicizes the word *this* (UK, 67).

[64] Cf. Hegel's description of this event of the God's entry into the temple as the "lightning-flash of individuality that smites its way into the inert mass, permeating it with its presence." *Vorlesungen über die Ästhetik* (Frankfurt: Suhrkamp, 1986), vol. I, 117–18.

> at the same time gathers around itself the unity of those paths
> and relations in which birth and death, disaster and blessing,
> victory and disgrace, endurance and decline acquire the shape of
> destiny for human being. The prevailing expanse of these open
> relations is the world of this historical people. From out of and
> within such a world this people first comes back upon itself for
> the fulfilment of its vocation. (H, 31)

The temple is not just an isolated object among others; it is not at all an "object" in any sense. For it is not a "mere thing" set or "thrown" over against human beings, something people might come to view as a "beautiful work" of architecture, perhaps, but that would remain fundamentally a matter of indifference for their existence as a whole. The temple is not something to which human beings in general might relate just as they choose, in some arbitrary manner, or whenever they feel like doing so. According to Heidegger, the temple first articulates and gathers all fundamental relations that a people might assume toward things. It first opens up a world, from out of which and within which people understand themselves and their limits, beyond any particular comportment toward this or that. The temple itself is the site and institution of an enigma, a mystery, a concealment that draws people toward it, thus first drawing them together in relation to one another, founding a historical community. Such a community is historical only if it has some intimation of the *event* that is set into the work here: the presencing of the god. The temple is the sacred site of a promise, of something that appears in concealing itself, of something that, as thus apparent in its enigmatic concealment, is yet to come. The power of time, of the originary future, the power of that which bestows and prevails over life and death comes to presence in a finite being, in the temple as a work. The power of destiny, of the coming into being (*poiēsis*) that exceeds and first grants human doing and making, directing it onto its own particular paths, itself comes to presence in and as the divinity of the temple. In the face of such destiny, "birth and death, disaster and blessing, victory and disgrace, endurance and decline" are at stake and have to be struggled for by human beings (via their *technē*). What a people is called to, its historical vocation, is always already dependent upon such destiny, but also, of course, upon the response of humans to such vocation. There is no history, and no historical deed, without finite human *praxis*.

In opening up a world, that is, the manifestness of beings as a whole, the work of art first lets beings be seen in their own particular significance and meaning; it lets them be seen in relation to one another, and each in their own proper, historically articulated limits. It first grants beings their look and appearance, the way in which they appear to one another:

The temple, in its standing there, first gives to things their look [*Gesicht*] and to human beings their outlook [*Aussicht*] upon themselves. This view [*Sicht*] remains open as long as the work is a work, as long as the god has not fled from it. It is the same with the sculpture [*Bildwerk*] of the god, a votive offering of the victor in the athletic games. It is not a portrait [*Abbild*] whose purpose is to make it easier to realize how the god looks; rather, it is a work that lets the god himself presence and thus *is* the god himself. The same holds for the linguistic work. In the tragedy nothing is staged or displayed theatrically; rather, the battle of the new gods against the old is being fought. (H, 32)

Heidegger here draws attention to the *time* that belongs to the being of a work: what is granted in the opening up of a world—namely, the reciprocal look of things, the way in which (as he would later express it)[65] they thus come to "mirror" and reflect one another in their belonging together in a specific temporal and spatial "play"—this look of things as granted by the work "remains open as long as the work is a work, as long as the god has not fled from it." The Greek temple, which opens up a specific historical world, is, as a singular work of art, bound to a specific place and to a specific historical era of a specific people or community, here, the Greeks of the classical age. Such an artwork, as a singular event of "great art" (H, 29), cannot be understood in what it properly is or once was—or better, in what it properly *does,* in its proper accomplishment—if it is merely regarded as an object of aesthetic appreciation that can be accommodated in a gallery. Yet nor can its proper accomplishment be understood simply by our visiting it at its original site, perhaps in Paestum, because its *world* "has perished" (H, 30). The *time* of such an artwork is thus inseparable from its being. But the great work of art does not merely—indeed does not at all—"reflect" a particular historical era. It does not reflect, portray, or depict (*abbilden*) anything; rather, according to Heidegger, it first *inaugurates* the time of a world and of a community. The essence of the theatrical spectacle of a tragedy is likewise not the depiction or representation of something (such as the already written plot); rather, its essential power lies in the singular and sensuous appearance of the epiphany of the gods that prevail over human destiny, an epiphany that is brought about in and through the struggle of the tragedy itself.

The temporality of the work of art is thus nothing less than the temporality of world. Yet how can this be? The artwork is a particular entity, a "thing." World, on the other hand, is neither a thing nor a mere aggregate

---

[65] See in particular the essays "The Thing" (VA, 171ff.) and "The Turning" (TK, 42ff.), both from 1950.

of things, but the manifestness of beings as a whole. Of such manifestness little remains to be said but that it occurs. *"World worlds ... "* (H, 33–34); its happening cannot be explained in terms of anything else[66]—unless perhaps in terms of the work of art. Consider Heidegger's description of how the work opens up a world in the sense of "setting it up":

> This setting up [*aufstellen*] is an erecting in the sense of dedication and praise. Here "setting up" no longer means a mere placing [such as the placing of a work in an exhibition]. To dedicate means to consecrate, in the sense that in setting up the work the holy is opened up as holy and the god is invoked into the openness of his presence. Praise belongs to dedication as doing honor to the dignity and splendor of the god. Dignity and splendor are not additional properties behind which the god then stands. Rather, in such dignity, in such splendor the god comes to presence. In the radiance of this splendor that which we named world gleams, that is, is cleared. (H, 33)

World is not to be understood, then, as an already existing openness within which the artwork, as one particular being, would then become accessible. World is rather an event, a happening, an occurrence whose divine presencing unfolds *in* the work of art. Just as the god himself *is* the work, so the enigmatic presencing of divine splendor, radiance, and glory—as an event unfolding in excess of any already existing openness of an already existing world—manifests or "clears" world as this very unfolding, this very presencing in which something also remains unclear, uncleared, and yet to come—in which something in excess of manifest presence announces itself in its very withdrawal. The power of this epiphany transforms, transfigures the way in which other beings themselves come to presence. They come to be seen in an ever-new, ever-radiant light; the play of their presencing enters a radiant buoyancy and lightness—"as long as the work is a work, as long as the god has not fled from it."

The work sets up a world: it "erects" a world in opening up and consecrating the holy—in invoking the god, calling him into the openness of his presence, calling upon him to come, to arrive in the midst of beings themselves, and in praising and attending to his presence. Erecting a world, Heidegger explains, is to be understood literally in the sense of "e-recting" (*er-richten*): "Opening up that which is right in the sense of a directive and guiding measure, as a manner in which that which is essential gives directives" (H, 33). In bringing the presence of the divine, the work of art plays an ethical role, in the originary sense of *ēthos:* in the presence of the

---
[66] Cf. "The Thing," VA, 172.

god, human beings are raised beyond themselves toward something greater, something excessive, something that prevails over them. Thus raised beyond themselves toward the splendor of the divine, humans themselves acquire an uprightness, a stance, a dignity and nobility of their own, in response to the work's divine presencing. Their stance is determined in each case from where they stand, from where they reside, from their dwelling—with things and with one another—in the presence of the divine. The work of art such as the temple, in opening up a world in which all beings come to presence and are themselves cleared, "grants to things their look and to human beings their outlook upon themselves." We find here the same disclosure of ethical responsibility as in ancient *theōrein* itself, whether that disclosed to the *theōros* who visits an oracle, or to the *theōros* as participator in a festival.[67] Yet what is especially significant in all this is that an originary ethical directive in each case emerges from the presencing of things themselves: it is disclosed by beings themselves in their presencing in the midst of a world, of a world illuminated by divine epiphany as it occurs in a distinctive being, in the great work of art.[68]

In the opening up of a world "all things come to acquire their lingering and hastening [*ihre Weile und Eile*], their remoteness and nearness, their scope and their limits" (H, 34). The time and space of a world, of beings as a whole, is thus granted in and through the work of art. Yet why must the opening and setting up of a world occur *in* a work of art, in and through a particular entity? Why is the happening of world not an act of purely ontological disclosure? Because the work not only opens up a world, but grants it a singular time and space, grants it a place, grants it a stay. "Towering up within itself, the work opens up a *world* and holds [*hält*] this world in its abiding sway" (H, 33). "The work holds open the openness of a world" (H, 34).

The world thus opened up maintains its constancy and stability, its sway over human beings, as long as the god has taken up residence in the temple itself, as long as the god has not fled, but abides in his presencing. The temple itself, erected upon the Earth, has its constancy and stability in what we normally call its "materiality." Yet whereas materiality, fashioned to serve a particular end, is properly concealed in items of utility, disappearing in what is most proper to it, the temple first lets such materiality emerge,

[67] Cf. Rausch, *Theoria,* especially 18–21 and 27–37, and our remarks on 263–67 above.

[68] Beginning from here, and extending Heidegger's understanding of the work of art to the context of his readings of Hölderlin, one might question the claim made by Véronique Fóti concerning "Heidegger's neglect and obscuring of the ethical import of the responsive relationship between human being and the enigma of manifestation." See *Heidegger and the Poets* (New Jersey: Humanities Press, 1992), 113. On this relationship, see also "The Look of the Other," below.

and indeed in an enigmatic manner. It lets its materiality presence in such a way that, as Heidegger describes it:

> the rock first comes to bear and rest and so first becomes rock; metals come to gleam [*blitzen*] and shimmer, colors to glow, tones to resonate, the word to tell. All this comes forth as the work sets itself back into the massiveness and heaviness of stone, into the firmness and pliancy of wood, into the hardness and luster of metal, into the illumination and darkening of color, into the resonance of tone and into the naming power of the word. (H, 35)

This elemental materiality that comes forth in the work of art, and into which the work "sets itself back," that is, in which it finds a constancy, a foundation and support, Heidegger terms "the Earth."[69] The Earth does not simply refer to the Greek *phusis,* but to a fundamental trait thereof, namely, its self-concealment. It refers to the self-concealing that elemental materiality itself is, and which cannot be overcome except at the cost of destruction, of total transformation:

> A stone presses downward and manifests its heaviness. But while this heaviness exerts an opposing pressure upon us it denies us any penetration into it. If we attempt such a penetration by breaking open the rock, it still does not display in its fragments anything inward that has been opened up. The stone has instantly withdrawn again into the same dull pressure and bulk of its fragments.... The Earth thus lets shatter every attempt to penetrate it. It lets every merely calculative encroachment turn into a destruction. (H, 35–36)

The elemental materiality of things can certainly be analysed and resolved in scientific and calculative fashion into mathematically determined relations between atoms. Yet even the "atom"—supposedly indivisible—can, like every particle, in principle be divided into ever smaller, subatomic particles. But in this ongoing process of splitting, a process that is in principle infinite, we never reach an "inside" of things. In the face of the Earth's withdrawal and self-concealing, every scientific and technical attempt to penetrate the Earth "remains an impotence of the will." All such analysis results in a deformation and transformation of the materiality of things

---

[69] On the presence of elemental materiality in Heidegger's discussion of the Greek temple, see John Sallis, *Stone* (Bloomington: Indiana University Press, 1994), chapter 4.

themselves, of the power of the Earth—that is, of the *Heimat* or originary dwelling place of the worldly and historical being of human beings (H, 32).[70]

This elemental materiality of the Earth, however, does not merely refuse itself or close itself off from all discovery. It does not merely mark the absolute limit of all scientific-technical appropriation. Rather, it is itself disclosed, uncovered in what is proper to it (i.e., in its very self-concealment) in and through the work of art. For the work of art not only "sets up" a world, but in doing so, it therewith "sets forth" the Earth: "The work moves the Earth itself into the openness of a world and maintains [*hält*] it there. The work lets the Earth be an Earth" (H, 35). The Earth thereby shows itself, comes to appear, precisely as that which conceals itself. "To set forth the Earth means: to bring it into the open as that which closes itself off" (H, 36). The work of art itself thus proves to be the site of a "strife" between world and Earth, between the Earth's striving to conceal itself and the world's striving to open itself. World and Earth are "essentially different from one another, and yet never separate. The world grounds itself on the Earth, and Earth rises up through world" (H, 37). The work of art maintains this strife, this occurrence of un-concealment as such; in setting up a (possible) world and setting forth the (singular) Earth, the work itself "accomplishes" (*vollbringt*) this strife. This accomplishing is the happening of *alētheia*, of "truth" as an event of un-concealment setting itself to work, of its being "at work"—of its coming into its own in the work of art.

The terms "setting itself to work" and "being at work," as used by Heidegger in this context, allude not only to the Greek *en-ergeia* thought

---

[70] This sense of *Heimat,* which Heidegger finds poetized in Hölderlin, is traced most persistently throughout the three lecture courses on Hölderlin's poetry given in 1934/35 (GA 39), 1941/42 (GA 52), and 1942 (GA 53). As *Being and Time* had already shown, the initial "home" of human beings, as the everyday Dasein of *das Man,* is fundamentally *unheimlich;* the "not being at home" of Dasein is, in its everydayness, covered up and concealed, becoming manifest only through fundamental attunements (in each case a being attuned to ground or *Grund*), such as that of "anxiety." But such attunement thereby also manifests the possibility of a more originary dwelling within the finitude of the happening of world. The *Unheimlichkeit* of being-in-the-world cannot properly be opposed to the everyday dwelling of *das Man,* since the latter is, fundamentally, never entirely "at home" in any case. The tranquillity of *das Man* is but a concealment of the happening of *Un-heimlichkeit* as a happening of world. The temporal finitude of this happening of world—in *Being and Time* still conceived in part in a "transcendental" manner, oriented by the ontological "difference"—is, from the mid-1930s, thought by Heidegger (in dialogue with Hölderlin) as the power of the Earth, as the strife between world and Earth that manifests itself *in beings themselves.* The philosophical attunement of a wakeful anxiety thus also shows itself to be attuned already by a "sacred mourning" (in Hölderlin's words) for the Earth: anxiety is originarily *poietic* in that in its *Un-heimlichkeit* it *manifests,* and thus first opens and transforms, the presencing of world. Yet the philosophical *logos,* attuned since Plato to describing being (beingness) as something that "is," is no longer in tune with the originarily poietic saying of language.

otherwise than in its Platonic-Aristotelian usage, but seek to bring out the event-like happening that the work of art itself is.[71] In the phrase "the work of art," the felicitous ambiguity in the English word "work," undecidable with respect to its nominal or verbal sense, conveys better than the German noun *Werk* precisely what is at issue for Heidegger. "The work of art" refers primarily not to an entity, but to an accomplishing, an event. And yet this event, this dis-closive accomplishing—far from being a purely ontological occurrence—unfolds precisely in the midst of beings themselves, in and through the elemental materiality of Earth, in and through a singular, historical manifestation of Earth. The "work" of art has a singularity, a finitude: as an "event" (*Ereignis*), it is not to be understood in terms of movement as opposed to rest or *stasis*.[72] Rather, it is itself a specific *ec-stasis*, a "displacement" in the sense of a transport or rapture that is not that of a (calculable) displacement *in* space, but of an opening up of spatiality itself, an ecstatic opening of temporal spacing, an *Ereignis* of "timespace" (*Zeitraum*). In the period immediately following "The Origin of the Work of Art," in the *Beiträge zur Philosophie: Vom Ereignis* (1936–38), the site of this event is repeatedly identified as the *Augenblick*, in which site (*Stätte*) the strife of world and Earth occurs.[73]

The work of art rests in itself, in its own singularity, it holds itself within its own limits, within what is proper to it; it holds itself back in its very accomplishment. This repose (*Ruhe*) of the work of art is, as Heidegger puts it, "an intimate gathering [*innige Sammlung*] of movement, thus supreme movedness" (H, 37). The work of art, the work of the work, as the instantiation of the strife between Earth and world, is "the steadfastly self-exceeding gathering of the movedness of the work," or, as Heidegger also expresses it, using a word from Hölderlin, that of an *Innigkeit*, the simplicity of a gathered intimacy (H, 38).

Hitherto, Heidegger's account has focused on the great work of art itself as such, with the goal of understanding the being of the work solely in terms of itself. The relation of the work of art to human beings was touched upon only in passing, and then only in terms of the work's belonging to a

---

[71] See the Postscript and Epilogue to the essay (UK, 91–101).

[72] H, 28, 49, 53; see also the 1956 Epilogue (UK, 99–100).

[73] See GA 65, 29–30, 96–99, 260–61, 310–11, 349, 371, 391, 506–10. On the *Ereignis* of "timespace" see GA 65, 30, 260–61, 323, 354, 371–88. See also "Time and Being" (SD, 14ff.), and "The Essence of Language" (US, 208ff.). Heidegger elsewhere alludes to the path of the *Beiträge* as begun "in the '*Augenblick*' of an attempt to say the truth of being in a simple manner" (GA 9, 313). His highlighting of the word *Augenblick* here indicates that it is central to this attempt, and not to be understood in the ordinary sense of "moment." Far from shifting away from the *Augenblick*, the *Beiträge* thus maintains it at the very center of Heidegger's thought. See David Michael Levin, "Decline and Fall," in *Modernity and the Hegemony of Vision* (ed. Levin), 191.

historical world that it itself opens up. This belonging to a historical world Heidegger will later call the preservation of the work. Yet to the work of art there belongs not only its "reception," but also its "creation," its having been created. We shall now try to explicate these traits of creation and preservation specifically with respect to the temporality of the work of art that is indicated in Heidegger's account, in order then to approach the question of the kind of human knowing or *technē* appropriate to the being of the artwork.

Not only does the artist's "activity" of creating belong to the genesis of the work, but the fact of its having been created belongs to the being of the work in its worldly presencing. Indeed, the specific way in which this "fact" comes to the fore in the work of art is something that distinguishes it from other things that have been "made" or "produced." Whereas in an item of utility, its having been created disappears and becomes unobtrusive in its subordination to a particular purpose, in the work of art "its having been created is expressly created into that which is created, so that it explicitly emerges from what has thus been brought forth" (H, 53). In the great work of art it is not the fact that it has been created by an artist, even a great one, that distinguishes it (after all, the artist becomes recognized as "great" only by virtue of his work), but the simple fact that such a work *is:*

> It is not the *N. N. fecit* that is to be made known. Rather, the simple *factum est* is to be held forth into the open in the work, namely this: that unconcealment of a being has occurred here, and first occurs as this event that has occurred; this: the fact that such a work *is* rather than not being. The shock that the work is, as this work, and the unrelenting nature of this improbable thrust, constitute the steadfastness of the work's resting in itself. (H, 53)

If only this "simple fact" were so simple! The sheer being, the "that it is" comes to the fore in such a work of art as the singular being of the work as *this* work. Being itself is disclosed in its singularity, in the finite being of a particular entity. Yet the work of art, in accomplishing this disclosure of being, manifests not only the "that it is" of this work, but in so doing discloses also the "nothing," the fact that such a work is rather than is not. The possibility of nonbeing that intrinsically belongs to being is itself manifested in and through the work of art. The work itself, in the presencing of its elemental materiality, holds us enraptured in transporting and holding us into this "nothing" that emanates so enigmatically from it. In the presence of the great work of art, we are held, in "unrelenting" fashion, by the power of this play of being and nonbeing that issues from the work. We are held enraptured by something "improbable" (*unscheinbar*), by something that, in its shining forth, also does not shine, or does not yet shine—by the approach of an event that could not have been foreseen. The shock and thrust (*Anstoß, Stoß*) that emanate from the work in its very being, in its presencing, are also a kind of interruption, an opening that announces—in the manner of a sign (*Zeichen*)[74]—the concealed approach of something constantly withheld, always yet to come, thus constituting the very steadfastness or constancy (*Beständigkeit*) of the work's resting in itself, of its self-withdrawal in its approach.

In the presence of the work of art—of the great work of art—what is disclosed, as we have seen, is not only "the fact that it is rather than not being" with respect to this particular being. In this opening up of the play and tension of being and nonbeing, in and through this particular work, what is also thereby opened up is something excessive: the openness of a world as such, of the being of beings as a whole in relation to the possibility of nonbeing.[75] The great work of art thus acts as the shock and thrust, the stimulus of a steadfast reminder or recollection of the play of being and nonbeing, prompting our wonder and astonishment. It transports us into an attunement of *thaumazein*.

Yet the simple fact of the being of the work of art conceals something that is perhaps still more astonishing. The event that holds us enraptured in disclosing the play of its being and nonbeing is not a happening that, as it were, has its origin in nothing. What is still more astonishing in the work of art is this: "that unconcealment of a being has occurred here, and first occurs as this event that has occurred [*und als dieses Geschehene erst geschieht*]. . . ." The improbable, unforeseeable event of the work's coming into its own presencing precisely in withholding such presencing as always yet to come (so long as the work remains the work that it is)—this event first occurs as something that has already occurred. Its first happening is thus *also* something that has already happened: its first occurrence is always already "secondary," that is, ec-static, an "always already" that "is" (presences) as a "not yet." This does not of course mean that every work that could be has factically already been, but simply that the work of art, once it is, has necessarily also already been: that it necessarily bears the trait of this secondariness as that of its worldly being. In this sense, its first coming is already its second coming. The occurrence of this event, of this *Ereignis*, is the extraordinary happening of that which has always already been and nevertheless has not yet been, but remains unforeseeable:

[74] On the relation of the sign to the originary meaning of *theōros*, see Rausch, 18f.

[75] On the relation between the Nothing and the possibility of world, see our earlier comments on the temporality of *Angst* as that which holds the *Augenblick* at the ready, brings it before the possible retrievability of a worldly having-been (chapter 4, 132–34).

the nonsimplicity of the originary future, of that origin and enigma which in the present essay is called "art."[76]

By contrast with the being of most beings, that of the great work of art is distinctive, unique. The simple fact of the "that it is," which pertains in its own singular way to everything that "is," to every being, is ordinarily concealed from us in our habitual comportment and conduct with beings; in the case of an item of utility, it disappears in that item's becoming subordinate to a further end. In the "business" of our habitual, everyday existence, such a "simple fact" is scarcely worth our attention, especially since we think that it can be said of everything in the same way:

> Yet what is more commonplace than this, that a being is? In the work, by contrast, this—the fact that it *is* as such—is what is unusual. The event [*Ereignis*] of its having been created does not simply reverberate subsequently through the work; rather, the work casts before it this event [*das Ereignishafte*]—namely, that the work is as this work—and has constantly cast it around itself. The more essentially the work opens itself, the more luminous becomes the singularity of the fact that it is rather than not being. The more essentially this jolt comes into the open, the more strange and solitary the work becomes. (H, 53)

The great work of art like the Greek temple comes to presence as an event that constantly precedes itself. Its own presencing goes before it. It carries and sustains its own future—yet only up to a point, for it is unable to relate to that future *as such,* that is, to have the possibility and necessity of decision, of human *praxis.* But this is also to say that its own presencing is in a sense "freer" than that of human beings: It does not have a responsibility for and of freedom, of the world—of having to care for the being of others. Its being is not that of *Sorge,* care, that is, of *standing in* and in this way being the site of a clearing for beings as a whole. And this is why, as we shall see shortly, the work cannot *be* without preservation. The event that the work casts before it and has always already cast around itself is the singular and enigmatic presencing of the work itself. It belongs to what Walter Benjamin would call the "aura" of the work.[77] Heidegger's analysis makes visible this "aura" not as a property of an already existing thing, but as an event of being, an event of presencing that shrouds the work itself

---

[76] See the opening lines of the Postscript to the essay, where Heidegger indicates that the task is not to solve the enigma, but simply "to see the enigma" (H, 66). On enigma, see also Heidegger's 1937 discussion of the eternal return in Nietzsche's *Thus Spake Zarathustra,* discussed in part 3 above.

[77] See "The Work of Art in the Age of Mechanical Reproduction," in *Illuminations,* ed. Hannah Arendt (New York: Schocken Books, 1969), 217ff.

in its promise and its refusal. The shining of such singular presencing in its self-concealing—the shining that is ordinarily referred to as "beauty" (H, 44)—manifests the work itself as something "strange," "solitary," even uncanny. It discloses something extraordinary.

The work of art first brings to presence the event of unconcealment as such, in letting the Earth be an Earth, in first letting the most profound concealment of beings as a whole (of world) be "seen" as such concealment, as the concealment that belongs to the presencing of beings themselves as their provenance, their origin, the site of their emergence. World and Earth thus belong inextricably to one another in their presencing in the event that unfolds in the great work of art. "Earth is not simply that which is closed, but that which emerges as self-closing." Likewise, world is not simply the openness of the clearing, but an openness that remains in, and only in, its strife with concealment (H, 43–44). Yet the concealment (in fact a double concealment) that belongs to beings themselves is for the most part itself concealed:

> We believe ourselves to be at home in the immediate sphere of beings. Beings are familiar, reliable, ordinary [*geheuer*]. And yet the clearing is pervaded by a constant concealing in the double form of refusal and dissembling. At bottom, the ordinary is not ordinary; it is extra-ordinary [*un-geheuer*]. (H, 43)

Concealment, Heidegger has clarified, can be the dissembling that characterizes error, namely within the realm of that which has already been cleared or revealed, as when a being appears as something it is not, thus concealing its true being. Yet concealment does not pertain simply to cognitive knowledge (*Erkenntnis*) as its limit, or to the realm of *logos*. In its more profound sense, concealment belongs to the being of things themselves, to their very presencing; in this sense, it is the "provenance" of all clearing (H, 42–43). In manifesting concealment as such, in the event of the un-concealment of concealing, that concealing that is ordinarily concealed in our everyday activities comes to light. The extraordinariness of beings themselves becomes manifest. It becomes manifest in and through "the tranquil thrust" (*der stille Stoß*) of the work's having been created coming to the fore in the presencing of the work itself (H, 54; UK, 74).[78]

Yet how precisely does this coming to the fore, this singular emergence and manifestation unfold? At this point something extraordinary occurs in the unfolding of Heidegger's own essay. The essay invites us to "accomplish the step toward which everything thus far said tends" (H, 54). This step concerns the relation of human beings to the event of unconcealment that

---

[78] The word "tranquil" (*stille*) appears to be added in later editions.

occurs in the work of art; it concerns what Heidegger calls the "preserva-tion" (*Bewahrung*) of the work. Until the third part of the essay, as we noted, the relation of the artwork to human beings had been broached only indirectly. And even in the third part, which opens with the question of the "creating" of the work, the role of the human being is initially and deliberately marginalized as Heidegger continues to focus on the being of the work itself by asking how createdness, that is, having been created, be-longs to the work as such. "The more solitarily the work ...stands in itself, the more cleanly it seems to cut all ties to human beings, the more simply does the thrust of the fact that such a work *is* come into the open, and the more essentially is the extraordinary [*das Ungeheuere*] thrust to the surface and what seems long-familiar and ordinary [*geheuer*] thrust down" (H, 54). Yet, Heidegger indicates, even the fact of its having been created does not exhaust the "actuality" or most proper being of the work. For the sud-den irruption and interruption of this simple fact occurs as a "transport" (*Entrückung*) of the work itself into the transformed openness opened up by it, as a "displacement" (*Verrückung*) that invites our attentiveness, that invites our response. It is the transport of a displacement from the ordinary, a displacement that human beings are called upon to follow:

> To follow this displacement means: to transform our accustomed
> relations to world and Earth and henceforth to restrain all usual
> doing and prizing, knowing and looking, in order to tarry [*ver-
> weilen*] within the truth that is happening in the work. The
> restraint of such tarrying first lets what has been created be the
> work that it is. This: letting the work be a work, we call the
> preservation of the work. It is only for such preserving that the
> work yields itself, in its having been created, as the actual work,
> which now means: presencing in the manner of a work. (H, 54)

Face to face with the presencing of a great work of art such as the Greek temple, our usual doing and assessment of things, our familiar knowing (*Kennen*), our ordinary seeing and looking (*Blicken*) at things, governed as they are by the *doxa* of everyday interpretation, are called to a halt, to an interruption. Such presencing invites us into what is originarily at issue in such *doxa*, namely, the self-showing of beings themselves in their radiance and shining, in their glory and nobility, in their dignity and restraint.[79] The work itself, in its enigmatic shining, looks at us as something extraor-dinary. It invites us into ourselves, so to speak: it calls upon us to "hold to ourselves" (*ansichhalten*), calls us to a "restraint" (*Verhaltenheit*), to a

---

[79] On the manifold meanings of *doxa*, see EM, 75ff.

tarrying in its presence.[80] As Gadamer puts it in his introduction to the essay, the work of art "presents itself in its own being in such a way that the one who is contemplating it is compelled to tarry in its presence" (UK, 116).[81] The presencing of the great work of art thus first calls us into our own time—but that means, into a time that is first brought about, a time that first comes to be, via the work itself.

The call that issues from the work itself to tarry in its presence, in the face of the extraordinary, of the divinity of the Earth, i.e. of what we might call the Earthworld, thus invites a response akin to that of ancient *theōria* itself. The call to *let* the work be a work by tarrying in its presence, granting it time by responding to the possibility of its time, entering our own time as that of the work, as the presencing of an extraordinary being—this call, as a call to preservation, is the call to essential knowing, to *Wissen*. The work itself cannot properly be, that is, come to presence, without such knowing. Essential knowing, as preservation, first grants a time to that which has been. As a "having-seen" (*Gesehenhaben*) it tarries in the presence of that which it has seen, first letting it come to its full presencing, to the presencing of its own self-concealing. As a knowing having-seen, the preservation of the work is a letting be seen of the "extraordinary" event occurring in the work: "Preservation of the work, as knowing [*Wissen*], is a sober standing within the extraordinariness of the truth that is happening in the work" (H, 55). Such "standing within" (*Inständigkeit*) the openness occurring in the work first lets the extraordinariness that has come to a stand in the work unfold into its full and proper steadfastness, into its own time. Knowing as preservation, as having-seen, is, however, equally a having-heard, namely, having heard the call of the work itself, of that which approaches us in the work.[82] It is thus not to be taken in the narrow sense of seeing as opposed to hearing, as merely one form of sensory apprehending, but is a gathering of our entire being (of what Plato and Aristotle called the "soul" or *psuchē*) into the event of presencing disclosed in the work.

Yet such knowing, Heidegger emphasizes, is also not to be understood as merely opposed to "willing," that is, to what modernity characterizes as the distinctive essence of "praxis." Rather, this originary knowing is itself a willing, and willing, when thought appropriately, is this knowing. "Whoever truly knows beings knows what he wills to do in their midst." Willing is not

---

[80] On the attunement of *Verhaltenheit* see especially the *Beiträge zur Philosophie* (GA 65). In a later essay, "What is that—Philosophy?" (1955), Heidegger characterizes *Ansichhalten* as a possible response to astonishment and wonder (*Erstaunen*).

[81] The significance of such tarrying is already seen by Kant, with respect to the pre-subjective (i.e., worldly) appearing of the beautiful as an intensification of presence that founds a *sensus communis*: "We *linger in* [weilen bei] our contemplation of the beautiful...." See the *Critique of Judgment*, §12.

[82] Cf. our remarks in chapter 1 on the "sameness" of having-seen and having-heard.

conceived here as a prior decision, or as the application of prior knowledge, nor is it conceived in terms of "the action of a subject positing himself as end." Heidegger relates it, rather, to the "ecstatic" analysis of resolute openness, or un-closedness, in *Being and Time:* "Willing is the sober and resolute openness [*Ent-schlossenheit*] of an existent going-beyond-oneself that exposes itself to the openness of beings as such openness is set into the work." Knowing, "as having-seen, is itself a being resolved [*Entschieden-sein*]" (H, 55–56).

In what way is knowing as having-seen to be thought as a resolute un-closedness? And why does it mean "being resolved"? What is meant by *Entschiedensein*—having been decided—here, and what calls for such decision? Heidegger's characterization of disclosive resoluteness as an "exposure" to the openness of beings, as such openness happens in the work, underlines the element of a prior address or call that issues from the work itself. The openness of *Ent-schlossenheit,* hyphenated by Heidegger to bring out the sense of un-closedness, is intrinsically ambiguous, even *undecidable,* because it refers on the one hand to the stance demanded of human beings— namely, opening oneself in advance to the address of the work—and on the other hand to the opening up of the work itself in its very address, in its claim upon us. To have seen the work in its own proper presencing is to have said "yes," to have already given oneself over to something, to have *let* oneself be claimed in advance by the approach of the work (and indeed by the second coming of the work). It is to have been decided in one's being, as "an ecstatic letting oneself into [*Sicheinlassen in*] the unconcealment of being [*Sein*]" occurring in the work (H, 55). It is a standing—having come to a stand and to a halt—in the presence and approach of *das Ungeheure,* of an extraordinary coming to presence.

The preservation of the work, in transporting us into the openness of a world that unfolds in and through the work itself, thrusts human beings into the presencing of a world that is not merely that of an "individual experience," but that addresses and is accessible to a community. It "thus grounds our being for and with one another as an historical *Ausstehen* of *Da-sein* on the basis of our relation to unconcealment." The word *Ausstehen,* literally "standing out," here suggests at once ecstasis and steadfastness. Yet whence the necessity of decision? Being resolved, already being "decided" in the sense just indicated does not mean that there is no room or need for human freedom or for decision in the active sense. Heidegger's point, rather, is simply that all decision in the active sense always already presupposes a more originary "passivity" or dependence. It presupposes that human beings are always already sustained and carried by the presencing of other beings, by the concealed presencing of the Earth. Thus the human being as apprehender of the work of art, that is, as knower and preserver, indeed acts in the originary sense; his knowing is itself already originary *praxis* in being a *response* that is called for by the work itself, but that has no intrinsic necessity (although it is indeed necessary if the work is to be properly preserved). The work itself, Heidegger emphasizes, can fall into decline or oblivion; but even then it "awaits" its preservers. Its forgotten-ness or oblivion is still a preservation (*Bewahren*) in the sense that its truth (*Wahrheit*) remains preserved for them (H, 55). In the temple's standing there, beings as a whole are brought into unconcealment "and held therein. To hold [*Halten*] originarily means to take into protective heed [*hüten*]" (H, 44). The unconcealment of a historical world is held and sheltered within the work itself, which demands a certain *Haltung* or stance on the part of human beings—whether one of neglect or attentiveness. But why does the work demand this? Why does it call human beings to decision? Because world is not simply the openness of beings as a whole. Because it cannot be without the Earth. And because neither can be in strife, in play and thus at stake (*auf dem Spiel*), without human beings. Without, that is, beings that can respond to something beyond presence, beings that can respond to concealment:

> The world is the clearing of the paths of those essential pointers [*Weisungen*] with which all decision complies [*in die sich alles Entscheiden fügt*]. Every decision, however, is grounded in some-thing not mastered, something concealed, confusing, otherwise it would never be decision. (H, 43–44)

> The emergent world brings out what is as yet undecided and without measure, and thus discloses the concealed necessity of measure and decisiveness.... World demands its decisiveness and its measure, and lets beings come into the openness of its paths. (H, 51)

With the emergence of world, the Earth, as that which constantly con-ceals itself and yet sustains all beings, itself appears. It does so in and through the work, appearing precisely *as* that which conceals itself. In the presence of the work, the Earth, that is, concealment itself, calls and brings itself to bear as that which is—as that which is without measure, as that which has always yet to be decided.[83] The Earth itself shows itself as that which remains undecided, as that which constantly calls us toward her— as the originary future, as she who grants birth and death, natality and mortality. And yet she cannot show herself without those who are her own offspring, at once of the Earth and yet excluded from her—for a time.

---

[83] On the call of the Earth as song and as *Dichtung*, see Michel Haar, *Le chant de la terre* (Paris: Éditions de l'Herne, 1985).

We are now better able to understand Heidegger's "definition" of *techne* as knowing and as "having-seen." *Technē* as "creating" does not just refer to an "activity" of making or producing, because it is originarily the same having-seen that occurs in the preservation of the work. *Technē,* we recall, as a knowing having-seen, is to be taken "in the broad sense of seeing, which means: apprehending something present as such." Its Greek essence lies in *alētheia,* in that revealing which "sustains and guides" all comportment toward beings:

> *Technē,* as a kind of knowing experienced by the Greeks, is a bringing forth [*Hervorbringen*] of beings in that it brings forth [*her*] what is present as such out of concealment expressly before [*vor*] us and into the unconcealment of its outward appearance; *technē* never means the activity of making. The artist is not a *technitēs* because he is also a craftsman, but rather because both the setting-forth [*Her-stellen*] of works and the setting-forth of items of use occur in that bringing forth before us which in advance lets beings come before us [*vor kommen*] into their presencing in terms of their outward appearance. Yet all this happens in the midst of beings that emerge and flourish of their own accord, namely, *phusis.* (H, 48)

As in the later essay on technology, *technē* is here understood as a kind of *poiēsis,* a bringing to the fore from out of concealment into the unconcealment of an appearance. Yet this kind of *poiēsis,* unlike that of *phusis,* happens as an explicit engagement with, and indeed an interruption of *time.* It is at once an interruption of *phusis,* that is, of that which unfolds of its own accord, and an irruption into the temporality of the emergence of beings into unconcealment. In other words, it occurs as an originary *praxis* that, in constituting or "founding" a beginning, assumes a responsibility for that which is to come forth in its responding to it. It has always already entered the clearing. Such *poiēsis* must "let beings come before it" *in advance,* that is, prior to their emergence into a world, in advance of their full presencing in and through the Earth, as a worldly presencing that will be accessible to others, to a community. But what is the outward appearance or "look" that must already have been seen in advance by the "creator" of the great work of art, by the one who brings forth such a work into unconcealment, the human being who—precisely in great art— "remains something inconsequential compared to the work, almost like a passageway [*Durchgang*] that annihilates itself in the creative process for the emergence of the work" (H, 29)? Both the craftsperson and the artist let beings come forth in advance in terms of their outward appearance.

But in the case of the craftsperson, the outward appearance is itself already seen as subservient to a useful purpose or end, to a *telos* of utility. The item of utility is brought forth with a view to such an end, and as brought forth, its elemental materiality, its own presencing, and its own origin are literally overlooked in our orientation toward some future end. Yet precisely such things are what emerge as such in the great work of art. The work has no extrinsic goal; in positive terms, what is created "into" the work, as Heidegger puts it—that which the work points toward and lets emerge—is everything that pertains to the extraordinariness of its coming to presence, including, of course, the concealment in such presencing. What the artist as creator of the great work must have seen in advance is precisely *das Ungeheure,* the extraordinary. But the latter is itself the event of the singular work that has or will have been created, the work itself as the happening of an extraordinary unconcealment. The non-simple origin of the origin, of its origination, with everything that pertains to such origination, is what is created into the great work of art. That which has already come in advance of its first coming (of its proper, ultimate, that is, finite coming)—the extraordinary event of such a being—comes to presence in the work of art. The artist *responds* to such an extraordinary coming; he *lets* such an arrival itself come to the fore in the look of the work. The artist is the site of this letting, of this giving way that yields another path (other than that of *phusis* alone) to presencing. He or she occupies this ancient site of *technē,* this site of concealment itself, of the originary future. To be this site is the vocation of the human being as historical, the vocation of a worldly belonging to the Earth that is "poetized" into the work, "the latent vocation of historical Dasein itself" (H, 63).[84]

Heidegger's essay on the origin of the work of art thus focuses on the coming into being of the work itself in such a way as to avoid the reduction of the being of the work to a matter of human knowledge or aesthetic judgment. The happening of un-concealment in the radiant and shining presencing of the great work is neither the product of a human subject who would be its origin, nor is it simply dependent on subjective judgments of taste. The polarized thinking of modern subjectivity is thought more originarily in showing how *both* "creating" and "preserving" are themselves intrinsically poietic, grounded in knowing as a having-seen, namely, having seen the concealment and finitude at work in the finite happening of the un-concealment of a being. Creating and preserving are inseparable; each implies the other. The determination of art as "the setting itself to work of truth" is, Heidegger notes, deliberately ambiguous. It refers both to the

---

[84] Cf. the closely parallel interpretation of *technē* in the 1935 course *Introduction to Metaphysics* (EM, 122).

establishment of unconcealment in the work as a singular being, that is, to creating, and to bringing the being of the work into play (*in Gang*), to letting it happen, that is, to preserving (H, 59). The creator of such a work is intrinsically also a preserver; and the preserver of the work of art is no less a creator; for, like the creator, he or she must first let happen the singular strife between world and Earth, in coming to see—thus to have seen—the extraordinary event of presencing that a great work is. This entails not only a tarrying in the presence of the work, but a tarrying in the presence of (i.e., a coming to know) its specifically historical claim, the claim of its historical world.

The establishing of truth as unconcealment in the work is, Heidegger emphasizes, "the bringing forth of a being such as never was before and never will come to be again." Such a being is an event. The bringing forth of the work brings forth the singular event of un-concealment in "placing this being into the open in such a way that that which is to be brought first clears the openness of the open into which it comes forth." Such bringing is not the bringing of something already existing, but "rather a receiving and removal": it receives and takes from concealment that which comes, that which has yet to come, accompanying it on its way, on the path to unconcealment (H, 50–51).

Concealment, as the "provenance" of all clearing, is the provenance of precisely that which is "not yet," that which is un-revealed (UK, 67).[85] And this more profound, more primary concealment is what appears in the presence of the great work of art—appears in its presencing and with-drawal. Yet as we have seen, this event first happens as something that has happened. Its presencing presupposes its prior withdrawal. It must always already have withdrawn, have made way for itself, so as thereby to let itself appear. And this always already having made way—given way, opened up the timespace of presencing as the pathway of all paths—is what has always already been at work wherever a world is opened up. It is the event of the extraordinary, of *das Ungeheure*. An event that is always excessive, that is, originary.

Art as originary *poiēsis*, as *Dichtung*, is thus characterized by Heidegger toward the end of the essay as "founding" in the threefold sense of "bestow-ing, grounding, and beginning." Art as founding is a bestowal in the sense of an "excess": "The setting to work of unconcealment thrusts the extraor-dinary into the open and thrusts down the ordinary and what we believe to be ordinary. The truth that opens itself up in the work can never be documented or derived from what went before" (H, 62). The latter, indeed, is "refuted" (*widerlegt*) in its claim to exclusive actuality by the work.

---

[85] This elucidation appears to be an addition to later editions of the essay.

Such refutation should be compared to the "responding" (*Erwidern*) and "revocation" (*Widerruf*) that in *Being and Time* are said to be intrinsic to Dasein's historicality, as a historical existing in the *Augenblick* (see chapter 4 above). The comparison indicates a shift in emphasis vis-à-vis *Being and Time:* the originating power of Dasein (which was still open to being appropriated and misinterpreted in the sense of the modern, active power of the will) is still more decentered in relation to that of other worldly beings; origination occurs primarily as an event of world in its strife with Earth, even though this strife occurs only in the site (*Stätte*) of the *Augenblick,* the site that Dasein itself is. This shift also accords greater import to the having-been of world, while the originary future, the "power of death," as the site of birth and mortality, is no longer conceived as Dasein's own, but as belonging to the Earth in the *Ereignis* of its strife with world. This also implies, as our subsequent reflections will indicate, that with regard to the *Augenblick* the moment of having-seen, now in the sense of having been looked upon, assumes a priority over any human "act" of looking. The human activity of looking is always secondary, responsive, even though there can be no *technē* (thus also no historicality and no *praxis*) without it. The 1934–36 meditations on the origin of the work of art and on the essence of *technē,* which include the 1934/35 course on Hölderlin (GA 39) and the 1935 *Introduction to Metaphysics,* thus open the way for a more originary thinking of the *Augenblick* that will be more fully and explicitly developed in the *Beiträge* and in the 1936–37 courses on Nietzsche. These meditations remove any remaining connotations of the *Augenblick* as an "active" or "perceptive" seeing that would belong in the first instance to Dasein as its own originating accomplishment—connotations that, as we noted, still play a role in *Being and Time,* even though such activity cannot there be understood in any sense of a modern or "strong" subjectivity. "The Origin of the Work of Art" understands the being-at-work of art as first giving rise to the ecstasis of human seeing and apprehending, which must therefore be thought as a primarily responsive activity.

Art as founding is thus intrinsically an unmediated beginning (*Anfang*), unmediated not in the sense that it comes from nowhere or from a sheer nothingness, but in the sense that, as the coming to pass of a singular event, it has already exceeded (or "leapt over") everything that has yet to come from that beginning. The origin that the work of art itself is, the origin that is "at work," is not "caused" by something already present that acts upon it; rather, it *lets* itself occur from out of the "not yet" of unconcealment, in its having already departed from presence, in its opening of time and of timespace. The beginning "always contains the undisclosed fullness of the extraordinary, and that means, of conflict with the ordinary" (H, 63). Finally, art as an origin is intrinsically "grounding" in the sense that the projection of unconcealment, that is, of being itself in its historical manifestation, occurs in a being, in the work, and does so as a response to an already existing world, a response to something concealed therein—to something bestowed and destined—a response that, as a beginning, creates the world anew in being set to work (H, 62–63). What is most extraordinary about Heidegger's essay is that it itself seems to be such a beginning, or, as a "thoughtful knowing" (H, 65), the preparation thereof.

Art as originary *technē*, as *Dichtung*, the founding of unconcealment as such, is thus not limited to "artworks" in the narrow sense of the fine arts. Unconcealment happens in the being that the work of art itself is, but also in other ways: in "the deed that founds a political state"; in "the nearness of that which is not at all a being, but that which most is in beings" (the "last god" as the presence of the "nothing" in being); in "the essential sacrifice," as an exceptional deed in which the entire being of a human being is at stake; or "in the questioning of the thinker, as a thinking of being" (H, 50). Thus, at the end of the essay, Heidegger indicates that the bringing forth of the new in its historical significance is precisely the setting itself to work of unconcealment, the event in which the enduring claim of a *world* is opened up, in which the world as we have hitherto known it is transformed:

> Whenever beings as a whole, as beings themselves, demand to be grounded in openness, art comes into its historical essence as founding. This happened in the West for the first time in Greece. What was in the future to be called being [*Sein*] was set into work in a manner that gave the measure. Thus opened up, beings as a whole then came to be transformed into beings in the sense of that which was created by God. This occurred in the Middle Ages. Such beings were again transformed at the beginning and during the course of the modern age. Beings became objects that could be controlled and become perspicuous through calculation. On each occasion a new and essential world irrupted. On each occasion the openness of beings had to be established in beings themselves by setting truth into place in the figure [of a work]. On each occasion unconcealment of beings occurred. Unconcealment sets itself to work, which setting is brought to accomplishment by art. (H, 63–64)

The Greek beginning maintains its power today precisely through the claim to truth of modern science, as a particular transformation of the desire to see, and through the dominant sway of modern technology as a further transformation thereof in which the production of presencing becomes an end in itself. Yet science, Heidegger indicates, "is not an originary happening of truth, but always the cultivation of a realm of truth already opened ..." (H, 50). Paradoxically, given its relentness pursuit of the new, it thereby cultivates indirectly the oblivion of the origin, of that *poiēsis* which first lets human beings exist as originary *praxis*. For such *praxis* is truly originary only when it has taken the time and the care to know itself, or in Hölderlin's words, with which Heidegger closes his essay, to "dwell near the origin."

The Look of the Other

Our considerations of ancient *theōria* pointed to the originary sense of *theōria* as an exceptional manner of human comportment characterized by an attentive and respectful tarrying in proximity to the presencing of the divine, an apprehending of the coming of the god, a catching sight of an event of divine epiphany. Heidegger's account of the radiant splendor emanating from the great work of art in "The Origin of the Work of Art" helps us to understand such epiphany in terms of the event of presencing itself, in terms of the happening of concealment in the un-concealment of beings themselves. The attentive and respectful heed that marks the stance of ancient *theōria* is a respect for boundaries and limits, for origins: it shows respect for the sacred inviolability of the presencing of the other being, an honoring of the dignity of other beings in their otherness. The great work of art proves to be an exceptional being, an exceptional event of un-concealment, because in and through it there occurs the happening of a world, of the timespace of a world that calls human beings into their historical dwelling (their *ēthos*) in opening them to what is supremely worthy of question, and thereby to the happening of their own finitude in the midst of other beings. This accomplishment is the distinctive achievement of *technē* as an exceptional kind of *poiēsis*. For of its own accord, *phusis* does not let the Earth be an Earth: it does not found (*stiften*) the strife between world and Earth. *Phusis* turns to and calls upon *technē* (in its originary sense, as the disclosure of worldly finitude) to accomplish this. Letting-be (*Seinlassen*), the letting-be of beings as a whole—which is not to be understood as the mere passivity of "letting things happen" or of "leaving things alone"[86]—occurs only at the site of such originary *technē*, that is, only where there is both an opening up of beings themselves as a whole *and* the express acknowledgement of the finitude of beings in their presencing. But such acknowledgement of finitude—which entails a prior knowledge, the thoughtful recollection (*Gedächtnis,* the gathering of thought that has been) of a having-seen—is also the precondition of human *praxis* in the

---

[86] See UK, 97.

originary sense we have given this word.[87] Acting in and from out of an acknowledgement of one's own finitude entails a dwelling not merely in proximity to such finitude, but in its midst. It entails already having come to stand within the coming of concealment itself, thus within the event of un-concealment. It entails a relation (of knowing, of having seen) to one's own presencing as a presencing from out of concealment, of a concealment that is not one's own, but that belongs to the Earth.

The felicitous strife between *phusis* and *technē*, between Earth and world, the disclosive play of un-concealment as the event of a radiant shining in the sensuous presencing of a worldly being—all of this transpires not only in the great work of art. It comes to pass in an even more enigmatic way in the sensuous presencing of human beings themselves, of those who, according to Heidegger's translation of the opening lines of the famous choral ode from Sophocles' *Antigone*, "loom and stir" as "the most uncanny" amid all beings, as *to deinon* (EM, 112). In his 1942 lecture course on Hölderlin's hymn "The Ister," Heidegger ventures a more extensive discussion of the words *ragend sich regt*, "looms and stirs," as he again translates the Greek verb *pelein* that describes the uncanny presencing of the human being. The words *ho pelas*, he recalls, mean "the neighbor," the one who presences nearby, in the immediate vicinity, and actively stirs in such presencing; *pelagos* names that which stirs of its own accord, "remaining and abiding in itself," and is thus the word for the sea. In the closing lines from Hölderlin's "most sublime" elegy, "The Archipelagus," Heidegger hears, in his own thoughtful remembrance, the poetizing of something that continues to stir in the spirit of the poem:

> Aber du, unsterblich, wenn auch der Griechengesang schon
> Dich nicht feiert, wie sonst, aus deinen Woogen, o Meergott!
> Töne mir in die Seele noch oft, dass über den Wassern
> Furchtlosrege der Geist, dem Schwimmer gleich, in der Starken
> Frischem Glüke sich üb', und die Göttersprache, das Wechseln
> Und das Werden versteh', und wenn die reissende Zeit mir
> Zu gewaltig das Haupt ergreifft und die Noth und das Irrsaal
> Unter Sterblichen mir mein sterblich Leben erschüttert,
> Lass der Stille mich dann in deiner Tiefe gedenken.

> Yet you, immortally, though even Greek song itself
> No longer celebrates you as before, from your waves, O god of
>   sea!
> May you ring yet often in my soul, that over the waters

---

[87] On *Gedächtnis*, see also "Absence of the Body" below.

Fearlessly may spirit stir, like the swimmer, practise
Fresh fortune of the strong, and know the language of the gods,
    know
Change and becoming, and if the time that tears
Should seize too violently my head, if need and errancy
Among mortals disrupt for me my mortal life,
Leave me then to remember the stillness in your depths.[88]

In this poetic disclosure Heidegger hears a sense of presencing that is at once close to and yet different from the presencing of one's neighbor that for Aristotle discloses itself in the momentary stillness of a *theōrein*.[89] Whereas Aristotle's *theōria* tends toward an emphasis on the being of the Other that is *disclosed* in such *theōrein*, the poetic disclosure, Heidegger's reading suggests, points toward the event of disclosure itself and thereby toward that which in such disclosure resists and withdraws from being brought to a standstill. The stirring (*pelein, sich regen*) poetized in the poetic spirit of the waters, Heidegger remarks, "here means the concealed presencing of stillness and tranquillity [*das verborgene Anwesen der Stille und Ruhe*] amid constant and unconcealed absencing and presencing." In such a manner there stirs also, he adds, that uncanniness (*Unheimlichkeit*) which is itself nothing human, and yet continues to stir in human beings, a supreme uncanniness from out of which they emerge and presence as the most uncanny, *das Unheimlichste:*

> Uncanniness does not first arise as a consequence of humankind; rather, humankind emerges from uncanniness and remains within it—looms out of it and stirs within it. The uncanny itself is what looms forth in the essence of human beings and is that which stirs in all stirring and arousal: that which presences and at the same time absences. (GA 53, 89)

Unheimlichkeit is here to be thought as a unique manner of dwelling, an intrinsically poietic dwelling that is itself a journeying of "coming to be at home" in one's own, that is, in that which is properly *unheimlich,* which for its part can be encountered only in and through an exposure to the foreign, to what is other than one's own.

It is in the *Parmenides* course from the following semester, however, that Heidegger addresses the presencing of the other human being specifically in terms of the look. The discussion occurs in the midst of an extraordinarily rich and complex analysis of unconcealment and its relation to "seeing," an

---

[88] Cited at GA 53, 88.
[89] See "The Theoria of the Ancients" above.

analysis that we cannot hope to treat adequately here.[90] We shall restrict our comments to a few remarks that bear directly on our theme.

The context in which Heidegger's discussion of the look of the Other is broached is an interpretation of a myth (*muthos*), of the concluding myth of Plato's *Republic* which, Heidegger claims, is the last telling of concealment (*lēthē*) in Greek thinking as the classical age comes to an end. It is the "last word" of the Greek era to "name *lēthē* in its essence" (GA 54, 140). In the same context, Heidegger again recalls Aristotle's testimony concerning the first philosophers, the original "thinkers": namely, that they know (*eidenai*) things that are astonishing, difficult, "daimonic" (GA 54, 148). Yet here Heidegger follows Aristotle's testimony not in the direction of philosophy as the "science of being," but toward the Presocratic experience of wonder. The "daimonic," Heidegger argues, is to be understood as the nonordinary, the "extra-ordinary," *das Un-geheure*. As such, it means "being as it shines into everything ordinary, that is, into beings, and that in its shining often only brushes across beings like the shadow of a cloud silently passing.... The extraordinary is the simple, the inconspicuous, ungraspable by the claws of the will, withdrawing itself from all artifices of calculation, because it surpasses all planning" (GA 54, 150). The extraordinary shines, inconspicuously for the most part, into beings themselves; it is something that, as human beings, we "always have in view," yet seldom catch sight of as such. It looks at us from out of beings themselves in their enigmatic shining.

What is the look, as in the look proceeding from another being? In Greek, Heidegger remarks, to look means *theaō*. Notably, this verb is familiar to us only in its medial form, *theaomai,* usually translated as to "behold" (*anschauen*) or "spectate" (*zuschauen*). Yet the Greek, medial sense of this verb implies "bringing the look [of something or someone] toward oneself, namely, the look [*Blick*], *thea,* in the sense of the view [*Anblick*] in which something offers and presents itself" (GA 54, 152). *Theaō* does not mean looking in the sense of "looking at" something, and especially not

---

[90] The *Parmenides* discussion is of particular interest in the context of the present study, since the emphasis on "seeing" as a relation to being has again led to accusations of a latent Platonism in Heidegger's thought. See, for example, Jacques Taminiaux, *Lectures de l'ontologie fondamentale,* 178–79. Similarly, David Krell, commenting in *Daimon Life* (Bloomington: Indiana University Press, 1992) on this passage, remarks that "Heidegger holds to Platonic theory, theater, and theism" (301). But may one conclude that "Platonism" is present wherever theory and visual presentation are in play? At the other end of the scale, the *Parmenides* analysis of the look has been described by Véronique Fóti as "proto-Levinasian" (see "Aletheia and Oblivion's Field: On Heidegger's Parmenides Lectures," in *Ethics and Danger,* ed. Dallery & Scott [Albany: State University of New York Press, 1992], 71–82), although her book *Heidegger and the Poets* is sceptical that Heidegger leaves room for a genuine encounter with alterity.

the kind of modern looking in which we direct ourselves toward an object of representation and thereby "grasp" it. Looking, in this sense, is not the subjective activity of an "I" or subject; rather, it is that "looking" in which things, beings themselves, look, that is, show themselves, appear, and "are there." Furthermore, we do not originarily experience our own looking in any form of "reflexivity"; rather, Heidegger observes, "even human looking, experienced in an originary manner, is not the grasping of something, but that self-showing with respect to which a grasping looking first becomes possible." In other words, an emergence into unconcealment is the precondition for any looking in the active sense; and only because we are already addressed, looked upon by beings themselves, can we respond to them in the manner of looking "at" them. The human look in the active sense, such as that promoted by modern subjectivity, is in fact always responsive, secondary, dependent upon the prior presencing of beings themselves.

In the present context, Heidegger illustrates this by reference to the look of another human being:

> If the human being experiences his own looking, that is, here the human look, not in "reflection" upon himself as the one representing himself looking; if the human being instead experiences the look in letting it be encountered in a manner that is free of any reflection, as the way in which a human being coming toward him looks at him, then it becomes apparent that the look of the human being we encounter shows itself as that in which one human being awaits and approaches [*entgegenwartet*] the other, that is, appears and is. (GA 54, 153)

To put it in modern terms, the look, *thea,* is not the activity of a "subject," but the way in which another being (whose presence is likewise not reducible to that of an "object")—in this case a human being—emerges and comes toward us, awaits us. Yet such emergence, in which the ground of the human essence is revealed as a distinctive and exceptional kind of approach and "waiting," is ambiguous:

> Looking is showing oneself, namely, that self-showing in which the essence of the human being we are encountering has gathered itself and in which the human being we encounter "emerges" in the double sense that their essence is gathered together in the look as the sum of their existence, and [in the sense that] this collectedness and straightforward whole of their essence discloses itself in the look, yet does so only to let concealing and the abyssal ground of their essence be present at the same time in what is thus unconcealed. (GA 54, 153)

The look is the emergence, the presencing of the Other, in which emergence the other being is precisely gathered into his or her own being, into themselves in their presencing, their unconcealment. Emergence is at once the way in which the self that shows itself becomes absorbed and merges into its own presencing, its own self-showing, at any particular moment, and this self-showing itself. Yet such presencing, at any given moment, is also a concealment of that which is past and that which has yet to come (so long as there is anything left to come) from the Other: in particular, of the possibilities of action. Such concealment, however, is not a mere "nothingness"; it announces itself in and through the look of the Other, in the presencing of the Other as look. The gathered coming into presence of the other human being in the look at each moment "lets presence" a concealing and the "abyssal ground" of their essence. Concealment itself, as the freedom of this being, announces its presence and its power in and through the un-concealment of the look.

The human look, thought in terms of the unconcealed look of the Other who comes toward us and which presents the Other in his or her being, is thus inevitably also a look of withdrawal, of concealment.[91] But what is the nature of this specific event of un-concealment that occurs in the look of the Other? The human being, claims Heidegger, is "distinguished" (*ausgezeichnet*) by such looking. Yet not—precisely not—because it is we human beings who (actively) look and thus "have" or possess this capacity for looking. Rather, the human can be distinguished by such looking only because this looking, which "shows or points to being itself," is "nothing human, but belongs to the essence of being itself as a coming to appear in what is unconcealed" (GA 54, 153–54). In what sense is the looking of the other human being "nothing human"? What is at issue is not a dehumanizing of the human being, but rather a decentering of the human as determined by subjectivity. Heidegger does not claim that the *look* of the other human being is nothing human: indeed, this look, as we have heard, precisely reveals the human "essence," reveals what is proper to this particular being at any given moment. The claim, rather, is that the *looking,* that is, the presencing of the look, is itself nothing human, but belongs to "being itself," to an event of presencing that exceeds it (namely, in the direction of a world), an event that, as such, is not the property of the human being.

---

[91] Such is the case even and especially where human activity unfolds into its most intense self-presentation and presence, in being fully given over to an action (cf. the actions of a stage-actor or musician, where the performance, the *praxis* itself, is everything). What would all superlative performance be, as an event of un-concealment, were it not held and continually surrounded in advance by the suspense and tension of ongoing concealment, of the fragility of the possible?

Everything that appears and presents a view of itself does so, Heidegger notes, in the realm of "the ordinary" (*das Geheure*), in the realm of beings. The fundamental Greek experience of the way in which beings come to presence in this realm is a visual experience (the Greeks, as Heidegger often recalls, were *Augenmenschen,* visual beings): things presence by way of their look (*Blick*), their face or countenance (*Gesicht*). Yet this very experience of being indicates that being itself is understood in terms of the way things show and reveal themselves, their coming into presence, into unconcealment (*alētheia*). This alone can let us comprehend what is otherwise, as Heidegger puts it, "incomprehensible": namely, the fact that Plato, "toward the end of the Greek world," thinks being in terms of the "look" that a thing presents, its *eidos* or *idea.* Being is that which shows itself in, and looks at us from out of all things. That which properly looks, however, in looking into the realm of the ordinary, is for the Greeks, Heidegger indicates, nothing less than "the divine," the so-called "gods":

> That which looks into everything ordinary, namely the extra-ordinary [*das Un-geheure*], as that which shows itself in advance, is that which originarily looks in a distinctive sense: *to theaon,* that is, *to theion;* we translate this "correctly," but without thinking in Greek terms, as "the divine." *Hoi theoi,* the so-called gods, those who look into the ordinary and look everywhere within the ordinary, are *hoi daimones,* those who show and point. (GA 54, 154)

To theion in its originary sense, Heidegger suggests, demands to be understood as *to theaon,* as that which looks into and out of things themselves in the manner of the extraordinary. *Thea,* the look that something presents, and *theā,* the goddess, are one and the same word for the Greeks, if we heed the fact that the Greeks wrote without accenting words, and were attentive to the ambiguities that resonate from the similarity in sound of words such as these (GA 54, 160).

As in the case of the work of art, the "extraordinary" or the "divine," the god, is not to be understood as an entity, as a thing or being that looks. Rather, as that which "looks," the divine is to be thought as the appearing of concealment in the presencing or un-concealment of a being. Such concealment *looks* at us in and from out of things themselves, marking them and pointing them out (*daiō—daimones*) in their singularity,[92] in the extraordinariness of their being, which is ordinarily covered over in ordinary appearances. Here, as in "The Origin of the Work of Art," the

---

[92] See GA 54, 151ff. for Heidegger's discussion of the intrinsic relation between daimonic looking and pointing or marking.

"divine" refers (points) to the Earth itself, to the primary and most profound concealment that pervades the presencing of things; the gods that
appear are gods of the Earthworld. The divinity that thus looks in and from
out of things themselves is worldly in the sense that it can appear in any being. In the presencing of the gods looking in, Heidegger remarks elsewhere,
the Greeks experienced "the most uncanny and enchanting face-to-face: *to
deinon*" (SG, 140). Yet among those beings in which such divinity itself
presences, the human being appears as even more extraordinary, even more
uncanny, than other beings. The human being has a special distinction:

> The one who looks appears in the look [*Anblick*] and "appear-
> ance" [*Aussehen*] of the ordinary, of beings. That which attends
> [*das Gegenwartende*] amid the ordinary through his or her look
> is the human being. Therefore, amid the ordinary, the vision
> [*Anblick*] of the god must gather itself within the essential do-
> main of this human looking, and its figure must be established
> therein. Human beings themselves are those beings that have
> their distinction in being addressed by being itself, so that in
> the self-showing of human beings, in their looking and in their
> look, the extraordinary itself, the god, appears. (GA 54, 154–55)

The vision of the "gods," the look of the divine, gathers itself not simply
within the human look or face, but within the essential domain of human
existence, within the world of human beings. It is gathered also, as we have
noted, in the appearance of the great work of art. Heidegger indeed uses
the same words here that were used in the essay on the work of art: the
"figure" (*Gestalt*) of divine presencing must become established or "set up"
(*aufgestellt*) within the domain of human vision, within the world that is
visible to humans.

Yet the face of the human being is not simply a look in and through
which the divine appears, showing itself in its self-concealment—something
that also happens in an exceptional way in the work of art. Human beings
have their distinction, according to Heidegger, in "being addressed [*ange-
sprochen*] by being." The human being is the one who, through his or her
look, attends amid the ordinary. We use the word "attend" here to render
the German *Gegenwarten*, which suggests a waiting (*warten*) in response
to (*gegen*), coming to presence in the manner of a responsive awaiting, an
"attending."[93] The human being is a being who waits, a being that tarries

---

[93] As noted earlier, Heidegger suggests this sense of waiting as intrinsic to the time
of the *Augenblick* already in *Being and Time*, where he writes the presence of the
Augenblick as *Gegen-wart*, a waiting that first lets us "encounter" something in its time
(SZ, 338).

in presence, a being that in its very essence (its relation to concealing) has left time, "left" in the double sense of having exited from, and thereby been given time. For what? For being. Time to be, to respond to the address of being, of the being of other beings and of oneself, to dwell in the presence of beings themselves.[94]

The fact that the human being "attends" through, or by way of his or her look—that the look of the human being is thus a site of passage for a dwelling—means, however, that this look itself must be distinct from the looks of other beings, from the look of a being that presences only by way of *phusis* (but not by way of *technē* or *praxis*), and indeed also from the look of the work of art. This also implies, however, that the human look is not yet sufficiently determined in what is most proper to it, most distinctive of it, if we simply understand it as the letting-presence of a concealing. The latter is characteristic of the look of any being when we attend to its singularity. But the presencing of the human being is also not merely the opening up or setting up of a world in the manner of the great work of art. The human being is a being that itself has a relation—a relation of being as "care"—to world, and thereby also to Earth.

The human being, as Heidegger has indicated, not only "has" a look in the way that other things have a look (their *eidos*), but exists as a looking. Yet in this context everything depends on not interpreting this "looking" as the activity of a subject, or of an already existing self. The looking in question is not yet to be conceived as the (discursive) apprehending or grasping of something, that is, it is not yet a "looking at," but is a more subliminal, and indeed prediscursive "catching sight" (*Erblicken*) of something. And as such, it is a distinctive mode of disclosure, of self-disclosure (thus of a certain *poiēsis*) as presencing. There is certainly also an *activity* "at work" here; but Heidegger's point is that this level of activity is one of *response:*

> That which comes to shine and appears to our catching sight of it is the look that looks at and solicits the human being in addressing him. That catching sight of ... which is accomplished by the human being in relation to the look that appears to him is already a response [*Antwort*] to the originary look, to the look that first elevates the human catching sight of [things] into its essence. Thus, as a consequence of the prevailing of *alētheia,* and only thereof, looking is the primordial way of emerging into the clear [*ins Lichte*] and of coming, that is, of shining into the unconcealed. (GA 54, 158)

---

[94] Thus, Heidegger elsewhere writes of the human being as the one whose essence is to be "affected" by presence: "der Mensch, der von Anwesenheit Angegangene ..." (SD, 12).

Human looking as self-showing is a primarily responsive activity. It occurs as a responding to and catching sight of, namely, of what Heidegger here calls the "originary look" that solicits and addresses us in its appearing, in its coming to shine (*erscheinen*). This originary look, as the looking of that which is more originary than the human look, is that of the "extraordinary," of the presencing of *das Ungeheure*, as that looking which "shows" or points to being itself (to the possibility of presence), but as such is "nothing human" (GA 54, 154). And yet—this more originary look is not simply other than human. It is the look of that which appears only in and through the look of the other human being, of human beings themselves as those who have always already been, always already come to presence. As Heidegger already indicated above, it is within the essential domain of human looking that the look of the divine is "gathered": "Human beings themselves are those beings that have their distinction in being addressed by being itself, so that in the self-showing of human beings, in their looking and in their look, the extraordinary itself, the god, appears" (GA 54, 155). Likewise, in the present context Heidegger emphasizes that "We must, however, understand looking in the originary Greek manner, as the way in which a human being encounters us in looking at us and in looking gathers himself into this self-disclosive emergence and, without holding back a remainder, lets himself 'emerge' in presenting his essence" (GA 54, 158). In a human being's looking at us (*anblicken*) there is already a more originary looking (*blicken*)—neither purely human nor purely divine, but "daimonic," that is, monstrative—that is a gathering into self-disclosure. The presence and presencing of the human being is decisive for the appearance of the divine, of *das Ungeheure*. And this also implies that the first emergence of the human being into presencing by way of "looking" would always already be a response to the presencing of the Other, specifically, to the originary looking of the "extraordinary" in the Other, in the radiant shining and appearing of other human beings. Such shining would be the look and address of being itself, of "the being of [i.e., addressed to] that being which those looking themselves are" (GA 54, 153).

Yet have we not indicated that *das Ungeheure* can in principle come to appear in any being? Have we not seen the presence of *das Ungeheure* as distinctive of the work of art? What is so distinctive about the look and looking of another human being? Presumably, such distinctiveness lies in the fact that no other being has been "addressed" by being itself, by presencing as such. Presumably it lies in the fact that no other being has gathered itself in the face of such an address. What is meant by such an address, and what constitutes its uniqueness?

According to Heidegger's interpretation here, this subliminal human looking that is itself responsive to *das Ungeheure* is "more originary than the presence of things." Indeed, it "first enables presencing," and does so because the human look, in showing itself as looking, as emergent, "at the same time shelters and conceals within it that which is undisclosed." By contrast, "the thing that does not itself look appears only in such a way that it crops up amid the unconcealed, yet itself has nothing to disclose, and thus nothing to conceal either" (GA 54, 158).

An important claim is made here. Originary human looking (and the context makes it clear that *human* looking is intended), Heidegger asserts, *first enables presencing.* In which case, there would be no presencing without this human participation, without the activity of this distinctive responsiveness to being, to presencing, to the originary presencing of *das Ungeheure.* It is not that "presencing" itself first "exists" somewhere or somehow and we *then* respond to it; rather, presencing (which never occurs independently of beings) itself happens or comes about only in and through a responsiveness. And it can be seen from this that the distinctive human accomplishment of this responsive activity must thus lie in letting presencing be, in a letting-be. But this is so, Heidegger remarks, because such activity shelters and conceals within it something undisclosed. Unlike the thing that "crops up," human coming into presencing, human emergence, has something to disclose: precisely the presencing of that which is concealed. But self-concealment marks the presencing ("worlding," the event of world) of all beings upon this Earth. And the highest—the primordial and ultimate—vocation of human beings is, according to "The Question Concerning Technology," precisely to protect (*hüten*) such concealment. In letting presencing be, in letting beings be in their presencing, human responsiveness *thereby first lets concealment be, lets there be concealment.* It first lets there be concealment: there in the "there," the *Da,* of *Dasein.*

Astonishingly enough, the "enabling" activity of such letting-be is thus not that of an already existing "subject" or "self." It is, rather, an ongoing responsiveness to an event of origination: to the approach of *das Ungeheure,* of the radical irruption of the "extraordinary," of the irruption that the "extraordinary" itself is (i.e., what we have earlier called the originary future), and *thereby* of the possibility of that which is not yet, of the "new" as that which can come to presence, that which may yet await us.

In the activity of originary looking, a human being emerges into presencing, shows him- or herself "without holding back a remainder." What this originary human looking conceals, therefore, is not a human selfhood or "subjectivity," but the Earth, the concealment that awaits us in all beings. It conceals it precisely in sheltering it. The fact that human looking, unlike the presencing of a thing, has something *to* reveal and something *to* conceal also indicates that such revealing and concealing is for human beings *a task,* something to be accomplished, something oriented toward a future, toward the possibility of coming and of origination, toward concealment itself. In its elevation, the face in Heidegger thus shows or indicates the coming into presence of a *world* whose provenance remains enigmatic, concealed, and yet haunts the face in an exceptional way, in the manner of an exceptional and distinctive shining. The haunt of this haunting is the dwelling of an *ēthos* whose habitat is, in an exceptional way, close to the Earth.

The distinctiveness of human looking in its originarily disclosive presencing lies, on this account, in an exceptional relation to un-concealment. The human look itself thereby also has an exceptional relation to concealment itself. This relation indeed constitutes the distinctiveness of its shining. As we have seen in our discussion of the work of art, the shining of the sensuous occurs as the presencing of concealment. Yet this "occurrence," this singular event of presencing, is different in the case of different kinds of beings. The self-showing of the stone that crops up "naturally" on the beach is different from the presencing of the temple of stone; the presence of a cat or a dog is not that of another human being; among the latter, the presence of a friend is not that of an unknown stranger, although both appear as human beings having something in common that distinguishes them from the pebble or from the cat. And certainly, we would not experience the human as human unless we had also experienced other beings. In order to highlight what is distinctive of the human look, Heidegger discusses briefly that kind of being which seems in many ways to be closest to us, namely, the animal.

If we compare the pebble that does not actively look (that is, emerge from itself in showing its self-concealment) to the human being who does, we notice, as Heidegger puts it, that the animal has a "peculiar intermediate position" in this regard:

> People say that animals "look at us" [*sehen uns an*]. But animals do not look [*blicken*]. The animal's "peering" or "furtive glance" or "gaping" or "staring" is never a self-unconcealing of being [*Sein*]; the animal in its so-called looking never brings along with it any emergence of itself into a being [*Seiendes*] that is disclosed to it. It is always we who first receive into what is unconcealed such "looking," and from our perspective attribute a looking [*Blicken*] to the way in which animals "look at" us [*uns "ansehen"*]. On the other hand, where humans experience being and what is unconcealed only in a vague manner, the animal "look" can concentrate in itself a special power of encounter. (GA 54, 158–59)

This passage makes a fundamental distinction between the looking of human beings and the "look" that an animal may present to us. "Looking" here is still to be thought in the sense of originary emergence, coming to presence, and not yet as an activity of apprehending or grasping, not yet as a "looking at. . . ." Strictly speaking, animals do not "look" (*blicken*) in the way that humans do. They present a visage, as do all beings, but this presentation is not a *self*-presentation in the way that human looking is. The look of the animal never "brings with it" an emergence *of itself* into an entity that is disclosed to it. It is not an emergence *of itself into itself* in the manner of self-disclosure, of a disclosure that discloses—that brings into unconcealment—its self as such, as being a self, as a being. It is not the kind of human self-disclosure that is a precondition for ethical life, for *bios* over and beyond, or rather, outside of and excentric to *zēn*. Which is another way of saying that the being of the animal, and thus also of its look, is not ec*static:* it does not "stand" or "dwell" outside of itself as an entity that it can relate to *as* the other of/in itself, as the other of itself within itself.[95] And this implies that it cannot relate to what is concealed as being concealed: it has no relation of being to concealment; it does not stand or dwell within concealment itself, and thus, as Heidegger later puts it, "is excluded from the essential realm of the strife between unconcealment and concealment" (GA 54, 237). The human being, by contrast—the presencing of the human body—is extraordinary in being an emergence of itself into itself as a being that is disclosed to it. It is the emergence of a body that would otherwise be concealed from itself as such into un-concealment. In this emergence into an entity, a being—the manifest self—that is disclosed to it, human presencing becomes something other, outside of itself, ecstatic. Yet this going outside of itself, this emergence into exteriority, is not, on Heidegger's account, an entry into what is commonly understood as interiority, but—paradoxically enough—an entering into, and coming to dwell within concealment itself. But not self-concealment.

How does this exceptional emergence manifest itself in the human face, in human looking? Human looking, in the originary sense of emergence, is always an attending in the sense indicated. It is a tarrying in the face of that which is yet to come, of that which has announced itself in already having withdrawn, of that which, in the trait (*Zug*) of this withdrawal (*Entzug*), thus continues to promise and to hold promise: *das Ungeheure.* Human looking, as emergent presencing, thus bears this trait: It is intrinsically and always already monstrative, "daimonic," a showing and pointing. Unlike the presencing of the animal, which displays an exceptional self-sufficiency or self-containedness (thus also an exceptional "unconcernedness" with the

---

[95] We pursue this thesis in greater detail with respect to Heidegger's earlier work in "Life Beyond the Organism: Animal Being in Heidegger's Freiburg Lectures, 1929–30," in *Animal Others,* ed. H. Peter Steeves (Albany: State University of New York Press, forthcoming).

ways of being and of the world that concern us), the human presencing shows—in its very temporality—an exceptional unrest: it shows itself as that which has always yet to come, always yet to happen. It already dwells in such a way as to have being (being in the world, in the realm of ethico-political existence) as its task, as its "to be." The originary emergence, the coming and approach of human looking, has the task of both disclosing and concealing: in disclosing itself as a being, it points to its own dwelling in concealment, to the locale of its dwelling as a concealment that is radically open, undecided, always held open as long as we continue to be. The human being attends the presencing of things, of beings as a whole, in such a way as to accompany them in their presencing, to let them be, to let them come to presence. Human looking sees that which is unconcealed precisely as *un-concealed,* as that which has to be revealed or sheltered in its concealment, kept and maintained there. It dwells in the possibility of disclosing or concealing, in the possibility of language, but can do so only because it can relate to, that is, let presence, that which is concealed as such, as concealed. Human dwelling in concealment is the tarrying of an enduring responsiveness to the approach of language, to the promise, an awaiting of the imminent withdrawal of the word.

On the basis of these reflections, we can better understand the initial description of the look of the human being as a self-showing in and into which their entire being has "gathered itself," as a "collectedness" of their existence (GA 54, 153). This having been gathered is the coming to presence of language itself (which is not to be understood here primarily or exclusively as enunciation), of *logos,* the looking that has been gathered into presencing in advance in bearing the trait of that which withdraws, of that which thus presences in its withdrawal in the manner of a showing, a pointing in the direction of absence: in the direction not merely of that which is not already and not yet present as such but concealed, but primarily toward concealment itself as such. The latter appears in the emergence of the look as the presencing of the divine, the extraordinary; it "looks from out of the figure of the 'human being' [i.e., of the being who is thus not "merely" human], the figure that is gathered in the look [of the divine]" (GA 54, 161). The human being is a being that has already been gathered into presencing in being gathered into the self as disclosed, as un-concealed, in relating to this very concealment or finitude by way of language, by allowing it to presence in language. The letting-presence, the letting come to presence of that which is otherwise concealed that occurs in and through language means that the "daimonic," *das Ungeheure,* the extraordinary and the divine *gathers itself* in and through human looking. It does not first need to be gathered (*legein, logos*), that is, to be explicitly gathered into presencing for human beings, for oneself and for others; it does not first need to be interpreted or "layed out" (*ausgelegt*), made visible for others, in order for it to presence. The "daimonic" presencing of this entity called the human being presences, rather, of its own accord wherever human beings already exist. But precisely this is not the case with the work of art (not even with the "great" work of art), which *needs* preservation, the act of *Bewahrung,* in order to be what it most properly is, to let it be, to let it come into its own being. Prior to being gathered into such preservation, its being lies in dispersion, in a play of unconcealment in which concealment dominates. And this is indeed the case with every other entity apart from the human being: the stone, the animal, every other being is in need, and calls for, our response in order to let them be, that is, to protect (*hüten*) them in first letting them be seen in their own proper concealment (their own resting in themselves) in each singular case.

Thus, Heidegger argues, "It is first and only in the word, as a revealing, that the look emerges into what is unconcealed." The look here refers to the look that any being presents. But, "The look [*Anblick*] itself looks and is the self-showing appearing that it is only within the realm of revealing that is the word, a telling apprehending" (GA 54, 169). And so too a statue of Apollo or a Greek temple could not look at us in their divine epiphany without the word; these "works" "only *are*" in the "medium of the word":

> The statue and temple stand in silent dialogue with the human being in the realm of the unconcealed. Were there not the *silent word,* then the god that looks as the look of the statue and of the traits of its figure could never appear; without standing in the disclosive domain of the word, the temple could never stand there as the house of the god. (GA 54, 172–73)

"The word" is not to be understood here as enunciation, or as the communicative exchange of information. Indeed, in itself it is not even, or not yet, something human. For even the "silent word"—which does not refer to the absence of speaking, or even of human thinking or philosophizing, but to the word in its keeping (something) silent, preserving in silence— even the silent word remains a call: the call of things themselves as they beckon us. The *daimonion,* as the claim of the divine (*theion*), appears and shows itself as looking only through the originary element of the word, the originary saying of "myth" (*muthos*). For "myth" makes manifest that which is astonishing, wondrous, that which in its appearing exceeds human comprehension even as it claims it, pointing humans toward it as a supreme phenomenon of being. The appearing of the daimonic indicates our relation to being, to being in its ultimate manifestations, to the being of beings as a whole. And this, Heidegger suggests, is why the original sense of *daimonion* still resonates in the Platonic-Aristotelian usage of *eudaimonia:* the originary sense of "the *eu* that prevails in the appropriate measure—the appearing and presencing of the *daimonion*" becomes transformed into "a mere quality of the human soul." The *daimonion* in the originary sense, by contrast, has nothing to do with the interiority of a "spirit" or "mind"; the Socratic way of discussing the daimon as an "inner voice" may be read, rather, as indicating that the daimonic here appears not from an entity that is already present before us, but from the invisibility of being (GA 54, 173–74). The Platonic-Aristotelian appropriation of philosophy, in interpreting this invisibility as something that is, something already there waiting to be discovered by the right vision and the appropriate *logos,* grants the seeing of the right measure only to a *theōria* turned away from the sensuous, toward the nonsensuous. And this demands that one undertake a search, that one investigate (*zētein*).

Prior to this turning, this transformation of being itself, the Greek human being is not yet governed by this more active desire for knowledge, this more active desire to see. He is the one who "apprehends beings," as "The Age of the World Picture" already expressed it: the one who, looked upon by beings that open themselves to him, has the task of fulfilling his being by "gathering (*legein*) and saving (*sōzein*), receiving and preserving in its openness that which opens itself, in remaining exposed (*alētheuein*) to all its sundering confusions" (H, 83–84).[96] Such apprehending, over and beyond the originary looking of self-emergence, is certainly also an activity. But the apprehending look that "takes hold" of (*erfasst*) beings is, Heidegger suggests, primarily determined by the originary look of self-disclosure, the look of another being that we encounter. It too is a primarily responsive activity. It is expressed in the medial form of the verb *theaō,* namely, *theaomai:* "letting the look one encounters come toward oneself, that is, catching sight of it [*erblicken*]" (GA 54, 159). Letting the look one encounters come toward oneself in this manner, thus to tarry in its presencing—this look of encounter, Heidegger emphasizes, is a kind of seeing with which we are still familiar today, just as the Greeks too are not purely passive beings, but also actively look in this manner of taking hold of and grasping things—which kind of grasping, of course, is thoroughly different from, and yet related to, the grasping look of modern science.

The apprehending look of encounter is expressed not only in the medial *theaomai,* however, but—Heidegger recalls—also in the early sense of *theōria:*

> The look [*Anblick*] of being that looks into beings is in Greek called *thea.* The looking that grasps in the sense of seeing is in

---

[96] Cf. GA 54, 160. On "The Age of the World Picture," see part 2 above.

Greek *horan*. To catch sight of the encountering look, in Greek, *thean – horan*, is *theoran – theōrein, theōria*. (GA 54, 219)

Accordingly, "theory" refers to the "relation of human apprehending to being, a relation that human beings do not produce or set forth, but into which the human essence is placed by being itself." "Of course," Heidegger remarks, "when later ages and especially we of today say 'theory' and 'theoretical,' everything primordial has been forgotten" (GA 54, 219). In *theōria*, the Greeks experienced directly, and not first by way of some "practical" utility or applicability, "an essential relation to the *theaontes* and to the *theion* and to the *daimonion*," a relation not yet removed from "the look of being" (GA 54, 219–20).

Because being itself demands to be thought as un-concealment, in Greek, as *a-lētheia*, the site of concealment (*lēthē*) is an exceptional locale where *das Un-geheure*, the extra-ordinary, presences in its "daimonic" power. Concealment itself, as the locale from which beings emerge into presencing and to which they return, is a *daimonias topos,* a daimonic site, an "extraordinary locality" (GA 54, 174). And because language, in its originary gathering and saying, does not grasp (in the "concept") that which conceals itself in showing itself, but can only point toward it, the *muthos*, according to Heidegger, is "the sole appropriate kind of relation to being in its appearing" (GA 54, 166). For in *muthos* "the *daimonion* appears" (GA 54, 173).[97] The philosopher cares for the appropriate measure of things, he has "an eye for the essential," as Heidegger here translates the pre-Aristotelian sense of *phronēsis* in Plato's myth.[98] The myth of the plain of *lēthē*, the last *daimonias topos* at which the travelers arrive at the end of Plato's *Republic* before beginning a new death-bound journey on Earth, points to *lēthē* as an exceptional *topos,* an exceptional site or locale (*Ort*). Not because *lēthē* is sheer concealment, but because:

> The "awayness" of what has withdrawn itself presences in the essential prevailing [*Wesen*] of withdrawal.... The site remains empty.... The emptiness of the site is the look that looks into and "fulfils" it. (GA 54, 176)

The emptiness of the site *is* the look: Singular look, of the *Augenblick* of world, no doubt, in which, via the detour of radiant presencing, desire is at once fulfilled and displaced, to return, eternally, in our visions of others....

---

[97] Indeed, Aristotle himself recalls that the *philomuthos* is in a sense a *philosophos,* "since myths are composed of wonders [*thaumasiōn*]" (M, 982 b19).

[98] On the pre-philosophical and tragic origins of *phronēsis*, see Pierre Aubenque, *La prudence chez Aristote*, part 3 (153ff.). Heidegger discusses tragic knowledge as a *phronein* most incisively in his 1942 interpretation of *Antigone*. See GA 53, part 2, especially 130ff.

Absence of the Body

Among those beings who presence amid the sensuous in the manner of the
human look, there are some whose powers of vision are nevertheless exceptional, whose eye is drawn not merely to the enigmatic presencing of
other beings, but toward this empty site of withdrawal, toward the concealments of destiny at work in that very presencing. They are seers and
prophets, ancient precursors of the philosophers whose distant offspring is
the modern scientist. In foreseeing and foretelling the future, these ancient
visionaries play a pivotal ethical and political role within a community,
providing directives for leadership and action. Prophetic vision of this kind
is of course documented much earlier than the philosophical turn that the
vision necessary for leadership was to take in Plato and Aristotle, the turn
whereby *theōria* claimed to discover "true being" as something already existing behind appearances and events themselves. The word *theōria* and its
cognates are not found in Homer (the first recorded example appearing in
Theognis, as we mentioned); yet just as Presocratic senses of the divine and
daimonic continue to resonate in the philosophical connotations of *theōria*
and *to theion*, of *daimonion* and of *eudaimonia*, so too a transformation of
the claims of prophetic vision belonging to the Homeric world is unmistake-
ably present in the philosophical appropriation of seeing. Something of the
prophetic and visionary sense of *eidō* as documented in Homer continues
to speak in the *eidenai* pursued by philosophy and science in the direction
of an increasingly withdrawn and monotheistic *theōrein*. But what kind of
future is foreseen in ancient prophecy? And what is its relation to the seer
himself? We have already noted how the sense of "future" opened up by
the modern scientific Cartesian turn, with its philosophical and theological
roots, becomes not only increasingly monotheistic, one-worldly, a movement
that attains its consummation in the modern, technological appropriation
of science; it also becomes increasingly *nonworldly,* ever more withdrawn
from the claims of ethico-political singularity and immediacy. Absolute self-
mediation has arrived; the future is now and henceforth always will have
been now: in this sense Hegel's vision was indeed prophetic.

In his 1946 essay "The Anaximander Fragment," Heidegger, seeking
to understand the meaning of the Greek *ta eonta* (beings), undertakes a
digression into Homer. He turns specifically to lines 68–72 of Book I of the
Iliad, where Achilles calls upon Kalchas the seer to interpret the cause of
the pestilence that rages amid the Achaeans. Citing these lines, Heidegger
comments:

> Before he lets Kalchas speak, Homer designates him as the seer.
> Whoever belongs in the realm of seers is such a one *hos ēidē* . . .

"who knew . . .": *ēidē* is the pluperfect of the perfect *oiden,* he
has seen. Only when someone has seen does he truly see. To see
is to have seen [*Sehen ist Gesehenhaben*]. Whatever is seen has
arrived and remains in sight for him. A seer has always already
seen. Having seen in advance, he sees ahead. He sees the future
from out of the perfect. When the poet narrates the seer's seeing
as a having seen, he must tell in the pluperfect tense of the fact
that the seer saw: *ēidē,* he had seen. What is it that the seer has
come to see in advance? Manifestly, only that which comes to
presence in the clearing [*im Lichten*] that his vision traverses.
What is seen in such seeing can only be that which is present
in the realm that is unconcealed. Yet what is present? The poet
names something threefold: *ta t'eonta,* that which is in being
[*das Seiende*], *ta t'essomena,* also that which is coming to be
[*das Seiend-Werdende*], *pro t'eonta,* and also that which once
was [*das vormals Seiende*]. (H, 318–19)

The pluperfect *ēidē* and the perfect *oiden* come from the verb *eidō,* to
see. Having seen in advance, the seer sees ahead. At first glance, the seer's
vision may seem no different, at least in its formal structure, from the
philosophical seeing instituted by Platonic-Aristotelian thought: having-
seen the *eidos* determines in advance what can come to presence. Of course,
Aristotle's insight (itself a *philosophical* insight) into practical vision shows
that the prior determination of being as *eidos* precisely breaks down, or can
at most be an indirect and always fragile guideline, in the realm of ethico-
political existence. In *phronēsis,* what one has always already foreseen in the
Augenblick of practical vision is the presence of an ongoing concealing happening here and now, the possibility of the present in which I am involved
becoming other at any moment, thus calling for an appropriate response. In
phronēsis one has already foreseen and anticipated the concealment at work
not only in the presence of other human beings (in political or communal
life), but in the presencing of all beings (in philosophico-ethical existence).
How does the Homeric vision of Kalchas the seer compare to these philosophical interpretations of seeing?

Heidegger's first point in explicating this passage is to show that *ta
eonta* refers to that which presences and is present (*das Anwesende*) in a
broad sense which, as the context indicates, is not restricted to that which
is immediately present during the immediate "while" within the open region of unconcealment. *Ta eonta,* that which is present, means that which
can be encountered as coming to presence within this open region. It does
not simply mean that which is present immediately or "now," but refers
also to "the past" and "the future," that is, to the presence of that which

is not immediately present, but rather present in its absence. Yet whatever is absent in this way is (presences) *as* absent only insofar as it can arrive, and can announce its arrival, within the open region where all presencing occurs. In its presencing, it is thus essentially related to and drawn into that which is presently present within this region (*das gegenwärtig Anwesende*). The *gegen* in *gegenwärtig*, Heidegger elucidates, should here be taken to mean not the oppositionality of an object or *Gegenstand* as standing over and against a subject; rather, what is presently present approaches and is encountered in a site where there is no "subject" (in the modern sense), namely, in the open region or *Gegend* where it comes to presence in lingering for a while (*Weile*). Such presencing is to be thought in the Presocratic sense of *para*, which names the being-alongside of whatever appears in unconcealment and can thus be accompanied for a while: "What is presently present the Greeks also named more precisely *ta pareonta; para* meaning 'alongside' [*bei*], namely having come alongside into unconcealment" (H, 319).[99] Having thus come to presence for a while in the open region of unconcealment is, Heidegger remarks, "authentic arrival, the presencing of what is authentically present" (H, 320).

Heidegger points out that these reflections show how *ta eonta* has an ambiguous meaning for the Greeks, encompassing both that which is presently present, and that which can come to presence from beyond the field of what is presently present. Thus, the meaning of *ta eonta* is explicitly situated in Homer's text in relation to *ta t'essomena* and *pro t'eonta,* to that which is coming to be and that which once was. "The Anaximander Fragment" is in large measure a meditation on this very ambiguity of *ta eonta* and its consequences in the subsequent history of being, although we shall not have the occasion to pursue this here. We shall confine our remarks to just

---

[99] Cf. the important discussion of the Presocratic sense of *para* in *Was heißt Denken?* (WD, 143–45). Discussing the sense of Parmenides' *eon emmenai,* Heidegger translates the meaning of *para*—which, he claims, is implicitly heard in the Presocratic word for being, *einai*—as *herbei:* coming closer, approaching or coming alongside. Coming to presence, enduring (*wesen, währen*) bears a trait that is sometimes explicitly named by the *para:* "to come close by, to presence close by in strife with absencing [*her-bei-,* ... *an-wesen im Streit mit dem ab-wesen*]." The *bei* that helps to translate the *para* here means, Heidegger indicates, "nearness in the sense of a shining into unconcealment, a shining from out of unconcealment." This sense of *para* belongs to those traits of presencing from out of which the Greeks thought that which is present or presences (*das Anwesende*), traits which include "lingering [*die Weile*], gathering, shining, restfulness, the concealed suddenness of possible absencing." And yet, Heidegger remarks, the Greeks never gave thought to these traits themselves, never came to question presencing as such. And this implies that they never came to question the meaning of the *para,* which under the influence of Plato and Aristotle acquired the sense of *Vorhandenheit,* of presence-at-hand, commensurate with the "technical" interpretation of thinking. The *para* in *parousia* was implicitly understood as the alongsideness of the *ergon,* the presence-at-hand of the "work" brought forth via *technē.* Cf. NE, Book VI, and part 1 of the present study.

a few pages of the essay. In the present context, our interest concerns the seer's relation to what he sees and the nature of his prophetic vision. Following these comments on the meaning of *ta eonta*, Heidegger turns his attention from what is and has been seen by Kalchas to consider the kind of seeing that the Homeric seer embodies. Kalchas' visionary power, Heidegger relates, is a kind of *mania:*

> The seer stands in sight of what is present, stands in its uncon-cealment, which has at the same time cleared the concealment of what is absent as that which is absent. The seer sees inas-much as he has seen everything as present; *kai,* and only on that account, *nēess' hēgēsat',* was he able to lead the Achaeans' ships to Troy. He was able to do this through his God-given *mantosunē.* The seer, *ho mantis,* is the *mainomenos,* he is manic [*der Rasende*]. But in what does the essence of mania consist? The one who is manic is beside himself, outside himself [*außer sich*]. He is away. Away? Where to and where from? Away from the pressing nature of whatever merely lies before him, of what is merely presently present, away to what is absent and thereby away at the same time to what is presently present, insofar as the latter is only ever the arrival of something that is going away. The seer is outside himself in reaching into the unitary expanse of the presencing of that which presences in whatever way. This is why he can at the same time return from his reach-ing "away" into this expanse and come back to what has just presented itself as the raging pestilence. The mania of the seer's being away does not consist in the one who is manic raving, rolling his eyes, or tossing his limbs. Visionary mania can go to-gether with an inconspicuous tranquillity of bodily composure [*der unscheinbaren Ruhe der leiblichen Sammlung*]. (H, 320–21)

The seer stands within the clearing of presencing and absencing, the clear-ing of un-concealment. Such clearing is itself an event, and not simply or primarily an already given site. The seer stands within this event of the coming into presence of that which presents itself and of its passing away into concealment. Yet this stance of the seer, as Heidegger describes it, is a being-outside-himself, a standing outside himself, an ec-stasis. Such ecstasis does not, however, mean that the seer abandons his embodiment; and yet, his ecstasis is manifest in the most inconspicuous way, for it does not at all entail what are commonly regarded as the signs of an "ecstatic experience." What Heidegger describes, rather, is an ecstasis of embodied existence, an ecstasis that, as a seizure and rapture of the body, can accompany and go together with the tranquillity of the seer's bodily composure. The seer is an embodied being, and as such is someone present, someone who "in an exceptional sense belongs to the entirety of that which presences" (H, 323). His embodiment is present and presents itself to others, but it is not merely present as a body *within* the field of presence accessible to others. The body of the seer is outside itself, away, held into and within an ecstasis that transports it away from all that presses around it and presses in upon it. It departs from all this, departs from all that is presently present around it (including its own presencing), and is transported "away," toward what is absent—and yet, in having thus departed from the already constituted field of sensuous presencing round about it, the embodied seer is *also*, as Heidegger puts it, "thereby away at the same time to what is presently present, insofar as the latter is only ever the arrival of something that is going away." The seer's ecstatic departure from the scene of presence is not an abandonment of presence, but precisely an event that first opens up an access to presence as such, to the presence of whatever can be present in the broad sense of *ta eonta.*

Yet the bodily presencing of the seer not only departs from the unified scene of all presencing: it has *already* departed from the field of presence. The seer is able to see what is presently present around him only insofar as he has already departed from the field of presence, so as to be able to return to there in the rapture of his *mania.* He is also thereby removed in advance, always already, from every possible constituted or determinate presence, also from that which can become present as absent: the past and the future insofar as they can appear and come to presence. This removal, this transport, is indeed the precondition for his seeing.

In what way does Kalchas see? In his rapt transport, the seer is altogether away, outside himself, "absent." He is one already gone: "The seer is outside himself in reaching into the unitary expanse of the presencing of that which presences in whatever way." And only because he is already gone, "away," can he come back to what presents itself around him and see it as the raging plague, sent as it is from the wrath of Apollo. Yet this return of the seer is not a factical return, nor an abandonment of the "unitary expanse" into which his being is transported. He does not at all abandon his "awayness," his departedness, his *mania.* On the contrary: he is *held* there, he sees always *from* there, and must remain in that site in order to be able to see as he does. Such removal—a removal from presence into concealment—is indeed a precondition for all seeing of something as present (in the broad sense of *ta eonta* elucidated), for it first *lets* that which is un-concealed come to presence as present, as unconcealed. It first enables human beings to be those who are affected by *presence* as such (and not merely by that which is present). But the seer is a seer, that is, somebody who sees in an exceptional manner, because he is able to let himself—his own bodily presencing—be collected explicitly into that site, into the site of concealing as the clearing of un-concealment, the site from which he is first granted his visionary power. He has an exceptional insight into the event of presencing as such.

Heidegger's analysis of the ecstatic being of Kalchas the seer in "The Anaximander Fragment" at once recalls and invites comparison with the ecstatic-temporal analyses of the being of Dasein in *Being and Time* and in the Marburg and early Freiburg lecture courses. In his being, Kalchas is "outside himself" in standing outside the presencing of what is present as such. His being is futural in the sense of being already transported away from ... that which is already present in such a manner as to be able to come back to ... the presence of what presents itself, back to such presence as the presence of that which has already been, and thereby to be able to "be" (dwell) alongside or with (*bei*), in the presence of ... that which is present.[100] His removal is an *Ent-rückung,* a being transported into the unitary "expanse" (*Weite*) in terms of which Heidegger had earlier characterized the open "horizon" of ecstatic temporality, the open and unitary expanse of "world," of beings as a whole in their presencing.[101] And such removal is itself at the same time a return to being affected by the presencing of that which thus presents itself, a movement of what Heidegger elsewhere calls *Be-rückung,* a being enraptured.[102] The ecstasis of the seer is none other than that of the temporality of the *Augenblick* as that "look" in which Dasein was earlier said to be held open for the happening of a world, the look of "resolute openness" that first opens and holds open the horizon of ecstatic presence for that which can become "bodily [*leibhaftig*] present," as *Being and Time* expressed it.[103] As such, the resolute openness (*Entschlossenheit*) of the *Augenblick* implies precisely a gathering of one's being in the unitary direction of what is coming to presence, a gathering and opening up of one's being in the direction of world. In the ecstasis of vision whose temporality is held in the manner of the *Augenblick,* as a being held open for the presence of the world, one's bodily being is gathered into "an inconspicuous tranquillity of bodily composure." Such tranquillity and gathering presumably prevails in the very midst of human presencing, as the *stasis* of the *Augenblick* itself, for the most part in a concealed

[100] In relation to the structural moments of "away from ... ," "back to ... ," and "in the presence of ... ," cf. Heidegger's discussion of the ecstatic structure of temporality in *Being and Time* (SZ, 328–29).

[101] On the notion of horizon as an open expanse (*offene Weite*), see especially the analyses of horizonal temporality in GA 26 and GA 29/30.

[102] See the *Beiträge zur Philosophie* (GA 65); also NI, "The Will to Power as Art."

[103] This reference in *Being and Time* to what can be "bodily" present is also an implicit critique of Husserl's conception of *Leibhaftigkeit.* See GA 25 for the broader context.

manner that rarely shines, and is seldom seen as such. As a temporalizing, the *Augenblick,* Heidegger had noted in the *Beiträge zur Philosophie,* "itself prevails only as the gathering of the moments of ecstatic transport [*als die Sammlung der Entrückungen*]" in the opening direction of the future, of decision. But equally, the *Augenblick* is itself held within the "embrace" (*Umhalt*) of an originary enrapture (*Berückung*) that lingers with and gives space to that which has already been opened (GA 65, 384).

Heidegger's discussion of the Homeric seer not only maintains a continuity with the earlier analyses of ecstatic temporality, however; it also moves beyond those analyses in thinking the event of presencing differently in a decisive respect. For, as we noted in the context of our reading of "The Origin of the Work of Art," the finitude that was earlier conceived in terms of Dasein's being-toward-death, and that could be appropriated as such, as finitude, in a movement of anticipation (*Vorlaufen*), is in the later thinking of *Ereignis* no longer conceived as potentially Dasein's own. It is seen, rather, as belonging to the event of presencing itself, as a finitude of world in its "strife" with Earth. Visionary anticipation anticipates, therefore, one's belonging to a finitude that will not have been one's own, a finitude that from the perspective of one's own presence can be seen rather as disappropriation: as a finitude that occurs, beyond calculation or appropriation, in the destinal turnings of presencing itself. The finitude of one's own presencing occurs only in a responsive belonging to the finite presencing of other beings as a whole. This responsive belonging is what, in "The Origin of the Work of Art," was traced as the poietic strife of world and Earth, as the poietic-linguistic delineation of presence that occurs as the event of the work of art.

How does "The Anaximander Fragment" think the event of presencing in relation to the seer's seeing? The seer is transported into the unitary expanse where he dwells in seeing the presencing of all things. But this expanse itself, as a finite opening of and for presencing, is itself neither something present, nor the presence of what is present. It is the prevailing of an absence in which the seer is held, held precisely insofar as he is called back into presence by the presencing of those beings from which he has always already departed. He first comes into presence, first presences in his own being, in coming toward and responding to that which presences round about, presences in its very withdrawal, in its unfathomable and multiple concealments. His absence, his departedness, is his very belonging. Unlike other human beings, the seer is turned away from that which merely presences in presenting itself before him. He is turned toward an absence, toward the presencing of a concealment at work in the abyssal grounds of all presencing. Transported into the clearing as a clearing of concealment (*lēthē*), as a clearing of self-concealing presencing, the seer can see that what is presently present is only ever "that which arrives of something that is going away." Presencing for a while is a going, a passing from concealment into unconcealment and back into concealment, a passing in which whatever presences lingers for a while in coming to the fore and passing away; it is a transition or "going over" from arrival to passing away (H, 322–23). Yet the coming and going of this or that presence, thought only in terms of such presence, does not constitute the passage itself, the *poros* in which this coming and going passes. The passage itself occurs as the sheltering and preserving work of concealing, of *lēthē*—of the concealing in un-concealing.

Heidegger emphasizes the unified nature of the gathering that explicitly comes to the fore in the seer's vision: "For the seer, all things that come to be present or absent are gathered into *one* presencing, and are preserved [*gewahrt*] there" (H, 321). The body of the seer too, as manifest, as something that presences, is gathered into this one site of presencing, as is all that presences. All that presences or can presence is gathered into the site of the seer's vision, in a gathering or coming together that first lets all things present accompany one another: "When that which presences stands in view in advance, then everything presences together, one thing brings another with it, one thing lets the other go" (H, 322). A *bringing-with* and a *letting-go* characterize the relationality between manifest beings themselves, thought from out of their being gathered into a singular site, their entering into world. And yet this belonging together of events in their presencing can no more be calculated in the end than can the actions of another human being. One thing brings another with it, one thing lets the other go; but whence these events emerge, to where they return, no one has seen.

We can now perhaps characterize more appropriately the nature of Kalchas' seeing. Transported into the raptures of time, Kalchas thus sees in and from out of this removal, this awayness, this ecstatic transport. The Homeric seer, himself an exceptional being, is called upon in exceptional circumstances. He is called upon to communicate an ethical directive to his community, whose world is threatened and brought back to its proximity to the Earth by the concealed yet manifest presence of the plague at work in the community. In his god-given *mantosunē*, his task is to divine and foretell what should be done, on the basis of what he has foreseen. The seer's having-seen in advance, on the basis of which he sees ahead, does not therefore have the character of an "ontic" prediction or prophecy. It is not an attempt to predict—let alone to control and order—what will be on the basis of having seen what now is. Prophetic vision is thus not a having seen the truth of beings (as in the philosophical seeing of the *eidos*); yet nor is it a philosophically informed seeing of oneself as an origin of *praxis* (although the seer also sees himself as implicated in the worldly presencing of that which presences round about him). What Kalchas has seen, rather, as Heidegger's analysis clarifies, is the belonging together and mutual implication of all beings in their coming to presence and in their withdrawal (H, 323). The seer must have seen precisely this finitude of presencing as such, this finitude of events, this finitude that is a happening of concealment and absence. What he sees and has seen is not a truth of beings, of that which now is, but a truth of *events*, a truth of presencing—of the presencing of events that are not primarily within human control, but to which human beings can and must respond. Kalchas' task of divining the why and wherefore (*heneka*) of the plague,[104] as an event that affects this particular community at this particular time, is thus quite unlike the scientific-"technical" foreseeing (*theōrein*) of the ground that will be binding for the presencing of something in its infinite repeatability. His seeing is in this respect closer to the kind of seeing found in *phronēsis,* and yet it is not attuned in advance to a horizon of presence discerned in a philosophical *theōrein,* but to the withdrawal already at work in all presence and presencing. He sees and reads the signs of the divine, communicating them to others, in a manner more akin to the role of the *theōros* who consults an oracle. Kalchas' prophetic seeing and soothsaying, because they attend to the *unforeseeable* turnings of events themselves—that is, to that which necessarily withdraws in the presencing of events and in the event of presencing—do not foresee or foretell what will be, and thus are necessarily equivocal. As Michael Naas expresses it in his inspired study of the *Iliad,* the soothsayer is always already turned toward the turnings of events themselves; thus turned toward the turnings of time, seeing both forward and backward, "the prophet sees only because he is already half-dead." "Prophecy takes place at the limits of life," and so the seer's communication plies itself in advance to the turnings of time, he "foretells what *will have been* on the basis of what *is.*" He lets what is and has been follow the turning of language itself, always already turned toward the future, toward a turning beyond calculation, an incalculable turning of destiny or twist of fate.[105]

"The Anaximander Fragment" recalls not only the analyses of ecstasis from *Being and Time.* It also reinvokes and extends a number of themes from "The Origin of the Work of Art," and indeed from other essays too. In particular, it takes up again the conceptions of preservation (*Bewahrung*), of an in-standing (*Inständigkeit*) within the clearing, and of resolute openness (*Ent-schlossenheit*) in hinting how they may be thought in relation to human seeing. Heidegger writes:

---

[104] *Iliad,* 1.110.
[105] See Michael Naas, *Turning: From Persuasion to Philosophy* (New Jersey: Humanities Press, 1995), 53–61.

The seer is the one who has already seen the totality of that which presences in its presencing. Said in Latin, *vidit;* in German, *er steht im Wissen* [he stands in knowing]. Having seen is the essence of knowing. In having seen there is always something else at play other than the completion of an optical process. In having seen, our relation to that which presences has gone back behind every kind of sensuous or nonsensuous grasping. From there, having-seen is drawn to self-clearing presencing. Seeing is not determined by the eye, but from out of the clearing of being. Standing [*Inständigkeit*] in this clearing is the configuration [*Gefüge*] of all human senses. The essence of seeing as having seen is knowing. Such knowing retains vision. It remains mindful [*eingedenk*] of presencing. Knowing is the thoughtful memory [*Gedächtnis*] of being. This is why *Mnēmosunē* is the mother of the muses. Knowledge is not science [*Wissenschaft*] in the modern sense. Knowledge is the thoughtful maintaining of being's preserve. (H, 321–22)

Originary knowing as a having-seen is a preservation of being, of the presencing of beings in their togetherness, in their belonging together in a worldly and historical context. The seer who, as a human being, reaches into the divine, apprehending the concealments of presencing, interprets the hidden forces concealed in and borne by events themselves. In his ecstatic transport, he dwells in and tends to the intrinsic concealments of events as they unfold before him. He himself has already been gathered into the unitary expanse of all presencing, into the poietic happening of timespace in which concealment itself is at work. He has learnt the art of letting himself be expressly transported into such dwelling, there to preserve the presencing of beings in tending to their concealments. Thus Heidegger recalls that the word *wahr*—the root present in *Bewahren* (preservation), but also in *Wahrheit* (truth) and *Wahrnehmen* (in modernity usually translated as "perception," but, Heidegger suggests, having the more originary sense of "taking into preservation": *in die Wahr nehmen*)—comes from the Old High German *war,* implying protection (*Hut*). The verb *wahren* suggests a "sheltering that clears in gathering." "Truth," in the originary sense of the un-concealment of being, may thus be thought as the "preserve" (*Wahrnis*) of being as presencing. The seer tends to this preserve, and thus to the presencing of that which presences, the latter encompassing that which is presently present, that which once was, and that which is yet to come. Drawn into this preserve—into the concealing sheltering in un-concealment—from out of which he sees and has seen the presencing of that which presences, the seer's telling and prophecying is attuned from there. His telling is thus itself ambiguous; it tells in making manifest that which simultaneously conceals itself, in saying the turning of events in which concealment is at work. "From out of the preserve [*Wahr*] of that which presences the seer speaks [*sagt*]. He is the sooth-sayer [*Wahr-sager*]" (H, 321). But his speaking or saying, his telling and foretelling, based on the turn that events seem to be taking in their unfolding, in their coming to pass, itself only "responds" (*entspricht*) to this preserve of presencing, to the gathering of concealment that points the direction in which events seem to be turning. Kalchas is the "shepherd" or custodian of presencing; yet he is this only insofar as he "holds the place of nothing," recalls Heidegger, using a phrase from the 1929 lecture "What is Metaphysics?" The seer is held out into the "nothing," he holds the place of nothing, insofar as his being—his bodily presencing—is itself gathered into and held by the site of concealment itself as a concealing at work in the presencing of all beings as they accompany one another in their coming and going. And this, Heidegger adds, is possible for the human being only within a resolute openness, "only within the resolute un-closedness [*Ent-schlossenheit*] of Da-sein" (H, 321). It is possible only within an opening onto concealment that is an emergent gathering of one's own being into presencing in response to the self-concealing presencing of a world that always already calls upon us. Beings as a whole "slip away" (to use an expression from the 1929 lecture) in the gathering of their very presencing. What the philosophy of modernity calls the "will," when thought more originarily than as an activity of subjectivity or as a causality, is nothing other than this emergent and responsive self-gathering into presencing: a self-gathering that *preserves* its relation to concealing as such, that can thereby "see itself" as this very finitude of its own presencing, and thus have the possibility of *praxis* in the originary sense.

Standing and assuming a stance within the clearing of presencing can thus be seen as the "configuration" or "jointure" (*Gefüge*) of all human senses insofar as all senses and sensibilities of human beings have always already been drawn in advance toward presence: drawn not only in the sense that they have always already inclined in that direction, but also inasmuch as this leaning is also a kind of delination or figuring, in which the being that is "drawn" in this way is also cast into and takes on a distinct form, a self-limitation and a finitude *in* presencing. With emergence into a world there occurs—not simultaneously, but in response—a drawing back, a being thrust back, *and* a holding oneself or catching oneself, a catching sight of oneself—for a moment or *Augenblick*—in that very withdrawal.[106]

---

[106] On the event of this drawing as the poietic "work" of language in "The Origin of the Work of Art," see Christopher Fynsk, *Heidegger: Thought and Historicity*.

What we apprehend via the senses is always already emergent in a relational context of other beings that also come to presence in the same moment— come to presence precisely in their self-concealing. Our having-seen this emergent presencing of beings as a whole, of world, has already "gone back behind" any kind of sensuous or nonsensuous grasping not only because it is prior to the sensuous/nonsensuous distinction, but insofar as our originary "relation" (*Verhältnis*) to that which presences (a relation of letting-be) has already withdrawn, is already "away," "gone," in such a way as to first let us respond in an active or "grasping" manner to that which presences in its presencing.

If the human being is the one who is and can be affected by presence as such, it is because he or she is in each case a coming to be open for that which is coming to presence, a coming into the openness of one's own being—thus, a coming into one's own presencing—in response to the event-like approach of presencing as the presencing of other beings, of a world. This also implies that the human being is one who, in being, is being affected by absence, indeed so profoundly that one is thereby held by and continues to dwell in the approach and happening of such absence, in what "The Origin of the Work of Art" named "the silent call of the Earth." One is always already called by the presencing of that which withdraws. Yet even though this call may first occur factically *through* or by way of other human beings, it is not on that account reducible to a purely human call. For through such a call, in responding to such a call, one never entirely knows to what or to whom one is responding. Through such a call, one is called into the open (that is, also indeterminate) presencing of a *world,* into an opening for the possible presencing of beings as a whole. One is called in the first instance by the being of beings as a whole, by the opening of a world in its strife with the Earth, and *not yet* by any particular being. For how will one determine the human being, or the call, *as* human, unless other beings have also already been opened and come to presence in their being? Is one not thereby called into an infinite and unfathomable, indeterminable responsibility, into the possibility of an impossible, yet no less binding responsibility?

Visions of Stillness

Toward the end of a long dialogue with Western philosophy, in a lecture entitled "On the Question of Determining the Matter of Thinking" (1965), Heidegger contrasts Plato's thinking of presence in terms of light and the visible with a more originary way of seeing which he once again finds documented in Homer, this time in the *Odyssey:*

THE GLANCE OF THE EYE

Let us think back to Homer, who likewise, almost intuitively, already relates the presencing of that which presences to light. We may recall a scene that marks the homecoming of Odysseus. When Eumaeus has left, Athene appears in the form of a beautiful young woman. The goddess appears to Odysseus. His son Telemachus, however, does not see her, and the poet says: *Ou gar pōs pantessi theoi phainontai enargeis* (*Odyssey*, XVI, 161). "For it is not to all that the gods appear *enargeis*." (BSD, 16)

Enargeis, notes Heidegger, does not simply mean "visible," as it is sometimes translated. *Enargeia* comes from *argos*, meaning "radiant" (*glänzend*); it means a brilliance, a shining, a lighting up, a radiance proceeding from things themselves as they presence. The same word is still used in Plato's *Phaedrus*, alongside *ekphanestaton* and *erasmiōtaton*, to characterize the beautiful as that which is most luminous, that which radiates most brightly (*enargestata*), although the shining of the sensuous has by now been brought into discordance with the *theōrein* of the nonsensible ideas.[107] In being displaced into the nonsensible idea, the true being of the sensible no longer shines of its own accord, but becomes dependent upon human apprehending via the *logos*.[108] By the time of the Romans, the divine radiance of the sensuous that once spoke in *enargeia* has given way to an ascendency of human apprehending. Heidegger indicates the abyss that has opened up in that time:

"For it is not to all that the gods appear *enargeis*." Some translate this word as "visible" [*sichtbar*]. However, *argos* means radiant. That which radiates shines of its own accord. Whatever shines in this way, presences from out of itself. Odysseus and Telemachus see the same woman. But Odysseus apprehends the presencing of the goddess.

The Romans later translated *enargeia*, shining of one's own accord, by *evidentia; evideri* means to become visible. Evidence is thought in terms of human beings as those who do the seeing. *Enargeia*, by contrast, is a characteristic pertaining to things themselves in their presencing. (BSD, 16)[109]

---

[107] *Phaedrus*, 250d. See Heidegger's incisive and nuanced analysis of this in "The Will to Power as Art" (NI). See also our comments in "Traces of Discordance: Heidegger—Nietzsche."

[108] See especially *Introduction to Metaphysics* (EM); also "Plato's Doctrine of Truth" (W, 109–44).

[109] In "The End of Philosophy and the Task of Thinking," discussed briefly below, Heidegger indicates that the translation of *enargeia* into *evidentia* is undertaken by

It is not to all that the gods appear in their radiant presencing. Not all humans see the divine presencing of a beautiful young woman—not even when one and the same woman appears before them—but presumably only those who have a fitting eye for the divine, for the astonishing and the wondrous, for the appearing of the *thaumasta* at a particular moment. Odysseus and Telemachus, as Heidegger reminds us, see the same woman. But Odysseus apprehends the presencing of the goddess. Indeed, according to Homer, not only Odysseus sees the goddess, but "the hounds too," although, having sensed her approach, they do not tarry in her presence, "but with whining slunk in fear to the further side of the farmstead."[110]

An extended and yet unitary trajectory leads from the originary sense of *enargeia* to the "evidence" that, via experimentation and the projection of probabilities, feeds modern science. Yet does not Plato, over and beyond the human apprehending of that which presences as *eidos* or *idea,* think that which enables such presencing, namely, through what is usually read as the "metaphor" of light?[111] The question remains, however, as Heidegger reminds us, of what it is about the Platonic experience of presencing that allows for and even demands this image. The preeminence of the image of light is indicative of a thinking of presence that starts from the visible, from the outward appearance or look (*Aussehen, eidos*) as something present, in order from there to think the ground that enables it. Yet Heidegger's dialogue with the Platonic interpretation of being that dominates Western philosophy has shown that presence as such is not appropriately thought in what is most proper to it when we think it starting from things present and their visibility.[112] Presence as such has no intrinsic or necessary relation to light: "The presence of that which presences, as such [presence], has no relation to light [*Licht*] in the sense of brightness. But presence is referred to what is light [*das Lichte*] in the sense of the clearing [*Lichtung*]" (BSD, 17).

Heidegger elucidates what is meant by *Lichtung* via the well-known example of a clearing in a wood. A clearing in a wood is as it is not on account of the presence of light in the sense of brightness; the clearing persists even in the dark. "Clearing" here means that the wood "can be passed through" at this point, it is *durchgehbar.* The clearing is thus a site

Cicero (SD, 73). See Cicero, *Academicorum* II, 17: quod nihil esset clarius ἐναργείᾳ, ut Graeci: perspicuitatem aut evidentiam nos, si placet, nominemus ["there was nothing clearer than *enargeia,* as the Greeks call it: let us term it perspicuousness or evidentness"].

[110] *Odyssey,* Book XVI, 162–63.

[111] The "metaphoric" reading is of course problematic inasmuch as it presupposes the opening up of the Platonic *chōrismos* between the sensible and the nonsensible, the literal and the metaphoric meaning.

[112] On the Platonic interpretation of visibility or *Sichtsamkeit,* see especially the 1931/32 course on Plato's *Republic* and *Theaetetus* (GA 34).

of passage, a site that one can traverse and pass through, the site of a *poros.* Heidegger insists that *Lichtung,* thought in terms of the issue to be considered, does not mean illumination, even though the root *licht* could be taken to mean "bright, illuminated." For *licht* carries two different senses, in the same way as the English *light,* to which it is related. Heidegger writes:

> The light [*Das Lichte*] in the sense of the bright and the light [*das Lichte*] in the sense of the clearing [*Lichtung*] are different not only with respect to their issue, but in what they say. "To lighten" [*Lichten*] means: to make free, to give to be free, to let be free. "To lighten" belongs to "light" [*leicht*]. To make something light, to alleviate it means: to push aside whatever resists it, to bring it into a realm without resistance, into a free realm. *Den Anker lichten* [To weigh anchor] means: to free it from the bed of the ocean that envelops it and to raise it into the free realm of the water and the air. (BSD, 17)

Whatever is "light" in this sense is that which is free, that which has been made light in the sense of buoyant, that which has overcome resistances, been released and brought into a free realm (*das Freie*), a clearing. Such a clearing marks a site of freedom, it occurs as the site of a passage, a *poros* of materiality and elementality that has already made way, given way—given way to the coming to pass of the presencing of things themselves.[113] It occurs as a site in which all things that presence appear in their buoyancy, in a play of presencing that marks their own proper freedom. Presence, remarks Heidegger, is referred to this clearing as "granting the preserve of a free realm for the presencing and tarrying of that which presences" (BSD, 17).

Is the talk of the "clearing" also merely a "metaphor"? Heidegger's discussion here wards off any attempt to think the clearing starting from light or from the visibility of something visible.[114] If we attend to the matter to be thought, such a "clearing" should not be understood as simply "read off" from the phenomenon of a clearing in the wood. It is not a transference of the image of a clearing in a thicket over onto something else that would also be present. The forest clearing is "something present" in the forest that is itself present. But the clearing as granting the preserve of a free realm for presencing and for the lingering of whatever presences "is neither something present, nor is it a property of presence" (BSD, 17). The clearing of presencing should not be understood, therefore, as an entity or as

---

[113] On the alleged "oblivion" of the elemental in Heidegger, see Luce Irigaray, *L'oubli de l'air* (Paris: Éditions de Minuit, 1983).

[114] On the "metaphoric" in relation to vision, see SG, 86–89.

something that "is," but as the realm or preserve of an event of granting, as a giving and giving-way of presencing in its finitude, as a happening of the originary finitude of temporality and spatiality, of "timing" and "spacing" (BSD, 18).[115]

In a closely parallel text, "The End of Philosophy and the Task of Thinking" (1964) Heidegger again recalls the meaning of the Greek *enargeia* in asking "whether the clearing, the free and open realm, is not that wherein pure space and ecstatic time and everything that comes to presence or absence within them first have their all-gathering, sheltering locale [*Ort*]." All shining forth and all light, including that of the *lumen naturale*, "traverses" (*durchmißt*) this locale, but does not first constitute or create it. The openness of this locale "alone grants any giving or taking, and all evidence, the free realm within which they can reside and must move" (SD, 73). Clearing as such is neither dependent upon, nor to be thought starting from, visibility or light; it is equally a clearing for sound, resonance, and tone, indeed "for all that comes to presence or absence" (SD, 72).

If the clearing that prevails in presence is that which remains unthought in all philosophy—for all metaphysics, including its counterpart positivism "speaks the language of Plato," whose thinking thinks presence starting from the visible self-showing of beings in their *eidos*—Heidegger nevertheless hears it named at the beginning of philosophy, in Fragment I of Parmenides which, albeit unheard, "continues to speak today in the sciences into which philosophy dissolves":

> ... *chreō de se panta puthesthai*
> *ēmen Alētheiēs eukukleos atremes ētor*
> *ēde brotōn doxas, tais ouk eni pistis alēthēs.*

> ... you, however, are to experience everything:
> both the untrembling heart of well-rounded unconcealment,
> and the opining of mortals too, which lacks the ability to trust
> in what is unconcealed.[116]

What could be meant, Heidegger asks, by the "untrembling heart" (*atremes ētor*) of unconcealment? Thought in terms of the matter of thinking, it must refer to unconcealment itself in what is most proper to it:

---

[115] "Giving-way" should here be understood in the double sense of opening up a way or path, and of a concealing that comes to pass in such opening, as when the presence of one thing "gives way" to or is superceded by the presence of another. Cf. Heidegger's discussion of *Bewëgung* and *Weg* in the 1959 essay "The Way to Language" (US, 239ff.).

[116] Parmenides, Fragment I, ll.28ff. Cited at SD, 74. Note Heidegger's subsequent correction of the misleading implication that Parmenides himself might have heard what Heidegger hears, that is, that he might have "explicitly pondered" the being of beings or "experienced" (SD, 74–75) unconcealment as such, that is, in terms of its belonging to concealment (VS, 133ff.).

the locale of silence, of tranquillity or stillness (*der Ort der Stille*), as the clearing of the open realm that "gathers within it" that which first grants unconcealment. The clearing grants before all else the possibility of a path to presence, grants the possible presencing of presence itself. "The tranquil heart of the clearing is the locale of stillness, from out of which the possibility of a belonging together of being and thinking, that is, presencing and apprehending, is first given" (SD, 75). The heart of the clearing, of unconcealment, demands to be thought as concealment itself, as *lēthē,* which "belongs to *A-lētheia* not as a mere addition, not as does the shadow to the light, but as the heart of *Alētheia.*" Whereas a shadow is dependent upon the presence of light for its existence, concealment itself is of another order than presence; it is not a function of presencing or unconcealment, but prevails as that which shelters and maintains itself as such in and throughout all presencing. The clearing would thus demand to be thought as a "clearing of self-concealing presence, clearing of self-concealing sheltering" (SD, 79). Concealment, as the heart of the event of un-concealment, thus shows itself, as concealing, to be not of the order of being, not of the order of presencing. And yet it speaks in (and only in) the call of the presencing of things themselves, calls also upon a thinking that would seek to think being as such. The thing itself, the singular "thing" or *Sache* that is the matter of thinking, would thus be thinkable only in and through a thinking of "the things themselves," of *die Sachen selbst,* of the things that were originally to be approached by phenomenology.

Heidegger's thinking of the concealment that inhabits presencing as the clearing of un-concealment turns toward the unthought of Greek philosophy and of the subsequent itinerary of Western knowledge. If the visibility of the visible, the first and enduring philosophical paradigm of the being of beings, always already depends on that which is visible first having come into the light and come to presence, the event of such presencing itself has nevertheless always already made way for beings, always already departed from the scene of presence, withdrawn in advance into its own self-sheltering concealment. The presencing of the visible, thought in its temporality, presupposes the event of clearing, of a concealing that not only first opens the visible in its visibility, letting it be—letting it come to presence, letting it be seen—but that remains at work in the presence of the visible. Far from making presence impossible, it precisely enables a human dwelling in the presence of "the things themselves," in the presence of other beings. In the course of Heidegger's thought, the time of vision, the "simultaneity" of seeing and having seen, shows itself to be a finite dwelling in the presencing of the visible, a dwelling in the stillness of time, in the concealed presencing of the irreducible concealment at work in all presencing: a dwelling in the time of the *Augenblick.* The human being, the one possessed by concealment, the one who tarries for a while in such stillness, has the task of revealing, of letting presence that which would otherwise be concealed, of responding to the call of the presencing of others.

Turning toward the unthought of philosophy is thus a turning toward the presencing of concealment in the history of philosophy itself, an attentiveness to that which philosophy itself calls upon us to think. For this reason, the "unthought" of philosophy is not at all to be regarded as a lack or fault, as something to be corrected, something for which thought henceforth should have to compensate. Yet nor is philosophy's unthought something that could be accessed by turning elsewhere, by turning away from the history of philosophy, and least of all by turning away from the ancients. The task, rather, is to turn toward the history into which we have been cast, to turn into philosophy in an appropriate manner. Even, and especially, when philosophy is at an end. In "The End of Philosophy and the Task of Thinking," Heidegger characterizes the end of philosophy as "the triumph of the controllable establishment of a scientific-technological world and of the social order proper to that world. The end of philosophy means: the beginning of the world civilization grounded in Western-European thinking" (SD, 65). As such, the end of philosophy is equally "the locale [*Ort*], that end wherein the whole of philosophy's history is gathered into its most extreme possibility" (SD, 63). Understood as the consummation (*Vollendung*) of philosophy's original task, the modern scientific-technological world itself directs us toward what remains unthought in philosophy's beginning: the event of presencing as such. For what comes increasingly to the fore in and through modern technology if not the event-like character of presencing, of un-concealment? Is not thinking thereby called to the site of presencing itself, to the clearing? In attending to the clearing as the site of historicality—as the specific locale and time of the historicality of our modern world and its socio-political configuration—questioning might attain "a way" toward the task of thinking at the end of philosophy, toward the task—and thus the future—of a thinking that is "perhaps more sober than the unceasing rush of rationalization and of cybernetics as it tears us away" (SD, 79).

Would the task of thinking, thus understood, still be a quest for knowledge? The German word for task, *Aufgabe,* suggests something given, given over to us, allotted and left to us. The task of thinking would thus be something left to those known as thinkers, those who, as in the beginning of philosophy, continue to have an eye for the inhabitual and the astonishing, the difficult and the daimonic; those whose seeing, before and beyond the desire to see, has already been drawn toward something astonishing, something wondrous, extraordinary, something uncanny at work amid all presencing. "To know means: to have seen"; but to have seen entails an ongoing

openness, an attentiveness toward that which conceals itself in its presencing as it concerns and affects us. In another, earlier text from the 1935 course
"Introduction to Metaphysics," many of whose themes are echoed in the
later essay "The End of Philosophy and the Task of Thinking," Heidegger
gave another formulation, another apparent definition, of what is meant by
knowing. "To know," he wrote, "means: *to be able to learn.*"[117] Yet being
able to learn, in turn, "presupposes being able to question" (EM, 17). And
the latter? The same text concludes, after an extensive journey of thought,
by recalling that what is properly given us as a task (*das Aufgegebene:* a
term used by Hölderlin) is "that which we do not know," that which, insofar
as we know of it in a genuine manner, namely, know of it *as* a given task,
"we only ever know *in questioning.*" Just as knowing is not the same as the
passing acquaintance offered by a glimpse of something, so too questioning
must remain, must tarry within an openness toward the concealment of
that which has called it, toward the concealment of its own vocation, ever
mindful of its own finitude. The 1935 course ends with the following words:

> To be able to question means: to be able to wait, even for a
> lifetime. In an era, however, that considers what is real to be
> whatever can be quickly attained and grasped with both hands,
> questioning is held to be something "alien to reality," something
> that doesn't pay. But what is essential is not what pays, but the
> fitting time, that is, the fitting moment [*der rechte Augenblick*]
> and the fitting endurance.

> "Denn es hasset
> Der sinnende Gott
> Unzeitiges Wachstum."

> "For the god that muses
> Hates
> Untimely maturation."[118]

To wait, as we have noted, can mean not only to await some event or
something yet to come in a projected future. To wait can mean to wait
upon, in the sense of attending to something or someone.[119] The thinker's

---

[117] Cf. "The Word" (1958): "To learn means: to become knowing. Knowing is, in Latin,
qui vidit, whoever has seen, caught sight of [*erblickt*] something, someone who never
again loses sight of what has been caught sight of. To learn means: to enter into such
catching sight of ..." (US, 223).
[118] EM, 157. The poetic fragment is from Hölderlin, *Homburger Folioheft.*
[119] Early in his philosophical career, in a 1921/22 course, Heidegger had already identified the ability to wait with a sense of time, of the time of the *kairos:* "The kairological—
'time.' Sitting still, being able to wait, that is, to 'give time,' within the world and its
history" (GA 61, 139).

attending to the task of thinking may take a lifetime, and, no doubt, the work of a lifetime. It entails an enduring attentiveness toward something that itself endures amid the time of a life: a concealment that belongs to the heart of the fitting moment, of the living *Augenblick* from which the thinker's work itself emerges.

Selected Bibliography

For works by Aristotle, Gadamer, and Heidegger cited by abbreviation see pp. xiii–xvii.

Aeschines, *The Speeches of Aeschines*. With a translation by Charles Darwin Adams. London: Heinemann, 1919.

Ambrosii, S. *De Bono Mortis*. Translated by W. T. Wiesner. Washington: Catholic University of America Press, 1970.

Aphrodisias, A. *Commentaria in Aristotelem Greca*. Vol. II, 1. Edited by Wallies. Berolini, 1883.

Arendt, Hannah. *The Life of the Mind*. New York: Harcourt Brace Jovanovich, 1978.

———. *The Human Condition*. Chicago: The University of Chicago Press, 1958.

———. *Between Past and Future*. New York: Penguin, 1993.

Aristotle. *The "Art" of Rhetoric*. With a translation by J. H. Freese. The Loeb Classical Library. Cambridge: Harvard University Press, 1926.

———. *The Athenian Constitution*. With a translation by H. Rackham. The Loeb Classical Library. Cambridge: Harvard University Press, 1952.

———. *The Categories*. With a translation by H. P. Cooke. The Loeb Classical Library. Cambridge: Harvard University Press, 1938.

———. *History of Animals*. With a translation by D. M. Balme. The Loeb Classical Library. Cambridge: Harvard University Press, 1991.

———. *Magna Moralia*. With a translation by G. C. Armstrong. The Loeb Classical Library. Cambridge: Harvard University Press, 1935.

———. *On Interpretation*. With a translation by H. P. Cooke. The Loeb Classical Library. Cambridge: Harvard University Press, 1938.

———. *Parts of Animals*. With a translation by A. L. Peck. The Loeb Classical Library. Cambridge: Harvard University Press, 1955.

———. *The Physics*. 2 vols. With a translation by P. H. Wicksteed & F. M. Cornford. The Loeb Classical Library. Cambridge: Harvard University Press, 1957.

———. *The Poetics.* With a translation by W. H. Fyfe. The Loeb Classical Library. Cambridge: Harvard University Press, 1932.

———. *Posterior Analytics.* With a translation by H. Tredennick. The Loeb Classical Library. Cambridge: Harvard University Press, 1960.

———. *Prior Analytics.* With a translation by H. Tredennick. The Loeb Classical Library. Cambridge: Harvard University Press, 1938.

———. *Problems.* With a translation by W. S. Hett. The Loeb Classical Library. Cambridge: Harvard University Press, 1936.

———. *Protreptikos.* Edited by I. Düring. Frankfurt: Klostermann, 1969.

Arnou, R. *Praxis et Theoria.* Paris: Libraire Félix Alcan, 1921.

Aubenque, P. *La prudence chez Aristote.* Paris: Presses Universitaires de France, 1963.

Augustine, St. *Confessions.* 2 vols. With a translation by William Watts. The Loeb Classical Library. Cambridge: Harvard University Press, 1912.

Bacon, Francis. *The New Organon.* Edited by F. H. Anderson. Indianapolis: Bobbs-Merrill, 1960.

Bambach, Charles R. *Heidegger, Dilthey, and the Crisis of Historicism.* Ithaca: Cornell University Press, 1995.

Becker, Otfrid. *Plotin und das Problem der geistigen Aneignung.* Berlin: De Gruyter, 1940.

Beierwaltes, Werner. "'Εξαίφνης oder: Die Paradoxie des Augenblicks." *Philosophisches Jahrbuch* 74, no. 2 (1967): 271-83.

Benjamin, Walter. *Illuminations.* Edited by Hannah Arendt. New York: Schocken Books, 1969.

Bernasconi, Robert. *Heidegger in Question: The Art of Existing.* New Jersey: Humanities Press, 1993.

———. "Heidegger's Destruction of Phronesis." *The Southern Journal of Philosophy* 28, Supplement (1989): 127-47.

———. "Technology and the Ethics of Praxis." *Acta Institutionis Philosophiae et Aestheticae* 5 (1987): 93-108.

Bernstein, Richard J. *Philosophical Profiles: Essays in a Pragmatic Mode.* Philadelphia: University of Pennsylvania Press, 1986.

Birmingham, Peg. "Ever Respectfully Mine: Heidegger on Agency and Responsibility." In *Ethics and Danger,* ed. Arleen B. Dallery & Charles E. Scott with P. Holley Roberts, 109-82. Albany: State University of New York Press, 1992.

———. "The Time of the Political." *Graduate Faculty Philosophy Journal, New School for Social Research* 14, no. 2–15, no. 1 (1991): 25-45.

———. "Logos and the Place of the Other." *Research in Phenomenology* 20 (1990): 34-54.

Blumenberg, Hans. *Die Legitimität der Neuzeit.* Frankfurt: Suhrkamp, 1996.

————. *Das Lachen der Thrakerin: Eine Urgeschichte der Theorie.* Frankfurt: Suhrkamp, 1987.

Boll, Franz. "Vita Contemplativa." *Sitzungsberichte der Heidelberger Akademie der Wissenschaften,* 3-34. Heidelberg, 1920.

Bröcker, Walter. *Aristoteles.* 5th ed. Frankfurt: Klostermann, 1987.

Brogan, Walter. "Heidegger and Aristotle: Dasein and the Question of Practical Life." In *Crises in Continental Philosophy,* ed. Arleen B. Dallery & Charles E. Scott, 137-46. Albany: State University of New York Press, 1990.

————. "A Response to Robert Bernasconi's 'Heidegger's Destruction of Phronesis'." *The Southern Journal of Philosophy* 28, Supplement (1989): 149-53.

Cicero, Marcus Tullius. *Academica.* Edited by J. S. Reid. Hildesheim: Georg Olms, 1966.

Derrida, Jacques. "Geschlecht: différence sexuelle, différence ontologique." In *Martin Heidegger,* ed. Michel Haar, 419-30. Paris: Éditions de l'Herne, 1983.

Descartes, René. *Discours de la méthode.* Paris: Garnier-Flammarion, 1966.

Ferguson, John. *Callimachus.* Boston: Twayne Publishers, 1980.

Figal, Günter. *Heidegger: Zur Einführung.* 2nd ed. Hamburg: Junius Verlag GmbH, 1996.

Fóti, Véronique. *Heidegger and the Poets: Poiesis, Sophia, Techne.* New Jersey: Humanities Press, 1992.

————. "Aletheia and Oblivion's Field: On Heidegger's Parmenides Lectures." In *Ethics and Danger,* ed. Arleen B. Dallery & Charles E. Scott with P. Holley Roberts, 71-82. Albany: State University of New York Press, 1992.

Foucault, Michel. *Surveiller et punir.* Paris: Gallimard, 1975.

————. *Histoire de la sexualité.* Vol. I. Paris: Gallimard, 1976.

Fynsk, Christopher. *Heidegger: Thought and Historicity.* Expanded edition. Ithaca: Cornell University Press, 1993.

Gasché, Rodolphe. "Towards an Ethics of 'Auseinandersetzung'." In *Enlightenments,* ed. H. Kunneman & H. de Vries, 121-40. Kampen, the Netherlands: Kok Pharos Publishing House, 1993.

Glazebrook, Patricia. "Heidegger's Philosophy of Science." Ph.D. dissertation, University of Toronto, 1994.

Haar, Michel. *Le Chant de la Terre.* Paris: Éditions de l'Herne, 1985.

Hegel, Georg Wilhelm Friedrich. *Vorlesungen über die Ästhetik.* 3 vols. Frankfurt: Suhrkamp, 1986.

Irigaray, Luce. *L'oubli de l'air.* Paris: Éditions de Minuit, 1983.

Jaeger, Werner. *Aristoteles: Grundlegung einer Geschichte seiner Entwicklung.* Berlin: Weidmannsche Buchhandlung, 1923.

Jaspers, Karl. *Psychologie der Weltanschauungen.* 2nd ed. Berlin: Julius Springer, 1922.

Jay, Martin. *Downcast Eyes: The Denigration of Vision in Twentieth Century French Thought.* Berkeley: University of California Press, 1993.

Jonas, Hans. "The Nobility of Sight." *Philosophy and Phenomenological Research* 14, no. 4 (June 1954): 507-19.

Kant, Immanuel. *Kritik der reinen Vernunft.* Hamburg: Felix Meiner, 1971.

————. *Kritik der Praktischen Vernunft; Grundlegung zur Metaphysik der Sitten. Werkausgabe* vol. 7. Edited by W. Weischedel. Frankfurt: Suhrkamp, 1991.

————. *Kritik der Urteilskraft. Werkausgabe* vol. 10. Edited by W. Weischedel. Frankfurt: Suhrkamp, 1990.

Kerkhoff, Manfred. "Zum antiken Begriff des Kairos." *Zeitschrift für Philosophische Forschung* 27, no. 2 (1973): 256-74.

———— and Amelung, E. "Kairos." In *Historisches Wörterbuch der Philosophie,* ed. J. Ritter & K. Gründer. Darmstadt: Wissenschaftliche Buchgesellschaft, 1976, 667-69.

Kierkegaard, Soren. *The Concept of Anxiety.* Translated by Reidar Thomte. New Jersey: Princeton University Press, 1980.

Kisiel, Theodore. *The Genesis of Heidegger's* Being and Time. Berkeley: University of California Press, 1993.

———— and van Buren, John, eds. *Reading Heidegger from the Start: Essays in His Earliest Thought.* Albany: State University of New York Press, 1994.

Koller, Hermann. "Theoros und Theoria." *Glotta* 36, no. 3/4 (1958): 273-86.

Krell, David Farrell. *Intimations of Mortality: Time, Truth, and Finitude in Heidegger's Thinking of Being.* University Park: The Pennsylvania State University Press, 1986.

————. *Of Memory, Reminiscence, and Writing: On the Verge.* Bloomington: Indiana University Press, 1990.

————. *Daimon Life: Heidegger and Life-Philosophy.* Bloomington: Indiana University Press, 1992.

Levin, David Michael. *The Opening of Vision.* New York: Routledge, 1988.

————, ed. *Modernity and the Hegemony of Vision.* Berkeley: University of California Press, 1993.

Liddell, H. G. & Scott, R. *A Greek–English Lexicon.* Oxford: Oxford University Press, 1989.

Lobkowicz, Nicholas. *Theory and Pratice.* Indiana: University of Notre Dame Press, 1967.

McNeill, William. "Heidegger and the Modification of *Being and Time*." Ph.D. dissertation, University of Essex, 1986.

———. "Metaphysics, Fundamental Ontology, Metontology." *Heidegger Studies* 8 (1992): 63-79.

———. *Heidegger: Visions. Of Animals, Others, and the Divine.* University of Warwick: Center for Research in Philosophy and Literature, 1993.

———. "The First Principle of Hermeneutics." In *Reading Heidegger from the Start,* ed. T. Kisiel and J. van Buren, 393-408. Albany: State University of New York Press, 1994.

———. "Traces of Discordance: Heidegger—Nietzsche." In *Nietzsche: A Critical Reader,* ed. P. Sedgwick, 171-202. Cambridge, MA: Blackwell, 1995.

———. "Care for the Self: Originary Ethics in Heidegger and Foucault." *Philosophy Today* 42, no. 1/4 (1998): 53-64.

———. "Life Beyond the Organism: Animal Being in Heidegger's Freiburg Lectures, 1929-30." In *Animal Others: Continental Philosophy and the Status of Non-Human Animal Life,* ed. H. Peter Steeves. Albany: State University of New York Press, forthcoming.

———. "A 'Scarcely Pondered Word'. The Place of Tragedy: Heidegger, Aristotle, Sophocles." In *Philosophy and Tragedy,* ed. M. de Beistegui & S. Sparks. London: Routledge, forthcoming.

Naas, Michael. *Turning: From Persuasion to Philosophy.* New Jersey: Humanities Press, 1995.

Nietzsche, Friedrich. *Die Fröhliche Wissenschaft. Werke, Kritische Gesamtausgabe,* vol. 5/2. Edited by Giorgio Colli and Mazzino Montinari. Berlin: Walter de Gruyter, 1973.

———. *Der Wille zur Macht.* Stuttgart: Kröner, 1964.

Ott, Hugo. *Martin Heidegger: Unterwegs zu seiner Biographie.* Frankfurt: Campus Verlag, 1988.

Plato. *Parmenides.* With a translation by Harold North Fowler. The Loeb Classical Library. Cambridge: Harvard University Press, 1926. In German: Platon, *Werke.* Band I.2. Translated by F. Schleiermacher. Berlin: Akademie-Verlag, 1985. Reprint of 2nd. edition (1818).

———. *Phaedrus.* With a translation by Harold North Fowler. The Loeb Classical Library. Cambridge: Harvard University Press, 1914.

———. *The Republic.* 2 vols. With a translation by Paul Shorey. The Loeb Classical Library. Cambridge: Harvard University Press, 1937.

Plotinus. *Enneads.* 6 vols. With a translation by A. H. Armstrong. The Loeb Classical Library. Cambridge: Harvard University Press, 1966.

Pöggeler, Otto. *Der Denkweg Martin Heideggers.* Pfullingen: Neske, 1963.

———. "Destruktion und Augenblick." In *Destruktion und Übersetzung,* ed. T. Buchheim, 9-29. Weinheim: VCH, Acta Humaniora, 1989.

Rausch, Hannelore. *Theoria: Von Ihrer Sakralen zur Philosophischen Bedeutung.* München: Wilhelm Fink Verlag, 1982.

Redlow, Götz. *Theoria: Theoretische und Praktische Lebensauffassung im Philosophischen Denken der Antike.* Berlin: Veb Deutscher Verlag der Wissenschaften, 1966.

Ruin, Hans. *Enigmatic Origins: Tracing the Theme of Historicity through Heidegger's Works.* Stockholm: Almqvist & Wiksell International, 1994.

Sallis, John. *Double Truth.* Albany: State University of New York Press, 1995.

———. *Stone.* Bloomington: Indiana University Press, 1994.

———. "...A wonder that one could never aspire to surpass." In *The Path of Archaic Thinking,* ed. K. Maly, 243-74. Albany: State University of New York Press, 1995.

Schürmann, Reiner. *Heidegger on Being and Acting: From Principles to Anarchy.* Bloomington: Indiana University Press, 1987.

Seubold, Günter. "Bemerkungen zu 'Destruktion und Augenblick'." In *Destruktion und Übersetzung,* ed. T. Buchheim, 31-38. Weinheim: VCH, Acta Humaniora, 1989.

Sheehan, Thomas. "Heidegger's 'Introduction to the Phenomenology of Religion,' 1920-21." *The Personalist* 60, no. 3 (July 1979): 312-24.

Taminiaux, Jacques. *Lectures de l'ontologie fondamentale.* Grenoble: Millon, 1989. Translated by M. Gendre under the title *Heidegger and the Project of Fundamental Ontology.* Albany: State University of New York Press, 1991. (Translation includes additional material.)

———. *La fille de Thrace et le penseur professionnel: Arendt et Heidegger.* Paris: Éditions Payot, 1992.

———. "Poiesis and Praxis in Fundamental Ontology." *Research in Phenomenology* 17 (1987): 137-69.

———. "The Origin of 'The Origin of the Work of Art'." In *Reading Heidegger: Commemorations,* ed. J. Sallis, 392-404. Bloomington: Indiana University Press, 1993.

Thucydides. *Historiae.* Edited by Henry Stuart Jones. Oxford: Oxford University Press, 1942.

Tillich, Paul, ed. *Kairos.* Darmstadt: Otto Reichl Verlag, 1926.

Van Buren, John. *The Young Heidegger: Rumor of the Hidden King.* Bloomington: Indiana University Press, 1994.

Villa, Dana R. *Arendt and Heidegger: The Fate of the Political.* New Jersey: Princeton University Press, 1996.

Volpi, Franco. *"Dasein* comme *praxis:* L'assimilation et la radicalisation heideggerienne de la philosophie pratique d'Aristote." In *Heidegger et l'idée de la phénoménologie,* ed. F. Volpi et al., 1-41. Dordrecht: Kluwer Academic Publishers, 1988.

Von Herrman, Friedrich-Wilhelm. *Subjekt und Dasein: Interpretationen zu "Sein und Zeit."* 2nd, expanded edition. Frankfurt: Klostermann, 1985.

Weiss, Helene. *Kausalität und Zufall in der Philosophie des Aristoteles.* Basel: Verlag Haus zum Falken, 1942.

Wohlfart, Günter. *Der Augenblick: Zeit und ästhetische Erfahrung bei Kant, Hegel, Nietzsche und Heidegger mit einem Exkurs zu Proust.* Freiburg: Karl Alber Verlag, 1982.

Wood, David. *The Deconstruction of Time.* New Jersey: Humanities Press, 1989.

Index of Names

Index of Subjects

science (*continued*)
  modern
    as experimental, 81, 168,
      174, 201, 249
    future of, 182–87, 251
    grounding of, 81–82, 163,
      166–70, 247–51
    as industriousness, 168
    as institutional, 144–56,
      162–64, 168
    and method (*see* method)
    and National Socialism,
      147–48
    as panoptic, 176–77
    and progress, 181–87
    as research, 167–69, 250–51
    and rigor, 167–68
    and specialization, 146–47,
      168, 181
    and thematization (*see*
      thematization)
    and philosophy (*see*
      philosophy)
    See also *epistēmē;* objectivity
seeing
  circumspective (*see*
    circumspection)
  as ecstasis, 72–73, 119–23,
    132–35, 242, 244, 271–79,
    302, 323–26 (see also
    Augenblick)
  as *eidenai* (see *eidenai*)
  as grasping, 178–81, 319
  as historically determined,
    80–81, 161–65
  as mode of access to being,
    4–9, 20, 66, 76, 109–11
  in modern science, 81–83,
    173–78
  of oneself, 107–14, 142–43,
    241, 255, 269–71, 321 (see
    also *phronēsis*)
  of others, 109–14, 141, 241,
    255, 269–71, 303–19
  phenomenological, 71, 94,
    96–98, 100, 110–111,
    161–62
  in *phronēsis* (see *phronēsis*)
  as poietic, 260 (see also *nous;*
    theōria)

priority of, ix–x, 1–2, 5, 8, 20,
    76, 83, 93, 162, 309
  prophetic, 320–31
  as responsive, 214–18, 301,
    307, 311–13, 319
  and simultaneity (*see*
    simultaneity)
  and subjectivity, 169–73, 175
  in *technē* (see *technē*)
  as touching (*thigein*), 175
  See also *Augenblick;* clearing;
    contemplation; insight;
    theōria
shining (*Scheinen*)
  as divine, 260–62
  of human look, 315
  of the sensuous, 259–61, 282,
    290–95, 299, 304, 306,
    311–12, 332–33
  See also radiance
silence (*Schweigen*), 122–23, 317,
    335–36. See also stillness
simultaneity (*hama,*
    Gleichzeitigkeit)
  as finite dwelling, 231–32
  and seeing, 8, 46n. 30, 128–30,
    275–76, 336
  and work of art (*see* art, work
    of)
solicitude (*Fürsorge*), 69, 109–12
  authentic, 114, 135
  See also being with others,
    Dasein as
solipsism, accusation of, 97, 101
solitude (*Einsamkeit*), 222, 222n. 3,
    269–70. See also
    individuation
sophia
  in Aristotle, 1, 26–29, 37–38,
    47–54, 55, 93, 105–7,
    127–31, 243–45, 253–58,
    269–71
  and *epistēmē*, 28–29, 37–38
  and experience, 267–71
  and *phronēsis* (see *phronēsis*)
  Presocratic, 10, 268–69
  and *technē* (see *technē*)
  and *theōria* (see *theōria*)
spectator
  and *Augenblick*, 221–27,
    275–76, 278